Sheridan in the Shenandoah

SHERIDAN
IN THE SHENANDOAH

Jubal Early's Nemesis

SECOND EDITION

Edward J. Stackpole

Commentary by D. Scott Hartwig
Foreword by William C. Davis

STACKPOLE
BOOKS

Published by
STACKPOLE BOOKS
Cameron and Kelker Streets
P.O. Box 1831
Harrisburg, PA 17105

Printed in the United States of America
Second Edition

10 9 8 7 6 5 4

Cover art: "Sergeant's Valor" by Don Stivers

Cover design by Caroline Miller

Maps by Colonel Wilbur S. Nye, USA Ret.

Illustrations from the Kean Archives

Library of Congress Catalog Card Number 61-14913

CONTENTS

LIST OF ILLUSTRATIONS

These illustrations were made by artists and photographers accompanying the armies in the field; and have been prepared from contemporary sources by the Kean Archives, Philadelphia.

LIST OF MAPS

FOREWORD

Consciously or otherwise, the novice who undertakes the exciting task of writing an account of a Civil War campaign or battle might as well make up his mind that he has trapped himself in the unrelenting jaws of an avocation from which there is no release. The additional fact, that in pursuit of such mission it becomes necessary to live the life of a hermit or risk the accusation of one's friends that he has turned antisocial, is purely coincidental.

The wealth of source material, both primary and secondary, is so extensive as to be bewildering. The problem consequently becomes a matter of ruthless selectivity if it is the author's intention to complete the self-assignment within his alloted life span.

The writer of this book caught the Civil War fever in 1954 without realizing what a tenacious bug had laid hold upon him. Gettysburg led to Fredericksburg, then Chancellorsville, with complete indifference to chronological consistency; then back to Second Bull Run and Antietam, at which time was cherished a flickering hope that the fever had subsided.

It was not to be so. Try it and see for yourself. Every road, stream, line of hills, field, undulation of the terrain, mountain peak, ravine, obtrusively suggests or recalls to mind a similar natural feature that played a significant part in one or another of the more than five thousand battles or engagements between the forces of the North and South. There appears to be no escape, once committed, but on the asset side it should be noted parenthetically that a more fascinating or rewarding time-consumer would be difficult to find.

FOREWORD TO THE SECOND EDITION

It is a truism in Civil War history that there are many areas and subjects, ripe with human interest, excitement, and drama, that for some reason no one writes about. Literally hundreds of books have dealt with Gettysburg or Lincoln. Only a pitiful handful have taken on Atlanta or Jefferson Davis. Why this phenomenon exists is hard to explain, but that it exists cannot be denied.

Another proof of its existence is the 1864 campaign in the Shenandoah Valley of Virginia. The characters involved compose a virtual pantheon of the Civil War's most interesting and dynamic leaders—Philip H. Sheridan, George A. Custer, John S. Mosby, George Crook, John C. Breckinridge, and Jubal A. Early. There are hairbreadth battles like Cedar Creek. There is the great Confederate raid on Washington that took Rebel forces within sight of the Capitol dome and brought even President Lincoln under fire. There's the controversial burning of Chambersburg, Pennsylvania, and the incredibly dramatic "Sheridan's Ride," an event most Americans have heard of without knowing where or when it happened.

Despite all of this, the 1864 Valley Campaign is among the least studied of all the major and secondary campaigns of the war. Only in the past few years have scholars started to address it seriously. Yet thirty years ago General E. J. Stackpole, who had already produced a series of very popular histories of major Civil War battles and campaigns, turned his attention to what he called *Sheridan in the Shenandoah*. It was the first book in decades to look at the epic contest between the ruthless Sheridan and the bold yet flawed Jubal Early, and it achieved instant success.

This new edition brings Stackpole's book up to date thanks to the efforts of Scott Hartwig. Every book sooner or later shows its age. There are outdated conclusions to be altered, dates and numbers to be amended, and new scholarship to be taken account of. Hartwig has noted such changes in his commentary, while retaining unaltered the direct, matter-of-fact approach and style that make General Stackpole's books so popular.

The Valley Campaign is a model of the indirect effect a seemingly peripheral campaign can have on the course of major events. Early succeeded at first in throwing into the North one of its greatest scares of the war and in the process saving the vital Shenandoah crops Lee needed to feed his army. But when Sheridan attacked him that fall, Early was no match for him, and the loss of the Valley eliminated what had been the vital protection of Lee's experienced left flank. This may not have had great repercussions on the events at Petersburg, where Lee was already effectively besieged. But when it came time for the Army of Northern Virginia to attempt to break out, Lee's loss of the Shenandoah left him too many closed roads.

Sheridan in the Shenandoah is today, as it was thirty years ago, an excellent introduction to the climactic events in the storied Valley of Virginia, to the men who struggled there, and to the cause they served. It is history as it ought to be — clear, direct, exciting.

William C. Davis

ACKNOWLEDGMENTS

In reflecting on the factual material from which this account of the Shenandoah Valley Campaign of 1864 was constructed, the author finds that to a great extent he has relied on a few primary source books, small in number but comprehensive in coverage. Aside from the *Official Records* and the personal accounts of participants to be found in *Battles and Leaders of the Civil War*, sufficient unto the mission for research and analysis were the *Memoirs of Philip H. Sheridan* and *The Autobiography of Jubal A. Early*, commanders of the opposing armies; *Reminiscences of the Civil War*, by General John B. Gordon, and the *Autobiography of General George Crook*, two of the prominent corps commanders; and the meticulously detailed accounts written by two captains in the Union Army, Henry A. DuPont and John W. DeForest, both of whom were unusually observant officers whose status afforded opportunity to record events of the campaign in broad perspective.

Specific acknowledgment is gratefully made to the author's Alma Mater for permission granted by the Yale University Press to freely use material from *A Volunteer's Adventures* by John William DeForest, which first appeared in *Harper's Monthly* in the year 1865 and was republished at New Haven in 1946.

Thanks are due Dr. Francis A. Lord for his courtesy in lending from his extensive private library a number of rare books which have been used in checking facts and filling out some details.

An unexpected nugget of historic value was derived from a friendly correspondence with Mr. Alan du Bois of Honolulu, whose grandfather, Henry A. du Bois, served on Sheridan's staff throughout the Wilderness Campaign, the Valley Campaign, and on to Appomattox. That officer's first-hand appraisal of General Sheridan, taken from one of his letters, can be found in Chapter 5, thanks to the helpful courtesy of grandson Alan.

Another windfall served to add a touch of whimsy to the several references to Colonel John S. Mosby, gadfly of the armed forces of the North. Appreciation in that connection is made to Mr. Stewart M. Walthour of Worcester, Massachusetts, a Civil War buff. His grandfather, Cornelius Raver, was a colorful Union soldier whose letter to his wife fitted in very nicely in Chapter 15.

I am indebted to the Rev. Sheridan Watson Bell, prominent Methodist minister of Harrisburg, who made available several letters from his grandfather, Sergeant L. L. Bell, a member of the 110th Ohio Volunteer Infantry, who fought at Cedar Creek and informed his family as to just what Sheridan really said at the end of his famous ride from Winchester (Chapter 13).

Grateful thanks are expressed to Mr. and Mrs. George E. Lippincott of Germantown, Pa., for making available extracts from the unpublished diary of Brigadier General Clement A. Evans, Mrs. Lippincott's father, and in particular the highly pertinent letter of October 18, 1864, in which the General described to his wife the significant reconnaissance of October 17 to Three Top Mountain in company with General John B. Gordon and Jed Hotchkiss.

I am also deeply indebted to Robert H. Fowler, Editor of *Civil War Times*, for a meticulous job of editing whereby the manuscript was made infinitely more palatable than would otherwise have been the case.

My heartfelt appreciation for assistance rendered is reserved for two colleagues without whose otherwise unsung contributions neither this book nor any of its predecessors would ever have come to pass:

To Colonel Wilbur S. Nye, U.S.A. Retired, author, Civil War editor, and cartographer emeritus who fears not to tangle with such famous map sources as Jed Hotchkiss, Matthew Forney Steele, and the Official Atlas; who was singlehandedly responsible for conceiving and executing the maps accompanying the narrative. Furthermore, he was instrumental in uncovering and pinpointing much useful source material found in the Library of Congress and elsewhere. Finally, his knowledgeable editing pointed a diplomatic red pencil at cliches and redundancies that cried out for deletion to avoid being pounced upon by sharp-eyed reviewers. To Bill Nye I owe a debt of gratitude which is here expressed, with the hope that he will not feel encouraged thereby to dream up any additional ideas to put this author immediately to work on still another project.

To Cora Martin Weeber, my long-time secretary, who manages uncomplainingly and always smilingly to take such punishment as should never be visited on any human being. How she contrives to decipher the long-hand pencil scribbling that falls to her lot in transcribing manuscript notes, deletions, corrections, et al., passeth all understanding. Withal, a growing familiarity with the foibles of a would-be author has conditioned her to the stage where her own use of the dictionary leads to an occasional exchange of differing views which proves quite stimulating to both parties. Without Cora I should be a lost soul, and for these several reasons I pay grateful tribute for her invaluable assistance.

E.J.S.

In the text the names of Confederates and their units are *italicized,* in order to assist the reader to differentiate readily between Confederates and Federals. This is not done on the maps, where the symbols make this clear.

MAP 1. THEATER OF OPERATIONS

FEDERALS DESTROYING LEE'S GRANARY IN THE SHENANDOAH

CHAPTER 1

LEE FACES A PROBLEM

IT was the middle of May, 1864. Two military giants, General *Robert E. Lee* and Lieutenant General Ulysses S. Grant, for, the first time recently had come face to face in Northern Virginia. The Battle of Gettysburg was ten months in the past. George G. Meade still led the Army of the Potomac, but the post had become a nominal one when Grant, to whom President Lincoln had recently given supreme command over all the Union armies, chose to make his headquarters with Meade's army. There had been a considerable amount of maneuvering for position and several inconclusive engagements between Meade and *Lee,* but little fighting of major importance had occurred during the fall and winter of 1863-64 in the Virginia theater of operations.

1

It had taken a long time for Lincoln to find his general in Ulysses S. Grant, and the able *Lee* had made the most of the delay. Now the assurance of Confederate victories was a thing of the past, as the inevitable tide of ultimate Union supremacy rose slowly on all sides of the shrinking island that the Confederacy had become. *Jackson* and *Stuart, Lee's* "right arm" and "the eyes of his army," were dead. *Longstreet* had been severely wounded, and *Ewell* was no longer physically able to stand the strain of combat. Hardpressed by Grant's grinding war of attrition, the *Army of Northern Virginia* could no longer count on replacements, either of men or animals. It had become a serious question whether the impoverished South could much longer supply sufficient food and clothing to enable *Lee* to maintain his steadily diminishing army in anything like fighting shape.

In the midst of these discouraging conditions the unquenchable spirit of the imperturbable Southern commander rose to its supreme height, somewhat like that of the Thoroughbred horse that responds to the urging of its rider even though its great heart is on the verge of bursting. Perhaps there was still a faint hope for Southern independence, although not through a victory by arms, which by this time had become a practical impossibility in the opinion of sound thinkers on both sides of the Mason-Dixon line. The apparently unlimited manpower and industrial strength of the Northern States, on the basis of simple mathematics, was a virtual guaranty that the South could not win. It was that premise on which Grant was operating, doggedly, and, as it seemed, without regard to Union losses. Inhuman as it appeared to some, this was sound warfare; the inability of the South to sustain equal or even fewer losses per battle than the North being implicit in Grant's overall strategy.

Nevertheless a faint hope of victory still existed in the minds of the Confederate leaders. This was based on the very real possibility that the Democratic party, with George B. McClellan as its standard-bearer, and supported by the proponents of peace—with or without honor—would win the fall election and take over the Government from the strong hands of the unyielding Abraham Lincoln. If that should happen, the entire picture could change overnight. McClellan's favorites among the Union generals would supplant Grant, Sherman, and others, particularly in the grade of corps commander. Stanton and Halleck would immediately be eliminated (not an unmixed blessing, perhaps), and the slow motion of Grant's Union Juggernaut would come to a jarring halt. At the very least, the still dangerous Confederate armies would be granted a respite. There were still vivid memories of the good old days when the team of *Lee, Jackson, Longstreet,* and *Stuart* consistently outmaneuvered, outmarched, and outfought the Army of the Potomac under less aggressive commanders than Grant. During such an interlude a war-weary North, with a new President who when he was an army commander could never quite make up his mind that to win a campaign it was necessary to fight and kill a lot of people, might be persuaded to accept a negotiated peace, even though the price should be recognition of the Southern States as an independent nation.

The tactical honors in the series of battles during May were clearly *Lee's,* in that he was able, week after week, like a ball of mercury, to sideslip his army from Grant's imminent grasp while inflicting greater losses than his own on the enemy. Nevertheless, even as *Lee* countered Grant's every move to work around his right flank, Grant's strategy was slowly but steadily succeeding as the two armies sidled ponderously towards Richmond. Ultimately *Lee* would have to make a stand, at which time the unlimited supply of men and materials that the North was able to furnish must prove decisive.

After four weeks of matching wits with his new antagonist, *Lee* had not seen any evidence that Grant possessed a magic formula for success, although the Confederate ranks had become conscious of a new spirit that had been infused in the Army of the Potomac. The Yanks kept coming at them, an experience the Rebs had not previously encountered. There was foreboding in such Federal persistence, but that was a matter for the generals to worry about, and General *Lee* didn't seem to be too concerned about the unaccustomed bulldog tenacity of their old enemy—at least not that the men in ranks could observe. Nevertheless many Confederate generals began to have misgivings about the future in the actions of this new man, Grant,who never paused for breath and who appeared to be unimpressed by his frightful losses. There was something quite awesome in fighting a general who acted as had no other Union general in the experience of the veterans of the *Army of Northern Virginia*. Grant's predecessors among the army commanders, after a major battle habitually retired to regroup, refit, and think it over. But not this one. His only reaction, apparently, was to hitch up his britches, light a fresh cigar, and hit his enemy again.

Lee Plans a Strategic Diversion

Robert E. Lee knew perfectly well that the odds against him had mounted until only a miracle could save the Confederacy from the crushing weight that had been available to the North from the very beginning, had its military leaders only been intelligent enough to employ its strength properly. Nevertheless, there was still a chance for such a miracle. A diversion in the Shenandoah Valley might duplicate *Jackson's* successes there in 1862. By such means Grant might be compelled to divert part of his army to assuage the fears of the Administration in Washington, and so relieve the pressure against the *Army of Northern Virginia.*

It was against the foregoing background of events that General *Lee,* master of the calculated risk and past master in the art of evaluating the capabilities and divining the probable intentions of his opponent, made the bold decision to detach an important segment of the *Army of Northern Virginia* for transfer in early June, 1864, to the Shenandoah Valley. To recover that vital granary and hold it for the Confederacy, at the very least until the year's harvest of grain could be brought in, was almost mandatory for the Southern cause. If the expedition and its commander could also emulate *Jackson's* "foot-cavalry," to throw Washington into a state of shock once again, the two-fold strategic success might prolong the ebbing life of the Confederacy.

The temporary cessation of active fighting afforded *Lee* an opportunity to do some necessary reorganizing of the reduced *Army of Northern Virginia. Richard H. (Dick) Anderson* was commanding the *First Corps* during the convalescence of the wounded *Longstreet. Richard S. Ewell* was stubbornly resisting removal from command of the *Second Corps,* although it was apparent to practically everyone else in the corps and at army headquarters that his health had deteriorated to the point where his staff did much of his thinking for him. The Confederate Congress on May 31 passed an act which authorized the temporary promotion of general officers, similar to the advanced brevet rank conferred on Union officers by way of reward for outstanding service. This timely legislation simplified *Lee's* problem to a certain extent, so that he promptly made *Anderson* a temporary lieutenant general,

5

which left only the top position in the *Second Corps* to be filled.

The solution of the latter problem was found in a bit of diplomatic maneuvering on *Lee's* part whereby *"Old Baldy" Ewell,* after a talk with *Lee,* was for the time being placed in command of the *Department of Richmond.* Although he objected to the proposed transfer, insisting that he was fully able to perform field duty, he was the only one who thought so. For *Ewell,* after recovering from the loss of his leg at Groveton in August, 1862, had in the opinion of his colleagues suffered deterioration of both mental and physical powers. This condition had been compounded by a bad fall from his horse in the snow during January of 1864 and again on May 19, when he was severely injured by having his horse shot under him during the final stages of the fighting at Spotsylvania Court House. *Lee* had been concerned for a long time about *Ewell's* health and ability to withstand the rigors of campaigning. *Old Baldy* was a conscientious leader who, in spite of his physical handicap, insisted on sharing the discomforts of field service with his men. He was in the habit of sleeping on the ground in all kinds of weather, with the result that he suffered occasional intestinal upsets. Forced to ride with his wooden leg strapped to the saddle, his equestrian balance was so affected that he was in danger of serious accident every time he mounted his horse. His marriage to the Widow Lizinka Brown, which took place after his new leg had been fitted, was undoubtedly a contributing factor in effecting a transformation in *Baldy Ewell.* For it was common belief that the happily married general had come so fully under the domination of his wife's aggressive personality that she, rather than *Ewell,* dictated corps policy and made the decisions.

On several occasions Major General *Jubal Early,* senior division commander of the *Second Corps,* had been assigned as acting commander of that corps when *Ewell* fell ill, notably during the Mine Run Campaign of November, 1863. Again during the final stages of the Battle of the Wilderness, when *Powell Hill* was ill, *Lee* selected *Early* to take command of the *Third Corps,* which he led at Spotsylvania Court House. The corps reverted to *Hill* as soon as he had partially recovered. Back with his own division after fulfilling a brief assignment in the Shenandoah Valley, *Early* barely had time to become readjusted to the old position when he was again elevated to corps commander. Only this time it was to supplant *Ewell,* who was transferred to Richmond. Young *Stephen Dodson Ramseur* took command of *Early's division.*

In spite of *Early's* caustic tongue and propensity for making enemies, he was a fighter. He had proven his loyalty and capacity on many battlefields, and in *Lee's* opinion deserved advancement. Consequently, on May 31, the date of the passage of the enabling Act, *Early* was made a lieutenant general and given command of the *Second Corps* until *Ewell* could resume the post.

EARLY'S PROFILE

Born in Franklin County, Virginia, November 3, 1816, *Jubal Anderson Early* was graduated from West Point in 1837, resigning after a brief service against the Seminole Indians to take up the practice of law at Rocky Mount, Virginia. Entering politics, he was elected to the House of Delegates, served a term as Commonwealth's Attorney, and was a Major of Volunteers during the Mexican War.

A man of positive opinions, he never hesitated to express them freely, usually in a blunt, satirical vein which tended to offend many who could otherwise have been his friends. He was a strong supporter of the Union, not hesitating to argue its case privately and publicly. But when Virginia finally joined her sister states in the Act of Seces-

7

sion, even though he had voted against it in 1861, *Early* espoused the cause of the Confederacy with the same aggressive vehemence that had characterized his earlier contrary position.

Of all the military leaders who walked or strutted across the stage of the Civil War, it would be difficult to find a

LIEUTENANT GENERAL JUBAL A. EARLY, C.S.A.

more unique subject for searching analysis than *Jubal A. Early*. Tall, angular, and somewhat bent with rheumatism acquired during service in Mexico, he was 45 when he threw in his lot with his native state. A confirmed and crusty bachelor, with snapping black eyes and a black beard streaked with gray, he was profane and irreligious, chewed tobacco constantly, was reputedly fond of applejack, and possessed a sharp wit to match his sharp tongue. An ambitious, self-sufficient nonconformist, he recognized the necessity of discipline, but resisted it when applied from above to himself, a paradoxical attitude the inconsistency of which never appeared to bother him.

DISTINGUISHED COMBAT RECORD

Upon returning to active duty, *Early* was assigned as Colonel, *24th Virginia Infantry,* in which capacity he led the *6th Brigade* at the First Battle of Bull Run, where the spirited action of his troops on the Confederate left flank provided the impetus to a counterattack that started McDowell's army on its retreat to Washington. *Early's* reward for conspicuous service in this first engagement came immediately in the form of a promotion to brigadier general, dating from July 21, 1861. At the head of his brigade in the Peninsular Campaign he was wounded at Williamsburg, but returned to duty in time to succeed the invalided *Elzey* in command of a brigade of *Ewell's division.* He fought well at Cedar Mountain, where *Stonewall Jackson's corps* defeated Banks' Federal corps of John Pope's newly constituted Army of Virginia in the prelude to the Second Battle of Bull Run.

In the maneuvering that occurred between the two battles, as *Lee* was feeling his way around Pope's right flank along the Rappahannock, *Early's brigade* was briefly in peril when *Jackson* sent him across the river below Sulphur Springs to establish a bridgehead, only to have his brigade cut off by the rising waters. Fortunately his immediate opponent, Union General Sigel, was more nervous than *Early,* believing that the whole *Confederate Army* was after him, so the affair had a happy ending for *Early's* men. They were able without punishment to recross the Rappahannock to rejoin *Jackson's* main force the following

9

morning, after having spent an uncomfortable night in dangerous isolation.

As part of *Jackson's Second Corps, Early's brigade* participated in its circuitous flank march around Pope's army, through Thoroughfare Gap to Manassas and back to the vicinity of Groveton, where *Ewell* lost his leg in the fight with King's division of McDowell's corps. In the next day's battle of Second Bull Run, *A. P. Hill's division* was hard pressed and close to disaster in the course of the savage fighting along the unfinished railroad occupied by the *Second Corps*. At the critical moment *Early* from a position in support brought his brigade in at a run with leveled bayonets, hit Kearny's division on the extreme right of Pope's line, and threw it into confusion. Thus he restored the balance to save the day for *Jackson* and *Lee*.

THE CAPITOL AT WASHINGTON IN 1863

Little more than two weeks after Pope had been driven back to Washington and *Lee* was proceeding with his first invasion of Northern soil, the two armies met in the bloody Battle of Antietam, where McClellan failed to grasp his great opportunity to defeat *Lee's* widely scattered forces in detail before they could be reassembled. Still with *Ewell's division* (now commanded by *Lawton*) of the *Second Corps*, *Early's brigade* accompanied *Jackson* from Harpers Ferry and was in the thick of the fighting on the heights north of Sharpsburg, where the corps suffered heavy losses in the massive attacks that were repeatedly thrown against *Lee* from the north, east, and south. When *Lawton* was wounded, *Early* succeeded to the division command. Reduced to about 600 men as a result of casualties, his *division* was confronted with a charging attack by Sedgwick's division of 6,000 men, and would have been wiped out had not the Confederate *divisions* of *McLaws* and *Walker* arrived in the nick of time to counterattack Sedgwick's flank and drive his division from the field. Nevertheless *Early* had managed to hold the line against ten times his strength long enough to prevent what would otherwise have been almost certain disaster for *Lee's army* and in all probability the opening wedge for a resounding McClellan victory.

Early remained in command of *Ewell's division* through the major battles of Fredericksburg, Chancellorsville, and Gettysburg, and throughout the Wilderness Campaign of 1864, always as a part of the veteran *Second Corps*. Whether it was due to chance, or habitual alertness, *Early* seemingly had the knack of always appearing at the point of decisive action at a critical moment in the battle. This happened too consistently to be wholly accidental, so that his reputation as a fighting general became more firmly established with each major battle. It was a common saying among his men that if another outfit found themselves in trouble, they called on *"Old Jube"* to come to the rescue, as for example at Fredericksburg, when Meade's division had punched through *A. P. Hill's* defenses only to be hit hard by *Early* and driven back to its starting point.

In the Chancellorsville campaign, when *Lee* moved west from Fredericksburg to meet Hooker's dangerous threat to his left rear, he took his entire army with him except for *Early's division,* reinforced by *Barksdale's brigade* of *McLaws'* division, which remained on Marye's Heights to keep Sedgwick's reinforced corps occupied while *Lee* dealt with the main body of the Union army. With his 10,000 man force outnumbered at least 2½ to 1, *Early* put up such a bold front against his West Point classmate that Sedgwick withheld his attack until he received peremptory orders from Hooker, with the result that *Lee* was given time to send *Jackson* on his famous and successful flank march which rolled up the Union right, quenched Hooker's ardor, and left him cowering in the Wilderness at Chancellorsville with his back to the Rappahannock, all the fight gone out of him. By the time Sedgwick had driven *Early* off the Fredericksburg heights and advanced to Salem Church, *Lee* was able to march a part of his army back from Chancellorsville, to engage and drive Sedgwick across the river, where the rest of Hooker's army joined him the next day, leaving *Lee* master of the field.

Early was in the van of *Lee's* second invasion of the North when in early June, 1863, *Ewell's corps* moved up through the Cumberland Valley to gather supplies, cattle, and horses and to threaten Harrisburg, the capital of Pennsylvania. The *Second Corps* spread itself widely over the countryside, alarming the inhabitants, levying tribute, throwing Washington and Baltimore, and even Philadelphia and New York, into a state of nervous panic. When the advance of the Army of the Potomac under Hooker's successor, General Meade, forced *Lee* to pull his army together, *Early's* division hastened back from York to reach the field at Gettysburg on the afternoon of July 1, in time to add its weight to the meeting engagement between the gathering forces of the two armies. Swinging down the Harrisburg road to the outskirts of the crossroads town, *Early* threw his brigades in a slashing flank attack against Howard's Eleventh Corps, already hard pressed by earlier Confederate arrivals. When Howard's line broke and his men fled into and through Gettysburg, the Union First Corps on the Chambersburg Road was uncovered and forced to retreat. The first day's battle came to an end with a victory for *Lee* practically assured if *Ewell* could exploit the initial success by seizing Culp's Hill and Cemetery Hill, thus making Cemetery Ridge untenable for the disorganized Federals who had taken refuge on the two eminences and were extending along the ridge to the south as fast as fresh divisions reached the position.

The historic fact is that *Ewell* failed to act, for reasons which he probably considered good. The Gettysburg campaign was his first experience as a corps commander. Having been indoctrinated under *Stonewall Jackson,* who gave simple, direct orders to his division commanders that allowed them little latitude in execution, *Ewell* was illprepared for the discretionary instructions which *Lee* was in the habit of issuing to his corps commanders in the expectation that they would carry them out in their own way, in accord with his general plan. *Jackson, Longstreet,* and *Stuart* had by long experience and intimate association with the *Commanding General* learned that his directives were usually framed as wishes which allowed plenty of leeway so long as the desired result was achieved. But it was a new experience for *Baldy Ewell* and it found him in a state of uncertainty that led him to rely heavily on the judgment of his close friend and long-time associate, *Jubal Early,* whose temperament was such that he felt no hesitancy in advising his corps commander how to act in the situation that existed on the Confederate left on the evening of the first day at Gettysburg.

It was Lee's opinion that if *Ewell* attacked Meade's right on the morning of July 2, Culp's Hill could be captured and Meade's position on the ridge made so v ilnerable that he would be forced to withdraw. At an evening conference attended by *Lee, Ewell, Early, Rodes,* and possibly others, *Early* assumed the role of spokesman, venturing to disagree with *Lee* by arguing that the correct procedure would be to attack Meade's left to occupy the Round Tops, which he insisted were the key to the Union defense. *Ewell* and *Rodes* concurred. *Lee* accepted their viewpoint, but was neither happy about the defensive attitude of the *Second Corps* generals nor convinced of the wisdom of their conclusions. In light of what occurred on July 2 and 3 during *Lee's* frustrating experience in attempting to execute his battle plans through corps commanders, who had never before functioned so inefficiently or at such cross purposes, division commander *Jubal Early* may unwittingly have set a pattern of nonconformance with *Lee's* more mature military judgment that adversely affected the outcome of the Battle of Gettysburg and consequently the subsequent course of the war itself.

Affairs did not always work to *Early's* advantage, as had seemed to be the case in so many of the earlier battles in which he participated and which had shed luster on his combat record. Perhaps his most humiliating experience occurred in November 1863, when Meade's army sprung a surprise night attack that caught *Early* and other Confederates napping. The defense of the sector that included Rappahannock Bridge, where the Orange and Alexandria Railroad crossed the river, was assigned to *Jubal Early.*

The Federals outguessed the defending Confederates, one of *Early's brigades* was overwhelmed, and the way was open for Union General Sedgwick to throw two corps across the river. *Lee's army* was forced to retreat, found itself unable to hold between Culpeper and Brandy Station, and kept going until it was safely beyond the Rapidan. The *Second Corps* lost more than 2,000 men, 1,674 of them in *Early's division* alone, but it was typical of *Early* that he declined to accept responsibility for the disaster. Instead he commented, ungenerously, that General *Lee* had concluded that the enemy lacked the enterprise to stage a night attack, conveniently overlooking the fact that it was his duty to look after his own defenses rather than attempt to shift the blame to others for his own obvious failure. This unattractive trait had shown itself on previous occasions, and would do so again, since it was one of the ingrained characteristics that made *Early* as paradoxical a personality as existed in the Confederate hierarchy.

The combination of ambition, combativeness, intolerance, self-assurance, an inquiring mind that sought to penetrate directly to the heart of every situation, a restiveness under disciplinary supervision of superiors, and finally—above all else—that caustic wit whose barbs were never dull, all tended to set *Early* apart from his associates. He was an individualist whose good qualities far outweighed the bad, but the latter were of a character to overshadow the former in the minds of some of his colleagues and ultimately the general public in the Southern States. None doubted his courage or toughness, for he proved both during four years of combat; but there were a great many who questioned the soundness of his judgment.

Closely identified throughout the war with the *Second Corps of the Army of Northern Virginia, Early's* relations with its first commander, *Stonewall Jackson,* had been cor-

15

rect but never intimate, in which respect he differed from that equally aggressive fighter, *Ambrose Powell Hill,* whose fiery temper caused him to clash with both *Jackson* and *Longstreet.* Perhaps *Jackson's* austere manner and unapproachableness overawed *Early* as a mere brigade commander. Or his respect for his corps commander may have been such that *Early* found nothing to criticise. With General *Ewell, Jackson's* successor, the situation was entirely different. The long friendship of the two officers, during which the expansive, good-natured *Ewell* came to be intellectually and even militarily dominated by his more quick-witted subordinate, lasted until sometime during the spring of 1864, when it was put to severe strain by a remarkable change in *Baldy Ewell,* wrought by his "fall from grace" in marrying the Widow Brown. Thereafter *Ewell* came increasingly under his wife's influence, effecting a transformation that was almost anathema to *Early,* whose confirmed bachelorhood evidently caused him to believe that his friend had played him false by creating a three-way relationship wherein *Early* would experience only dissatisfaction and discomfort. Furthermore the *Ewell* team may have developed a suspicion that *Early's* unconcealed ambition, particularly after he had been given opportunities to command the *Second Corps* during *Ewell's* absences, was leading him to covet that command on a permanent basis. In any event, smouldering doubts brought about one day an occasion which led *Ewell* to place *Early* under arrest for some alleged fault. Nothing ever came of it, because *Lee* promptly nullified the action, but the damage was done and the close comradeship between the two generals was never again the same.

The ambitious individual as a rule is one who is likely to be wary of potential rivals and, if ruthless by disposition, to take advantage of every opportunity to deprecate or at least avoid measures to elevate the presumed competition. When the character trait of intolerance is added to that of ambition, it becomes easier to evaluate the motives that conceivably lie behind words and actions that may otherwise be difficult to understand. A case in point was the relationship between *Jubal Early* of Virginia and *John B. Gordon* of Georgia, both of whom achieved distinction. The individual stories of both men are bound up with that of the *Second Corps,* in which each served successively as brigade, division, and finally corps commander, with the rank of lieutenant general. Until near the close of the war, *Early* was always one grade ahead of *Gordon,* his subordinate, and on the surface there was no conflict of personalities nor open differences of opinion, at least not until the Shenandoah Valley campaign in the fall and winter of 1864. Hard feelings were engendered by bachelor *Early's* violent and freely voiced objection to the presence of officers' wives in the field near their husbands. Mrs. Gordon followed her husband whenever it was practicable. There were also three notable occasions when General *Gordon* was convinced that his superior, by his attitude of overcaution or because of faulty judgment, or both, threw away glorious opportunities to win victories or to exploit those already won. These were the first day at Gettysburg, July 1, 1863; the last day of the first phase of the Wilderness Campaign, May 6, 1864; and the Battle of Cedar Creek, October 19, 1864, an account of which will be found later in this book. In the two first-named incidents, *Ewell* was the corps commander, *Early* a division commander, while *Gordon* was a brigade commander in *Early's division.*

At Gettysburg *Lee's army* had defeated the only two Union corps that had reached the field and it was the *Commanding General's* expressed wish that *Ewell's corps* wrap up the victory in the late afternoon by seizing Culp's Hill and East Cemetery Hill, which would have deprived

Meade of the strong Cemetery Ridge position upon which he was to make his stand on July 2 and 3. *Early* strongly opposed *Lee's* plan for the follow-up attack on July 1 and *Ewell* concurred, both generals having strangely developed a defensive viewpoint, which *Gordon* and other generals of the *Second Corps* regarded as a tragic reversal of its traditionally aggressive role when *Stonewall Jackson* was at the helm.

In the Battle of the Wilderness, at the eleventh hour, a voluntary reconnaissance by *Gordon,* whose brigade, together with *Hays'* and *Pegram's,* all part of *Early's division,* was posted on the left of *Lee's* line, disclosed the fact that Sedgwick's wing on the right of Meade's army was exposed and lacked depth. Unable to persuade *Early* to grasp the opportunity, *Gordon* appealed to *Ewell,* who as usual supported *Early's* view. Hours later, *Gordon* found occasion to explain the situation to General *Lee* himself, who, according to *Gordon's* account, promptly overruled *Ewell* and *Early* and ordered the attack to be made. By that time, however, darkness was but minutes away, the Federals had redistributed their troops, and the attack ended in mutual confusion. Nevertheless *Gordon's* impact on that part of Sedgwick's line so surprised the defenders that couriers rushed to Grant's headquarters with reports that the army right had crumbled in disorder. And so it had, initially, for *Gordon's* attack captured several hundred Federals including two brigadier generals, and killed several hundred more, with minor losses in his own brigade.

Naturally there were two sides to each story, as is always the case when controversies arise that are predicated upon battles in which each participant sees only the part in which he himself is engaged; battles during which conditions change momentarily; in the course of which items of both friendly and enemy intelligence necessitate on-the-spot decisions and actions that may not be known to others

18

until the fighting is over and the reports filed. Both instances in which *Gordon* believed *Early* to be lacking in enterprise involved matters of judgment. In both cases, *Early* vigorously defended his position and may have been right. *Gordon* thought otherwise, then and later. It would appear that *Lee* concurred in *Gordon's* judgment as opposed to *Early's,* if we are to judge by events in the closing weeks of the war, when *Early* was relieved of command while *Gordon,* by that time a lieutenant general commanding the *Second Corps* in place of *Early,* would be found holding a position of trust and importance as one of the few remaining high ranking officers with the *Army of Northern Virginia* when *Lee* surrendered.

Attention Focuses on the Valley

Lee's attention during the early part of June, despite preoccupation with his immediate problem of fighting off Grant's superior force as the Confederate army was interposed on successive positions between the Army of the Potomac and Richmond, was drawn as though by a magnet to the military situation in western Virginia and the Shenandoah Valley. In that area a small Union army under 62-year-old Major General David Hunter, an intimate friend of Secretary of War Stanton, posed a threat to the Confederacy that *Lee* could not afford to ignore.

When *Breckinridge's* small *Confederate division,* aided by the cadets of *Virginia Military Institute,* had combined with *Imboden's cavalry brigade* to defeat Sigel's Federals at New ·Market on May 15, it had appeared safe for *Breckinridge* to rejoin *Lee,* leaving *W. E. ("Grumble") Jones* with *Imboden's* help to handle the situation in the Valley as best he could. With Union General Hunter, a far more able soldier than Sigel, in overall command of the Federal forces, *Jones* had his work cut out for him. Hunter's force, consisting of Sullivan's infantry division, Stahel's cavalry division, and four batteries of artillery, added up to a strength of 8,500 men, somewhat more than *Jones* could gather together from the scattered units in various parts of the Valley. Hunter marched on Staunton as a preliminary to crossing the Blue Ridge, disrupting *Lee's* supply lines and wreaking as much damage as possible on depots and industrial installations. *Jones* assembled a mixed force of 5,000 men, marched to block Hunter, and was decisively defeated at Piedmont on June 5. In this battle *Jones* was killed and his force badly broken up, to the disappointment of General *Lee*, who had written *Jefferson Davis* that he hoped *Jones* and *Imboden* would succeed in defeating Hunter.

The loss of Staunton, heretofore a symbol of Confederate resistance which had loomed as a Gibraltar to baffle all Yankee attempts to occupy it during three years of war, was a premonition of impending disaster. It was clear to *Lee* that if he could not restrain Grant on the James River and Richmond should fall, the Valley could not be held; but if Grant were defeated, the Valley could then be recovered. Logically the Valley was secondary in a strategic sense. The ideal solution would of course be to accomplish both a repulse of Meade's army and the recovery of the Shenandoah Valley. The situation called for the most meticulous kind of figuring on troop dispositions, and wherever *Lee* looked, he was short of men. Grant's strategy of simultaneous pressure at every point was working to *Lee's* serious disadvantage, but he was still far from being licked.

The Union Supreme Commander's pause following Cold Harbor on June 3 coincided with a similar pause by Hunter's Valley force after the seizure of Staunton on June 6, although for different reasons. Reinforcements were on the way to join Hunter, and while awaiting their arrival he proceeded systematically to destroy everything in Staunton of value to the enemy except private property—factories, mills and foundries—and to remove from the stores of the town all merchandise beneficial to the Confederate cause. The railroad station was burned and the tracks of the Virginia Central Railroad were torn up for miles in either direction.

On June 7 *Lee* decided that the time for evaluation was past. Encouraged by his army's decisive repulse of Grant's hopeless assault at Cold Harbor, and confident of his own ability to parry further blows, *Lee* sent *Breckinridge* back to Lynchburg with his reduced infantry division, to team up with *McCausland's* cavalry, gather in what additional strength he might be able to recruit in an area that knew the former Vice President *(Breckinridge)* well, and do what he could to halt the depredations of Hunter's army.

In further pursuit of his policy of hammering away at *Lee* wherever opportunity seemed to offer, and in the expectation that Hunter would succeed without difficulty in capturing Lynchburg and moving on to destroy the Central Railroad eastward from Charlottesville, Grant on June 6 dispatched Sheridan, with Gregg's and Torbert's cavalry divisions, to wreck the railroad from the east. The plan was for the two Federal forces to unite somewhere along the line, complete the destruction of trackage and the canal as far as Hanover Junction, and rejoin the Army of the Potomac.

As soon as word reached *Lee* that Sheridan was on the loose, he countered by sending *General Wade Hampton,* in command of the cavalry since *Jeb Stuart's* death from wounds at Yellow Tavern, with his own and *Fitz Lee's* divisions to forestall Sheridan's designs, whatever they might might be. The opposing cavalry tangled in several lively fights at Trevilian Station and vicinity, but the junction of Sheridan's force with Hunter's never materialized; first, because Hunter was destined never to penetrate beyond the western outskirts of Lynchburg, and secondly because *Hampton's Confederate cavalry* occupied Sheridan's attention to such an extent that the latter began to run short of ammunition and decided on June 12 to retrace his steps, encumbered with his own wounded, about 500 captured Rebels, and a horde of pathetic Negroes who had attached themselves to his column as a hoped-for guaranty of freedom from bondage.

EARLY IS GIVEN A MISSION

On June 12 *Jubal Early*, Lieutenant General commanding the veteran *Second Corps, Army of Northern Virginia,* was summoned from his reserve position at Gaines Mill, in rear of *Powell Hill's Third Corps,* to the quarters of the *Commanding General.* He was quietly briefed by General *Lee* on the general situation, following which *Lee* unfolded a plan that would have brought the usually undemonstrative *Stonewall Jackson* to his feet in a burst of uninhibited enthusiasm. *Early* was told that he was to take his corps on an independent mission, employing as much secrecy as practicable, hasten to the defense of Lynchburg, dispose of Hunter's Federal force in the Shenandoah Valley, and then move down the Valley, cross the Potomac, and threaten Washington.

That same evening his oral orders were confirmed in writing, attaching two battalions of artillery to the *Second Corps,* directing him to move at three o'clock the next morning, and advising that *Breckinridge* would receive instructions to report to *Early* for orders and that his force would be attached to the *Second Corps* for the march into Maryland.

In his *Reminiscences,* where he tells of the receipt of *Lee's* orders and describes his own actions in putting his corps in motion, *Early* makes no reference to his personal reactions, whether he was elated at the prospect of leading his own army in an exciting adventure that offered a rare opportunity for fame and solid achievement; or whether the heavy responsibility with which *Lee* had charged him, and the grave risks that might involve his own force in failure and possible destruction, were uppermost in his mind. It was only later, when the war was over and events could be studied in retrospect, that *Early* recorded his ex post facto opinion that he had been selected to lead what he described as "a forlorn hope."

VICTORIOUS CONFEDERATES IN THE SHENANDOAH

CHAPTER 2

HUNTER FLEES BEFORE EARLY

HOWEVER *Jubal Early* may have felt about the far-ranging mission that General *Lee* had just given him, to many of the enlisted men of the *Second Corps* it was cheering news. After three years of fighting and severe losses the ranks of the corps still numbered hundreds of men who had marched with *Stonewall,* up and down the Shenandoah Valley, the garden spot of Virginia which was home to many of them, and moreover an area that for purposes of campaigning was infinitely to be desired over the rugged Wilderness or the Tidewater Country.

Early and his staff had plenty of business to attend to in

24

the few hours that remained before the advance elements of the *Second Corps* were scheduled to move out, in the early hours before dawn of the next day. These included procurement of supplies and ammunition; disposition of the sick and those whose physical condition might not be equal to the rigors of a long, fast march; determination of the troop order for the march; and many other matters that required attention for such an expedition. The famous old *Second Corps* was about to cut loose from the main army for a long march of unspecified duration, on a mission that offered great potential for exciting achievement.

Information of the enemy was meager. Hunter's cavalry had cut the railroad and telegraph lines between Charlottesville and Lynchburg, while Sheridan's horsemen were similarly engaged between Charlottesville and Richmond. *Early* knew that Hunter had been reported at Staunton and his force augmented by Crook's infantry and Averell's cavalry, but the exact strength of the Union army in the Valley could only be estimated. He knew also that Sheridan's cavalry was somewhere along his own line of march and might interfere with his movement, a danger that was somewhat lessened by the probability that *Hampton's* cavalry would keep Sheridan from causing him any real trouble.

The whereabouts of *Breckinridge's* infantry was uncertain, although he was supposed to be at Waynesboro or Rockfish Gap. *Early* wasn't sure what *McCausland's* or *Imboden's* cavalry might be doing or just where they were operating at the moment, but in light of his low opinion of the capabilities of cavalry, an obsession well-known to the rest of the army, it may safely be assumed that the extent of its cooperation and support did not enter materially into his calculations. *Lee* had suggested that *Early* march via Charlottesville through Swift Run Gap in the Blue

Ridge, to come in on Hunter's rear at Staunton. If *Breckinridge* were actually at Waynesboro and could delay Hunter's march eastward until the *Second Corps* could get behind him, the chances were good that Lynchburg would escape destruction and Hunter be brought to battle in the Valley.

Taking account of stock as he prepared for the movement, *Early* observed that his three infantry divisions could muster a total of only 8,000 muskets* (exclusive of the two artillery battalions); that divisions had been reduced to the size of normal brigades and brigades to regimental strength by losses in the recent Wilderness Campaign and the battles of Spotsylvania and Cold Harbor; and that most of his general officers were leading new commands because of casualties and the resulting promotions and reassignments.

Although the projected third Confederate march of the war into Maryland (this one via the Shenandoah Valley) hardly qualified as an invasion, since it had only limited objectives and strategically was staged primarily as a diversion to relieve the pressure on *Lee's army* at Petersburg, its importance in the Southern commander's thinking was evident in his selection of the veteran *Second Corps* to carry out the assignment. It may be granted that it was now but a gaunt shadow of the proud corps that had served under *Jackson* and *Ewell*. Nevertheless it remained a redoubtable combat outfit. The passage of years and the loss of thousands of its best men at Bull Run and Antietam, Fredericksburg, Chancellorsville, Gettysburg and the Wilderness had not impaired its capability either for long, fast marches or sustained fighting.

----

* Apparently *Early*, like some other Confederate commanders, was forced to rely on scanty, irregular, and incomplete strength returns. It seems likely that his figure of "8,000" referred to the number of muskets available in the battle line.

A more distinguished group of major generals than those composing *Early's* command would be hard to find. Each had proven his worth on many battlefields. *Early* and *Ramseur* were graduates of West Point, the former in 1837, the latter in 1860. *Rodes* claimed Virginia Military Institute as his Alma Mater and *Breckinridge* was a graduate of Center College, Kentucky. *Gordon* had spent several years at the University of Georgia, but left college before graduating. *Ramseur* at 27 was the youngest of the five, *Early* the oldest at 48; *Breckinridge* was 43, *Rodes* 35, and *Gordon* 32.

Rodes would be the first of the quintet to die, at Winchester on September 18, 1864. The second, *Ramseur,* carrying wounds received at Malvern Hill, Chancellorsville, and Spotsylvania Court House, and destined to receive the fourth, a mortal one, at Cedar Creek on October 19, was the youngest West Pointer in the Confederate armies to become a major general, having received his second star on the day following his 27th birthday.

Breckinridge and *Gordon* were lawyers, without previous military education or training, but both possessed qualities of leadership which come from within rather than from books or academic halls, however helpful the latter may be in providing the basic foundation.

There were other similarities between *John C. Breckinridge* of Kentucky and *John B. Gordon* of Georgia. The former was a magnificent physical specimen whose personality and driving force had carried him to the Vice Presidency of the United States in 1856 when he was only 35 years of age. The latter, who by the end of the war had come to be recognized as perhaps the most distinguished of all the Confederate officers who hailed from Georgia, was a tall, slender man of strong character and great personal

Maj. Gen. John C. Breckinridge

Maj. Gen. John B. Gordon

Maj. Gen. Stephen D. Ramseur

Maj. Gen. Robert E. Rodes

courage, an accomplished horseman who looked every inch the natural military leader that he proved himself as he rose to brigade, division, and corps command. Both generals served their respective states in the United States Senate, *Breckinridge* resigning as Vice President in order to take his seat in 1859, while *Gordon's* public service came after the war, when he was welcomed back to Georgia as a hero for whom nothing was too good that his state had to offer. An appreciative public elected him to the Senate for three terms, interrupted only by a tour of duty as Governor of the State.

Breckinridge and *Gordon* were two Confederate generals who by the quality of their soldierly leadership would disprove the narrow conception that only an officer trained at West Point or other military institution such as V.M.I. could possibly qualify for command of large bodies of troops. Made a major general in early 1862, the ex-Vice President fought at Shiloh, Vicksburg, Murfreesboro, and Chickamauga, and was commanding the Department of West Virginia when the spotlight was again turned on the Shenandoah Valley in the summer of 1864. Both *Lee* and *Jefferson Davis* reposed great confidence and trust in *Breckinridge,* so much so that the Confederate President called him to Richmond to the post of Secretary of War in February 1865, in which position his brilliant political-military career came to a close two months later with the abandonment of the Capital and the surrender at Appomattox.

For his chief of artillery, *Early* was fortunate in having Brigadier General *Armistead L. Long,* an experienced and skilful artilleryman who had served as General *Lee's* military secretary from the spring of 1862 until after the Battle of Gettysburg in 1863. A West Point graduate, class of 1850, he married the daughter of General E. V. Sumner in 1860, but the family relationship did not preclude his resignation to join the Confederacy. *Long's* excellent judgment in the placement and tactical employment of gun batteries led *Lee,* although with reluctance at losing a good secretary, to assign him to command the artillery of the *Second Corps,* with which he served until the end of the war. His selection was solid assurance that the twenty-four guns that would accompany the expedition would be ably commanded.

THE SECOND CORPS MOVES OUT

At 2 a.m. on June 13, an hour ahead of schedule (as though *Jubal Early* was determined to prove to *Lee* that he had selected the right man to fill the shoes of *Jackson* and *Ewell*), the *Second Corps* commenced its march, covering eighty miles in four days to reach the Rivanna River near Charlottesville on June 16. En route, the troops passed over the scene of the recent cavalry fight at Trevilian Station, but by then both *Hampton's* and Sheridan's troopers had moved back towards Richmond. At Charlottesville *Early* found a telegram from *Breckinridge,* reporting that Hunter had reached Bedford County, about twenty miles from Lynchburg, to which place *Breckinridge* had hastened from Rockfish Gap when he learned that the Union force had bypassed Waynesboro, crossing the mountains to the south on a direct route from Staunton through Lexington.

Breckinridge reached Lynchburg from Rockfish Gap with his small division on June 15, attached the VMI cadet battalion to his command, and proceeded to strengthen the defenses of the town to meet the expected attack from the oncoming Hunter. Angered by the Federal general's wanton destruction of property in the course of his advance, the Confederates put their hearts into the task of hastily throwing up emplacements in a semicircle on the western outskirts of Lynchburg. It was obvious, however, that the poorly mounted scratch cavalry of *Imboden and McCausland,* hovering on the fringe of Hunter's advance, could hope to do little more than slow him down. When the Federals were ready to brush the cavalry aside and assault the weak defenses of Lynchburg in earnest, *Breckinridge's* tiny force, vastly outnumbered by Hunter's 18,000, would be able to hold out little longer than it would take Hunter to develop his greatly superior forces for action.

Early Races Against Time

The fate of Lynchburg rested with the clock, and the enterprise of the Federal commander. Would *Early's corps* arrive in time? With sixty miles of road marching still to be covered between Charlottesville and Lynchburg, as against only twenty for Hunter, to *Early* the situation looked unpromising. In fact, the Federal troops may already have reached Lynchburg, 24 hours having passed since the dispatch of *Breckinridge's* telegram. Fortunately for the Confederates, the damage to the wire communications between the two towns was slight and had been quickly repaired.

Early went into action as soon as he read *Breckinridge's* telegram of the sixteenth, starting his artillery and wagon trains on the highway in the direction of Lynchburg. Only one train stood on the tracks at Charlottesville, about to pull out for Waynesboro. It was no time to stand on ceremony. *Early* promptly commandeered it and sent wires to the railroad authorities directing them to dispatch all passenger and freight trains without delay to Charlottesville to meet the emergency. While awaiting the arrival of the requisitioned rail equipment, *Early* encountered some old friends in Charlottesville, one of whom invited the general to join him in a drink. Apparently one good turn deserved another, for after several hours *Old Jube* had become a bit mellow, as reported by a member of his staff, *William Allan,* who was heard to remark that it was the only time he had ever seen *Early* even slightly under the influence. Another member of his staff saw to it that his general met an afternoon engagement for tea at the home of a university professor, so that by evening things were again normal and running smoothly at the temporary army command post.*

In spite of the urgency of *Early's* need, it was not until early the following morning, June 17, that additional rolling stock became available, and then only enough to provide accommodations for half the infantry. At sunrise *Ramseur's* division and one of *Gordon's* brigades were loaded on box and stock cars. The rest of *Gordon's* and all of *Rodes' division* were ordered to march along the railroad until the first troop serial could be unloaded and the empty trains returned to pick them up. *Early* boarded the first train with *Ramseur's* troops and off they went.

The trip was made with agonizing slowness, so that it was one o'clock in the afternoon of the seventeenth before the first train puffed into the Lynchburg station, and hours later before the others reached their destination. But Hunter had been even slower, *McCausland* and *Imboden* with their cavalry having harassed his advance. *Early* was pleasantly surprised to find no Federals at Lynchburg, but he soon discovered that the defense arrangements had bogged down somewhat because *Breckinridge* had been forced to take to his bed, suffering from an injury caused by a fall from his horse at Cold Harbor.

Several convalescent generals happened to be sojourning in Lynchburg, among them Major General *Daniel H. Hill*

---

* *Stonewall's Man, Sandie Pendleton,* by W. G. Bean, Chapel Hill, N. C., p. 204.

and Brigadier General *Harry T. Hays,* the latter convalescing from a wound received at Spotsylvania. Both had volunteered their services and assisted in staking out a defense line along the western edge of town. Accompanied by *Hill, Early* rode over the ground and decided that sounder tactics would be to place his own divisions well forward from the close-in defense, in order to avoid enemy shell fire directed against the buildings in Lynchburg.

Hunter's Actions, June 8 to 16

The instructions Hunter had received from Grant afforded wide scope for his projected operations. His primary mission was to cause maximum damage to the railroads and the James River Canal. Collaterally his activities would serve to attract strength from *Lee's army,* keep enemy forces in the Valley occupied, and quite possibly invest Lynchburg, if only temporarily, for the psychological impact such seizure would have on Confederates everywhere and, as a practical measure, for the purpose of destroying it as a key supply base for Southern armies.

Brigadier General George Crook's "Army of West Virginia" (two small divisions) and Brigadier General William W. Averell's cavalry division joined Hunter at Staunton June 8, increasing his force to approximately 18,000 men. Thus reinforced, Hunter, after a short stay in Staunton, had marched on Lynchburg, halting at Lexington June 11 long enough to burn the buildings of the Virginia Military Institute, presumably in retaliation for the sturdy fight the cadets of the Academy had put up in helping to drive Sigel's force from New Market on May 15. *Governor Letcher's* residence and the homes of other prominent citizens were also put to the torch. But when Hunter ordered his incendiary detachment to ⋅burn Washington College, originally endowed by George Washington, many

Union officers, among whom was Captain William McKinley, protested so vigorously that that venerable institution was saved for the time when General *R. E. Lee,* putting off his uniform, would become its distinguished postwar President.

Hunter dallied in Lexington three or four days, indulging his propensity for burning and destruction, and in so doing forfeited the opportunity to reach Lynchburg before

MAJOR GENERAL DAVID HUNTER

the virtually undefended city could be prepared for defense and secured by the arrival of the regular Confederate forces that were converging on it from several directions.

There was no logical reason for the sluggish manner in which Hunter made his march from Staunton to Lynchburg. He was not the most aggressive of generals, but neither was he a timid soul. It is conceivable that the process of destroying valuable Confederate installations as he moved east may have induced him to become more cautious, in the face of conflicting reports on the defensive strength that he would encounter at Lynchburg. Of Virginia ancestry, although not a native himself, Hunter had many relatives living in the country that he was presently engaged in devastating, among them Confederate Secretary of State *R. M. T. Hunter* and Major *Robert W. Hunter* of General *John B. Gordon's* staff. He had been a vehement opponent of slavery in the South and he knew that he was cordially hated on that score alone. His recent acts in Staunton and Lexington had added nothing to his stature in the eyes of Virginians. Reputed to have been a skilled duellist in his younger days and to have killed two men in the exercise of his specialty, the fact that *Jefferson Davis* once served as his second would not be likely to mitigate Southern hostility. If dubious thoughts of his personal safety, should he fall into the vengeful hands of infuriated Confederates, may have crossed the Federal general's mind, that would partly explain his growing anxiety to keep his troops concentrated and to move with caution until he could learn if reports of a strong force hastening to secure Lynchburg were true or false. Even at that, six days had elapsed from the time he reached Lexington until his arrival before Lynchburg, indicating that he couldn't have covered much over 10 miles a day on the average.

General Crook's subsequent account of Hunter's campaign referred in scathing terms to the ineffective service of Averell's cavalry during this period. It seems that Hunter on approaching Lexington from the north had sent Averell to cross Black River higher up, to come in on the rear of the *VMI cadet battalion* that was opposing the Union advance. This Averell failed to do, allowing the cadets to escape to Lynchburg. As for General Duffie, who commanded part of the cavalry, instead of pursuing the mission assigned him during Hunter's occupation of Lexington, that officer, according to Crook, "had spent his time pilfering, including robbing refugees of some Staunton City bonds which, after the war, he tried to dispose of." Duffie's side-adventure, Crook said, in consequence delayed the advance one or two days. Whatever the cause, or combination of causes, David Hunter was in no great hurry to get to Lynchburg, a city that could have been taken with very little resistance any time up to the morning of June 17. So fearful had Hunter become of the outcome of the inevitable battle, which his imagination conjured up as occurring when his force should meet the "heavy reinforcements" coming up from somewhere, that he ordered his large wagon train to return to the comparative safety of the western side of the Blue Ridge. This precautionary measure reflected little confidence in a Union victory.

Hunter's Column Pauses Before Lynchburg

As though he hadn't wasted enough time already, Hunter lost one more day in sending his column across the Blue Ridge by way of the lofty Peaks of Otter rather than by the direct road from Lexington to Lynchburg, which indirect approach, instead of bringing him into the latter town from the northwest, put him on the Salem road, southwest of Lynchburg. By midday June 17, Crook's infantry and Averell's cavalry, pushing *Imboden's* harassing cavalry ahead of them, were four miles from Lynchburg, proceeding as the advance of Hunter's army. Crook halted near an old Quaker meeting house, at which point instructions were received from Hunter not to attack until the rest of the column had closed up.

When the afternoon was about gone, and no additional troops had arrived, Crook became impatient. He and Averell put their heads together, cooked up a combined maneuver, and moved out, the Union cavalry coming in on *Imboden's* flank. The threatened attack was sufficient to panic *Imboden's* troopers, who started for the rear.

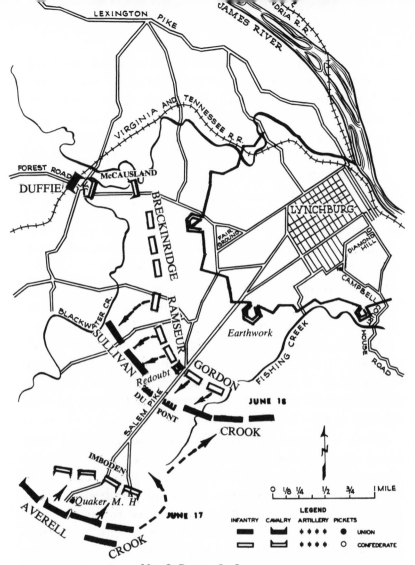

MAP 2. BATTLE OF LYNCHBURG

Near the Quaker Meeting House is shown the action on June 17, 1864, in which the Confederate cavalry under Imboden, attempting to delay Hunter's advance on Lynchburg, is driven back by Averell and Crook. On this day Breckinridge's infantry is inside the earthworks which have been thrown up to protect the city against attacks from the west.

The action on June 18 is shown, in which Ramseur and Gordon attack Sullivan, and bluff Hunter into withdrawing during the night. On this day Duffie's cavalry division drives McCausland back along Forest Road to the vicinity of a railroad bridge. Here McCausland, reinforced by infantry, stops Duffie's further advance.

This map is based on Plate 83 (7) of the Atlas.

37

It was at that juncture that *Early* and *Hill* rode out from the town to examine *Imboden's* situation, which they quickly discovered to be entirely fluid. *Early* sent back word to *Ramseur* to bring his division forward from its temporary bivouac just west of Lynchburg. Two of *Ramseur's brigades,* with two guns, responding to the order, met *Early* at a redoubt two miles out of Lynchburg, where they were thrown at once across the road as an obstacle to possible Federal pursuit of the retiring Confederate cavalry. A short time later *Ramseur's* other *brigade* and that portion of *Gordon's division* which had come on the first trainload, were fed into an extension of the defense line.

Crook has left in a few brief sentences a vague, unsatisfactory account of what occurred. Referring to his enforced delay in attacking the opposing Confederates, he wrote: "After waiting until nearly dark, I had to do all the work as it was; for I got no material assistance from anyone else. I defeated their troops, captured their artillery, and drove their troops off the field. It became too dark to go into the town, so we had to go into camp."

Crook neglected to identify his opponents, but they could only have been *Imboden's* small cavalry force, for *Imboden* reported the skirmish at the Quaker Church as having caused him casualties of over one hundred in killed and wounded, adding that his men retired to the fortifications of Lynchburg "unpursued by the enemy." In view of the indefiniteness of Crook's narrative, one may be pardoned for being somewhat skeptical that he "captured their artillery," if for no other reason than that *Imboden* would be most unlikely to be accompanied by guns on the kind of mission upon which he was engaged at the time.

Crook's account must be further discounted because he makes not the slightest reference to the arrival of Sullivan's division and DuPont's artillery, in company with which troops his own attacked *Early* the following day,

June 18, without being able to break his resistance. The probability is that Crook became so disgusted with Hunter's timid leadership and so disgruntled at being associated with a group of ineffectual division generals such as Sullivan, Averell, and Duffie, for none of whom he had the slightest respect, that he wanted to forget the whole thing, and therefore gave the Lynchburg expedition bare mention in his autobiography.

Apparently nothing much had happened after Crook drove *Imboden's* weak force of cavalry away from the Quaker Church except a desultory exchange of artillery fire. *Early* was entirely satisfied that his display of force *(Ramseur's brigades)* astride the Salem Road had prevented the Union infantry and dismounted cavalry from an attempt to take Lynchburg after dark.

On the Forest Road to the north, *McCausland's cavalry,* performing a similar mission to that of *Imboden's* on the Salem Road, was slowly pushed back by a Federal detachment, probably Duffie's cavalry preceding Sullivan's division of Hunter's force. There, too, the advance halted for the night, leaving Lynchburg untouched, as *Early* waited impatiently for the slow-acting railroad authorities to transport the still marching remaining brigades of *Rodes'* and *Gordon's divisions* to the worried city.

That night Crook's men heard trains coming into Lynchburg from the side of the town opposite them, bringing reinforcements as they naturally supposed. They also heard the Confederates cheering, which completed the illusion that their imagination conjured up. For it was no more than that, a ruse devised by the wily Confederates to dampen Federal ardor for aggressive action, a desire that happened to be strangely nonexistent in the mind of the troubled General Hunter. The trick was not a new one, to run a detached engine with an empty car noisily up and down the tracks, but it usually worked.

Jubal Early was still in a dangerous spot and he knew it. Counting *Breckinridge's* scratch force, the cadets, and a scattering of home guards, but with all the artillery and half of the infantry of the *Second Corps* still absent he had fewer than 8,000 men all told to counter Hunter's 18,000. If he should try to man the semicircular defense line necessary to cover all the roads that Hunter might decide to use, his defense, lacking depth, would be dangerously thin all along the line. The most likely point of danger would be the Salem Road, where he was already in contact with Crook and Averell, but a flank maneuver from the north against Lynchburg could not be ruled out.

Early compromised by moving *Breckinridge's infantry* and *artillery* forward to prolong *Ramseur's line* to the north, but even then it fell somewhat short of reaching the Forest Road. He would have to rely on *McCausland's* dog-tired troopers to watch the enemy on that avenue of approach. The direct road from Lexington would have to be entirely unguarded. If Hunter should send troops by that route, *Early* would be forced to do some rapid sideslipping to meet the threat, which at the moment did not seem imminent.

Early had no choice but to remain on the defensive until the rest of his corps arrived, however ambitious he may have been to take the offensive. Even when the delayed troops should all be up, Hunter would still have a substantial margin of strength in his favor. Instinct and the opinion of one or two of his division commanders favored a prompt attack to gain the initiative, but *Early* considered it too grave a risk. Granted that Hunter had shown no evidence of boldness, Lynchburg was in fact open to attack from three sides and it was possible that a flank maneuver by the Federals might lead to a Confederate disaster. *Early* therefore bided his time, visiting his lines repeatedly as

June 18 came, and almost went, before there was any sign of a Union attack.

Hunter's mental fog persisted all through the seventeenth of June and until the morning of the following day. He couldn't seem to make up his mind what to do. His mission was clear enough, but the hesitation that paralyzed him was based chiefly on uncertainty as to the augmented strength of the enemy in his front. The novel thought finally occured to him, to send a number of reconnaissances in force to cause the enemy to show his hand. In that way, perhaps, he could develop the Confederate strength and would then be able to decide upon an intelligent battle plan. At least it was a positive step, however elemental militarily. Three roads ran to Lynchburg within operating distance of Hunter's position on the Salem Road: the one he was on; the Forest Road about three miles to the north; and a third road which came up from the South through Campbell Court House. Orders to effect the desired reconnaissances were issued in the early morning of June 18.

Except along the Forest Road, where Duffie on his own responsibility had already moved against *McCausland's* blocking cavalry, nothing much happened. Possibly command efficiency at Hunter's headquarters had suffered from the irresolution of the general commanding, for as late as nine o'clock in the morning Duffie had heard nothing from Hunter or Averell, whose cavalry division was supposed to be the nearest to Duffie's line of advance. However, he went right ahead, this time vigorously pressing his independent battle, and finally succeeded in breaking *McCausland's* resistance, forcing him to retire after damaging a bridge that crossed the railroad tracks. Duffie followed *McCausland* as far as Blackwater Creek, where the Confederates occupied a strong position on the far side of the stream, obviously part of the entrenchments that had been thrown up to serve as *Early's* main line of defense. Duffie ordered several attacks, with artillery support, on this position, but each was repulsed. Still out of touch with army headquarters, whence no orders had come, the cavalry officer figured he had gone as far as he could, or should; so he settled down to hold where he was and await clarification from his so far uncommunicative commander.

The ordered reconnaissances on the center and south roads were feebly undertaken, without achieving their purpose. *Early* could scarcely believe that a superior force like Hunter's would show so little energy or spirit. What Hunter was doing most of the day was one of the unsolved mysteries of the expedition. *Early's* Confederates, stalling desperately for time, threw bluff after bluff, repeatedly marching detachments back and forth to give the impression of arriving reinforcements.

During the night Sullivan's division, having finally joined Crook's troops was assigned to position on the left of the Salem Turnpike, with Crook on the right, and Du Pont's artillery in the center astride the pike. Towards noon, when it seemed to *Early* that Hunter was never going to make up his mind to attack, the Confederate general determined to provoke an assault in the hope that Hunter in his apparently perplexed state might be encouraged to make a false move that could be exploited.

Suddenly Confederate batteries opened fire. Du Pont's Federal guns responded, and for a time the artillery duel raged. Then from the entrenchments the men of *Ramseur's* and *Gordon's divisions* leaped to their feet and charged the Union lines. The unexpected attack caught Hunter flatfooted, routed part of Sullivan's division, and was on the verge of breaking Hunter's line when some of Crook's troops were rushed over from the right to restore the balance; after which *Early's* venturesome warriors returned to their entrenchments, happily content with the success of their surprise attack.

42

If anything more had been needed to take the final bit of starch out of the passive Hunter, that roaring Confederate attack did it. Hunter concluded that Lynchburg was not for him; West Virginia offered a much healthier climate. Taking precautions not to advertise his intentions to *Early*, orders were transmitted, before darkness fell, to all elements to take the road to the west as soon after dark as the troops could be put in column.

Late that day *Rodes' division* and the rest of *Gordon's brigades* had finally arrived by rail. The artillery and trains were still marching by road. The noise the Federals made as they moved out could be heard by the Confederates, but *Early* had no way of knowing their direction, which conceivably could be a shift in position for the purpose of coming in on Lynchburg from the south. He toyed with the idea of a night attack, but thought better of it. It would still be a risky venture, and *Early* was acutely conscious of his second mission, upon which General *Lee* counted heavily: to divert Washington's attention from Petersburg and Richmond. He decided to hold off till morning, by which time his quarry had put many miles between the Confederates and himself. Crook's infantry, more reliable than Sullivan's, brought up the rear, bivouacking the night of June 19 at Liberty,* twenty miles west of Lynchburg, Crook all the while complaining that Hunter gave him all the tough jobs.

General *Gordon*, a firm believer in attacking whenever a choice existed, had been convinced that the calculated risk of a night attack should be taken when Hunter's men were discovered to be on the move. In urging *Early* not to delay, *Gordon* prophesied that otherwise by morn-

---

* Now Bedford City.

ing his quarry would have taken flight. As it happened, *Gordon* was right, but the effect of a night assault would have been problematical. It might have caused such havoc in Hunter's marching columns as to ruin him entirely as an organized force; conversely it could have disrupted *Early's* own *corps* in the darkness so that an effective pursuit would be delayed for hours.

In early daylight the Confederates piled out of their defenses and took off after the Federals. *Early* sent the *Second Corps* along the Salem Road. *Breckinridge's* small *division* followed the Forest Road, while the combined cavalry brigades under command of *Robert Ransom,* whom *Lee* had just sent to *Early* for that purpose, took the road that led past the Peaks of Otter, with instructions to get around Hunter to seal off his escape.

To Hunter's credit, his retreat, humiliating as it was, was skilfully conducted. On only one occasion were the pursuers able to interfere with the Federal race for sanctuary. That was when *McCausland's cavalry* barged in on the fleeing column at a mountain pass known as "Hanging Rock," capturing prisoners and ten pieces of artillery. With that exception, Hunter got off scot free, passed through Buford's Gap and never stopped until his bedraggled army reached safety on the Kanawha River in West Virginia. His exhausted troops arrived at Charleston June 29, sadly in need of food and clothing, many of them barefoot. During the retreat Hunter had directed that the wagons be abandoned, but Crook disregarded the order by retaining a part of his, with the result that his men fared slightly better than the rest of the army.

It was with a feeling of relief that *Early* saw Hunter take the route to Lewisburg, which meant that he was headed for the Kanawha Valley and would be out of the way for some time at least. Had the enemy turned in the direction of southwestern Virginia, *Early* felt that he would have had to follow him because of the unguarded supplies in that area.

EARLY SWEEPS THE VALLEY CLEAN

The first phase of his mission had been speedily fulfilled. The Shenandoah Valley was cleared of Federal troops, and *Early* was ready to undertake the second phase. *Lee* had couched his instructions for the raid on Washington in his usual diplomatic language, advising *Early* to use his discretion as to whether to risk the attempt. *Early* decided that he would continue the march, but only after giving his troops a short rest following their three-day, sixty-mile chase after Hunter.

On June 22 the Confederates enjoyed at Botetourt Spring a 24-hour period of relaxation, only to resume the march the following day. That night the column reached Buchanan, passing over the route Hunter had taken on his return march from Lynchburg. Early described the conditions in which the country had been left:

The scenes on Hunter's route from Lynchburg had been truly heart-rending. Houses had been burned, and helpless women and children left without shelter. The country had been stripped of provisions and many families left without a morsel to eat. Furniture and bedding had been cut to pieces, and old men and women and children robbed of all the clothing they had except that on their backs. Ladies' trunks had been rifled and their dresses torn to pieces in mere wantonness. Even the negro girls had lost their little finery. We now had renewed evidences of the outrages committed by Hunter's orders in burning and plundering private houses. We saw the ruins of a number of houses to which the torch had been applied by his orders. At Lexington he had burned the Military Institute, with all its contents, including its library and scientific apparatus; and Washington College had been plundered and the statue of Washington stolen. The

45

residence of Ex-Governor Letcher at that place had been burned by orders, and but a few minutes given Mrs. Letcher and her family to leave the house. In the same county a most excellent christian gentleman, a Mr. Creigh, had been hung, because, on a former occasion, he had killed a straggling and marauding Federal soldier while in the act of insulting and outraging the ladies of his family. These are but some of the outrages committed by Hunter or his orders, and I will not insult the memory of the ancient barbarians of the North by calling them "acts of Vandalism." If those old Barbarians were savage and cruel, they at least had the manliness and daring of rude soldiers, with occasional traits of magnanimity. Hunter's deeds were those of a malignant and cowardly fanatic, who was better qualified to make war upon helpless women and children than upon armed soldiers. The time consumed in the perpetration of those deeds, was the salvation of Lynchburg, with its stores, foundries, and factories, which were so necessary to our army.

The distance down the Valley from Buchanan to the Potomac was two hundred miles. Once across the big river and into Maryland, the *Second Corps* would have to march scores of additional miles in enemy country, with the risk of stirring up a Federal hornet's nest of violent opposition, the closer the Confederates came to the Union capital. General *Lee,* as an old campaigner, was fully aware of the magnitude of *Early's* assignment and may have had second thoughts about the practicality of the projected raid even though its potential strategic implications still loomed large in his planning. At intervals after the fight at Lynchburg *Early* received messages from the General inquiring whether he still considered the march on Washington advisable, in each case giving *Early* the choice of going through with the plan or returning to the army at Petersburg.

A less determined general than *Jubal Early* might have

read into these dispatches a weakening of *Lee's* purpose; a less self-assured character could have interpreted them as indicating a doubt whether *Early* and his men had the staying power to execute so far-reaching a mission. Many a pair of shoes had already been worn out and so far no replacements had caught up with the expedition. Roads were dusty, the heat of summer would soon become oppressive, rations were not always at hand, and the troops had been on the go virtually without intermission since the start of the Wilderness campaign seven weeks earlier. All of these things were in *Lee's* mind as he repeatedly offered *Early* an honorable out.

Weighing all the factors, *Old Jube* set his face towards Washington with, it may be assumed, the hearty concurrence of such able fighting leaders as *John Breckinridge, John B. Gordon, Robert Rodes,* and *Dodson Ramseur.* In view of the size of the job and the uncertainty of the outcome, it was of the first importance that the troops be reshod, that all excess baggage be discarded, and the column stripped down to bare essentials.

Reaching Staunton on June 26, *Early* spent the day sorting out for elimination every bit of transportation not considered certain to stand up under pressure, inspecting guns and horses to weed out those unfit for service, remounting horseless troopers, and distributing provisions that came up that day from Waynesboro. *Early* took advantage of the pause at Staunton to make a number of officer and organizational adjustments. One was to give General *Breckinridge* a command commensurate with his position and rank by assigning *Gordon's* and *Elzey's* divisions (the latter temporarily under *Vaughn* because of *Elzey's* relief at his own request) to a provisional semicorps under *Breckinridge.* Another was to assign Colonel *Bradley T. Johnson* to command the cavalry brigade of the late General *W. E. Jones,* to which was attached the *bat-*

CONFEDERATES CUTTING THE CHESAPEAKE AND OHIO CANAL

talion of Maryland cavalry that had come up with *Johnson.*

The strength returns at Staunton, *Early* reported, revealed about 10,000 foot soldiers, 2,000 troopers (with horse artillery), and three battalions of artillery (40 guns), including that of *Breckinridge* and the two from the *Second Corps.* Leaving empty wagons with instructions to follow the column as soon as the requisitioned shoes arrived, *Early* resumed the march on June 28 with seven days' rations on the wagons and in the men's haversacks. *Imboden's cavalry* was detached from *Ransom's command* and sent ahead through Brock's Gap to destroy the railroad bridge over the south branch of the Potomac and all the bridges on the Baltimore and Ohio Railroad as far as Martinsburg. The main body proceeded north by the Valley pike, reaching Winchester on July 2. At that point *Early* received a telegram from *Lee* telling him to remain in that vicinity until everything could be put in readiness for the dash into Maryland, meanwhile destroying as much of the Baltimore and Ohio Railroad and the Chesapeake and Ohio Canal as possible.

The cavalry brigades of *Johnson* and *McCausland* were sent out from Winchester by different routes to get beyond Martinsburg, combine forces, and cut off the retreat of Sigel's Federals, stationed at Martinsburg. On July 3, *Early* split his infantry and artillery into two echelons, to move by different roads on Martinsburg, the idea being to pocket Sigel in that town and force his capitulation. The mere threat was sufficient to cause the wholly undependable Sigel to retire with his troops. The Union general retreated rapidly to the Potomac, crossed at Shepherdstown, and found lodging on the bristling Maryland Heights that looked down forbiddingly at strategic Harpers Ferry on the southern shore.

Early's force passed the 4th of July closing in on Harpers Ferry, driving the garrison into the village, and occupying Bolivar Heights. That night the Federals evacuated Harpers Ferry, burned the railroad and pontoon bridges behind them, and joined Sigel on Maryland Heights under the protection of his artillery, whose guns discouraged the occupation of the town of Harpers Ferry itself by the Confederates. Under cover of darkness, however, *Early* was able to gather in a considerable cache of supplies which the Federals in their haste had neglected to destroy.

With the occupation of Shepherdstown and the fords over the Potomac, the stage was set for the great adventure —the objective, Washington, D. C.

FORT STEVENS IN WARTIME

CHAPTER 3

THE RAID ON WASHINGTON

THE direct route from Harpers Ferry to Washington was naturally the one *Early* chose for the further advance of the reinforced *Second Corps,* now committed to the raid on Washington. Time was all-important, for once across the Potomac and moving through Maryland, it would be fatal to dally. The North's extreme sensitivity over the safety of the Capital made it safe to assume that reinforcements would be rushed to the defenses of the city if there should be even the suspicion of a threat in that direction. The raiders would have to play it by ear as they moved along, since *Early* had not made up his mind in advance whether to attempt to penetrate Washington's defenses or merely threaten the heart of the city by getting as close to it as the situation should warrant. Either eventuality would satisfy *Lee's* purpose to give the Lincoln Administration its greatest scare since *Stonewall Jackson* kept the Capital in a state of continual alarm back in 1862. Surprise was the principal ingredient of the plan, and that in turn implied rapid movement.

General Grant and the War Department did not know the whereabouts of the Confederate *Second Corps,* after Hunter's repulse at Lynchburg and ignominious retreat to the fastnesses of West Virginia. Dispatches from Franz Sigel at Martinsburg and Max Weber, commanding at Harpers Ferry, only added to the fog of war without causing the Federal authorities at Petersburg and Washington any particular anxiety. The flurries of excitement were nothing new, what with frequent cavalry and guerrilla raids by the fast-moving and hard-hitting Rebel horsemen, particularly *Mosby's* men, so that the rumors of a large Confederate force moving towards the Potomac were taken as nothing more.

On July 3 Halleck wired Grant that Sigel had reported *Early* and *Breckinridge,* together with *Mosby's* guerrillas, to be moving down the Shenandoah Valley from Staunton, and that he had ordered Hunter up to the line of the Baltimore and Ohio Railroad, but had received no reply from the missing Hunter (who obviously hadn't as yet recovered his poise, and was still far away on the Kanawha River). Grant telegraphed a reply the same afternoon: "*Early's corps* is now here. There are no troops that can now be threatening Hunter's department, except the remnant of the force *W. E. Jones* had, and possibly *Breckinridge.*" And in a later telegram that evening, after checking with Meade's headquarters, Grant told Halleck: "I find no prisoners have been taken from it (*Early's Corps*) since its reported return. Deserters, however, from other commands reported that it returned about five or six days ago." If under instructions from *Lee,* Confederate intelligence personnel in the guise of deserters had entered Meade's lines for the purpose of deceiving Grant and pre-

51

serving the element of surprise for *Early's* expedition as long as possible, the ruse succeeded handsomely.

EARLY CROSSES THE POTOMAC

Early felt that it would be advantageous, before taking off for Washington, to maneuver Sigel out of Maryland Heights, to remove the danger attendant upon leaving that watchdog mountain peak in Federal possession on *Early's* flank and rear. To that end *Breckinridge's command* crossed the Potomac at Shepherdstown on the afternoon of July 5. The next day he sent *Gordon's division* across Antietam Creek to drive Sigel away or, if that failed, into the works on Maryland Heights, and concurrently to destroy the aqueduct of the Chesapeake and Ohio Canal. *Rodes'* and *Ramseur's divisions* followed. When *Gordon* completed his work of crippling the canal, *Breckinridge's* other division, now under *Echols'* command, joined *Gordon's* in the effort to dislodge Sigel. Finding the defenses too strong to overrun without serious loss and greater effort than *Early* felt was justified, *Old Jube* made a prompt shift of plans and decided to bypass the powerful Heights, take the longer route through the passes of South Mountain, and thence move through Frederick on Washington.

While *Breckinridge* and *Gordon* were making gestures at Sigel, *Early* sent the cavalry up the Cumberland Valley to clear out small parties of the enemy, reconnoiter the South Mountain passes, divert attention from the movements of his own infantry and guns, and incidentally make the Yankees pay the expenses of the expedition. *Bradley Johnson's brigade* occupied Boonsboro, while *McCausland* rode into Hagerstown, where he levied and collected a contribution of $20,000 from the citizens of that community.

By July 5 Grant had received more convincing intelligence from sources in the Valley and elsewhere to indicate that *Early* was indeed on his way to Washington. At 1 p.m. that day Meade informed him that two Confederate deserters that morning had stated it was being currently reported in Richmond and Petersburg "that *Early,* in command of two divisions of *Ewell's corps,* with *Breckinridge's command* and other forces, was making an invasion of Maryland with a view of capturing Washington, supposed to be defenseless."

Early meanwhile set up temporary field headquarters on the outskirts of Sharpsburg, a village of poignant memories to the *commanding general* and the living veterans of *Jackson's Second Corps.* On that very ridge, a short walk from Antietam Creek, *Jackson's* men had hastened up from Harpers Ferry on a fateful September day in 1862, racing to the help of the badly damaged, hard-pressed *Army of Northern Virginia* that was holding off McClellan's vastly superior Army of the Potomac in a battle that could have meant the extermination of *Lee's* grimly fighting divisions. Ahead loomed the high mountains through whose passes *Early's* men would shortly march over ground that was equally familiar. Beyond South Mountain lay a lovely valley, flanked on the east by Catoctin Mountain, the last to be crossed before striking open country that stretched invitingly to the front door of *Early's* target, the great city of Washington.

At Sharpsburg a message reached *Early* on July 6 by courier from *Lee,* advising him that on the 12th an effort would be made to free the Southern prisoners at Point Lookout, on the tip of the peninsula below Baltimore. There were 17,000 Confederates, the equivalent of a full-sized army corps, imprisoned there, and it would help greatly if they could be recovered to strengthen the diminishing ranks of the army. The details of the proposed coup were vague, but *Lee* indicated that in his judgment

Bradley Johnson would be a good man to lead the cavalry from *Early's* force to cooperate with the shadowy organization that would presumably be the one to make the principal effort to free the captives. It was the distance involved in this secondary mission, involving the Baltimore area, that was a major contributing factor, in *Early's* mind, in reaching his decision to utilize the South Mountain gaps for the approach to the Capital.

Lee's choice of *Bradley T. Johnson* for this special mission may have been based on the fact that he was a native of Maryland, would be familiar with the area to be covered, and knew personally many of the residents of Baltimore and other cities. Born in Frederick in 1829, he graduated from Princeton, then took up the practise of law, and was prominent in Democratic political circles, having served a term as State's attorney and in other official capacities. When *Breckinridge* ran for Vice President, *Johnson* was a strong supporter. As Colonel, 1st Maryland Infantry, he fought through the first two years of the war and was then given a variety of successive assignments that ultimately found him in the cavalry. After *"Grumble" Jones* was killed at Piedmont, *Johnson* was promoted to brigadier general, on June 28, 1864 and given the cavalry brigade that he now commanded.

Final preparations for the march included, among other matters, the distribution of shoes that had been received July 7 and sending a detachment back to Winchester to gather up and hold together the stragglers who had fallen behind. It would not do to have individuals or small groups wandering through enemy country in search of their organizations. That night *Early* issued his orders. The following morning the infantry moved out, *Rodes* to march through Crampton's Gap, *Breckinridge* through Fox's Gap, and *Ramseur,* accompanied by the trains, through Turner's Gap.

On the night of July 8 the troops bivouacked in the area: Middletown–Jefferson, in the shadow of Catoctin Mountain. *Ransom's cavalry*, in the advance as a covering force, had occupied Catoctin Pass between Middletown and Frederick on July 7 after encountering a mounted detachment of the enemy, with whom his troopers exchanged shots, with little serious damage to either side. The clash on the seventh was between *Bradley Johnson's brigade* and six companies of the Eighth Illinois (Union) Cavalry, a well-trained, finely disciplined former regiment of the Army of the Potomac, presently operating under General Augur, commanding the Department of the Potomac with headquarters in Washington. The Eighth was a highly reliable utility force that had been performing an important service under its commander, Lieutenant Colonel D. R. Clendenin, in fighting off the frequent raids of Confederate guerrillas, and its troopers had gained the respect of the redoubtable *John S. Mosby,* who tagged it as "the largest and finest regiment in the Army of the Potomac." At the first encounter the Confederates were driven back. *Johnson* then brought up his main body, pushed the enemy back to Catoctin Mountain, flanked them out of the pass, and took possession of the crest.

The situation was commencing to warm up, now that the Federal authorities were aware of the presence of a large Confederate force. *Johnson's* brush with the Yankee cavalry west of Catoctin Mountain was certain to result in spreading the alarm. *Early* would have to move fast if he were going to reap the hoped-for fruits of the expedition.

While *Early's* infantry, artillery, and trains were occupied on July 8 in moving eastward on their several assigned roads, over the South Mountain passes and across the Valley to their scheduled bivouac areas for the night, *Bradley Johnson* was having his troubles as the advance element of the army on the other side of Catoctin Mountain. It was part of his job, in addition to screening the march of the main body, to keep reconnoitering to the front in order to supply *Early* with timely information of the strength and dispositions of any enemy force that might be encountered. The town of Frederick, tactically important to the Federals, was likely to be garrisoned by militia units, in addition to the veteran cavalry regiment that had shown sharp teeth the preceding day in contesting *Johnson's* advance. It was essential to secure positive information, and that was *Johnson's* responsibility.

Johnson spent the better part of the day, July 8, gingerly feeling out the strength of his opposition in Frederick. The town where he had been born was being guarded, that much was certain, and after his experience with the Eighth Illinois he was cautious. Therefore it was late afternoon before contact was established and his dismounted cavalry exchanged shots with the mixed force in Frederick —infantry, cavalry, and what appeared to be a section of artillery. The defenders impressed him as being determined to fight, suggesting that it would require more than a mere show of strength to drive them out. After further deliberation *Johnson* decided to resort to the usually effective tactics—a holding attack by part of the command while the remainder moved to get on the enemy flank. At the very moment that he was about to launch his attack, however, the cavalry commander, General *Ransom*, rode up, appraised the maneuver as unduly risky, and ordered its abandonment. The disgusted *Johnson* was told to move back to Catoctin Mountain, with the explanation from *Ransom* that *Early* would be satisfied with the knowledge that these were local troops and not veterans from Meade's Army of the Potomac.

Early on the 9th the cavalry was sent off in several directions, fanning out towards Baltimore and Washington in advance of the infantry-artillery columns. *Johnson's brigade*, with a battery of artillery attached, moved east, around to the north of Frederick, with instructions to cut the railroads leading north and south from Baltimore, burn bridges, threaten Baltimore, and then strike for Point Lookout in order to release the prisoners if and when the main body should succeed in getting into Washington. *McCausland's* brigade was sent to the south, to cut the telegraph and railroad lines between Maryland Heights, Washington, and Baltimore, cross the Monocacy River and if possible seize the railroad bridge over the river at Monocacy Junction.

ENTER LEW WALLACE

Major General Lew Wallace, of later fame as the author of *Ben Hur*, was commander of the U. S. Army's Middle Military Department, with headquarters in Baltimore. His territory included the theater which *Jubal Early* had invaded, and he was of course promptly informed when the latter's cavalry started up the Cumberland Valley. Wallace, a good, solid type of officer, who much preferred field service to the type of administrative duty on which he was presently engaged, promptly emulated the erstwhile fire-department horse that paws the ground impatiently when he hears the clanging of the bell. Taking with him a member of his staff, Wallace ordered a locomotive to stand by for early departure, and after midnight of July 4-5 the two officers made off in the cab of their iron horse for Monocacy Junction, which the general felt was a logical point from which to observe and keep track of developments.

Wallace had reached Monocacy and was close enough to the mountains to hear the sound of firing between the opposing cavalry at Catoctin Pass on the seventh, while on the eighth he occupied what amounted to a front row seat from which to observe the defense of Frederick and to encourage the defenders to maximum effort. When Confederate cavalry commander *Ransom* jerked the frustrated brigade of *Bradley Johnson* back to the mountains, Wallace shared with the Federal troops the naive belief that they had won the skirmish, and so reported by telegraph to Washington.

Nevertheless it was chiefly due to his energy and initiative that *Early's* path to Washington was strewn with obstacles that in retrospect would be recognized by unprejudiced personnel of the War Department as having bought sufficient time for two army corps from Meade's army to be transported from Petersburg and Norfolk to forestall an actual attack on Washington. Although getting slightly ahead of the story, this is a pertinent fact to be kept in mind in following the events of the next few days after Wallace's arrival at Monocacy Junction. For it was at his instigation that the commander of the Eighth Illinois Cavalry, responsible directly to General Augur, willingly placed his regiment at Wallace's disposal and made the reconnaissance that established initial contact with *Johnson's* Confederate cavalry.

At the Junction, where he established a quasi-headquarters in one of the two block houses overlooking the Monocacy River, Wallace ordered up every loose aggregation of armed men that he could get his fingers on, and it *was* a motley group when assembled—Tyler's bobtailed brigade from Baltimore, the Eighth Illinois Cavalry, and a few militia units. But it proved to be enough, although scarcely exceeding 2,000 men, at first, to slow down the reconnoitering Southern cavalry long enough for Ricketts' division of Meade's Sixth Corps to hasten by rail to the Junction.

Appeals from the civilian brass in the Capital, urging Grant to send troops to stiffen the Washington defenses, had been assailing the ears of the General-in-Chief ever since *McCausland's cavalry* had crossed the Potomac and headed up the Cumberland Valley in the first days of July. Meade was thereupon directed to send a division; he had selected Ricketts, whose men detrained at Baltimore on the eighth. Finding that the Baltimore troops had already been summoned by Wallace, and after securing telegraphic authority from Halleck, Ricketts lost no time in reloading his division on the trains and heading it for the Monocacy.

The militarily perceptive Grant had been shrewd enough to size up *Early's* expedition into Maryland as the planned diversion that it was. Although reluctant to detach more than one division from his own forces, when he learned of the size of the raiding party and its passage through the South Mountain gaps the situation began to assume a graver aspect. Grant then went all out by ordering Meade to send the rest of Wright's Sixth Corps directly to Washington and also directing Emory's Nineteenth Corps (less one division), which was en route from Louisiana for assignment to the Army of the Potomac, to be diverted to the Capital from Fortress Monroe, where they had only just disembarked after their sea voyage.

Wallace, who was a good soldier, well knew what he was up against, although he had no way of gauging *Early's* strength except to be certain that he would be unable to meet him on anything like even terms. He was gambling heavily on Ricketts' approaching division, which would more than double his small composite detachment to give him nearly 6,000 men.

Withdrawal from Frederick to make a stand along the far bank of the Monocacy River at the Junction seemed to offer the strongest tactical defense by putting the river between him and the enemy, so Wallace gave orders accordingly. On the morning of the ninth of July his small force took position covering the river crossings, there to await their fate. The arrival of Ricketts' division on the night of July 8 was a godsend that gave Wallace and his thin line a measure of assurance that the Confederates would have to make a real fight of it if they insisted on continuing their journey direct to Washington, not over 50 miles distant.

EARLY SUFFERS A FATEFUL DELAY

Early's march order for July 9 placed *Ramseur's division* in the lead with instructions to push the enemy out of Frederick and clear the way for an unobstructed march directly on the capital. *Ramseur* encountered Federal skirmishers as his bridgades advanced in the early morning, but the latter were able to offer little resistance and quickly withdrew in the direction of the Junction. Unsure of the strength of his opposition, *Early* sent *Rodes* down the Baltimore Road, prepared to extend *Ramseur's* line to the left if it should be necessary for him to deploy his division. The other two divisions, *Gordon's* and *Echols'*, were halted in Frederick until *Ramseur* could develop the enemy strength and intentions.

The distance from Frederick to Monocacy Junction is about three miles by the Washington road as it was in 1864. The two roads that branched off to Harpers Ferry and Point of Rocks in a southwesterly direction did not enter into the calculations of either *Early* or Wallace. The Baltimore and Washington Roads were the vital highways. On both Wallace had established strong points with heavy concentrations of men at the river crossings. The Eighth Illinois cavalry was posted to cover the Federal left flank, believed by Wallace to be the more vulnerable because of the wooded ridges that afforded cover for an attacking force.

As *Ramseur's* advance elements moved south towards the Monocacy, his guns sent several exploratory ranging shells across the river. The Federal artillery reacted at once with retaliatory fire that exposed their locations. Confederate guns were wheeled into position and for several hours the gunners duelled, while *Early's* divisions were slowly deployed into battle lines for the attack which it was now apparent would require the employment of far more than a single infantry division and a couple of cavalry brigades.

During the early part of the morning, while his division commanders busied themselves with getting their men on the roads leading east and south from Frederick, shifting units from march column into open battle formations, and examining the terrain between the town and the river, *Early* conferred with the city fathers of Frederick. They were advised that $200,000 in cash must be paid or he would burn the town. It seems that *McCausland,* in levying only $20,000 on Hagerstown, had settled for ten percent of what *Early* had intended; this time *Old Jube* would avoid any such slip-up by figuratively holding his own pistol to the heads of the mayor and business leaders. Naturally they demurred, but when *Early* insisted, they requested and were granted time to look into their strong boxes and vaults and under their mattresses to see whether they could stretch a point and somehow gather together that much cash within a matter of hours. His financial negotiations disposed of for the time being, *Early* left several representatives in Frederick to receive the money as soon as it could be collected, and rode out to examine the situation to the south.

The Confederate commander observed through his field glasses a relatively open plain extending for several miles

61

from Frederick down to the river, with only a bit of fringe woods here and there. The tracks of the Baltimore and Ohio Railroad were clearly visible to the west of the Washington Turnpike where they paralleled the Monocacy River a few hundred yards north of the stream and then bent southeast of the Junction to disappear in the distance. Off to the east, about a mile or so from where he sat his horse, *Early* could see *Rodes' division* deploying astride the Baltimore Road, preparing to engage a force of the enemy that was guarding the bridge over the river at that point. At the Junction, two bridges arched the stream, the railroad bridge and, about 500 yards beyond, a wooden bridge that carried the Washington Turnpike, both strongly protected by Federal guns and infantry. Beyond the river could be seen cultivated fields, corn and wheat, and in the distance, ten miles away, loomed a tall, isolated ridge, called Sugar Loaf Hill, which extended almost to the Potomac.

It was a chronic weakness of *Early's* that he found difficulty in reading the topography of the ground and relating it to military tactics, but even an inexpert student of terrain could see that Wallace had done an efficient job of placing his defending troops to take advantage of the natural features at his disposal. As a brigade and division commander *Early* had been somewhat impulsive on occasion, rushing in to the attack without fully appreciating the lay of the land. As a corps commander he had grown more conservative, or perhaps it was simply that he had learned from experience the importance of the proper use of the ground in facilitating either attack or defense. In any event, despite his urgent need to get on to Washington, he took his time studying the terrain to his front and flanks, noting with interest and perhaps disappointment that the enemy had amassed a strong force to oppose him. *Early* overestimated Wallace's strength by a substantial margin when he figured it at 8,000 to 10,000 men, but he could see enough of the bluecoats through his field glasses to convince him that a frontal assault across so great an expanse of open fields, with the river obstacle still to cross, would be a serious mistake.

BATTLE OF THE MONOCACY

Time was slipping by as the skirmishers bickered with one another on the Baltimore and Washington Roads and in front of the three bridges. The artillery duel continued as *Rodes* and *Ramseur* pushed their main lines closer to the several crossings. The sun was high in the heavens when *Early* reached his decision. He would send *Gordon's division* to circle the enemy left by a concealed route *if* one could be found, and *if* a ford could be located at a convenient spot to enable the flanking troops to cross the river in order to reach the proper position from which to roll up the enemy left and open the direct road to Washington.

Early rode across the fields to the right on a personal reconnaissance to locate a ford that would solve his problem. About a mile downriver from the Washington Pike he was suddenly treated to a sight that gladdened his heart. Gray cavalrymen were fording the stream unopposed. They were *McCausland's* troopers, returning from their mission of cutting telegraph and railroad lines between Maryland Heights and Washington. According to earlier orders they were now aiming for the railroad bridge, unaware that General Lew Wallace had slapped a prior lien on that valuable property.

As *Early* watched, the troopers crossed the narrow river, dismounted, formed line, and attacked the Federal left, overran a battery, and then, outnumbered, were driven back in a counterattack before they could haul off the captured guns.

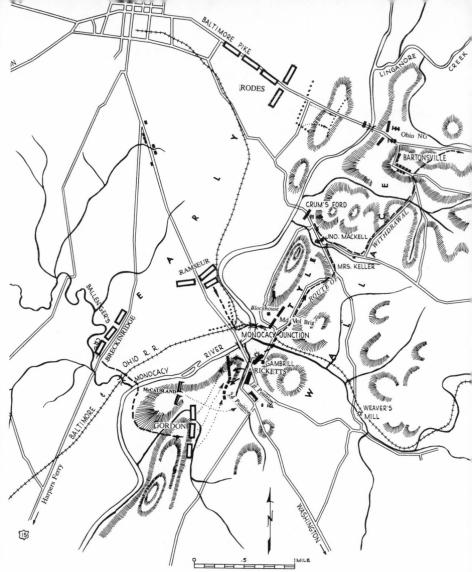

MAP 3. BATTLE OF THE MONOCACY, JULY 9, 1864

The basic topography of this map is from a U. S. Geological Survey modern map, scale 1:24,000, and all Civil War features are from the Union and Confederate maps, Plates 83 and 94, of the Atlas.

The situation shown here occurred at about 2:30 pm. when Gordon launched his assault on Ricketts. The battle was over by 4 p.m., the Federal route of withdrawal being shown.

Bradley Johnson's brigade of Confederate cavalry, a part of Early's force, is not shown on this map. Early on the morning of the 9th Johnson moved northeast from Frederick on his mission of cutting the railroads between Baltimore and Harrisburg and Philadelphia.

Frederick, Maryland was often called Frederick City, and this name appears on some of the contemporary maps.

Early's luck had held! An orderly was sent pelting back to *Breckinridge*, whose two divisions were relaxing in reserve while they watched the play being enacted on the plain before them. The order called for *Gordon* to carry out the plan already formed in *Early's* mind: to march by the flank, cross over the ford that *McCausland* had discovered, and attack the enemy left to secure the turnpike for the advance on Washington.

In *Gordon's* account of the part played by his division, the battle was "short, decisive, and bloody." *McCausland's* impromptu and premature attack had served to attract Wallace's attention to that flank, with the result that surprise was impossible; by the time *Gordon's* men had splashed through the stream and slithered up the steep, muddy, and slippery bank on the eastern shore, Ricketts had wheeled his line at right angles to the river, facing south. Instead of a flank attack, the Confederates were forced to make the assault frontally and alone, no supporting troops having been considered necessary for the maneuver that had suddenly gone awry. At the same time, the wooden bridge at the turnpike crossing went up in flames, when Wallace ordered its destruction. He wanted to hold the Confederates at the center of his position and to release some of the defenders at that point to bolster Ricketts' refused line.

As if that were not trouble enough, the fields over which *Gordon's brigades* advanced to close with the enemy were buttressed with strong lateral fences that would have to be climbed under fire (there was no time to tear them down), and most of the fields were dotted with stacks of recently harvested wheat. Under conditions where speed would not have been so essential, the stacks might have afforded welcome protection for advancing groups in extended order. But on this day they only broke up the co-

65

hesion of units and the alignment of regiments, and prevented volley fire.

At the first fence a withering volley from the Federals took a heavy toll of *Gordon's* men. On the Confederates went, ignoring losses, over the second fence and through the obstacle course of the wheatfield. Men and officers were dropping everywhere. It was sheer raw courage that inspired the Confederates to keep going. As they neared the first line of the bluecoats, who had been dealing out the punishment, a charge was ordered. The wild Rebel yell rang out as the lines rushed forward, overwhelming the defenders and driving them back on their second line. Bitter and prolonged fighting occurred in a ravine between the first and second Federal positions, where a small stream was crossed and recrossed repeatedly, as one side or the other gained the upper hand, until the water ran crimson and the killed and wounded were numbered in the hundreds.

Gordon was a savage fighter when battle was joined. He was also an experienced and skilful tactician and an inspiring leader of men. Although outnumbered by the Federals at that point, and faced with the almost impossible task of driving an enemy in a fixed position by direct frontal assault, his brigades responded with their accustomed bravery until all were engaged. Almost half of his division had been killed or wounded—and the Yankees still held the turnpike. One last supreme effort was needed. If he could manage to have one of the brigades that had not been so heavily engaged shift position, to slash in at a sharp angle against the Federal line, the maneuver might work. It did! The brigade took position, charged and sliced into the Federal line. Other units caught the excitement and lunged forward. Ricketts' line broke at the point of impact and retreated, unhinging the line. As his men commenced to stampede, Ricketts and Wallace, to avoid panic and disintegration of the entire force, ordered a withdrawal. This was executed in fairly good order, as the men were shepherded back across the turnpike and onto the Baltimore Road.

The pace of the retreat grew more rapid as Tyler's troops along the river caught the fever, but the Union officers kept their heads. Here and there groups and individuals recovered from the initial backward rush and responded to the discipline of the veterans of Ricketts' division of the Sixth Corps. When the Union retirement swept over the turnpike and across the tracks of the B&O, the uncovering of the railroad bridge opened the way for *Ramseur's* men to cross and join *Gordon* in the half-hearted Confederate pursuit.

The last thing *Early* wanted was an excessive number of prisoners to feed and guard. With the Washington Road open, he was satisfied to let Wallace go unpursued. As for the latter, who rightly considered that his men had performed a fine day's work, he led his broken regiments down the Baltimore Road, reflecting with satisfaction that Washington had been granted a full day in which to prepare for *Early's* visit, a respite that was probably more than the War Department had any right to expect.

It was four o'clock in the afternoon when the battle ended, too late for the Confederates to resume the march on Washington. *Early* decided to bivouac where he was, bring the rest of his army across the Monocacy, and make a fresh start the following morning after a night's rest. Before the sun went down the expedition was enriched by the $200,000 that he had demanded of the people of Frederick, who evidently concluded that, with Wallace and his troops no longer an ace in their hand, payment of the ransom was preferable to being burned out.

Although the Federals paid a stiff price for the 24-hour delay, almost 1,200 men killed and wounded and between

700 and 800 captured out of less than 6,000 engaged, it was more than worth the cost to the Union, which had suffered far more serious losses in many previous encounters without having anything but grief to compensate for the loss. *Early* reported only 700 killed and wounded, which is evidently a gross underestimate, in the face of *Gordon's* report wherein he stated that half of his division alone had become casualties.

THE SCENE SHIFTS TO WASHINGTON

A tall, loose-jointed figure in rusty-black garments, wearing a familiar stovepipe hat stood on the parapet of Fort Stevens, on the outer ring of the powerful fortifications that encircled the city of Washington. This northernmost link in the chain of forts covering the Seventh Street pike about two and a half miles south of Silver Spring, was being honored by a visit from President Abraham Lincoln on the morning of July 11, 1864.

This was no routine, run-of-mill inspection. The Capital was inflamed with excitement and considerable uneasiness because *Early* had reportedly reached Rockville, only a half-day's march to the north, and was about to threaten Washington itself at any moment.

THE WASHINGTON DEFENSES

If adequately manned by veteran troops, the Washington defenses by this time would have been impregnable. Every prominent point on a huge circle surrounding the city was occupied by an enclosed field-fort. All avenues of approach or depressions in the ground were swept by field guns, in position and zeroed-in. Trees in front of the earthworks had been cut down to provide open fields of fire, and covered rifle trenches with firing parapets connected all the forts, with a network of roads in the rear providing means

1864-5.

MAP OF THE DEFENCES OF WASHINGTON

SCALE OF MILES

MAP 4. WASHINGTON AND ITS DEFENSES IN 1864

The dotted line running south from Silver Spring (top center) is the present Georgia Avenue, an extension of Seventh Street. A number of the earth forts comprising the Civil War defensive works around Washington are discernible today in various wooded areas where buildings have not been erected. In recent years Fort Stevens has been restored, and is readily accessible. Its location is shown on the maps of Washington. Though it was surrounded by pastures, fields, and woods in 1864, today it is well within the built-up portion of the city.

The dotted line running north from Georgetown through Tenallytown is Wisconsin Avenue, or the Rockville Pike. Tenallytown, now called Tenly, is located approximately at the point where the River Road branches off from Wisconsin Avenue.

This is the map shown in Vol. IV, page 496, of *Battles and Leaders*.

for rapid transfer of troops to any threatened point. At the time of *Early's* raid, however, the garrison available for the strong defenses was composed chiefly of raw, untrained casual troops numbering fewer than 10,000. Actually there were twice that many soldiers in the Washington area, but they were mostly unorganized for combat and could at best offer but feeble resistance to a determined attack.

The President was not particularly worried that the raiding Confederates would succeed in penetrating the defenses, but he *was* concerned that something be done to punish the invaders. This business of frequent enemy forays in the direction of Washington tended to keep the Government off balance, and Lincoln was anxious that such adventures be made unprofitable for the Confederates. An exchange of telegrams between Lincoln and Grant, after *Early's* force crossed the Potomac, had led the Union general to detach two corps from Meade's army, the Sixth (Wright) and two divisions of the Nineteenth (Emory), just as *Lee* had anticipated. Lincoln expressed the opinion that Grant should leave a sufficient part of his forces to contain *Lee* and personally bring the remainder to Washington to destroy *Early*, but Grant felt that the two corps under Wright, combined with Hunter's augmented force from the Valley, would prove adequate to take *Early* out of circulation. On the afternoon of July 11 these reinforcements, some 15,000 men under the command of Major General Horatio G. Wright, were approaching the Capital as *Early* commenced to feel out the defenses of Washington.

Secretary of War Stanton fussed like a mother hen when Lincoln, despite the approach of *Early's* force, continued his practise of spending the night with his family at the Soldiers' Home in the northern part of the Capital. After driving Wallace from the Monocacy, *Early* had cut the direct telegraph wires between Frederick and Washington, generating a fog of war that for 24 hours prevented the Administration from knowing exactly where the Confederates were at any given moment. Stanton's jittery reactions failed to disturb Lincoln's equilibrium, but did cause him to yield reluctantly to the War Secretary's importunities to the extent of returning for the night of July 10 to a less exposed locale than the Soldiers' Home.

Not to be deprived of the personal satisfaction of observing the war at first hand, Lincoln had driven out from Washington on the morning of July 11 to be on hand for the opening scene at Fort Stevens, east of Rock Creek on the Seventh Street road. It was a hot summer day, without a breath of air stirring. There had been no rain for several weeks, so that marching troops stirred up choking clouds of dust that compounded for the already weary Confederate infantry the enervating effect of the sultry heat.

Early Approaches the Capital

Standing on the parapet of the fort, the interested President and Commander-in-Chief, looking to the north, could easily follow the approach march of *Early's* veterans by the dust clouds that rose, like the slowly undulating forward movement of a snake, from the Rockville-Silver Spring Road and thence south along the Seventh Street pike. In that long column could be observed *Early's* four infantry divisions together with three of the four cavalry brigades under Major General *Robert Ransom.*

Imboden's cavalry brigade under Colonel *George H. Smith,* leading the advance, was the first to arrive, shortly before noon. A small body of Federal cavalry briefly disputed the Confederate advance before retiring to the protection of the fort. *Smith* dismounted his men, deployed them as skirmishers, and waited for the supporting infantry to come up. Riding ahead of his infantry, General *Early*

71

came in sight of Fort Stevens shortly after noon, satisfied himself that the works were lightly manned, and promptly ordered *Rodes' leading division* to deploy against the fort.

CONFEDERATE ATTACK NEAR FORT STEVENS

In the course of these preparations, Confederate skirmishers opened a desultory, scattered fire to which the defenders replied. The tall figure of the President could have been a likely target for a Confederate sharpshooter had Lincoln not been warned by an officer standing nearby, who roughly told him, with more good sense than diplomacy, "to get down or he would have his head knocked off." Tradition has it that Lincoln's adviser was Oliver Wendell Holmes, Jr.

Early devoted the remainder of the day, July 11, to reconnoitering the forts along the northern fringe of the District of Columbia, seeking a weak point through which he might force a spearhead. By this time he knew that he had lost the advantage of surprise, but was as yet unaware that the defenses would in a matter of hours be strengthened by two corps from the Army of the Potomac. He wanted to have the pleasure of throwing Washington and the Government into confusion by penetrating to the heart of the city, if only briefly. That evening he held a council with four of his infantry commanders, *Ramseur, Rodes, Breckinridge,* and *Gordon,* informing them that it was necessary to do something at once before their line of retreat through the South Mountain passes or the fords of the Upper Potomac should be closed against them. The decision was to make an assault on the forts early the following morning, July 12.

"Undoubtedly we could have marched into Washington," later wrote General *Gordon,* who had ridden his horse into one of the breastworks to find it entirely unoccupied by Federal troops.* When he gave *Early* his orders *Lee* had stated his opinion that it would not be possible to capture Washington, and neither *Gordon* nor any other of *Early's* generals considered it advisable to make the attempt. "While General *Early* and his division commanders were considering in jocular vein the propriety of putting General *John C. Breckinridge* at the head of the column and of escorting him to the Senate chamber and seating him again in the Vice President's chair," added *Gordon,* "the sore-footed men in gray were lazily lounging about the cool waters of Silver Spring, picking blackberries in the orchards of Postmaster General Blair, and merrily estimating the amount of gold and greenbacks that would come into our possession when we should seize the vaults of the United States Treasury."

Gordon was right. The Confederates could not only have marched into Washington at any time during July 11, but could have done so with only minor casualties, and quite possibly have captured President Lincoln, burned the White House and other public buildings, and gotten away before Wright's troops arrived. It would have been

---

* *Reminiscences of the Civil War,* by General John B. Gordon; Charles Scribner's Sons, 1903.

a simple matter for *Early's* cavalry to accomplish such a hit and run raid, with incalculable psychological effect on the North. It is safe to assume that *Jeb Stuart* or *John Mosby* would not have missed the opportunity, despite *Lee's* opinion that it was not possible. But it must be remembered that the Confederates had already marched a very long distance in the heat of summer and had fought a stiff engagement on the Monocacy. *Early* couldn't have expected that the Capital would be denuded of trained troops, and had to weigh the chances of disaster if he should push his luck too far. Had he known on the morning of July 11 that Wright's veterans would not reach the city before midnight, the story would quite likely have had a different ending.

Early Calls off the Attack

During the night of July 11 *Early* received a message that two Federal corps had arrived and that probably more were on the way. The report came from *Bradley Johnson,* whose cavalry brigade was near Baltimore, engaged in the mission of cutting the Northern Central and the Philadelphia and Baltimore Railroads.

Johnson, whom *Lee* had personally selected as the officer best qualified for the delicate mission of releasing the Confederate prisoners confined at Point Lookout, had been informed that the garrison at that point was composed mostly of Negroes who would probably not offer a vigorous resistance. When, however, the arrival of part of Grant's forces had satisfied one-half of the purpose of the Confederate threat to Washington (the withdrawal of troops confronting *Lee* at Petersburg), the rescue project was abandoned.

Johnson's far-ranging cavalry brigade caused the usual excitement among the natives and had the pleasure of ripping up rails and destroying other railroad property. But

74

the Confederates weren't there long enough to do any permanent damage, and after they had gone the railroad men were able to make repairs quickly. *Johnson's* troops did succeed in temporarily capturing a train en route from Washington to Philadelphia, on which Union Major General W. B. Franklin was traveling, but in the haste of the raiders to rejoin *Early* their distinguished prisoner managed to escape.

Wright's appearance in Washington changed the complexion of affairs. The projected Confederate assault was called off, and the dream of capturing Washington dissolved. *Early* planned to initiate his withdrawal under cover of darkness but elected to remain in front of the fortifications during the daylight hours of July 12.

President Lincoln again visited Fort Stevens that morning, came under fire for the second time, and watched the Union artillery destroy several houses in their searching shell-fire for concealed Confederates out front. A Union officer was mortally wounded a few feet from the President, who this time showed greater caution by remaining seated on the ground below the parapet. Finally, as though in reward for his patience in waiting for a dramatic climax, Lincoln had the satisfaction of watching the newly arrived veterans from the Army of the Potomac move out in extended order in front of the line of forts as the retreating Confederates ran for cover to the wooded heights across the valley.

The Union reconnaissance in force, for it was no more than that, nevertheless had the desired effect of completely discouraging any offensive maneuvers that *Early* may still have contemplated, and by nightfall the fighting, such as it was, came to an end. The Confederates made good use of the darkness to cover as much distance as possible before daylight. Moving through Rockville and Poolesville, the long column crossed the Potomac at White's Ford above

Leesburg on the morning of July 14, without interference from Federal troops. After resting at Leesburg through the 15th, the Confederates resumed the return journey through Snicker's Gap to the Shenandoah Valley. At Berryville the weary troops went into bivouac.

EARLY RECROSSING THE POTOMAC AT WHITE'S FORD

Wright's pursuit of the retiring Confederates was so slow and ineffectual that the impatient President, keenly anxious to apply punitive measures, was thoroughly disgusted. The fault, however, belonged more properly on the doorstep of the confused and cumbersome command structure in Washington. Grant was too far away to influence the immediate action, Halleck as usual was reluctant to make a decision, and Lincoln had learned the wisdom of avoiding the issuance of direct orders to subordinate generals. In point of fact, the logistics of the situation were such that Wright, although an experienced and capable general, would have had considerable difficulty in blocking *Early's* retirement into Virginia. Without cavalry to circle him, throw up roadblocks, and force him to deploy while the Federal infantry caught up, about all Wright could do was to follow the Confederates in the hope that they would be slow in making their getaway. *Early's* wisely conceived night movement proved to be all that was necessary for him to make good his escape.

Stonewall Jackson, who rarely bestowed praise on his

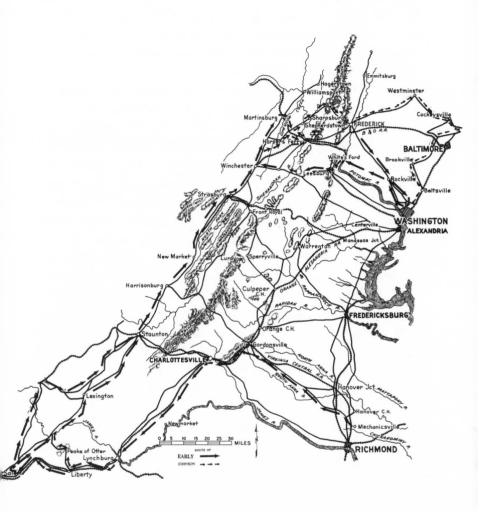

MAP 5. EARLY'S ROUTE, JUNE 13-JULY 21, 1864

This is based on a contemporary map (Plate 81, 4, 6) which, despite some inaccuracies, is convenient for portraying Early's march to Lynchburg, thence to Harpers Ferry, Frederick, and Washington, and return to the Valley. Except for Bradley Johnson's excursion from Frederick toward Baltimore, only the routes of the main infantry columns are shown.

As a matter of interest, this map shows two terrain features, which are usually mispronounced in the North: Opequon and Aquia. In Virginia these are called O-peck'-on and Ah-kwai-ah.

77

officers, would have been pleased with the manner in which his old *Second Corps* under *Jubal Early* carried out its mission on this occasion. His beloved Valley was once more safely in Confederate hands, the ability of the Southerners to penetrate deeply into Union territory almost at will and with relative impunity had again been demonstrated, and the strategic plans of the Federal high command had suffered a setback which would require considerable cost and effort to counteract. *Early's* long march through Charlottesville, Lynchburg, and Salem, down the Valley and through the South Mountain passes to the outskirts of Washington, driving en route the forces of Hunter, Sigel, and Wallace, was a feat that has seldom been equalled in war. In a period of exactly one month *Early's* little army marched 450 miles, defeated all the forces arrayed against it, saved Lynchburg, relieved the Shenandoah Valley, and came within an ace of capturing Washington. In their spare time, *Early's* hard-marching veterans had gathered in cash tribute, $20,000 at Hagerstown, $200,000 at Frederick, torn up a score of miles of Baltimore and Ohio Railroad tracks, damaged the Chesapeake and Ohio Canal, and put to the torch innumerable factories and workshops in retaliation for Union General Hunter's similar exploits in the Shenandoah Valley.

It was high time, Lincoln decided, that corrective measures be taken to remove the perennial threat to Washington implicit in Confederate control of the Shenandoah Valley, that vital invasion corridor which in Southern hands had too long been a loaded gun pointed directly at the Union heart in the Capital.

78

McCausland's Destruction Of Chambersburg

CHAPTER 4

GRANT GROPES FOR A SOLUTION

MORE than two years had elapsed since *Stonewall Jackson,* rocketing to military fame by virtue of his brilliant Valley Campaign in the spring of '62, had tied knots in the Union strategy, chased three separate, uncoordinated Federal army corps all over western Virginia, with their tongues virtually hanging out, and frozen the authorities at Washington into a congealed state of suspended animation.

One result of *Jackson's* amazing success in the face of overwhelming Union troop strength had been the lesson taught by the weakness of divided command in the field, which had not been lost on President Lincoln. Unfortunately for the North his selection of Major General Henry W. Halleck as General-in-Chief did not improve the situation. When Halleck failed to measure up, the Administration was right back where it had been from the beginning, only more so in that there was no real substance to the deceptive shadow of a united command under a single military head who was unequal to the task of exercising the authority vested in him.

79

Confusing directives were issued by Halleck and Stanton. Conflicting orders, letters, and telegrams flowed from the War Department to liaison-weak army commanders in the field. Direct communications went from the President to individual generals, couched in terms of advice which naturally had the effect of orders. For relief from such administrative insanity, what the Army and the country needed above all was a single-minded general of strong character, with steady nerves and an even temper, to grasp the reins of command and force the team to pull in harness.

The truth of the Clausewitz doctrine that war is an extension of national policy by other means suggested the foreboding corollary that continuation of the application of the "other means" could be assured only if the national policy remained firm in the determination to preserve the Union no matter how great the cost.

A New General-in-Chief Takes Hold

As General-in-Chief of the Union armies, Grant's military strategy was soundly conceived and beautifully simple. Relying on the North's vast numerical superiority, his plan was to concentrate his strength in two or three areas, operate simultaneously and unremittingly against the enemy armies in those areas, destroy his railroads and resources, and disregard the fringe maneuvers which in the past had been employed by the Confederates to divert attention from the major theaters and disrupt the Union campaigns. In this way a series of coordinated offensives on all fronts would serve to keep the Confederate armies engaged so that none could safely be weakened to come to the assistance of another. In effect Grant was applying in the East the successful western strategy which had cut the Confederacy in two and created islands of Confederate resistance, for which mutual support would become increasingly difficult as the Southern strength waned. The

RUINS OF BLAIR HOUSE

big question was whether the Northern voters would have the patience to wait for Grant's strategy to yield results.

On May 3, 1864 Grant launched his first campaign, as supreme commander of the Northern armies, against *Lee*, with the objective, not Richmond, but the destruction of that Confederate army which for three years had badly defeated or frustrated every single Union army commander before him. What had started out as a meeting engagement in the Wilderness, an encounter that neither Grant nor *Lee* had planned as such, quickly evolved into a succession of desperately fought battles, interspersed with marches and maneuvers in which Grant's battering-ram tactics were neutralized by *Lee's* prompt counter-moves and strong earthworks as Grant continually moved around *Lee's* right towards Richmond. The Battles of the Wilderness, Spotsylvania Court House, and Cold Harbor passed

81

into history within a month, leaving 56,000 Union and 20,000 Confederate casualties in their wake, and little else to show for them except the obvious fact that two equally able generals were finally locked in a combat that would cease only when one or the other would be shorn of his strength and forced to capitulate.

At Cold Harbor, however, even the obstinate Grant realized that there was a limit to the business of funneling masses of living men into certain death by frontal attack against a prepared defensive position. In the final assault which he ordered on the morning of June 3, more than 1,000 of his men were killed and an additional 4,600 wounded in a matter of minutes, while but 1,500 casualties were suffered by the defending Confederates. There was a great hue and cry throughout the North; morale in the Army of the Potomac took a serious drop, even though temporary; and Grant "the bulldog" was pilloried far and wide as a ruthless butcher of men. It was indeed a time for him to pause for reflection, reconsider the tactics which had so far failed to bring the clever Confederate fox to bay, and try a new approach.

Grant thereupon wisely decided to give his men a period of rest and recuperation, hold the position his army then occupied, send the cavalry to destroy the Virginia Central Railroad for a distance of twenty-five miles west of Beaver Dam, and after that, move the army to the south side of the James River with a view to resuming the offensive from that area. His experience of the past month in attacking *Lee's* strongly defended entrenchments had convinced him, as he wrote Halleck, that *Lee* considered it of the first importance to act purely on the defensive, behind breastworks, and to run no risks by assuming the offensive. "Without a greater sacrifice of human life than I am willing to make," added Grant (this was only two days after the Cold Harbor fiasco), "all cannot be accomplished that

I had designed outside the city (Richmond)." He then outlined to the Chief of Staff the plan described at the beginning of this paragraph.

The improved fortunes of the Union reflected in the Gettysburg, Vicksburg, and Chattanooga successes in 1863 appeared to have slipped somewhat in the spring campaigns of 1864. The outline of the pattern of final success had been sketched in, and Grant's strategy would in time prove correct. Nevertheless the political horizon for Lincoln was currently being darkened by storm clouds resulting from the indecisive character of Banks' operations in the Red River campaign and that of the politically-minded Butler in the James River area; as well as by Sigel's failure to maintain a firm grip on the Shenandoah Valley. The political picture was also made gloomy by the fact that neither the Army of the Potomac under Meade nor Sherman's armies in the South had yet created, in the public mind, the image of inevitable victory which would later emerge. Something dramatic was needed to reassure the Northern people, stiffen their backbones, and convince them of the soundness of the Administration's policies.

Lincoln was acutely aware of the danger. The President, never one to overrate himself, saw the possibilities perhaps more clearly than any other person. No stranger to politics, during more than three years of bitter strife he had acquired a fair working knowledge of military strategy as well. His faith in Grant continued unimpaired, but questions were now being asked and doubts had arisen in not a few Northern quarters, after the Wilderness Campaign, Spotsylvania, and more particularly Cold Harbor, whether even Grant could defeat an opponent of *Lee's* capabilities. Or whether the terrific cost in the lives of Union soldiers was worth the price. Lincoln needed a positive success in the field, if not a great victory, and needed it badly.

Grant's reluctance in early July to detach two corps from the Army of the Potomac to meet what he recognized as a diversionary expedient on *Lee's* part is not difficult to understand. He felt that the Washington defenses were sufficiently strong that *Early's* raid could achieve nothing more substantial than a psychological effect, whereas Lincoln, better able to judge the public temper, saw beyond the strictly military implications. As a result of Grant's seeming lack of political perception, the President began to wonder whether his trusted general might be indifferent to the prospect that he could very well fail of re-election. What was nearer the truth was that Grant's preoccupation with military strategy crowded from his mind all other considerations.

As it turned out, *Early's* threat to the Capital served the Union cause better than the Confederate in exposing the weakness of the Federal command structure in Washington. Too many cooks in the main kitchen were spoiling the broth, with the result that *Early's* command had escaped scot free when Halleck refrained from issuing orders. Grant was too far removed to take appropriate action, and a variety of independent or department commanders exercised separate jurisdiction over the Shenandoah Valley, the Washington defenses, the Baltimore area, and other sectors.

GRANT PROPOSES A SOLUTION

The solution proposed by Grant, in a letter to the President dated July 25,* was to appoint a single commander whose jurisdiction should include all four of the separate military departments concerned, to provide at long last the coordination that should have been in effect from the start. Halleck had the brains and the necessary

---

* *Official Records*, Vol. XXXVII, Part 2, p. 433.

ENTRANCE TO WASHINGTON FROM THE SOUTH—THE FAMOUS CHAIN BRIDGE

authority, but was hopelessly ineffectual and by this time had come to be universally recognized as little more than a glorified War Department administrator in the guise of Chief of Staff. But the problem remained, who should receive the appointment?

General David Hunter, senior among the general officers who commanded the several departments in West Virginia and the border country north of the Potomac, had, after retreating from the Valley, returned to Harpers Ferry. His timidity at Lynchburg, however, had demonstrated that he was not the man for the job. Grant offered the name of Major General William B. Franklin, but Halleck replied that Lincoln objected on the score that Franklin's record was unimpressive, and particularly that he had muffed his great opportunity as commander of Burnside's left wing at Fredericksburg. Grant then put forward the name of General Meade, a significant suggestion that may have revealed his real opinion of that general's capabilities. Grant's "Memoirs" are discreetly silent on the high-level exchanges between the Washington authorities and himself relating to this interesting episode, but elsewhere it is recorded that he sent his Chief of Staff, General Rawlins, to see the President personally, to explain that Meade had lost the confidence of his subordinates and that his valuable services could be employed to better advantage if he should be transferred from command of the Army of the Potomac. Grant's idea was to promote Hancock in Meade's slot, with Gibbon succeeding Hancock in command of the Second Corps; but Lincoln, unconvinced of the wisdom of the transfer, or at least wishing to give the matter unhurried thought, deferred giving his approval. While he was deliberating, during the latter part of July, *Early* again began to make threatening moves in the Valley; whereupon the President acted, without consulting Grant, to place the equivocal Halleck in command of the consolidated departments.

When the news of Halleck's appointment reached him, Grant's Chief of Staff was not at Headquarters and consequently unable to exercise his customary restraint in controlling the general's drinking habits. In the absence of the faithful and long-suffering Rawlins, Grant figuratively blew his top and went on a binge, his first real fall from grace since Rawlins had assumed responsibility for keeping his chief on the straight and narrow path of sobriety. The recent battlefield death of General McPherson, Grant's best friend and Sherman's most trusted subordinate, may have been a contributing factor, but the timing of events indicates that the primary cause of Grant's backsliding was the apparent unwillingness of the President to allow his field commander the complete freedom of choice and action in military matters that had been promised when he was brought in from the West. Heretofore the President had given him a free rein in a military sense, but Grant was fully aware of the feeling among the high ranking officers of the Army that there had been altogether too much political interference from Washington in the conduct of the war, and Lincoln's action in this instance may have created an impression in his mind that the President was slipping back into the old groove.

Where Grant made his mistake was in failing to take a quick trip to Washington in the early stages of the exchanges between the Capital and his field headquarters. Much lost time and misunderstanding could have been avoided by a personal conference with the President, and the end result probably achieved in a few hours without frayed tempers and with salutary effect all around. Lincoln had in fact urged Grant to come to Washington in person to take charge of the confused command situation, a request that the General-in-Chief sidestepped almost as though he were fearful of being contaminated by the militarily poisonous climate of the Capital, however temporary the visit.

Hunter Spars Feebly with Early

While *Early's* miniature army was paying its surprise visit to the outskirts of Washington in early July, Hunter's long, circuitous march through West Virginia and up the Ohio River had finally brought him back to Harpers Ferry, at which point he recrossed the Potomac to Virginia and made a feeble but fruitless effort to block *Early's* column on its return march. A portion of Hunter's force under General George Crook, joining Wright's pursuing Sixth Corps near Snicker's Gap, was directed by Wright to cross the Shenandoah River just west of the Gap and attack *Early,* with the promise that Ricketts' division would follow in support. Ricketts failed to move his division across the river when he observed *Early's* development in force, with the result that Crook's detachment was sacrificed in what the history books call the Castleman's Ferry fight. Crook lost over 400 men killed, wounded, and missing. In this engagement Colonel Rutherford B. Hayes, future President of the United States, was a participant as one of Crook's brigade commanders; as was a staff officer who likewise hailed from Ohio, Captain William McKinley, another future President.

With the escape of *Early's* force to the comparative security of the Shenandoah Valley, Wright's corps was ordered back to Washington for the purpose of rejoining the Army of the Potomac, while Hunter pulled his footsore travelers more or less together in the lower part of the Valley, where some disjointed fighting with elements of *Early's* command occurred during the latter days of July. At Kernstown, on July 24, the two forces met in a full-fledged but short-lived battle that ended with Hunter's troops, outflanked, being routed and pursued down the Valley Pike through Winchester, Martinsburg, and on to the Potomac River. Crook's autobiography covering this period makes scornful reference to the part played by Sullivan's division and Averell's cavalry, accusing the former of all the shortcomings in the book, including physical cowardice, and stating that the cavalry was of little assistance, with its commander getting drunk during the fighting.

By July 28 Hunter had withdrawn his force northward to an attenuated line along the Potomac, extending from Hancock, Maryland on the west to Harpers Ferry on the east, with the main body in the vicinity of the latter. Averell's cavalry division was posted to cover the Federal right flank, opposite *Early's* cavalry, which guarded the Confederate left in the vicinity of Berkeley Springs. For the second time within a month *Early* had virtually cleared the Valley of Federal troops, between times making his raid on Washington.

THE BURNING OF CHAMBERSBURG

While the authorities at Washington fiddled, and Grant dulled his frustrated sensibilities with his favorite whiskey, Chambersburg burned!

Jubal Early, flushed with the success of his Maryland tour and the fright into which his hit-and-run raid had thrown the Capital, concluded that he could keep the Union high command off balance by further harassing. On this occasion the target was Chambersburg, Pennsylvania, a conveniently situated town in the Cumberland Valley which seemed to have a magnetic appeal to the Confederates. *Jeb Stuart's* cavalry had spent a night there during his provocative ride around McClellan's army in October 1862; *Ewell* made his headquarters in the town in June 1863 while *Early's division* and other elements of the *Second Corps* of the *Army of Northern Virginia* were fanning out to the northeast to threaten Harrisburg and attempt a crossing of the Susquehànna River at Wrightsville; and a short time later General *Lee* with *Longstreet's* and *A. P. Hill's corps* occupied the area for several days before moving east through the South Mountain pass at Cashtown on the march that led to the Battle of Gettysburg. Chambersburg had indeed become a familiar place to the Confederates; a bustling county seat whose residents, farmers, and places of business were believed well able to pay tribute in goods and money to the Southern raiders.

Stuart's troopers and *Lee's* divisions had displayed exemplary behavior during their visits in 1862 and 1863, but this time Chambersburg would be less fortunate. When *Early's army* had returned to the Valley after the Washington raid and he learned the extent of the wanton destruction that Hunter had additionally visited on private property of Southerners while the Confederates were in Maryland, he concluded that the North needed a lesson. General *McCausland* was thereupon directed to take his mounted infantry brigade, reinforced by *Bradley Johnson's cavalry brigade* and a battalion of artillery, proceed up the Cumberland Valley to Chambersburg, Pennsylvania, and either collect a king's ransom or burn the town. The orders from *Early* were precise and unequivocal: to levy a tribute of $500,000 in United States currency or $100,000 in gold, and if the citizens failed to comply, to burn the town to the ground.

In selecting 27-year old *McCausland* as commander of the expedition, *Early* chose a willing instrument of destruction, stating freely that the raid was planned in direct retaliation for the burning of VMI and many private homes in the Shenandoah Valley under Hunter's orders, to the extent of $2,000,000 in property value, according to Confederate estimates. *Early* said later that his sole reason for selecting Chambersburg was that it was the only Northern town of any consequence within reach of his troops. The choice of *McCausland* to apply the torch, however, had a touch of poetic justice, for that general was a distinguished graduate of the Virginia Military Institute, class of 1857 who, following his graduation, had become an instructor in mathematics at the institution; and at the time of Hunter's depredations was operating with his horsemen against the latter's pyromaniacal digression in Staunton and elsewhere. *McCausland* could therefore be relied upon to carry out *Early's* orders with enthusiasm, and with the assurance that his officers and men would be adequately briefed on the retaliatory purpose of the planned destruction.

On the morning of Thursday, July 28, *Early* called *McCausland* in and handed him his orders, with a written demand for indemnity to be presented to the town officials at Chambersburg. At daylight the following morning, at

90

the head of his command of 2,900 mounted men, *McCausland* drove out the Federal pickets on his front, crossed the Potomac at Cherry Run and McCoy's Fords, rode rapidly north by way of Mercersburg, and before midnight had arrived on the heights two miles west of Chambersburg, where his troops went into bivouac for the night.

The mission of Major General William W. Averell's cavalry division, on the right flank of Hunter's force and directly across from *McCausland,* was to secure that flank and at least make an effort to prevent or delay such a movement as the Confederates were now making. *Early* had foreseen this and sent the divisions of *Rodes* and *Ramseur,* with *Vaughn's cavalry brigade* in the van, to cross the Potomac at Williamsport and demonstrate on Averell's left at the same time that *McCausland* slipped around his right and lunged for Chambersburg. Caught between the two, Averell had little choice but to withdraw or be pinched off, so he promptly marched north until he reached Greencastle, Pennsylvania, eleven miles south of Chambersburg, and about the same distance north of Hagerstown, Maryland, to which point *Vaughn's* Confederate cavalry followed, doubtless to convince Averell that he meant business.

Averell's division, numbering about 2,500 men, arrived at Greencastle at dusk and went into bivouac at the very hour that *McCausland* was completing his march on Chambersburg; an action that served rather well to confirm the inadequacy of Averell as a cavalry commander. He had repeatedly demonstrated that he was dilatory in obeying orders, slow to react when speed and aggressiveness would have paid off in Union successes, and entirely too ready to avoid combat or to press matters to a conclusion, once committed to action. This he had proven in his fight with *Fitz Lee* on the Rappahannock prior to the Chancellorsville campaign and again in the course of that campaign.

Crook was disgusted with his apparent indifference to his responsibilities during the recent skirmishes with *Early* in the Valley. The people of Chambersburg would very shortly blame him for dereliction of duty, in the conviction that he could have saved their community from destruction, but was too lethargic to stir himself in their defense. Finally, within a matter of months, Averell's performance in the Valley would be such that General Sheridan, who demanded efficient and bold service from his generals, would peremptorily relieve him from command.

For all practical purposes, the town of Chambersburg was wide open to capture and destruction, despite the fact that Major General Darius N. Couch, commanding the Department of the Susquehanna, made his headquarters there, and Averell's full division of Union cavalry had turned in for the night only nine and one-half miles to the south, in a grove a mile or so north of Greencastle. Couch's principal job as Department Commander at this stage of the war seemed to be to act as forwarding agent for newly organized militia regiments, many of them from the staging area for the northern states at Camp Curtin in Harrisburg, Pennsylvania. General Couch had made repeated efforts to organize a permanent force of trained men for the defense of the border areas, among them a 1,200 man provost guard regiment and six regiments of one hundred days' men (the latter shortly before the Chambersburg raid), but the long arm of the War Department pulled everything away from the Department of the Susquehanna for the Washington defenses or for Grant's forces as fast as they could be assembled, clothed, and armed.

Consequently on July 29 Couch had in Chambersburg nothing but one section of a field artillery battery, while the only other armed force in the entire Cumberland Valley that remained subject to his orders was a company of infantry with a strength of but 106 men, and that was stationed at Mercersburg, about twenty miles southwest of Chambersburg. Couch himself remained in the town until the last minute, expecting momentarily that Averell's cavalry would ride in to its defense in response to his repeated telegrams, even though Averell was part of Hunter's command and under normal conditions not subject to Couch's direction. When Averell failed to respond, Couch made the decision to remove himself and the handful of guns from Chambersburg to avoid certain capture and possibly to demonstrate to the Confederates that the place was completely defenseless and therefore not subject to attack under the accepted rules of warfare.

The suspense of waiting for something to happen, while not a new experience for the six thousand residents of Chambersburg, was sharpened by the expectation that the Union cavalry would gallop in at any moment to prevent the Confederates from making any further advance into Pennsylvania. As the night hours of July 29 passed without a sign of Averell's troopers, the fears of the townspeople began to mount. Nor was their confidence in the judgment of their military commanders improved as they stood on the streets and watched the large wagon train of General Hunter's force pass through the center of the town on its way to Harrisburg and safety from what Hunter evidently believed was another major invasion by the Confederates. The train took many hours to pass, and was guarded, according to eyewitness Jacob Hoke, a resident of Chambersburg, by "at least fifteen hundred cavalry and two hundred infantry." The helpless observers couldn't understand why General Couch did not exercise his authority to detach the train guard for the defense of the town, on the reasonable premise that the supply train would be perfectly safe from Confederate attack after clearing Chambersburg on its way to the Susquehanna. At the very least, 1,700 Federal troops could have forced the 2,900 Confederates to stage a battle for possession of their target and delay them long enough for Averell's cavalry to come up to give the Federals a substantial superiority.

An examination of the *Official Records* reveals, in the telegraphic dispatches between the War Department in Washington and the several department commanders in the field, how thoroughly confused the command situation had become, partly because of the inadequate reconnaissance and intelligence activities of the Union cavalry of Hunter's command. A typical example was Hunter's telegram of July 30 to Halleck, following a barrage of messages from the latter which sought to elicit information as to where Hunter's troops were and what he was doing to counter *Early's* unpredictable tactics:

Harpers Ferry, W. Va.
July 30, 1864-11 a.m.

Major General Halleck,
  Chief of Staff:

General Wright reports his corps so much fatigued and scattered as to be unable to move this morning. The whole command is now encamped at Halltown, but my information is so unreliable and contradictory that I am at a loss to know in which direction to pursue the enemy. If I go toward the fords over which he has passed to cut off his retreat by the Valley, he turns to the right, pushes toward Baltimore and Washington, and escapes by the lower fords of the Potomac. If I push on toward Frederick and Gettysburg, I give him a chance to return down the Valley unmolested. Please, with your superior chances for information with regard to the whole position of affairs, direct me what is best to be done. We shall be ready to move promptly in the morning, leaving most of our trains, and start in light marching order.

D. HUNTER,
Major-General.

General Hunter does not appear to have been a man of decision. Nevertheless his cavalry under Averell and Duffie should have done a more efficient job of keeping him informed of enemy movements. Instead of sending intelligence to Washington on what was happening in the field, the reverse was true. Hunter had come to rely heavily on Crook, so much so that he would make no move or take no action without first consulting his subordinate. On the other hand, there was a definite lack of rapport between Hunter and Averell, the former blaming the latter for the failure to take Lynchburg: "I should certainly have taken it," Hunter had written Grant, "if it had not been for the stupidity and conceit of that fellow Averell, who unfortunately joined me at Staunton, and of whom I unfortunately had at the time a very high opinion, and trusted him when I should not have done so."

About three o'clock in the morning of Saturday, July 30, Hunter's wagon train, General Couch, and the section of artillery having departed, the Confederates threw several shells into the town without doing any damage and with no reply from Chambersburg, where only the townspeople remained. Shortly thereafter, some 800 Confederates moved into town, leaving their main body of 2,000 and the six guns of the artillery on the ridge to the west where they had spent the night. Fanning skirmishers out to right and left, the invaders quickly occupied every street as the officer in charge, supported by a strong body of men, advanced to the center of town. Citizens who remained in the streets were assembled and directed to summon a number of the prominent residents so that General *Early's* demands could be officially presented.

The court house bell was accordingly rung, but the response was slim. It appeared that there would be a policy of passive resistance. Possibly the people recalled how the town of Gettysburg had received *Early* by professing inability to pay the ransom demanded when he passed through on his way to York, Pennsylvania, in June of

95

1863. The few citizens who did assemble were addressed by a Captain *Fitzhugh*, of *McCausland's* staff, who read *Early's* demand for $100,000 in gold or $500,000 in Northern currency; upon failure to pay which the town would be burned in retaliation for the private Virginia homes which Hunter had destroyed in June. The citizens stated that it was impossible for them to meet the demand, at the same time expressing freely their belief that the Confederates would not carry out the alternative threat. That seemed to annoy *Fitzhugh*, who advised them that they were very much mistaken, as they would soon discover.

Turning to his men, the order was quickly given, kerosene and matches appeared as if by magic, and within minutes the town of Chambersburg was burning in a dozen places. The Confederates went to work thoroughly and enthusiastically, as though determined to show the North that two could play at Hunter's game. A squad of men would approach a house, break open the door and start a blaze, at the same time telling the inmates to clear out at once. Most of the families were forced to escape with nothing but the clothes on their backs, while the sick and infirm had to be carried to the fields for safety. Children were separated from their parents and ran through the streets, screaming wildly.

Daylight came before the work of destruction commenced, or there would almost certainly have been a greater tragedy than the mere loss of property. The day was calm and sultry without a breath of air stirring. Black clouds rose straight up, and as new fires were started the columns of smoke spread and blended until the air above the town became one vast and lurid mass of smoke and flame, beneath which the crackling and crash of falling walls and floors mingled with the screams of horses, cows, and hogs caught in the burning barns and stables.

The work of the incendiaries was carried out so rapidly

that within an hour of striking the first match the major part of Chambersburg was burning fiercely. Only the outskirts remained standing, with a few exceptions in the heart of town where the buildings were isolated. The court house, bank, town hall, every store and hotel, every mill and factory in the marked area, two churches, and between three and four hundred homes were burned, leaving at least 2,500 residents completely destitute of dwelling or possessions.

Under such conditions it was not surprising that the normal restraint of human beings in dealing with others was removed. Robbery and brigandage was widespread, incited by drunkenness on the part of those Confederates whose captures included liquor, but there was no evidence of wanton cruelty or violation of womenfolk. On the contrary, numerous incidents occurred during the morning to indicate that the mission of destruction was thoroughly distasteful to many of the Southern host, both officers and enlisted men, whose innate sense of chivalry and decency rebelled against making war on unarmed, defenseless civilians who had not lifted a finger to oppose the will of the invaders. Several of the Confederate surgeons went so far as to publicly denounce the actions of their fellows as atrocities, one in particular replying to an inquiry as to who was his commanding officer with the remarks, "Madam, I am ashamed to say that General *McCausland* is my commander!" In fact there was open disobedience of the order by a number of officers, which probably explains why any portion of the town was spared from the flames. Colonel *William E. Peters,* commanding the *Twenty-first Virginia Cavalry,* one of those who refused to apply the torch, was placed under arrest for disobedience of orders, but was never brought to trial.

The year 1864 marked the one hundredth anniversary of the founding of Chambersburg, but the manner in which the centennial was celebrated was unappreciated by the people of the town. A conservative estimate of the loss, by a committee of townsfolk who subsequently made a meticulous survey of the destruction, building by building, placed the figure, including contents, at not less than $2,000,000 at replacement value.

For three hours the conflagration raged unchecked. At 11 a.m., their mission accomplished, the Confederates formed ranks and marched westward, leaving the ruins to the sad contemplation of the homeless and dejected sufferers. Then and only then did Averell and his division appear on the scene. At four o'clock in the morning, instead of coming directly from Greencastle to Chambersburg, Averell had marched his cavalry east to Greenwood, turned left on the Chambersburg-Gettysburg Road and ridden the remaining ten miles to the burning town, only to find that the Confederates had departed. Averell followed them, without haste, and without succeeding in catching up, a fitting finale to what can only be termed an ignominious episode in the history of the Union cavalry during the Civil War.

Averell's unheroic attitude and the damning implications that he could have prevented the rape of Chambersburg are related in letters from two reliable citizens addressed to Jacob Hoke, a resident of that community, who wrote and published a painstakingly researched book on *Lee's* Gettysburg campaign.* The first letter was from Thomas R. Bard, at the time agent of the Cumberland Valley Railroad Company at Hagerstown, who on the approach of *Vaughn's* Confederate cavalry had left Hagerstown for the telegraph office at Greencastle, where he watched Averell's Union cavalry pass through to its bivouac area just north of the town. Bard's letter, which has the ring of authenticity, follows:

-----
* Appendix to *Gettysburg, The Great Invasion of 1863.* Dayton, 1887.

General Averell left three "orderlies" at the telegraph office to convey to him all messages that might be received for him, and encamped his troops in a grove distant about one and a half miles north-east of Greencastle, and only nine and a half miles from Chambersburg. Late in the evening General Couch, commanding the Department of the Susquehanna, with head-quarters at Chambersburg, sent a message to General Averell, which was promptly handed to one of the orderlies, who quickly mounted his horse and rode off in the direction of General Averell's camp. Mr. B. Gilmore, the telegraph operator at Chambersburg, kept us informed constantly of all that was transpiring at that place, and of the movements of the Confederate force. It is quite probable that I was informed by one of the operators as to the contents of the message from General Couch. At any rate, at the time, I understood that General Couch informed General Averell that the Confederate forces were at or had passed through Mercersburg, Pennsylvania, and were moving toward Chambersburg; and that being without adequate forces to check the movement, he inquired whether Averell could be depended on for assistance. Later in the night two other messages were received from General Couch for General Averell, and were promptly delivered to the orderlies. The last of these messages was received probably about three o'clock in the morning of July 30th. These messages reported the rapid approach of the Confederates, and expressed great anxiety to learn if General Averell intended to render assistance for the defense of Chambersburg.

There had been no reply from General Averell, and learning that General Couch had made preparations for leaving Chambersburg, and that in all probability the communications with that place would soon be interrupted, I mounted a horse and hurriedly rode out to find General Averell. On the road, about half way to the camp, I met the orderlies riding leisurely toward Greencastle. In reply to my inquiry if they had delivered their messages, they said that General Averell could not be found, and that they did not know what to do with the messages. Hastily informing them of the importance of the dispatches, I took them in my own hands, and telling them to follow me, I spurred my horse and was soon at the grove. There was no sentry or guard to halt me. All was quiet. There was not a sound save the champing of the feeding horses; there were no lights or fires except the embers where the men had prepared their evening meal. I dashed into the middle of the encampment, and there found a solitary man to answer my inquiry, "Where is General Averell?" He could not tell me. An officer of a West Virginia regiment then appeared and said it would be difficult to find General Averell, but offered to aid me in the search. While he prepared to mount his horse, the booming of a cannon was heard in the direction of Chambersburg. The officer expressed surprise and asked, "What can that be?" I told him it supplemented the messages which I brought, and indicated that *McCausland* had arrived at Chambersburg. We rode hastily through the grove and soon found General Averell asleep by the side of a fence. On being awakened, he raised upon his elbow and heard the information I had brought. I had handed him the telegrams, but as there was no light I told him what they contained, and informed him that they had been delivered to his orderlies hours before. He made no reply, and, as I thought, was about to turn over and go to sleep. Minutes seemed hours to me, and growing impatient I said to him, "General Averell, if you wish me to convey any answer to General Couch, I beg you to let me have it quickly, for it is barely possible that I can get back before telegraphic communications will be cut off." Without rising to put his troops in motion, or without the slightest manifestation of interest in the condition of General Couch, or of the peril to which the loyal people of Chambersburg were exposed, he merely said, "Tell Couch I will be there in the morning." It was then, I think, about four o'clock, a.m. Returning to Greencastle, I found that already the Chambersburg office was closed, having first reported that General Couch had all his military forces and supplies on the cars, and that the Confederate advance was about to enter the town.

The other account is from H. R. Fetterhoff, M.D., of Baltimore, Maryland, but at the time of the war telegraph operator at Greencastle, Pennsylvania. Dr. Fetterhoff says:

"At the time these events transpired I was telegraph operator at Greencastle, and had the means of knowing what was going on generally. In the evening of Friday, July 29th, 1864, about eight o'clock, General Averell's command passed through Greencastle on their way from Hagerstown toward Chambersburg, and bivouacked for the night a short distance north of the town along the road leading to Chambersburg. If my memory serves me right General Averell reported his arrival to General Couch at Chambersburg. At least I so reported it to Mr. Gilmore, telegraph operator at Chambersburg. The General sent three or four orderlies to my office and informed me of his whereabouts. Mr. D. C. Aughinbaugh, operator at Hagerstown, Mr. T. R. Bard, and I think several other persons from that place, were at the office in the evening and at intervals during the night. The scouts reported that the Confederates had built camp-fires in the neighborhood of State Line, four miles south of Greencastle, and it was supposed that they had encamped there for the night. About midnight, or perhaps a little later, Mr. Gilmore informed me that the telegraph lines west of Chambersburg on the Pittsburgh turnpike had been cut, showing that the enemy after building the camp-fires at the State Line as a blind had moved in the direction of Upton and Bridgeport on General Averell's left flank. I immediately informed General Averell of this fact, when he sent me a message thanking me for the information, and requesting me to keep him posted in regard to any information I might obtain. About one o'clock A.M. July 30th, General Couch sent an order to General Averell directing him to 'Move on to Chambersburg at once.' I immediately sent this message with an orderly, but never heard from him again. In about a half hour General Couch repeated the message in the same words, and I sent another orderly with the message, but still no answer. The same order was repeated about every half hour until my orderlies were all gone and I had no one to carry the last message, when Mr. Bard came to my office and volunteered to deliver it. After searching for General Averell and finding him he delivered the message. I then learned that when I had sent General Averell the information that the Confederates

were in his rear, or on his flank, he moved his headquarters from the rear of his line, where it had been, up
into the line without informing the orderlies or any one
else, consequently no one knew where to find him, and
the messages had not been delivered and only reached him
near four o'clock A.M. when Mr. Bard delivered them.
The Confederates entered Chambersburg about this time,
and Mr. Gilmore bade me 'good-bye' and left the office."

SHERIDAN IS GIVEN A MISSION

The destruction of Chambersburg and the Union failure
to exploit the great mine explosion under the Confederate
entrenchments at Petersburg, occurring simultaneously on
the morning of July 30 although at widely separated points
and in no sense related, followed close on the heels of the
Halleck appointment and doubtless helped to convince
General Grant that further temporizing could not be
tolerated. The confused Union command system north of
the Potomac and in the Valley had brought about something akin to military chaos in those areas, the baneful
effect of which was being felt by the Army of the Potomac.
Grant's campaign of attrition before Richmond and Petersburg was being seriously interfered with because of the
necessity of diverting troops to cope with the fears and
alarms which *Early's* unchecked operations were causing
in Washington and throughout the North.

At the very hour that *McCausland* was burning Chambersburg, *Mahone's* Confederates were successfully counterattacking Ledlie's Federal division in the huge crater
caused by the mine touched off under *Lee's* lines at five
o'clock that morning. That "stupendous failure," as Grant
described it, had contained all the ingredients for a profit-
able breakthrough. Unfortunately it was badly mishandled
by Meade's last-minute replacement of Ferrero's division
of colored troops, through the drawing of lots, by an assault
division that had not been trained nor even briefed for
the job. Consequently instead of rolling up the Confeder-

ate line as a prelude to seizing Petersburg, all the Federals had to show for their labors were 4,000 casualties—killed wounded, and captured.

Characteristically, Grant wasted no time in dwelling on misfortunes. Orders crackled from his headquarters at City Point. Meade was directed to cancel the instructions that had dispatched one corps and the cavalry to move out to destroy twenty miles of the Weldon Railroad, which ran due south from Petersburg. Instead, additional troops would be embarked for Washington, earmarked for employment in the Valley.

The time for talking was past. There would be no more recommendations. Grant had decided to act. For some time he had been trying to convince the Administration that the four separate military departments should in the interest of efficiency be consolidated under one command. Although Lincoln agreed in principle, the Washington authorities had rejected each name that was suggested. When Halleck was temporarily put in charge by the President's order, Grant moved to circumvent the unacceptable expedient by a compromise proposal whereby Hunter would become the administrative head of the consolidated departments, with Major General Philip H. Sheridan commanding the troops in the field.

When Grant had earlier proposed Sheridan as his third choice, Secretary of War Stanton objected that he was too young, disregarding the fact that his age had not impaired his ability to lead the cavalry corps of the Army of the Potomac with such notable success that for the first time in their experience the Union troopers found themselves, to their keen satisfaction, consistently fulfilling a proper combat role. Under Sheridan's aggressive tactics they had managed in a few short months, in the spring of 1864, to nullify to a large extent the freedom of action that the

Confederate cavalry had enjoyed through the first three years of the war.

It was high time to clean house, have done with half-way measures, and put a general in charge who could be depended upon to take the action necessary to remove the perennial threat to Washington posed by Confederate armies operating from the Shenandoah Valley. Hunter on July 15 had asked to be relieved because Halleck told him to effect a junction between his own command and the troops detached from the Army of the Potomac under Wright, at which time the latter would be in charge of the combined forces. Sigel had already been relieved, as had Sullivan, one of Hunter's infantry division commanders, in the same Special Order that assigned Crook to the command of the active troops in Hunter's Department.

Ignoring Hunter's request for relief, Halleck had as early as July 17 transmitted to him a directive from General Grant which outlined the policy the General-in-Chief had decided to apply to the Valley, either through Hunter or his successor:

If Hunter cannot get to Gordonsville and Charlottesville to cut the railroads he should make all the valleys south of the Baltimore and Ohio a desert as high up as possible. I do not mean that houses should be burned, but every particle of provisions and stock should be removed, and the people notified to move out. * * * He wants your troops to eat out Virginia clear and clean as far as they go, so that crows flying over it for the balance of the season will have to carry their provender with them.

The foregoing order had had no effect on the bemused Hunter, who by that time had completely lost control of the situation in his Department. With some justification he attributed his difficulties to the War Department policy whereby Halleck and Stanton kept the field forces shifting to right and left as a shield between the Capital and the movements of *Early's* Confederates, with the result that the Union commanders, Hunter and Wright in particular, became mere automatons, without initiative and unable to carry out military operations with any degree of consistency.

On the morning of August 1, following a conference with Sheridan the day before, Grant sent a wire to Halleck that notified his civilian superiors in Washington, in a politely oblique fashion, that he was taking positive steps to correct what was fast becoming an intolerable military situation. The message informed Halleck that he was sending Sheridan "for temporary duty whilst the enemy is being expelled from the border," adding that "unless General Hunter is in the field in person, I want Sheridan put in command of all the troops in the field, with instructions to put himself south of the enemy and follow him to the death. Wherever the enemy goes let our troops go also."

Grant no doubt figured that Halleck would show the telegram to Stanton and Lincoln, and that his conditional proposal could hardly be rejected unless the Administration were willing to assume full responsibility for continuing the anomalous military situation. Without waiting for a reaction, however, Grant's headquarters on August 2 issued a Special Order temporarily relieving Major General P. H. Sheridan, commanding Cavalry Corps, Army of the Potomac, from duty in that Army and directing him to report in person without delay to General Halleck in Washington for orders. One division of the Cavalry Corps was also detached and ordered to proceed to Washington, to come under Sheridan's command as part of the provisional army which Grant planned to form in a major effort to dispose of the *Early* menace once and for all.

The following day, August 3, Lincoln sent Grant a cypher dispatch which went right to the heart of the problem and secured the result that the President had been striving for some time to achieve, which was that Grant come north in person to clear the military air. Grant was told that he was doing exactly the right thing, but was asked to discover, if he could, from any of the dispatches from Washington following Grant's August 1 telegram to Halleck, "that there is any idea in the head of any one here of 'putting our army *south* of the enemy' or 'of following him to the death' in any direction. I repeat to you it will neither be done nor attempted unless you watch it every day and hour, and force it."

On receipt of Lincoln's telegram, Grant replied that he would leave City Point in two hours. But instead of going to Washington he bypassed the Capital and headed for Frederick. There he found Hunter's command encamped along the Monocacy River, presumably protecting Washington but making no effort to flush out and engage *Early*. Grant asked Hunter where the enemy was. Hunter didn't know! Grant remarked that *he* would find out. He ordered Hunter forthwith to load all his troops except the cavalry and wagon trains on the available railroad cars and start at once for Halltown, four miles south of Harpers Ferry, the cavalry and trains to follow by road. That, said Grant, would reveal *Early's* whereabouts, because he was sure the Confederate general would be found opposing any Federal advance up the Shenandoah Valley.

Grant then proceeded to write out instructions for Hunter, suggesting at the same time that he establish Department Headquarters wherever he wished, but indicating that it would be well if Sheridan were given command of the field forces. Hunter told him frankly that he couldn't seem to satisfy Halleck and thought it best that he be relieved of his command. The idea suited Grant, who wired Sheridan in Washington to report to him at once at Monocacy Junction, where he would await his arrival.

106

Before leaving Washington, Sheridan visited the White House in company with the Secretary of War to pay his respects to the President who with customary candor remarked that when Grant had first proposed Sheridan for the job of fighting *Early*, Stanton considered him too youthful, and he, Lincoln, had agreed. However, said Lincoln, now that Grant had "ploughed round" the difficulties (meaning the face-saving offer to retain department autonomy under Hunter as administrative head), he was satisfied with the selection of Sheridan and "hoped for the best." When Stanton said good-by to Sheridan he took occasion to emphasize the political importance to the President of a military success in the Valley.

The lengths to which Grant was willing to go to avoid becoming involved in the political atmosphere of the wartime Capital was strikingly illustrated in this instance. The important thing was that a surgical operation was called for and the General-in-Chief was apparently the one surgeon who could perform it. Lincoln had seen the need for the operation but it took some doing to educate soldier Grant. Once convinced, however, the general's direct-action approach brought a quick solution by way of "ploughing around the difficulty," in Lincoln's homespun description. The result was that Lincoln gained his point, Grant carried out the Commander-in-Chief's wishes, and Philip Henry Sheridan, the doughty little Irishman whom Grant would later describe as the best general in the Army, was about to be turned loose with an independent command to show whether as leader of an army he could accomplish results comparable to those he had achieved as leader of the Cavalry Corps.

Now that the barnacles had been scraped off and the situation clarified, War Department orders were issued consolidating the Department of the Susquehanna, the Middle Department, the Department of Washington, and the Department of West Virginia into the Middle Military Division, with Sheridan in temporary administrative command on the one hand, and on the other reporting directly to Grant in his dual capacity as commander of the active forces of the unified Division. The way was finally open for vigorous action against *Early*.

UNHORSED TROOPERS DURING SHERIDAN'S RICHMOND RAID

CHAPTER 5

SHERIDAN'S BACKGROUND

SHERIDAN was no theoretician, nor a student of grand strategy and tactics as practised by the great exponents of the military art. His interest in books was limited, for there had been no one in his early life to inculcate in him a taste for good literature, although he developed a liking for history and did later on become a devotee of Shakespeare. Born of poor Irish parents in Albany, New York on March 6, 1831, he lacked the educational background of many of his classmates at West Point, where he had the good fortune to room with Henry W. Slocum, a studious type who proved a willing and helpful tutor to the backward Sheridan. Many a night after taps the two young men would hang a blanket over the single window of their room, when Slocum would patiently explain the intricacies of problems in algebra and other knotty subjects to his struggling roommate.

While Sheridan was still very young, his parents had moved to Somerset, Ohio, and in due course young Phil was sent to the village school, where an itinerant Irish dominie introduced him to such subjects as geography, history, arithmetic, and English grammar. Pursuing his studies until he reached the age of 14, Phil left school to earn a living at the village country store. His first job paid the munificent annual wage of $24, followed by a promotion to a better position at $120 a year in a dry-goods store, where he kept books and acquired a basic knowledge which may have proven to be the key that opened the door to opportunity when in 1861 he was selected by General Halleck to straighten out the administrative confusion existing in that general's midwest Department.

During boyhood, his small size and physical appearance made him an object of ridicule at the hands of larger boys, particularly the bully type whose attentions doubtless helped materially to develop in the young man a decidedly pugnacious temperament. At times this characteristic served a useful purpose, but on occasion it might later have gotten Phil into real trouble with his superiors in the service had it not been for the loyal devotion of friends who would go out of their way to cover up for his forthright but sometimes undiplomatic behavior.

YOUNG PHIL AT WEST POINT

At the age of 17 Sheridan managed to secure an appointment to West Point, fortunately passing his examinations for admission principally because the academic requirements were not rigorous. At the Military Academy he found himself in a class of sixty-three members, among whom were the aforementioned Henry Slocum and George Crook, with whom he would become closely associated during the later war years. There was little in the youth's physical appearance to attract the opposite sex. He stood no more than five feet five inches tall, and had inordinately long arms but short legs. A jutting jaw and a bullet-shaped head with a large bump in the rear made Sheridan one cadet who would be a losing gamble in a male beauty contest.

Sheridan finally graduated in 1853, thirty-fourth in a class of fifty-two, taking five years to complete the four years' course, although not through academic failure. The real cause grew out of an imagined affront administered to Sheridan on the parade ground by a cadet sergeant, which prompted the belligerent Phil to make after the noncommissioned officer with a lowered bayonet. The lethal weapon fortunately failed to pierce its human target only because Sheridan thought better of his impulsive attack just in time to put on the brakes. A year's suspension gave him time to think over this infraction of discipline, which he subsequently admitted deserved more severe punishment.

In spite of the embarrassment which he experienced in being forced to return to his home town in mild disgrace because of the year's suspension, Sheridan refused to let it worry him because he believed himself to have been the injured party, a victim of circumstances and unfair tactics at the hands of an upperclassman. Resuming his former job at the dry-goods store, Cadet Sheridan spent the year again looking after the boss's books, tucking under his belt some additional experience that was soon to stand him in good stead.

When he returned to West Point in the fall of 1852, his friends Slocum and Crook had graduated, but in his last year at the Point he made new acquaintances, among them a number of future officers who, like himself, would advance to the command of armies—James B. McPherson, John M. Schofield, and, on the Confederate side, *John B. Hood.* Sheridan's scholastic standing when he graduated was not high enough to afford him the opportunity to choose the branch of the service in which he would have liked to serve, so he was on July 1, 1853 assigned as a brevet second lieutenant to the First Infantry, stationed at Fort Duncan, Texas, where he served for a year in garrison and on frontier duty. The following year he became a full second lieutenant, was assigned to the Fourth Infantry, and served with that organization for the next seven years, part of the time in command of a detachment of dragoons (a cavalry element attached to the infantry regiment). The intervening years, until the outbreak of war, were interesting but comparatively uneventful. They were spent partly in Texas, but mostly in the Columbia River country of the far west making topographical surveys, hunting deer and small game, chasing bad Indians, building winter quarters for his men, studying bird-life, learning to speak Chinook (the Indian language among the coastal tribes), and performing routine chores.

During those years Sheridan developed a lasting friendship with Captain David A. Russell, a warm-hearted, solid officer of sound judgment and sterling character whose firm but friendly treatment of the Indians set a pattern which Sheridan was perceptive enough to emulate. A few years later, his good friend Russell, then a brigadier general and division commander serving under Sheridan, was to die on the battlefield of Winchester leading a charge against *Jubal Early's* Confederates.

His Slow Start in the War

Shortly after the firing on Fort Sumter, in April of '61, the Fourth Infantry was ordered east, but Sheridan, still a second lieutenant, was left behind in command of the post until relieved on September 1, 1861. During that five month period, expansion of the Regular Army and the wholesale resignation of officers who elected to join the Confederacy created vacancies whereby Sheridan was promoted to the rank of first lieutenant and then to a captaincy, with assignment to the Thirteenth United

States Infantry, Colonel William T. Sherman commanding.

Sheridan joined his new regiment at Jefferson Barracks, Missouri, but before he had a chance to get acquainted he was summoned to St. Louis by Major General Henry W. Halleck, the Department Commander, who was looking for an officer experienced in Army paper work, to head a board of officers detailed to audit the affairs of a host of inefficient disbursing officers for the purpose of correcting the almost chaotic administrative condition of the department in which Halleck's predecessor, General John C. Fremont, had left it. Although ineffectual as a field commander, Halleck was an efficient administrator, and the assignment given Captain Sheridan was a fine opportunity for him to show what he could do under the eyes of a prominent general who was in position, then and later, to advance the fortunes of the young Regular.

Halleck's Department was geographically a large one, embracing the States of Missouri, Iowa, Minnesota, Arkansas, Illinois, and all of Kentucky west of the Cumberland River. Halleck was so well satisfied with the manner in which Captain Sheridan executed his mission that as soon as the task was completed, in December 1861, he handed him another administrative job, this time in the dual capacity of Chief Quartermaster and Chief Commissary of the Army of Southwest Missouri, commanded by General Samuel R. Curtis, then organizing for the Pea Ridge Campaign. By hard work and intelligent application, Sheridan performed wonders in solving the transportation and supply problems of Curtis' army, following which Halleck gave him a roving commission to buy horses for the army, a task which occupied his attention until after the Battle of Shiloh, when Sheridan made up his mind that time was a-wastin' and he had better look to his own future if he was to advance in his chosen profession.

The upshot of his soul-searching was that he secured

a transfer to Pittsburgh Landing, Tennessee, in April 1862. There he reported to General Halleck at the latter's field headquarters, was assigned to duty with the topographical engineers, then as quartermaster for Halleck's headquarters, in which capacity he soon made things so comfortable for the general that, in Sheridan's own words, "I consider this the turning-point in my military career." He was now on active duty with an army in the field, with opportunity to visit the various divisions and to learn what was transpiring in the place of greatest interest to an officer who sought combat, which Sheridan certainly did. Among his friends was General Sherman, commanding a division in the army under Grant, who offered to secure for him the colonelcy of an Ohio regiment, a friendly gesture which came to naught when the Governor of Ohio selected another officer.

JOINS THE CAVALRY

Shortly after this disappointment, the Governor of Michigan, in casting about for a Regular officer to succeed Colonel Gordon Granger, just promoted to brigadier general, as commander of the Second Michigan Cavalry, learned of Sheridan's availability and offered him the post with the rank of colonel. After unwinding a bit of red tape General Halleck gave his approval. There was no time to lose in disposing of the formalities, for Sheridan's new command was even then under orders to make a raid south of the enemy, operating at Corinth, Mississippi, and the newly appointed colonel wanted badly to lead his regiment on this mission. Within a few hours he had borrowed a coat and trousers from an infantry captain, pinned on an old pair of colonel's eagles that had belonged to General Granger, mounted his horse, and, taking hasty command of the regiment, reported it to the brigade commander as ready to march.

This was indeed, as Sheridan stated, the turning point in his career, nor was he slow to demonstrate his capacity for combat leadership. His first field mission was handled so expertly that in the Battle of Booneville he achieved a decisive victory over a much larger Confederate force under General *Chalmers*. So impressed were his superiors by his aggressive activity and tireless industry that five of them, led by Brigadier General W. S. Rosecrans, sent off a dispatch to General Halleck on July 30 which said in part: "Brigadiers scarce; good ones scarcer. The undersigned respectfully beg that you will obtain the promotion of Sheridan. He is worth his weight in gold."

In thirty-five days after his promotion from captain to colonel, Sheridan was able to pin on his shoulders the stars of a brigadier general, and shortly thereafter was given command of the Eleventh Infantry Division of the Army of the Ohio, which he led at the bloody Battle of Perryville. The same qualities that won his spurs as a cavalry regimental commander were revealed in that battle; a keen tactical eye, a bull-dog tenacity in fighting the enemy to a standstill, a cool wariness in handling his troops to the best advantage. "Little Phil's" darkly brilliant eyes, surmounted by heavy, arched eyebrows, significantly reflected depths of character that came to the surface in the heat and excitement of combat. His stubborn defense and aggressive counter measures on this occasion finally forced his assailants to abandon the field.

Ten weeks after Perryville, the even bloodier battle of Stone's River saw Sheridan's division again covered with glory when it held steady against a massive Confederate turning movement which swept the two other divisions of McCook's corps out of action like tumble weeds. Here Sheridan's careful selection of ground and judicious use of his artillery enabled his guns to pour a devastating fire into the dense Confederate masses crossing Sheridan's front. This was followed by volley after volley of musketry that finally staggered the Confederate attackers, forcing them to break and flee, hotly pursued by a brigade of Sheridan's division, by which time his isolated troops had become vulnerable to a vicious counterattack by the redoubtable Confederate, *Pat Cleburne*, an Irishman like Sheridan. Sheridan reformed his division at right angles to its former position and, in spite of overwhelming Confederate numbers, repelled repeated onsets until his troops were out of ammunition and had suffered 1,633 casualties, including three brigade commanders, out of a total strength of 4,154. Still unperturbed despite his desperate plight, Sheridan launched a bayonet attack by one of his brigades, under cover of which the division was withdrawn from its precarious position. But the time gained by Sheridan's skilful maneuvering and aggressive fighting had delayed the enemy's advance for three hours and enabled Rosecran's hard-pressed army to reform on a battle line from which the Confederates were unable to dislodge it.

A FIGHTING DIVISION COMMANDER

There was little doubt in the minds of the officers and men of Rosecran's army that Sheridan's division had been the means of its salvation. He was clearly the hero of the battle and was almost immediately rewarded by promotion to major general. His reputation as a fighter was made, and additional laurels came to him at Missionary Ridge, although he missed a golden opportunity at Chickamauga when his division failed to take a direct road, the use of which might have brought him to the aid of hard-pressed General George H. Thomas in time to change the outcome of the battle. It was at Missionary Ridge, however, that Sheridan's gallant performance in the memorable assault which swept Bragg's army from the crest of the ridge brought his abilities forcefully to the attention of General Grant, who saw the whole affair in person and marked the young division commander as a hard-fighting leader upon whom he could strongly depend. It was only natural, when Grant was placed in command of all the Union armies and needed a new general to command the Cavalry Corps, that he accepted with enthusiasm Halleck's suggestion that Sheridan might be the man he was looking for. How Sheridan met his increased responsibilities as commander of the cavalry of the Army of the Potomac will be discussed later.

THE UNION CAVALRY'S EARLY HANDICAP

Back in the 1930's when the horse cavalry was something more than a nostalgic memory to the old-timers in the mounted arm of the service, hardbitten "yellow-legs" were wont to remark that the true cavalryman was born, not made. There was some truth in the statement, at least to the extent that in cases where a natural affinity existed between a man and his horse, the embryo trooper became a useful soldier with far less training than was required for the recruit who had never been on a horse and perhaps had no particular desire for the experience.

The Union cavalry in the Civil War was badly handicapped at the outset and until two years had passed, due to causes which served to retard its development to the point where it could pull its own weight as part of the combat team. Old General Winfield S. Scott, who was Chief of Staff at the outbreak, believed that horse cavalry would be ineffectual against the new type of rifled cannon; consequently he gave that arm of the service no encouragement. His successor, General George B. McClellan, did nothing to improve the stature of the mounted branch; on the contrary, he apparently approved of the policy whereby army and corps commanders utilized such cavalry units as were assigned to them in the form of escorts to the higher commanders, and as mounted messengers and occasional reconnaissance patrols, but mostly as security forces to picket the bivouac perimeters so that the infantry and artillery might rest undisturbed in their camps until time to march and fight.

Neither the horseflesh nor the would-be cavalrymen of the Northern states could compare with their counterparts in the South, where blooded horses were ridden by the young men almost as soon as they could walk. Much of the raw material for the Union cavalry was drawn from mines and offices, workshops and factories, men who in most cases had never made the acquaintance of a horse until they joined the cavalry. Even those who came from farms, and presumably had a working knowledge of horses, were not necessarily skilled riders. There was almost a complete lack of the cavalry spirit in the Union armies, a logical result of being treated as a poor relation or an unwanted guest. It is little wonder that the morale and effectiveness of the Union horsemen was at a low ebb during the early years of the war, when *Jeb Stuart* and *Fitzhugh Lee, Wade Hampton* and *Rooney Lee, Turner Ashby* and *Nathan Bedford Forrest, John S. Mosby* and *John Hunt Morgan,* and a host of lesser Confederates cavaliers were achieving fame, helping the Confederate armies to win victory after victory, and in the process making the Northern horsemen appear rank amateurs.

It was Major General Joseph Hooker, orginally an artilleryman, who took the first step to restore the self-respect of the Federal cavalrymen by giving them the chance to play their part as a combat arm. When Hooker succeeded Burnside in command of the Army of the Potomac after the Fredericksburg debacle, one of his initial reorganization moves was to rescue the cavalry from its attached, decentralized status as lackeys to corps and division infantry generals and to constitute a cavalry corps, under a single commander, whose mission would be to train intensively to function in accordance with the capabilities of that arm. As soon as it would be ready, Hooker promised to assign combat missions appropriate to the mounted arm.

The period of transition was slow, as was to be expected. But the morale of the Union cavalry rose perceptibly and after a period of trial and error, covering three or four months during the early part of 1863, a large Union cavalry force under General Alfred Pleasonton surprised *Stuart's* Confederate cavalry at Brandy Station in a swirling battle that came very close to inflicting a stinging defeat on that bold and heretofore uniformly victorious leader of the Southern horse. Although Pleasonton's cavalry was the first to retire, and *Stuart* naturally claimed a victory, *Jeb,* badly shaken, was subjected to violent criticism by the Southern press. Conversely, Pleasonton's reconnaissance in force had not only accomplished its primary mission, the gaining of valuable information that confirmed the fact of *Lee's* second invasion of the North, but—and this was of even greater importance—the Union cavalry had met the vaunted *Stuart* on even terms and shattered for all time the myth of Confederate invincibility so far as its cavalry was concerned.

During the period immediately following Brandy Station, a series of clashes occurred between the Union and Confederate cavalry at Aldie and other mountain gaps, as *Stuart* sought to screen from prying Federal eyes the northward march of *Lee's* divisions into Maryland and Pennsylvania. In all of those encounters the Confederates came off second best, and as a consequence *Stuart's* brigades were badly jaded even before he started off on his ill-fated, circuitous march via the outskirts of Washington toward a junction with *Lee's* main body, to which he finally caught up at the end of the second day of the Battle of Gettysburg, too late to render his accustomed service to *Lee's army* when he was most needed.

During the Gettysburg campaign, and for the first time in the course of the war, the Union cavalry under Pleasonton performed in a superior manner to cover the front and flanks of Meade's Army of the Potomac on its advance from Frederick, on June 29, 1863, to meet *Lee's* invading army at Gettysburg. By that time the Federal horsemen had come of age, and they proved it when Buford's division, fighting dismounted, held off *A. P. Hill's corps* on the first day, July 1, until Reynold's First Corps could come into action; again when Kilpatrick's division blocked *Stuart's* advance at Hanover; and finally, on the third day, when Gregg and Custer fought *Stuart* to a standstill three miles east of Gettysburg, to thwart the Confederate cavalryman's effort to create havoc in Meade's rear as Pickett's charge was being shattered against Cemetery Ridge.

And so it came about that when Phil Sheridan was assigned by Grant to command the Cavalry Corps of the Army of the Potomac on April 4, 1864, the Union cavalry was composed of veterans who had proven their competence and were armed and conditioned as a combat team capable of responding to the inspired leadership that Sheridan was so well equipped to furnish.

"Here was a Man who could Command Cavalry"

There must have been something electric about Sheridan, a magnetic quality that attracted enlisted men and officers alike, without apparent effort on his part. Like *Stonewall Jackson,* his mere appearance on horseback before his troops seemed to generate a spontaneous enthusiasm that puzzled his closest friends as well as himself.

At such times Lincoln's apt description of Sheridan's odd, almost grotesque physical shape, seemed strangely inappropriate. The President pictured the general as "one of those long-armed fellows with short legs that can scratch his shins without having to stoop over to do it."

Captain (Brevet Major) Henry A. DuBois, a graduate of Yale College in 1859 and the Yale Medical School in

Major General Philip H. Sheridan

1861, who served as a medical officer throughout the war, mostly with the cavalry, was a member of Sheridan's staff as assistant Medical Director of the Cavalry Corps from the time Sheridan took command until Lee's surrender at Appomattox. In a personal letter, written shortly after Sheridan's death in 1888 at the age of 58, DuBois recalled his first impression of General Sheridan thusly:

It was in 1864 shortly after Grant had taken personal direction of the Army of the Potomac and while that army

121

under the immediate command of Meade was at the beginning of the campaign which was to end the war, that Sheridan reported to General Meade to take command of the Cavalry Corps of the Army of the Potomac. At this time I was on duty at the Headquarters of the Army as a Medical Inspector and was quietly sitting in a small wall tent reading when my tent mate, Dr. Morris Asche, brought in a little man whom he had met in the Adjutant General's office and introduced me to him—the tent was small and a bed on either side left only a narrow space between for a table and no space for chairs.

The little man sat on one bed and Asche and myself appropriated the other. He talked freely, said little about himself, but seemed interested in the Army of the Potomac and in the character of its officers and in their current reputation. He drew both of us out and in return gave us his ideas of cavalry and how it could be used. I can now recall him seated on the low cot—his short legs and long body; his peculiar shaped head with a large bump on its back just where his cap fitted; his quiet and rather dull look when not speaking, and the sudden change which came over his face when speaking and the animation of his whole body and the sparkle of his eye when interested in what he was saying. The contrast was so great between his appearance in repose and when animated as to strike both of us as remarkable.

It was not long before I felt sure that here was a man who could command cavalry, a branch of the service that I had long served with and felt much interested in, and as I knew he had just been assigned to its command I felt a much greater interest in him than I otherwise should. As the conversation went on I felt strongly attracted toward him. He inspired me with confidence—but more than this I felt a personal liking for him—why I could not at the time understand nor can I after all these years explain.

He wore the uniform of a major general but there was no constraint in his manner in talking to us, although our rank was but that of captains—nor on the other hand did we feel any reserve towards him on account of his rank. At first I thought that this was due to politeness alone, but soon found it was his natural manner, that was absolutely destitute of any feeling of superiority on account of his rank, but even when I found this out it did not account for the feeling that I felt growing in me of personal attraction apparently without cause and which soon was so firmly fixed that before his orders had been made out and handed to him, I felt as if I had known him long and should have defended him, had he been criticized, as I only could have done for an old and personal friend.

He came into the tent an utter stranger and in less than an hour both of us not only believed in him but felt an affection for him, of the same kind as we would have felt towards one of our own rank. With me at least, this affection led to an exchange with an officer on the Cavalry staff leaving the headquarters of the army for that of a corps, and it has remained with me not only during the time I served on his staff but after I left it, also after I left the army until his death, and I still feel it now that he is no more.

I thought this very strange—this love at first sight, and without apparent reason, for I knew little of what he had done in the west. At the time I thought that it was peculiar to myself, for my companion, though greatly pleased was not affected to the same extent that I was. Soon, however, I found that others felt much as I did—that we had a personal ownership in him, that he would at all times acknowledge, and this without any feeling of superiority, though with an almost absolute reliance on his skill and judgement.

Later on I found that this same feeling was not confined to officers only but that the soldiers in the ranks felt much in the same way—that is to say—much as they would towards a brother in whom they had unlimited confidence and whose interests were also theirs. Nor was this feeling confined to those who had been with him for a length of time. It was felt by new troops placed under his orders for the first time in a very short space of time— men who scarcely knew him by sight. This magnetic influence seemed to spread by a peculiar infection to a whole army at times, in a moment—as at Cedar Creek. His appearance in front of the line of battle, without his saying a word, changed the character of every man in a moment, so far at least as his military utility in the pending battle was concerned.

Now this feeling was the more surprising as Sheridan never *tried* to inspire it and could not understand why he gave rise to it. He did not do as McClellan did, look personally after the comforts of his soldiers, talk to them at their camp fires and issue orders for their benefit. Sheridan once asked his brother about it after there had been great enthusiasm manifested by new men on his riding past. "Mike," he said, "do I affect you so?" "No, I know you too well," was his brother's answer, and to the general's question as to what he did that caused this feeling of enthusiasm in thousands of men at once, his brother replied that "he supposed the men saw he knew what he was about and had heard that he would not bother them." Notwithstanding all this Colonel Sheridan was not without this same feeling that we all had towards his brother.

This characteristic of Sheridan is to my mind the most noteworthy. Some men are great because of their actions, some because the ability lies latent ready when the occasion calls it forth—but few are great for both these reasons, as well as a third, the power of attracting men by their affections, as well as inspiring them with entire confidence in their earnestness in the cause in which they were both engaged, in their ability to guide them and in the absolute certainty of their success.

Sheridan had but one independent command. Could he have done better than he did? I know those who knew him best believe that had opportunity served he had that in him which was equal to greater things. His friends object to his being considered a cavalry leader only and say with truth that his reputation rests on actions fought by infantry rather than cavalry, that he knew how to use cavalry. Few will deny but they claim that he had power to give the rapidity of movement to infantry, when necessary, of cavalry and on other occasions to convert cavalry into infantry and to give them the steadiness and discipline of the latter—a far harder matter—but that his ability was only fully shown when in command of both arms. That his use of artillery was different from that in vogue in our army and that in his hands it was eminently successful. What other general ever made artillery take the place of cavalry in the pursuit of an enemy? Few ever got greater results from artillery placed in, or in advance of, the line of battle and whose safety depended on it being broken, and when this took place, keeping up their fire to the last moment when their guns were abandoned, not withdrawn, the men saving themselves if possible. The execution done with the last few shots at close range in Sheridan's opinion was worth more than the guns he lost. He promoted artillery officers leaving their guns provided they kept them in action until captured and then saved their men.

How Sheridan would have done in Grant's place can never be known, but that he had abilities fitting him for the command of a large army such as McClellan had I think will not be denied by those who have studied his military history and how differently in the circumstances the two men would have acted.

DuBois' appraisal of Sheridan's capacity for greatness pointed to the general's "power to give the rapidity of movement of cavalry to infantry, when necessary, and on other occasions to convert cavalry into infantry and to give them the steadiness and discipline of the latter—a far harder matter." Although Sheridan's basic arm after graduation was infantry, and he brilliantly commanded an infantry division for two years of the war, his initial combat was in command of a cavalry regiment, and he is best remembered as the successful leader of the cavalry corps of the Army of the Potomac. He was neither infantry-minded nor cavalry-minded in the narrow sense of that term. Realism, and a keen conception of the power, capabilities, and limitations of the three combat arms—infantry, cavalry, and artillery—combined with a comprehensive appreciation of the value of mobility and firepower when properly used—such were the tools that Sheridan possessed and employed with such notable success, regardless of the character of the troops he might happen to be commanding at the time. Like John Buford, Sheridan saw his cavalry as mounted infantry, and the horse as a means of more rapid locomotion rather than the lower half of a modern centaur. When the situation suggested a mounted charge as the best means of applying the principle of mass without concurrently violating the principle of economy of force, he did not hesitate to employ it. Unlike many of the Confederate cavalry generals, however, Sheridan failed to see in the mounted charge of large bodies of troopers the sine qua non of cavalry combat.

Sheridan Clashes with Meade

When Sheridan reported to General Meade, commanding the Army of the Potomac, of which the Cavalry Corps was an integral part, he was 33 years of age but looked even younger. Thin almost to the point of emaciation by the rigors of his campaign as an infantry division commander in the West, he weighed only one hundred and fifteen pounds, but was as hard and wiry as an Indian. In spite of his short stature and bantam weight, no one made the mistake of underestimating him; his reputation as a fighter was too well known, even in Virginia.

He found the Cavalry Corps at Brandy Station, twelve thousand strong, composed of three divisions commanded by Brigadier Generals A. T. A. Torbert, David Gregg, and, upon Sheridan's own recommendation, James H. Wilson. Twelve batteries of horse artillery were under the direction of Captain John M. Robinson as Chief of Artillery. To get a good look at his new command Sheridan, a few days after his arrival, ordered a review which showed the men in good health and satisfactorily equipped, but the horses thin and worn as the result of excessive picketing under the system in vogue in the Army of the Potomac.

This policy had plagued the Union cavalry from the very outset, even after Hooker had improved its lot early in 1863. Sheridan found that the cavalry pickets had been thrown almost entirely around the camps of the infantry and artillery on a continuous line that reached a distance of nearly sixty miles, although there was virtually no Confederate cavalry in contact at any point.

Determined to remedy the fault if at all possible, he sought an early interview with Meade, to whom he forcefully presented his own views on the proper use of cavalry, pointing out that major reliance must be placed on the horses and such wasteful employment as he had found impaired the ability of the corps to render the effective service of which it was capable. Sheridan argued that the cavalry should be kept concentrated, in the same way in which the Confederates traditionally husbanded their cavalry, so that it could be utilized for its primary mission of fighting the enemy cavalry. The shocked Army Commander wanted to know how he would protect the army trains and secure his camps if Sheridan's recommendations were followed, to which the latter replied in effect that if Meade would unshackle the cavalry corps he would guarantee to keep *Stuart's* cavalry so busy that they would have no time to harass the army infantry and artillery.

Meade remained unconvinced, and the divergent views of the two generals were never fully reconciled, although Meade did relax the picketing requirements sufficiently to give the horses a partial opportunity to recover their strength before the opening of the spring campaign on May 4.

The Virginia theater was entirely unfamiliar to Sheridan, all of whose previous service had been with the western armies, but he followed his established custom, in the time available to him, by an intensive study of the topography of the area over which he would be called upon to operate. His discovery that the country was heavily wooded and contained many parallel rivers and streams confirmed his fears that his cavalry would encounter unnecessary difficulties if forced to campaign in accordance with Meade's views. He thereupon made up his mind that operational independence for the Cavalry Corps was a basic requirement, and he never for a moment lost sight of that objective.

During the progress of the Wilderness Campaign, Sheridan found the operations of his cavalry divisions made difficult and on several occasions ineffectual because General Meade, although properly regarding Sheridan's corps as responsive to his orders as army commander, chose to treat the cavalry commander as a member of his own staff in the role of Chief of Cavalry, seeming to feel that it was perfectly proper for army headquarters to issue orders direct to elements of the cavalry command. At Todd's Tavern, for example, Meade modified Sheridan's orders to Merritt and Gregg without informing the corps commander, causing confusion and delay as well as raising Sheridan's blood pressure. Again, on the approach to Spotsylvania Court House, Sheridan's orders to his cavalry to seize Spotsylvania and the bridge over the Po River were changed by Meade, with the result that *Lee's* advance to that point was completely unobstructed, which in turn nullified Grant's modified strategy to sideslip his opponent and enabled the Confederate army to get there first.

These repeated irritations, to a pugnacious character like Sheridan, presaged a showdown with General Meade sooner or later. The smoldering resentment burst into flame when on May 8 Meade sent for Sheridan and dressed him down by making what the cavalryman felt were unjust criticisms and insinuations which implied that the cavalry was to blame for recent blunders, including the specific charge that it had impeded the march of Warren's Corps to Spotsylvania by blocking the road. Sheridan replied with equal pepperiness that if that were true, Meade had ordered the cavalry there without his knowledge, that "he had broken up my combinations, exposed Wilson's division to disaster, and kept Gregg's division unnecessarily idle, and further, that such disjointed operations as he had been requiring of the cavalry for the last four days would render the corps inefficient and useless before long."

The two generals at this meeting continued to argue for some time, until finally Sheridan, boiling over, told his superior officer that he could whip *Stuart* if Meade would only let him, adding in a burst of anger that since Meade insisted on giving the cavalry directions without consulting or even notifying him, he could henceforth command the Cavalry Corps himself—that he, Sheridan, would not give it another order.

GRANT TURNS SHERIDAN LOOSE

It appeared to Meade that Sheridan's campaign for relief from the army commander's control and for unrestricted freedom to carry out independent cavalry operations had led him to a point of no return, that his attitude had become insubordinate and rated a rebuke from General Grant. Whereupon Meade hastened to Grant's headquarters and repeated the conversation just concluded with Sheridan. When he came to the part where Sheridan had said that if turned loose he would lick *Stuart*, Grant's eyes twinkled. Brushing cigar ashes off on the lapel of his jacket, the General-in-Chief remarked calmly, "Did he say so? Then let him go and do it."

Sheridan's fight for freedom of action had been won and it was now up to his cavalry to make good as an independent force. Meade, a fair-minded and honorable man, took his defeat philosophically, secretly relieved, perhaps, because now his peppery cavalry commander would no longer be an annoyance. Within the hour an order was drafted and transmitted over the signature of Meade's chief of staff:

Headquarters Army of the Potomac.
May 8th, 1864—1 P. M.
General Sheridan,
 Commanding Cavalry Corps.

The Major-General commanding directs you to immediately concentrate your available mounted force, and with your ammunition trains and such supply trains as are filled (exclusive of ambulances) proceed against the enemy's cavalry, and when your supplies are exhausted, proceed via New Market and Green Bay to Haxall's Landing on the James River, there communicating with General Butler, procuring supplies and return to this army. Your dismounted men will be left with the train here.

A. A. HUMPHREYS,
Major-General, Chief of Staff

THE UNION CAVALRY TAKES THE INITIATIVE

Despite the hamstringing Sheridan's corps had experienced from army headquarters, it had functioned as cavalry was intended to operate, in a compact fighting mass. From the time Grant's army crossed the Rapidan into the Wilderness, the Union cavalry covered the army's front, flanks, and rear wherever it moved. It fought mounted or dismounted as the occasion required, assaulted and carried Confederate infantry entrenchments, seized strategic positions, cut enemy communications, destroyed his transportation, burned his supplies, and for the first time in the war seized and held the initiative by keeping *Stuart's* Confederate horsemen in a continuous state of uncertainty as to when or where to expect the next attack from their ubiquitous opponents. With Sheridan leading the Cavalry Corps, the bulldog grip that the Union Commander fastened on *Lee,* while it may have relaxed from time to time under stress of circumstances, never let go. The day of *Stuart's* exciting dramatic and successful raids around the Union army was over; now it would be the Union cavalry's turn to do the raiding, with the Confederate cavalry hard-pressed even in the performance of its primary missions of reconnaissance, counter-reconnaissance, and security of its army's flanks and rear.

Superior in numbers and vastly so in firepower by reason of the breech-loading repeating carbines with which most of the Union cavalry was now armed, the morale of Sheridan's troopers was fully equal to it if not better than that of the Southern cavalry, for whom horse replacements had become virtually impossible.

Sheridan's methods were bold and dashing. He believed in intuitive action and calculated risks, but his plans were carefully conceived and his officers and men had come to believe implicitly in his leadership. In Custer and Merritt and Wilson, and to a lesser degree in Torbert and Gregg, his cavalry brigades and divisions were led by the type of hell-for-leather horsemen of which the Northern armies had seen far too little until 1864. It is a historic fact that no cavalry force ever worked harder or fought more continuously than did Sheridan's corps during the months of May, June, and July. Scarcely a day passed without engaging the enemy cavalry, and there were frequent occasions when skirmishes were fought many times in a twenty-four hour period. This was gruelling work for the horses as well as the troopers; the Cavalry Corps was reported as requiring an average of 150 horses a day as replacements. The self-confidence and efficiency of the corps increased steadily, until it came to regard itself as invincible, and as the transformation occurred, the morale and aggressive spirit of *Jeb Stuart's* cavalry correspondingly decreased.

The words of one of Sheridan's best division commanders, Brigadier General James H. Wilson, whose opinion was based on personal experience, paint a clear picture of the Corps' activities and Sheridan's influence thereon:

There were times, in the year which led up to the crowning victory over *Lee*, in which the infantry commanders, and especially the rank and file, became despondent and faced the storm of battle with hopeless and dejected mien that foreboded failure; but there was never a day till the war ended when the cavalry corps did not go forth cheerfully and even gayly to its appointed tasks. A part of this was doubtless due to the greater freedom of action allowed to that arm of the service by General Grant, but it is simple justice to add that a much greater part of it was due to the untiring industry, the unflinching courage, the watchful care, and above all to the cheerful alacrity with which General Sheridan performed his own duties, and inspired every officer and man in his command to perform theirs. The benefits of this remarkable regeneration did not end with the Eastern cavalry, but spread in due time to that of the Western armies.

Wilson's opinion of Sheridan was confirmed by members of Grant's staff and Grant himself. "Little Phil's" physical courage, a source of great satisfaction to those who served under him, had much to do with his battle success. It was his practise to share the dangers of the front line with his men rather than send written attack orders up to the lines from a safe berth at the rear. This the troops appreciated as they always do, and it partly explains the alacrity with which they responded. The probabilities are that his remark to a staff officer on one occasion, when Sheridan seemed to be recklessly exposing himself and taking unnecessary risks, may have filtered down to the ranks. "I have never taken any command into battle," said Sheridan, "with the slightest desire to come out of it alive unless I won."

"Sheridan's courageous words and brilliant deeds encourage his commanders as much as they inspire his subordinates," Grant was reported to have said in an off-hand remark to several members of his staff. Which may have been one of the chief reasons why Grant so frankly admired Sheridan and allowed him such freedom of action.

As Sheridan's divisions were being readied for their big adventure on May 8, Grant added verbal instructions to Meade's written order. Sheridan was directed to pass around the left of *Lee's army* and attack his cavalry; to cut the two roads running west through Gordonsville and south to Richmond respectively; and when his rations and forage were exhausted, to move on to the James River for replenishment from Butler's supplies; then back to the Army of the Potomac.

Assembling his division commanders, Gregg, Merritt, and Wilson (Torbert was on sick report for the time being), Sheridan told them they were going out to fight *Stuart's* cavalry. "I know we can beat him," said the confident general, "and in view of my recent representations to General Meade I shall expect nothing but success." The line of march would be in one column in the direction of Richmond, down the Telegraph Road via Hamilton's Crossing, below Fredericksburg, a route that took the column well to the east of the Union and Confederate armies that were locked in battle around Spotsylvania.

This would be a radical departure from the type of infrequent raid to which the Northern cavalry had been accustomed in the past—the hit and run kind that involved mad gallops to burn a bridge or achieve some similar minor result that contributed little to the war effort, and exhausted men and animals in the process. The listening generals were surprised, but entered with enthusiasm into the spirit of the game, if game it could be called.

In column of fours the Blue horsemen moved out, early on the morning of May 9, an attenuated, but powerful force of at least 10,000 determined troopers that stretched thirteen miles. Sheridan set the pace, an unhurried walk, unheard of in their experience, but which inspired confidence among the old-timers that this little fellow knew what he was about. Sheridan's initial objective was the south side of the North Anna River, where forage could be procured, he hoped, before it would become necessary to fight *Stuart.*

The Union cavalry, well clear of *Lee's army* before *Stuart* learned of its departure, reached the North Anna with only minor interference from the Confederate horsemen. Custer's brigade, having been sent ahead to Beaver Dam Station to cut the Virginia Central Railroad, attacked a small enemy force engaged in shepherding to Richmond four hundred prisoners captured in the recent Battle of the Wilderness. The accidental encounter, a happy one from the Federal viewpoint, resulted in the recovery of all the prisoners and the destruction of the railroad station, two locomotives, three trains of cars, ninety wagons, supplies representing a million and a half rations, and nearly all the medical supplies of *Lee's army,* which latter had presumably been sent to that point for safe keeping.

Sheridan's steady march towards Richmond seemed to puzzle *Stuart,* who reached Beaver Dam Station after the Union column had passed. *Stuart* then made a forced march by a different route via Hanover Junction, in the hope that he could interpose between Sheridan and Richmond. The Confederate commander kept dividing his force, a part hanging on Sheridan's rear while the rest raced to get ahead of him. The Confederates, 5,000 strong, were run ragged while the 10,000 Federals conserved their strength in a steady march for the most part.

The two forces finally met in a showdown battle at the abandoned Yellow Tavern on the morning of May 11, with *Stuart's* troopers occupying a defensive position along a line of hills about six miles north of Richmond. During a period of four hours Sheridan threw repeated dismounted attacks at the Confederates without dislodging them. Late in the afternoon a combined mounted and dismounted assault broke the Confederate left, whereupon the center and right gave way as the graycoats were overrun and driven back.

THE DEATH OF JEB STUART

Jeb Stuart, galloping to the left to lend a hand where the fighting was hottest, rallied about eighty of the retreating Confederates and formed them in line as the 1st Michigan Regiment thundered by in the charge. Firing into their flanks as the Federal troopers rushed past, *Stuart's* little group watched with interest as the *1st Virginia Cavalry* countercharged the Michigan regiment in a grinding collision, from which the Blue troopers recoiled, many unhorsed soldiers hanging on to their comrades' stirrup straps as the Federals retraced their steps. *Stuart's* horse was up on the front line as the corps commander, drawing his pistol, fired into the withdrawing troopers, calling on his improvised detachment to follow his example.

A Union sergeant on foot, running to rejoin his regiment, paused a moment to fire one pistol shot at the Confederate officer on the big horse. Unaware of the identity of his important target or the fact that he had just made history, the soldier ran on, as *Stuart* swayed in the saddle, his hat jolted from his head. The bullet that passed through his liver would prove mortal within thirty-six hours, bringing to a close at age thirty-two the career of the superb cavalry leader who made one of the more notable contributions to the Lost Cause of the Confederacy.

Stuart's death-wound on the field of Yellow Tavern, significant as it was to the South, was only an incident, al-

135

though an important one, in the course of Sheridan's great raid. The battle had already been won when *Stuart* was stricken. The major part of the Confederate cavalry was driven in confusion toward Ashland, while a smaller segment headed for Richmond. *Fitz Lee* assumed temporary command in *Stuart's* place, as Sheridan pushed on to Haxall's Landing, below Malvern Hill, encountering aggressive but ineffectual opposition on the way, to complete his assigned mission, the greater part of which had already been successfully executed.

The temptation to lead his victorious divisions the few remaining miles into Richmond must have been an alluring prospect to Sheridan, since his route to Haxall's Landing took him into the area between the outer and inner fortifications of the Capital. *Bragg's* small force defending the city was composed largely of militia, old men, and government clerks, who could be counted on to offer only token resistance to Sheridan's veteran cavalry. There was always the possibility that *Beauregard's* force, presently in contact with Butler's Union army at Bermuda Hundred, would send troops to the aid of Richmond, and furthermore, there had been nothing in Grant's directive to Sheridan which even implied that he should attack the city or endeavor to occupy it. Sheridan was sure that he could move into the Capital and throw a mighty scare into its inhabitants, official and unofficial, but he also knew that the occupation would be fleeting and probably inconclusive. There would be casualties, and it was not Sheridan's way to sacrifice men in grandstand plays. He therefore set his mind sternly against the temptation, and that was that.

In due course the Cavalry Corps returned to Meade's army, rejoining at Chesterfield Station on May 24, having destroyed huge quantities of provisions and munitions of war, broken the two railroads between *Lee* and Richmond,

136

decisively defeated the Confederate cavalry and killed its brilliant leader, all within a period of sixteen days. Moreover, by way of additional benefits, the Army of the Potomac had been relieved for two weeks of the presence of enemy cavalry, and conversely, *Lee's Army of Northern Virginia* was deprived of *Stuart's* help in the Battle of Spotsylvania and during his march to the North Anna which followed. By the same token, Grant was also without the services of his cavalry during the period. On balance, however, the net gain from Sheridan's raid was of greater value to the Union.

During the absence of the Cavalry Corps, Grant's continuing battle of attrition, latterly at Spotsylvania, although unsuccessful in a strategic sense and at a frightful cost in Union casualties, was gradually wearing *Lee's army* down through losses that could not be replaced. Moreover, the Union general's policy of simultaneous offensives in every theater prevented *Lee* from shifting divisions from one area to another with the same facility as in earlier years. Over the weeks of massive sparring and footwork in the Wilderness he had suffered heavy losses among his general officers—*Longstreet* wounded (by his own troops in the same general area where *Stonewall Jackson* was shot by his own men), *A. P. Hill* on the sick list, *"Baldy" Ewell* close to breaking under the strain, *Edward Johnson* and *G. H. Steuart* captured, and nine brigadiers either killed, wounded, or in the hands of the enemy. Now *Jeb Stuart* was dead, a blow that *Lee* felt even more than the loss of the services of Corps Commanders *Longstreet* and *Hill,* whose return to the army would simply be a matter of time. "He never brought me a piece of false information!" *Lee* exclaimed in quiet anguish when the news of *Stuart's* death reached him at the very moment of the bitterest fighting at the "Bloody Angle."

Once again Grant decided to shift his army to the left,

as he had done between the Battles of the Wilderness and Spotsylvania, and once more *Lee* anticipated his intentions and moved to keep between the Army of the Potomac and Richmond. *Lee's* next natural defense line was the North Anna River, to which his *Army of Northern Virginia* repaired with skill and dispatch. Grant followed, and when the cavalry corps rejoined the army on May 24, Federals and Confederates were again facing each other, this time across the North Anna.

No Rest for the Cavalry Corps

But there was to be no relaxation for Sheridan's troopers, no matter how much they had earned a few days of rest. Grant hoped to maneuver *Lee* into attacking him on the North Anna, failing in which he decided to move again, still closer to Richmond, although by this time he had concluded that he could not succeed in interposing his own army between *Lee* and the Capital. With both armies fluid, Sheridan's cavalry again became active on reconnaissance, flank, and security missions, in the course of which, on May 31, Sheridan moved in advance of the infantry, drove Confederate troops out of Cold Harbor, and held it against enemy attacks until the supporting infantry was able to come up.

The ensuing battle, a frontal assault by the Union forces against strong Confederate entrenchments, was badly conceived, lacked coordination, and was roundly condemned by virtually all the participating Union generals as "the battle that never should have been fought." Even Grant admitted that it was an engagement he would not undertake if he had it to do over again.

Abandoning the attempt to defeat *Lee* north of Richmond, Grant transferred his army south of the James River, concurrently sending Sheridan with two divisions of cavalry to destroy the railroad between Charlottesville and Gordonville. At the same time General Hunter's Valley forces were instructed to proceed from Staunton to Charlottesville, where Sheridan and Hunter would join forces, complete the destruction of the railroad and canal, and then rejoin Grant's army.

Meanwhile *Lee* had detached *Breckinridge's* infantry, sending it back to the Valley to counter Hunter's destructive raids. When he learned of Sheridan's move, he sent cavalry under *Wade Hampton* to attend to Sheridan and block whatever he might be up to. The opposing cavalry tangled in a confused battle at Trevilian Station which resulted inconclusively for either side. Sheridan began to run short of ammunition. When he received information that Hunter was moving toward Lynchburg, in the opposite direction from Charlottesville, he concluded that the proposed junction of forces had become impracticable. Instead, he returned by slow marches to the Army of the Potomac, encumbered with prisoners, wounded, and several thousand colored folk who attached themselves to his column as a means to securing their freedom.

After further discomforts and occasional brushes with *Hampton's* cavalry, which clung to Sheridan's tail on the return march, the thoroughly wornout Federal cavalry crossed the James River on the morning of June 25, bringing to a conclusion their exhausting three weeks' long expedition.

With the historic Union failure to exploit the startling success of the exploded mine, the operations of the cavalry corps under Sheridan's personal command came to an end for 1864. On August 1, two days after the Petersburg fiasco, he was relieved of direct command of the corps and instructed to report to Washington for new orders which would transfer him to the Shenandoah Valley to deal with *Jubal Early*.

SHERIDAN'S HEADQUARTERS AT HARPERS FERRY

CHAPTER 6

SHERIDAN MOVES TO THE VALLEY

WHEN Sheridan on August 6 reported to Grant at the Monocacy, the latter simply turned over to him for execution the orders already prepared for Hunter, which read:

"Headquarters in the Field,
"Monocacy Bridge, Md., Aug. 5, 1864.

"General: Concentrate all your available force without delay in the vicinity of Harper's Ferry, leaving only such railroad guards and garrisons for public property as may be necessary.

"Use in this concentration the railroad, if by so doing time can be saved. From Harper's Ferry, if it is found that the enemy has moved north of the Potomac in large force, push north, following and attacking him wherever found; following him, if driven south of the Potomac, as long as it is safe to do so. If it is ascertained that the enemy has but a small force north of the Potomac, then push south the main force, detaching, under a competent commander, a sufficient force to look after the raiders and drive them to their homes. In detaching such a force, the brigade of cavalry now en route from Washington via Rockville may be taken into account.

"There are now on the way to join you three other brigades of the best of cavalry, numbering at least five thousand men and horses. These will be instructed, in the absence of further orders, to join you by the south side of the Potomac. One brigade will probably start to-morrow.

"In pushing up the Shenandoah Valley, as it is expected you will have to go first or last, it is desirable that nothing should be left to invite the enemy to return. Take all provisions, forage, and stock wanted for the use of your command. Such as cannot be consumed, destroy. It is not desirable that the buildings should be destroyed—they should, rather, be protected; but the people should be informed that so long as an army can subsist among them recurrences of these raids must be expected, and we are determined to stop them at all hazards.

"Bear in mind, the object is to drive the enemy south; and to do this you want to keep him always in sight. Be guided in your course by the course he takes.

"Make your own arrangements for supplies of all kinds, giving regular vouchers for such as may be taken from loyal citizens in the country through which you march.

"Very respectfully,
"U. S. GRANT, Lieut.-General."
"Major-General D. Hunter,
"Commanding Department of West Virginia."

Sheridan was as anxious as Grant that he get to his new command without loss of time, the troops having already left for Halltown. The meeting lasted less than two hours, with Hunter and his staff the only other officers present. Sheridan was informed that a new Union offensive on the James was in the making, and in the meantime Grant's strategy would be to conduct raids and reconnaissances in force north of the James River, coupled with operations on the railroad connecting Petersburg with Weldon, North Carolina, to keep *Lee* occupied and to discourage the dispatch of Confederate reinforcements to *Early's Valley Command*.

Sherman's famous (or infamous, if one is a Southerner) march through Georgia to the sea, which occurred later in the year 1864, is so much more familiar to readers of history than Sheridan's Valley Campaign in the summer and fall of that year that the points of similarity between them are frequently overlooked. Both campaigns represented a method of waging war, the strategy of which, while new on the part of Union generals, was as old as warfare itself. The scorched-earth policy, a radical departure from the more or less gentlemanly type of war that had been waged by both sides during the first three years, was Sherman's way of convincing the people of the South that war is certainly Hell. The mission that Sheridan was now about to undertake in the Shenandoah Valley was somewhat similar, although not so spectacular.

Grant's directive of August 5 made clear his purpose not only to remove *Early's army* as a factor in the war, but, what was of even greater importance, to strip the Valley clean of everything, animate and inanimate, that could contribute to the source of food supply for the armies of the Confederacy.

Description of the Shenandoah Valley

The beautiful Shenandoah Valley, vitally important to the South for strategic, logistic, and supply purposes, could if permanently controlled by Northern troops furnish the arena for a stab in the side of the Confederacy that would defeat *Lee*. From ten to twenty miles in width throughout much of its 150-mile length, extending from the Potomac on the north to well below Lexington, the Valley is flanked

142

on either side by rugged, heavily wooded ranges; on the west the Alleghanies, on the east the Blue Ridge Mountains, capable of being crossed readily by large bodies of troops only at the gaps which cut through them at convenient intervals. Between the Potomac and Strasburg the Valley is somewhat more than fifty miles wide, funneling down to its narrower conformation below the latter town. The north end of the Valley includes Martinsburg and Winchester, both of which played important roles in the maneuver plans of the opposing commanders, for reasons which a study of the map makes immediately obvious.

Throughout the war the Valley was a principal source of food for the Southern forces in Virginia, increasingly so as other parts of the State were gradually wrung dry by the marching and fighting armies. The gently rolling terrain, with fertile fields dotting the countryside, was drained by a myriad of small streams that empty into the north and south branches of the Shenandoah River. It was ideal cavalry country, and the partisan rangers of the Confederacy found its woods and dense forests a veritable Robin Hood's paradise for the peculiarly effective type of warfare waged by *Mosby* and his colleagues.

The destinies of armies have historically been related to roads, railroads, rivers, and mountains. The Shenandoah Valley boasted all four, but its picturesque mountains were perhaps the most significant in their influence on operations. The Shenandoah River, divided into two forks which unite at Front Royal, runs the length of the Valley to join the Potomac at Harper's Ferry. The road net was adequate for military purposes at the time of the Civil War, with a fine macadamized highway running north and south, known as "The Valley Pike," and smaller parallel roads to the west called 'the "Back Road" and the "Middle Road" respectively. Similarly the more important towns were connected by east-west roads of varying quality, which are noted on the maps in the endpapers.

An unusual topographical feature of the Valley is the Massanutten Mountain range. Splitting the Valley into two subdivisions, the easterly valley being known as the Luray, the tall range parallels the Blue Ridge from Strasburg almost to Cross Keys, affording opportunities for concealed troop movements which *Stonewall Jackson* had exploited in masterly fashion in the spring of 1862. This was home territory for the Confederates, a protected corridor for invasion of Northern soil with a secure line of communication and supply. Conversely it offered a logical route in reverse for Union advances into Virginia, the utilization of which had somehow invariably been mishandled by Northern generals, with assists by Stanton and Halleck, whose obsessive fears for the safety of Washington consistently blinded them to the military realities. *Jackson* had cleverly played on those fears and in so doing achieved undying fame through his ability to accomplish so much against so many with so little.

Now *Jackson* was gone, and by the summer of 1864 *Lee* no longer possessed the capacity to mount another invasion of Northern soil. By the same token, the agricultural resources of the Valley were more essential than ever, for without them it would be only a matter of months until the *Army of Northern Virginia* would wither away for lack of food. To recover control of the Valley from Hunter's troops had therefore become a matter of grim necessity, certainly for sufficient time to harvest the summer crops, and even at the expense of weakening *Lee's army* still further in its life-and-death struggle with Grant's forces before Petersburg. Hence the detachment in early June of the reinforced *Second Corps* under *Jubal Early,* who had so far succeeded remarkably well, as already noted, in executing *Lee's* orders in typical *Jacksonian* fashion.

Early's plan of action, after his July raid to the outskirts of Washington was, in his own words, "to keep up a threatening attitude toward Maryland and Pennsylvania, and prevent the use of the Baltimore and Ohio Railroad and the Chesapeake and Ohio Canal, as well as to keep as large a force as possible from Grant's army to defend the Federal Capital." As *Jackson* had done before him, *Early* determined to substitute mobility for relative inferiority in troop strength, and by shifting his forces rapidly from one area to another, to create an illusion of great strength.

In the execution of that policy he had succeeded in inflicting a sharp defeat on Crook and Averell at Kernstown on July 24. That was followed by *McCausland's* July 30 burning of Chambersburg. But the pattern of success was disrupted on Sunday, August 7, in the course of *McCausland's* return journey by way of Romney, West Virginia. On that morning, at Moorefield, Averell, urged by Hunter to bestir himself, partly retrieved his fallen fortunes by surprising *Bradley Johnson's* Confederate cavalry in its camps, giving that gentleman a severe trouncing and capturing some four hundred horses, four guns, a large quantity of small arms, twenty-seven officers, and almost four hundred enlisted men. It was a sad day for *Johnson,* who penned a bitter, vituperative denunciation of his superior, *McCausland,* whom he accused of lax discipline in his own brigade in contrast with the strict orders he had given to *Johnson.* "Every crime in the catalogue of infamy has been committed, I believe (referring to the acts of Confederate soldiers during the Chambersburg raid), except murder and rape," *Johnson* said, adding that "highway robbery of watches and pocketbooks was of ordinary occurrence . . . pillage and sack of private dwellings took place hourly."

General *Lee,* however, received the impression that

Johnson was responsible for the Moorefield defeat, and directed *Early* to relieve him of command if the facts warranted the action. *Johnson* had also charged that at the time of the attack *McCausland* had been asleep some distance from camp and that it had been the responsibility of *McCausland* as his superior to warn him of the approach of Averell's Federal cavalry. The Marylander felt so strongly on the subject that he demanded a court of inquiry, which *Early* ignored, probably discounting the stories of both cavalry generals in view of his own confirmed low opinion of the cavalry arm in general. The fact that *Johnson* spent the last months of the war at Salisbury, North Carolina, in charge of the prison stockade, suggests rather strongly that *Lee's* initial impression of the affair at Moorefield, combined with his characteristic distaste of the Chambersburg destruction, did nothing to raise *either Johnson* or *McCausland* in his estimation.

THE CONTESTANTS SQUARE OFF

The remaining weeks of August and the first half of September passed without a test of strength between the opposing commands of *Early* and Sheridan, as though both generals wanted to feel out the other's strength and dispositions before taking the plunge in a full-fledged battle. On *Early's* part such strategy was sound, for time was needed to harvest the crops, and it was more important to the Confederacy that use of the Canal and the Baltimore and Ohio Railroad be denied to the Federals than that a battle be fought. Furthermore, Sheridan's greater strength called for defensive Confederate tactics for the present. Therefore, as Sheridan assembled his forces in the vicinity of Harpers Ferry, *Early* pulled his divisions back from the Potomac to the Martinsburg area, there to mark time during early August, waiting to see what Sheridan proposed to do.

Arriving by special train at Harpers Ferry, where he planned to establish temporary headquarters for his new command, later known as the Army of the Shenandoah, Sheridan settled in the second story of what he described as a "small and very dilapidated hotel" and immediately summoned Lieutenant John R. Meigs, chief engineer of his inherited command, for the purpose of orienting himself on the geography and topography of the area over which his jurisdiction extended. Meigs was intimately acquainted with the Shenandoah Valley, even down to the location of farmhouses. And he was an articulate teacher. It was typical of Sheridan that he considered a thorough familiarity with the terrain over which his troops would operate to be of primary importance.

Nor was adequate appreciation of terrain the only factor that Sheridan considered. Characteristically, he made sure of his supplies and transport before making a move. Therein lay the secret of much of his success. What may have

HARPERS FERRY
When Used as a Quartermaster Depot by Sheridan

147

appeared to the more impulsive *Early,* and to many people in the Northern states as well, to be evidence of lack of aggressiveness was nothing more than the calculated deliberateness of a general who believed in leaving to chance nothing that could be provided by foresight and careful preparation.

His map studies and interrogations of Lieutenant Meigs satisfied Sheridan that the Valley was open to unrestricted troop movements across country almost as easily as on the roads, and that the numerous creeks and rivers were easily fordable at almost any point. Of special interest, however, were the easily negotiated passes that cut through the Blue Ridge Mountains on the east flank of the Valley, by which Confederate troops from the Charlottesville-Gordonsville area could move rapidly against the flank of Union troops operating west of the Blue Ridge. This advantage of being able to operate on interior lines had on several occasions served a useful Confederate purpose to the discomfiture of Federal generals. Sheridan took that topographic fact very much to heart in his preliminary studies.

Organization of the Army of the Shenandoah

As the opposing commanders took account of stock and began to size each other up, it appeared that the Union forces outnumbered the Confederate about two to one. Sheridan's own estimate gave him 26,000 men immediately available for Valley operations, with perhaps an additional 20,000 under his command in the Middle Division, the majority of whom were assigned to the essential duty of protecting the Potomac crossings and the railroad and canal which were the life lines of communication and supply to keep his army fed and equipped. His infantry-artillery combat command consisted of the Sixth Corps under Major General Wright, comprising three divisions led by Brigadier Generals David A. Russell, George W.

Getty, and James B. Ricketts; one division of the Nineteenth Corps under Brigadier General William Dwight, to be augmented within a few weeks by Brigadier General Cuvier Grover's division, with Brigadier General William H. Emory in command of the corps; and finally the West Virginia troops under Brigadier General George Crook (whose promotion to Major General came through a few days later), which were formed into two small divisions commanded respectively by Colonels Joseph Thoburn and Isaac H. Duval. Euphemistically designated "The Army of West Virginia," all of Crook's units added up to no more than a single medium-sized division, but for purposes of clarification and administration they would shortly be designated the Eighth Corps. The cavalry division commanded by Brigadier General Alfred Torbert had arrived from the Army of the Potomac and Averell's cavalry was under orders to join Sheridan, giving him two cavalry divisions, to which would shortly be added still another from the Army of the Potomac, under Brigadier General James H. Wilson.

Grant's confidence in Sheridan had grown to the extent that the General-in-Chief gave him a free rein in the reassignment or removal of officers in his new command. This was quite an innovation in the experience of Union generals, but it revealed a facet of Grant's character that showed his understanding of human nature and the vital importance of delegating authority in company with responsibility. Grant's appreciation of the part that the cavalry would play in the forthcoming Valley Campaign is reflected in a letter to Sheridan in which he advised: "Do not hesitate to give command to officers in whom you repose confidence, without regard to claims of others on account of rank. If you deem Torbert the best man to command the cavalry, place him in command, and give Averell some other command, or relieve him from the expedition and order him to report to General Hunter. What we want is prompt and active movements after the enemy, in accordance with the instructions you already have."

General Wright had been one of the several prominent officers who had "discovered" Sheridan as a promising young colonel in 1862. As commander of the Department of the Ohio in that year, he was one of the generals who had recommended to Halleck that Sheridan be made a brigadier general. In the early part of the war, Captain Phil Sheridan, then unknown, had served during the Corinth campaign as Quartermaster at Halleck's headquarters, an unglamorous and relatively unimportant assignment whose duties, however, he carried out with such fidelity and efficiency as to bring him favorably to the general's attention. Although in 1864 Wright ranked Sheridan as a major general by more than a year, the older general's character was such that he showed no resentment when the exigencies of the service required that he serve under a Regular officer junior to himself. Usually jealous of their alleged prerogatives, many an otherwise excellent general officer would under similar circumstances have protested vigorously, however ineffectually. It was to Wright's credit that he responded loyally to Sheridan's leadership and displayed no disappointment or chagrin.

Emory was a much older man who had graduated from West Point in 1831, the year Sheridan was born, but the latter thought well of the veteran, as he did of his third corps commander, George Crook, a boyhood friend who entered West Point in the same class as Sheridan. Sheridan had an open mind on Torbert, but believed him to be less aggressive than his two cavalry brigade commanders, Merritt and Custer, so he lost no time in transferring him upstairs to the post of Chief of Cavalry, where he could keep an eye on him and at the same time create an opening for Brigadier General Wesley Merritt to take Torbert's First

Maj. Gen. George Crook

Maj. Gen. William H. Emory

Maj. Gen. Alfred T. A. Torbert

Maj. Gen. Horatio G. Wright

151

Cavalry Division. Merritt, together with Custer and Farnsworth, had been among the dashing young cavalry captains who were jumped four grades to brigadier general for distinguished combat service just prior to the Battle of Gettysburg in June 1863. Farnsworth was killed in a fruitless but heroic charge in that battle, but Custer and Merritt lived to justify the confidence of their superiors and to lend Sheridan a constructive hand in the forthcoming struggle with *Early*.

Command and staff relationships within the reconstituted elements of the cavalry corps that served with Sheridan's Army of the Shenandoah were probably no better or no worse than in any other campaign. Army politics is a fact of military life; always has been and always will be, particularly among professional Army men whose competition for advancement reaches its zenith during a war, when expansion of the armed forces provides opportunity for rapid promotion. It is of more than passing interest in that connection to note that the nominal commander of Sheridan's cavalry, General Torbert, upon his assignment as Chief of Cavalry appointed Captain (Brevet Major) Marcus A. Reno as his chief of staff. In that position Reno was able to exercise considerable influence over the activities of the various division and brigade commanders, among whom was Brigadier General George Armstrong Custer, one of the fair-haired boys who had risen in meteoric fashion in the cavalry service while most of his army colleagues among the captains continued to wear the same insignia which had adorned their shoulder straps at the start of the war.

Reno graduated from West Point in 1857, four years ahead of Custer, and was therefore his senior in lineal rank in the Regular Army. Both distinguished themselves during the war, but Custer was the more dashing of the two and his dramatic exploits in many cavalry battles as brigade and division commander established a reputation that overshadowed Reno's. Much of the latter's war service was in a staff capacity, although he fought as a line officer in several of the important campaigns, was cited for bravery, and in 1865 was brevetted Brigadier General of Volunteers for his wartime service.

Whether fact or mere speculation, it has been said that a veiled hostility existed between Custer and Reno even before the war. If true, there is no evidence that it was permitted to seriously influence either during the Valley Campaign, nor that the fateful Battle of the Little Big Horn, fought in June 1876, cast a shadow backward across the years to afford any basis for the historic controversy that followed the extermination of Custer and his five companies of the 7th Cavalry on the heights and in the ravines of the Little Big Horn; a controversy in which Reno would be both proclaimed a hero and castigated as a coward responsible for the loss of half the regiment.

COMPOSITION OF EARLY'S ARMY

Early's army at the time Sheridan took command of the Union forces around Harpers Ferry was essentially unchanged from that which had unhorsed Hunter and flirted with Washington. It included his own corps whose divisions were commanded by *Ramseur, Gordon,* and *Rodes; Breckinridge's division* from southwestern Virginia; and the four cavalry brigades of *Imboden, McCausland, Johnson,* and *Jackson,* shortly to be consolidated as a division under command of Major General *Lunsford L. Lomax.* In view of the size of Sheridan's army, General *Lee* felt impelled to send reinforcements, which arrived during August, chiefly in the form of Major General *J. B. Kershaw's division* of *Anderson's corps,* and *Fitz Lee's cavalry division.*

153

The arrival of the Army of the Potomac's First Cavalry Division in the Valley was interpreted by General *Early* as presaging an offensive on Sheridan's part. Not wishing to allow his enemy to maneuver past his flank, *Early* withdrew twelve miles from Martinsburg to the vicinity of Bunker Hill. Here his right flank was less exposed but he still threatened the Baltimore and Ohio Railroad.

UNION TROOPS AT FRONT ROYAL

Moving out from Harpers Ferry on the tenth of August, Sheridan disposed his infantry along a line extending from Clifton to Berryville, with the cavalry well out to the front and flanks. His plan was to maneuver *Early* into a position whereby the Union forces might, without prematurely inciting *Early* to combat, work around his flank and attack from the southeast in the direction of Winchester with a view to cutting across the Confederate's line of retreat up the Valley and defeating him before reinforcements could reach him from *Lee's army*.

It was a good idea but it didn't work. *Early*, well posted on Sheridan's movements, declined to cooperate. Merritt's cavalry ran into Confederate horsemen on the Millwood-Winchester and Berryville-Winchester roads, drove them back and discovered that the Confederate infantry was retiring toward Strasburg. Sheridan at once ordered the cavalry to press the pursuit and harass the retiring columns, in the course of which one of Merritt's brigades tangled with a force of infantry near Newtown and was severely mauled.

For two days the Union cavalry snapped at *Early's* heels while Sheridan advanced his corps to Cedar Creek. There the movement was halted, when *Early's* main body was found to be strongly posted at Fisher's Hill, due south of Strasburg, on high ground that extended entirely across the narrow valley between North and Massanutten Mountains.

At this juncture Sheridan paused. His plan of maneuver had not worked out as hoped. He did not intend to allow a general engagement to occur on ground of *Early's* choosing. There was always the possibility of Confederate reinforcements coming through Chester Gap by way of Front Royal or Manassas Gap to the north and hitting him in flank while he was attempting to dislodge *Early* from Fisher's Hill. He thereupon decided to remain quietly on the defensive and await the arrival of Wilson's cavalry and Grover's infantry.

On August 14 Sheridan received a dispatch through Halleck from General Grant which stated in part: "It is now certain that two divisions of infantry have gone to *Early,* and some cavalry and 20 pieces of artillery . . . (Sheridan) must be cautious and act now on the defensive until movements here (at Petersburg) force them to detach to send this way. *Early's* force, with this increase, cannot exceed forty thousand men, but this is too much for General Sheridan to attack. Send General Sheridan the remaining brigades of the Nineteenth Corps."

155

CHAPTER 7

A STRATEGIC WITHDRAWAL

REPEATED rumors that Confederate reinforcements were marching to *Early's* aid from Culpeper having been confirmed by Grant's message, Sheridan ordered Merritt's cavalry division to Front Royal to oppose the approaching force, believed to be two divisions of *Anderson's (Longstreet's) corps* and *Fitz Lee's cavalry division.* At the same time he withdrew Wright's Sixth Corps to the north side of Cedar Creek as a precautionary move that would allow him greater flexibility to meet either *Anderson* or *Early,* depending on developments.

Sheridan's position at this moment, while not precarious, was at least uncertain. His mission was to destroy *Early* and strip the Valley clean, but his orders had not stipulated a time schedule for the operations. Good generalship implies more than mere willingness to attack. The enemy's capabilities must be carefully evaluated and the possible plans open to him weighed against one's own ability to counter each. The character of the terrain is also important. More often than not the victorious general is the one who appraises each facet of the situation accurately and commits his forces only at a time and place most favorable to himself.

Grant's warning to Sheridan to act on the defensive for the present was an unequivocal mandate. The latter's position on Cedar Creek exposed him to a possible Confederate attack from two directions. Grant's estimate of *Early's* total strength when the expected reinforcements should reach him— 40,000 men—indicated that the Confederates would then number 10,000 more than Sheridan's own available effective combat strength. The fact that Grant's estimate was greatly exaggerated was not then known to Sheridan.

A reexamination of his map of the Valley failed to show an adequate defensive position other than at Halltown, which lay several miles south of Harpers Ferry, where both flanks could be made secure on a river. That at least was Sheridan's opinion, and he decided to act upon it without delay by instituting a retrograde movement to the position from which he had moved south only a few days earlier.

The situation that confronted Sheridan at this early stage of his first campaign as a full-fledged army commander was reminiscent of the autumn of 1862 after the Battle of Antietam, when *Lee's Army of Northern Virginia* was recuperating on the banks of the Opequon twelve miles northwest of Harpers Ferry while McClellan's Army of the Potomac marked time on the Maryland side of the Potomac. The Lincoln Administration was then pressing McClellan to proceed vigorously against *Lee* in the confident belief that an aggressive campaign by the former, with his greatly superior strength, could cover Washington and at the same time bring *Lee* to battle somewhere between the Valley and Richmond, with favorable results to the Union cause.

The similarity between the two occasions lay principally in the fact that both times the Confederates had returned to the Valley after crossing the Potomac, invading Maryland, and raising the temperature of the Federal Government at Washington. The major difference was the size of

157

the opposing armies and the fact that in 1862 a reluctant, slow-to-fight McClellan was the Union commander; in 1864 it was a bulldog named Grant, who had selected a bull terrier named Sheridan who loved a fight and would go out of his way to seek it without being foolhardy in the execution.

It is not likely that Sheridan, in preparation for his Valley Campaign had either the time or the inclination to read up on the events immediately following *Lee's* unsuccessful first invasion of Northern soil in the early part of September 1862, between the Battles of Second Manassas and Antietam. Had the official reports and time to peruse them been available, he would have found at least one document interesting and pertinent as his own strategy evolved during his period of shadow-boxing with *Early*.

That document was a long letter that Lincoln had written to McClellan October 13, 1862, chiding him for being overcautious and "for assuming that he could not do what the enemy is constantly doing." Getting down to cases, Lincoln continued:

As I understand, you telegraphed Gen. Halleck that you cannot subsist your army at Winchester, unless the railroad from Harper's Ferry to that point be put in working order. But the enemy does now subsist his army at Winchester at a distance nearly twice as great from railroad transportation as you would have to do without the railroad last named. He now wagons from Culpeper Court-House, which is just about twice as far as you would have to do from Harper's Ferry. He is certainly not more than half as well provided with wagons as you are. I certainly should be pleased for you to have the advantage of the railroad from Harper's Ferry to Winchester; but it wastes all the remainder of Autumn to give it to you, and in fact ignores the question of *time,* which cannot and must not be ignored.

Again, one of the standard maxims of war, as you know,

is "to operate upon the enemy's communications as much as possible without exposing your own.' You seem to act as if this applies *against* you, but cannot apply in your *favor*. Change positions with the enemy, and think you not he would break your communication with Richmond within the next twenty-four hours? You dread his going into Pennsylvania. But if he does so in full force, he gives up his communications to you absolutely, and you have nothing to do but to follow and ruin him; if he does so with less than full force, fall upon and beat what is left behind all the easier.

There was much more in Lincoln's letter, having to do with the Virginia theater between the Blue Ridge and Richmond, but the quoted paragraphs, written two years before by the amateur military strategist in the White House about the identical terrain which was presently occupying the attention of General Sheridan, revealed a striking parallel. Whether Sheridan knew it or not, every move he made would unquestionably be viewed with a critical eye by a Commander-in-Chief who had acquired considerable knowledge about tactics and strategy in three years of war.

VIEW OF THE FRONT FROM UNION LINES NEAR HALLTOWN

For such a combative general as Sheridan, the decision to retire from an advanced position without throwing down

159

the gage of battle and to retrace his steps to Halltown demonstrated a high degree of moral courage. He knew the hopes that were pinned on this campaign by the Administration, and the extent to which his operations dovetailed with Grant's at Petersburg. He also knew what a lift would be given to Lincoln's political campaign for re-election as President were the Northern electorate to receive a shot-in-the-arm by a clean-cut victory in the field. These factors Sheridan evaluated in company with the strictly military implications, with the result that a strategic withdrawal, despite the certainty of public disappointment and loss of troop morale, seemed at the moment to be the wise decision.

Cavalry Ordered to Destroy Crops

This would in no sense be a retreat, although *Jubal Early* would choose to so regard it. Sheridan's long-range plans would not be modified, merely postponed to await a better opportunity. It was still his intention to attack *Early* from the east after maneuvering him into the desired position, preferably in the Winchester area. Meanwhile he would make a virtue of the necessity of his own withdrawal by initiating in conjunction therewith his secondary mission to destroy all the forage and subsistence that his troops could lay their hands on. Grant's original letter of instructions, handed to Sheridan at Monocacy Junction, had included the injunction that

Nothing should be left to invite the enemy to return. Take all provisions, forage and stock wanted for the use of your command. Such as cannot be consumed destroy. It is not desirable that buildings should be destroyed—they should, rather, be protected; etc.

The retrograde movement of Sheridan's army commenced the night of August 15, via Winchester, with Torbert's cavalry covering the rear. The cavalry was specifically instructed to destroy all the valley's wheat and hay south of a line from Millwood to Winchester and Petticoat Gap, at the same time seizing all the mules, horses, and cattle that could be useful to the Union forces.

"Get Mosby's Men!"

The following day, August 16, Grant wired Sheridan to send a division of cavalry, if it could be spared, through Loudoun County in northwestern Virginia east of the Blue Ridge, "to destroy and carry off the crops, animals, negroes, and all men under fifty years of age capable of bearing arms. In this way you will get many of *Mosby's* men. All male citizens under fifty can fairly be held as prisoners of war, not as citizen prisoners. If not already soldiers, they will be made so the moment the rebel army gets hold of them."

The guerrilla *Mosby*, who refused to accept the restrictions implicit in becoming a part of the regular Confederate forces, was practically a law unto himself, a thorny problem that the Federals were never fully able to solve. Operating from the extreme northwestern corner of Virginia, he invented his own tactics, holing up in the woods by day and sallying forth after dark to stir up trouble for Union troops. The territory from which he chose to operate became known as *Mosby's* Confederacy, wherein his "Irregulars" were given individual shelter by sympathetic residents. *Mosby's* men ranged in small groups like wraiths, rarely pausing long enough for pursuing Union troops to do more than catch a glimpse of them. For Sheridan, however, *Early* was Problem No. 1, while *Mosby*, although an irritant who could not be ignored, was secondary, to be given attention later on when Sheridan's cavalry could get around to it.

It is to be doubted that Sheridan, or for that matter the entire Union hierarchy of command, fully realized what a powerful deterrent to the execution of Federal military operations the *Confederate Rangers* were proving themselves to be, out of all proportion to their relatively small numbers. Their methods were so unorthodox, so at variance with accepted military procedures, so uniquely different from conventional doctrine as taught at West Point and other military schools, it was perhaps entirely natural for graduates of those institutions to discount the effectiveness of such methods of waging war.

The growing employment of guerrilla tactics during wars of the Twentieth Century, regardless of the fact that past rules of civilized warfare placed those who practised it beyond the pale, has forced modern armies to recognize its effectiveness and to include its techniques in their schools and instructional literature. The fact that guerrilla forces pose as civilians, never appearing in conventional military uniform, puts them in the same category as spies who may be executed without compunction if captured. Only the adventurous type dared to expose themselves to such sure retribution, and the daily life of danger led by the guerrilla tended to an indifference to life which inevitably reflected itself in his attitude towards those who crossed his path. It was a common occurence in the Valley to find Union soldiers with their throats cut, or shot through the back by one who posed as a harmless farmer, entitled to protection by uniformed troops, even those of the enemy.

Mosby was too intelligent not to be fully aware of the bitter hatred that his bushwackers generated in the minds of his country's enemies, military and civilian alike. In fact his partisan methods were distasteful as well to *Lee* and many other Confederates with decent instincts, and in time they came to be less popular with the people of Virginia, chiefly perhaps because of the furious retribution visited on the innocent by Federal commanders who found that no other method of retaliation seemed to be effective.

162

Whether adequately appraised by the Federal high command or not, *John Singleton Mosby* and his devoted followers were both will-o'-the-wisps and gadflys, worth to the Confederacy an undeterminable number of organized divisions of conventional soldiers. Their "now you see it, now you don't" tactics, developed by choice and long practise into a type of warfare all their own, both puzzled and frustrated Union troops upon whom they would suddenly pounce in terrifying hit-and-run fashion, from unexpected directions and at lightning speed. Reported to be in a certain area, *Mosby's* horsemen likely as not would be found miles away, perhaps in another county, scooping up men and horses and leaving a swath of dead and wounded Federals in their wake.

Mosby's depredations became so effective and his *Rangers* apparently so invulnerable to effective countermeasures that vastly greater Union forces were required than would normally have been the case in order to protect the lines of communication and supply for the successive Federal corps and armies sent into the Valley during the course of the war.

That Grant had at least a partial appreciation of *Mosby's* power was evidenced by his August 16 telegram proposing that Sheridan dispatch a cavalry division across the Blue Ridge to do a bit of cleaning out in Loudoun County. In due course Sheridan himself gained by trial and error a more realistic view of the *Mosby* threat to his own welfare and acted on that knowledge to organize a detachment of Union daredevils to emulate *Mosby's* feats and provide an antidote of sorts. But that is getting a bit ahead of the story. The extent to which activities of *Mosby's Rangers* were responsible for the scorched-earth policy that Sheridan would ultimately apply to the Shenandoah Valley is problematical. That they were a contributing factor is certain, but whether Hunter's initial incendiary actions, to which

Early responded by burning Chambersburg, represented the chronology of the chain reaction, or *Mosby's* continuous series of raids, coupled with Grant's progressively more grim evaluation of what was required to win the war, constituted the basic premise, will remain a matter of opinion.

FIGHT AT CEDARVILLE

FIGHT AT CEDARVILLE

On the afternoon of August 16 Sheridan moved his personal command post back to Winchester, from which more central point he would be able to direct the retrograde movement of his divisions. Upon his arrival there he received word from Merritt that the latter's cavalry had been attacked that morning by one of *Kershaw's* infantry brigades and two of *Fitz Lee's* cavalry brigades on the Front Royal Road at the crossing of the Shenandoah. The message stated that the Confederates had been repulsed with the loss of two battle flags and three hundred prisoners. It was a spirited little engagement, that fight at Cedarville, in which Merritt's cavalry lost 60 men killed and wounded, but managed to inflict total casualties of about 500 on the Confederates. This intelligence served to confirm the telegraphic information from Grant that *Lee* had dispatched reinforcements to the Valley and satisfied Sheridan of the wisdom of his temporary withdrawal and the tactical dispositions made to secure his left flank against attack from Front Royal.

The rearward march of the three Federal corps of Wright, Emory, and Crook was ably covered by the cavalry divisions of Merritt and Wilson, the latter having reported to Sheridan from Grant's army on August 17. Averell, who rarely moved quickly, did not reach the army from West Virginia until Sheridan's new line was stabilized north of Charlestown some days later. The several infantry corps were marched north by leapfrogging so that at all times Sheridan had substantial strength well in hand behind the cavalry screen to discourage any effort *Early* might make to disrupt the movement.

As Captain John W. DeForest of the Twelfth Connecticut Volunteers (Emory's Nineteenth Corps) wrote his wife a few days later:

Well, we tramped down the Shenandoah Valley, and we tramped back again. If ever I volunteer again I shall remember this vale of sorrows and shall specify that I am not to make war in it. Blazing hot marches, heavy guard duty, a diet of green corn and green apples have made a rough campaign of it so far.

Thus far General Sheridan is cautious about fighting, perhaps because of instructions from high political authority. With so many elections at hand, including the presidential, it would not do to have this army beaten and the North invaded. So, whenever Early is reinforced, Sheridan retreats to a strong position and waits to be attacked. It is to the enemy's interest just now to take the offensive, but we doubt if Early has enough men to risk it.

An order to fall in may come at any moment. Such orders generally arrive at night in the awkwardest moment possible. Then we march like fury for hours; and then nothing comes of it; we march back again. Of course the general understands it all, and perhaps Omniscience, but nobody else.

EARLY OBSERVES FEDERAL MOVEMENTS

A Confederate signal station on Three Top Mountain, the northernmost summit of the Massanutten range at Strasburg, where the north branch of the Shenandoah River bends to the east around the towering nose of that magnificent mountain, enabled *Early's* observers to watch every move of the Union forces. From that indestructible precursor of the early twentieth century's observation plane, *Early* was kept informed of Sheridan's movements. A small detachment from Sheridan's army had climbed the mountain and driven the handful of Confederates out; the latter returned with reinforcements and regained possession. When the Federals tried again and several small but lively fights ensued, *Early* strengthened the station with one hundred men of *Gordon's division,* too strong a force to be removed other than by a major Federal effort.

From that lofty observation post the Confederate commander learned on the morning of August 17 that the Union army was retiring. He at once took up the pursuit, that evening driving Torbert's cavalry out of Winchester and convincing Sheridan of *Early's* intention to follow him with his entire force. *Early* moved fast, and by the morning of August 18 had united with *Anderson's* reinforcing column in the vicinity of Winchester.

The vigorous Confederate pursuit, conducted more as a feeling-out process than an offensive maneuver, tested Sheridan's defense at various points without succeeding in developing a weakness that might justify a fully-mounted attack. The withdrawal tactics, by resting the Union flanks on Opequon Creek and the Shenandoah River in the occupation of successive delaying positions, offered *Early* no opportunity for surprise action, his major effort to turn Sheridan's flank having been foiled by the Confederate's misinformation as to the location of the enemy main body.

FIGHT AT SUMMIT POINT, AUGUST 21

Believing that the Federal commander had stationed his principal force near Summit Point, *Early* attempted to reach the enemy rear by crossing the Opequon bridge at Smithfield, but the projected attack landed in the air because the Union line was then in front of Charlestown rather than three miles further west at Cameron's Depot, as *Early* had supposed.

By August 22 the Army of the Shenandoah was back at Halltown, with Torbert's two cavalry divisions on the right of the line. On this position of readiness either to receive an attack by *Early* or for use as a springboard for the renewed offensive which Sheridan would launch in his own good time, his army covered Harpers Ferry, with both flanks firmly anchored on water, and threatened the main roads leading north to the Potomac via Martinsburg and Shepherdstown. That same day the Confederates reached Charlestown, pushing their advance elements up to the Union line where for the next three days spirited skirmishing between the two picket lines occupied the attention of the opposing forces.

CAVALRY COVERING FEDERAL WITHDRAWAL NEAR CHARLESTOWN

At this late stage of the war it had become standing operating procedure, in both the armies of the North and South, whenever the troops found themselves in an area where fighting might be possible, immediately to get to work erecting earthworks or artificial barriers of rail or stone fences blocking the logical avenues of enemy approach. When time permitted, the works were improved and made more elaborate, an activity which the men had learned from experience was sound life insurance as well as tactically advantageous when intelligently employed. It also served to keep the troops occupied and out of mischief.

DeForest paints a delightful picture of an all-night task in which his regiment was engaged at Halltown in anticipation of a Confederate attack:

"The men are so amused with this labor that they hew and shovel in the highest spirits. And we never tire of

168

looking at our fortification; we walk around it and discuss its merits by the hour; we are like little girls with a new baby-house. As you may lack entertainment at home (this was in a letter to his wife), let me instruct you how to make a fieldwork. Steal all the rails that you can find in a township; then build two parallel fences four feet apart and four and a half feet high; fill in with stones, earth, and green timber, and bank up the front with earth laid at an angle of forty-five degrees; then look across it and wish the enemy would come."

Early tested the Union line, found the Federals strongly entrenched, and decided against a frontal attack. Instead he left *Kershaw's infantry division,* with cavalry on either flank, dug in before the Union position while with the remainder of his army he marched around Sheridan's right flank on Shepherdstown, sending *Fitz Lee's cavalry* ahead to Williamsport with the avowed purpose of making still another raid across the Potomac. He figured that Sheridan would naturally follow the traditional policy of Union generals under such conditions by retreating to prevent being outflanked. If, however, his opponent should refuse the bait or move to attack the Confederate holding division, *Early* would then return and engage him on ground of his own choosing.

So *Early* reasoned! As it happened, Sheridan was merely biding his time, remaining on the defensive in accordance with the orders of General Grant, whose plan was to bring such pressure on *Lee's army* at Petersburg as to necessitate his calling back the troops sent to the Valley to reinforce *Early.* Grant had not however stipulated a *passive* defense in the Valley and Sheridan was not one to sit on his hands or permit his enemy to come and go as he pleased.

Aware that something was afoot when *Kershaw's* pickets opened a heavy musket fire all along the front on August 25, Sheridan sent Torbert, with Merritt's and Wilson's cavalry divisions, to Leetown to find out what was going on. Near that town Torbert encountered a small body of Confederate cavalry screening a column of infantry marching north on the road to Shepherdstown. As the Union cavalry broke through the thin screen they ran smack into *Breckinridge's infantry corps,* the head of which they attacked vigorously, causing *Early* to bring up all four of the divisions that he had with him. This was more than Torbert, who expected to encounter only Confederate cavalry, had bargained for. *Early's* counterattack threw the Union cavalry back in confusion, but he had now lost the element of surprise. While *Early's* main body was thus engaged, Crook with two divisions and Lowell's cavalry brigade moved against *Kershaw's* holding force, drove two brigades from their earthworks, captured a number of officers and men, and caused the withdrawal of the Confederate division from Sheridan's front. On top of that, *Fitz Lee's* maneuvers soon developed the fact that Sheridan's active cavalry was picketing the Potomac crossings and had taken position to bar the South Mountain passes east of Hagerstown, so he called the whole thing off and on August 26th pulled his troops back to their former position behind the Opequon at Bunker Hill.

Sherman's prophecy had not yet been fulfilled, that Sheridan would "worry *Early* to death," as the former had written to Grant when he first learned of "little Phil's" new assignment. The fact that Grant had applied a checkrein had much to do with cramping Sheridan's style, but he could afford to wait, even though it must have been galling to his fighting spirit to read the scornful criticism leveled at him by the Northern newspapers, which were of course uninformed that the Army of the Shenandoah was acting under orders. To the editors it looked like the same old story in the Valley, with the Confederates once again calling the shots. Even the Administration began to worry a bit, as the time for the Presidential election drew ever closer, with the McClellan political forces campaigning on a platform that called for peace at almost any price.

EARLY BECOMES OVERCONFIDENT

August gave way to September, and as the weeks of inactivity passed *Jubal Early* committed a serious error of judgment. He became overconfident, a cardinal military sin for the commander who misjudges his opponent by underrating his capabilities. *Early* had his good points; had demonstrated on many battlefields that he was a reliable, hard-fighting general as a brigade and later as a division commander. But he also had deficiencies, and there had been two notable occasions when he displayed faulty judgment, at Gettysburg and in the Wilderness, both of which represented lost opportunities for the Confederate cause. There were those among his fellow generals who were dubious about his qualifications for leading large forces such as the army he was now commanding in the Valley, and in the light of history it appears that, in company with many another infantry or artillery general, both Union and Confederate, *Early* failed to understand his cavalry or to employ it to the best advantage.

"The events of the last month (August-September) had satisfied me," *Early* says in his *Memoirs,* "that the commander opposed to me was without enterprise, and possessed an excessive caution which amounted to timidity." In light of subsequent events in the Valley, such an appraisal of the enterprising Sheridan indicated a lack of perception on *Early's* part or surprising ignorance of his opponent's combat record as an infantry division commander and as commanding general of Grant's Cavalry Corps in eastern Virginia. It was *Early's* opinion at the time that if Sheridan had thrown his whole force on the Confederate's line of communications up the Valley, *Early*

171

would have been forced to fight to cut his way through, since he could not escape to the right or left and was too weak to cross the Potomac, leaving Sheridan on his rear. To that extent *Early* was in agreement with Lincoln's evaluation, as outlined in the latter's 1862 letter to McClellan (see page 158), but warfare is full of imponderables, and few generals were infallible in their judgments.

GRANT VISITS SHERIDAN AT CHARLESTOWN
The two generals are standing on the porch

CHAPTER 8

GRANT'S DOUBTS ARE DISPELLED

THE waiting game that both Sheridan and *Early* were playing could only last so long, for one reason because experienced troops were too greatly in demand for any theater to be allowed to remain inactive indefinitely. Each of the commanders expected that the other's reinforcements would momentarily be recalled, with relative strength advantage to himself. When that should occur, it was inevitable that a full-scale battle would shortly follow, for both generals were anxious to bring the matter into the open and each was confident of his ability to knock the other out.

By reason of Grant's pressure on the Confederate lines at Petersburg in his grinding war of attrition, *Lee* was the first to yield in the war of nerves. During the first few days of September he ordered *R. H. Anderson's division* and *Fitz Lee's cavalry* back to the *Army of Northern Virginia*.

173

In the meanwhile, satisfied that *Early's* dispositions in the area west of the Opequon in the vicinity of Stephenson's Depot meant that he had given up the idea of again crossing the Potomac, Sheridan had for the second time moved his main body south from Halltown and was in the process of reoccupying the line, Clifton-Berryville, when *Anderson* started east on his march to rejoin *Lee* at Petersburg.

COLLISION AT BERRYVILLE

Moving out on September 3 from Winchester via Berryville with the intention of crossing the Blue Ridge at Ashby's Gap, *Anderson* unexpectedly ran into Crook's two Union divisions taking up their new positions near Berryville, on the left of Sheridan's line. The collision occurred about sunset, to the mutual surprise of both parties. The ensuing fight lasted but a short time, ending with *Anderson's* repulse. As soon as he learned of the contact, *Early* came up with three divisions at daylight September 4 to support *Anderson,* believing the Union opposition to be only a detached force. He soon discovered that Sheridan was present in full strength, whereupon he withdrew beyond the Opequon to the vicinity of Winchester, on the premise that this was no time to decrease the size of his army; *Anderson* would have to remain with him until a more favorable opportunity should be presented for his return to Petersburg by a different route.

Still biding his time, now that he had his army in a position of readiness, from Berryville north to Clifton, with *Early's army* facing him in the area between Winchester and Opequon Creek, Sheridan devoted the ensuing ten days to the task of preparing the plan of attack which had matured in his mind. He wanted to be certain that his generals knew exactly what was expected of their commands, and were thoroughly familiar with the terrain over which they would advance. This was to be a combined attack in

174

which his numerous cavalry would play an important role, suitable to the characteristics of the mounted arm. Now that Sheridan was free to employ his divisions as he saw fit, there would be co-ordinated action by the infantry-artillery-cavalry team.

SHERIDAN ORGANIZES SCOUT BATTALION

As he waited and planned, Sheridan gave thought to the need for a more effective intelligence system than that which he had inherited from the commander whom he succeeded in the Valley, General Hunter. In time the cavalry of the Army of the Shenandoah would become familiar with the topography, but it was hostile country whose inhabitants in the main were sympathetic to the Confederacy, and *Early's* intelligence, with the aid of *Gilmor, Mosby, Adams,* and other irregulars, was naturally superior to that of Sheridan.

To counter this disadvantage, Sheridan concluded that he would substitute a battalion of military scouts for the unsatisfactory system heretofore in vogue, under which citizens of doubtful quality and Confederate deserters were employed. Neither type of intelligence agent had proven effective. The battalion was promptly organized from the kind of volunteers who took naturally to the exciting and hazardous duties they would be called upon to perform. The right officer to lead them was found in the person of Major H. K. Young of the First Rhode Island Infantry, who entered with enthusiasm and efficiency upon his task of whipping the outfit into shape. An incentive system was introduced to the extent that payments in proportion to the value of the information gathered were promised from the Secret Service fund of the Federal Government. Confederate uniforms were to be worn when needed and before long Young's "guerrillas" would begin to cancel out the one-sided advantage so long enjoyed by the Confederates as the result of *Mosby's* successes.

Almost immediately Major Young struck pay dirt, when two of the newly organized scouts, delighted with their emancipation from routine soldier chores, uncovered the presence of an old colored man who lived just beyond the Union lines at Millwood and had been given a permit by

REBECCA M. WRIGHT

the Confederate commander to travel from his home to Winchester and back three times a week to sell vegetables to the townspeople. Having satisfied himself the Negro was intelligent and loyal, Young proposed to General Sheridan that the old man be employed to secure information from within Winchester. The approving Sheridan learned from General Crook, who was acquainted with some of the Union loyalists in Winchester, that a likely contact in the town was a school teacher by the name of Rebecca Wright, a Quaker woman whom he believed to be trustworthy.

176

The upshot of it was that the old Negro was brought in to Sheridan's headquarters by the two scouts and again questioned. He not only agreed readily to undertake the dangerous mission, but informed the general that he knew Miss Wright well and would carry a message from Sheridan on his next trip. As the plot thickened, the youthful Sheridan, in his best cloak-and-dagger manner, wrote out his message on a piece of tissue paper, wrapped it in tin foil, and instructed the old gentleman to conceal it in his mouth.

The project was carried out without a hitch. The messenger delivered Sheridan's note to Miss Wright early in the morning, stating that he would return for her answer that evening. This is what the understandably somewhat nervous school teacher read:

September 15, 1861

I learn from Major-General Crook that you are a loyal lady, and still love the old flag. Can you inform me of the position of Early's forces, the number of divisions in his army, and the strength of any or all of them, and his probable or reported intentions? Have any more troops arrived from Richmond, or are any more coming, or reported to be coming?

I am, very respectfully, your most obedient servant,

P. H. SHERIDAN, Major-General
Commanding.

You can trust the bearer.

Miss Wright replied as follows:

I have no communication whatever with the rebels, but will tell you what I know. The division of General Kershaw, and Cutshaw's artillery, twelve guns and men, General Anderson commanding, have been sent away, and no more are expected, as they cannot be spared from Richmond. I do not know how the troops are situated, but the force is much smaller than represented. I will take pleasure

177

hereafter in learning all I can of their strength and position, and the bearer may call again.

Very respectfully yours.

*****

Miss Wright's succinct report would have done credit to a well-trained intelligence officer. No unnecessary words, no speculation. Just the facts as she heard them from a convalescent Confederate officer who had called at her mother's house the evening before and talked out of turn! There had been conflicting reports about *Anderson's* force, a part of *Longstreet's corps*. This was important information that, in confirming the departure of *Kershaw's division,* put an end to the waiting game for Sheridan. His appraisal of the information at face value was evidence either of native shrewdness or satisfaction that he could now legitimately consider himself relieved from Grant's earlier injunction to move cautiously and remain temporarily on the defensive.

Kershaw had in fact moved on September 14, his division and *Cutshaw's battalion* of artillery, to Front Royal en route to Richmond via Culpeper Court House, but *Fitz Lee's* brigades remained with *Early.* Although Sheridan now felt free to launch his attack, he decided to wait another day or so in order to make certain that *Kershaw* should travel beyond recall distance.

Sheridan was getting one break after another, proving perhaps that patience is a virtue that even army commanders can afford to cultivate. The extra two days' delay following the receipt of Miss Wright's intelligence found *Early* at Martinsburg, to which place he had gone with *Gordon's division, Braxton's* artillery, and part of *Lomax's* cavalry to break up what was reported to be a Union working party engaged in repairing the break in the Baltimore and Ohio Railroad. The "working party" turned out to be Averell's cavalry division, which was driven out of Martinsburg, but the diversion indicated that elements of *Early's army* were pretty well separated on the eve of Sheridan's projected attack.

NORTHERN PRESS HOWLS FOR ACTION

On the political and economic front, meanwhile, storm signals were being hoisted that foretold trouble for Sheridan unless action should soon be forthcoming. The Northern newspapers were howling: "Why doesn't Sheridan do something?" Stocks were declining, the price of gold rising alarmingly, industrialists were getting jittery, the Administration was becoming increasingly worried. Spirits had risen in the North when Sheridan's army advanced from Harpers Ferry in the early part of August, but the subsequent inconclusive weeks of marching and countermarching that wound up in "the retreat" from Winchester to Sheridan's original starting point had aroused serious doubts whether the new army commander would do any better than the long list of repudiated Union generals who had previously lost their military reputations in the Valley—Fremont, Shields, Milroy, Banks, and Hunter.

Even Grant, whose confidence in Sheridan was founded on the solid reputation which the young general had built by his successful battle exploits as an infantry division commander and latterly as leader of the cavalry corps, became slightly infected with the virus of doubt. The more he thought about the situation, the more his impatience grew to know the truth. Instead of writing letters or sending telegrams, Grant took the more direct short cut of visiting Sheridan in the field, intending to hand him a plan of operations that would force him to take the offensive; if necessary, he himself would remain on the ground long enough to see the operation properly launched. Possibly Grant had forgotten that earlier message to Sheridan which advised him to play a defensive role in face of the reinforcements being sent to *Early;* or he may have assumed that, being a temporary measure, Sheridan would in due course exercise his own discretion once he became assured that his own strength exceeded that of his opponent, even with the latter's force augmented by *Anderson's* infantry and *Fitz Lee's cavalry.*

As a matter of fact, Grant's trip was less to reassure himself about Sheridan than it was a means of stepping up the pace of his long-range war of attrition in order to still the clamor of public opinion. In his own mind the demise of the Confederacy was simply a matter of time, for he had written of the South on August 16 that "Little boys and old men are guarding prisoners, railroad bridges, and forming a good part of their garrisons for entrenched positions. A man lost by them cannot be replaced. They have robbed the cradle and the grave equally to get their present force. Beside what they lose on frequent skirmishes and battles, they are now losing from desertions and other causes at least one regiment per day. With this drain upon them the end is visible if we will but be true to ourselves."

GRANT VISITS SHERIDAN

Grant's decision to pay Sheridan a visit proved wise in that it served to dispel any misunderstanding that may have existed between the two men, and confirmed the feeling of mutual confidence between these two forthright, soldierly generals. Fearful of possible interference from Halleck or Secretary of War Stanton, neither of whom had shown any hesitation about issuing orders that could and occasionally did conflict with his own instructions, Grant again bypassed Washington to go directly to Charlestown by way of Harpers Ferry, sending word to Sheridan to meet him there for a conference.

Grant left his headquarters at City Point on September 15. Miss Wright's letter reached Sheridan the evening of September 16. Sheridan's meeting with Grant took place at Charlestown on September 17. Sheridan was fully prepared for the conference, having already decided to move his army that morning to Newtown, now that it was certain *Kershaw's division* was on its way to Richmond.

The Federal cavalry had been kept busy the preceding week actively reconnoitering an area six miles deep between Sheridan's main body and *Early's* forces, which occupied the west bank of Opequon Creek. Sheridan wished to control this zone so that he could move his troops, without *Early's* knowledge, into a jumpoff position to attack. These reconnaissances involved considerable skirmishing with the enemy, during which McIntosh's Union cavalry brigade succeeded in capturing the *Eighth South Carolina Regiment (Kershaw's division)* at Abraham's Creek on September 13.

An eyewitness of the meeting between Grant and Sheridan has left this description:

On the 16th of September (or was it the 17th?), as I was strolling near one of the camps of the Sixth Corps, a Sergeant of the Vermont brigade eagerly called my attention to a couple of officers who were walking by themselves, engaged in grave tranquil conversation. They were undersized men, rather squarely built, but not portly or even heavy. The junior, who was also the shortest, had a distinctly Irish face of the puffy sort, with irregular profile and a swarthy grey complexion. He talked in a low silvery voice (the words quite inaudible to me), his elbows pressed to his sides, but gesturing slightly with fingers. The elderly man (Ed. note: he was in his early 40's), blond and sandy-bearded, his red-oak features perfectly inexpressive, his grey eyes fixed on the ground, listened without replying. "That youngest one is our General Sheridan," said the Sergeant, "Don't you know who the other is? That's G R A N T!"

He paused, gazed at the renowned chief with solemn eyes, and then continued pensively, "I hate to see that old cuss around. When that old cuss is around there's sure to be a big fight on hand."

I have often wondered whether that shrewd Vermonter lived through the battle that fulfilled his prophecy.*

As he spread out the map and explained his plan to General Grant, Sheridan exuded confidence. Referring to the message sent Grant on September 11, in which he had reported the Opequon crossings as deep, with steep banks constituting a formidable barrier that would make it difficut to attack *Early* in his position on the west bank, Sheridan now felt that his acquired familiarity with the terrain during the intensive reconnaissance of the past week had created a more favorable picture. Furthermore since *Early* had been weakened by the loss of *Kershaw's division,* now was the time to strike.

It was immediately apparent to Grant that here was a general who had made exhaustive studies of the ground, had considered all possible contingencies, and needed only his superior's approval to put the plan into immediate operation. Sheridan painted so convincing a picture of an assured Union victory if he were permitted to dispose his army across the Valley Pike south of *Early* at Newtown that Grant didn't even bother to mention his own plan of operations, which he had developed at City Point while waiting for Sheridan to get rolling.

The two generals then got down to specifics. "Could you be ready to move by next Tuesday [four days later]?" asked Grant.

"Oh, yes," Sheridan replied, "I can be off before daylight on Monday." That was enough for Grant, any lingering doubt about Sheridan completely dispelled. Sheridan

---

* *A Volunteer's Adventures* by John William DeForest, Yale University Press, 1946.

was told to proceed on those lines, in accordance with his own plan. "Go in," was the way Grant phrased what is probably the shortest directive ever issued in launching an army offensive.

Grant's inherent ability to go directly to the heart of a problem and the beautiful simplicity of his methods in finding a solution were again illustrated in this instance. Sheridan had been his own choice to do the job that had to be done in the Valley, but some people thought he was too slow in getting on with it. The thing to do was to make a personal reconnaissance; hence the visit to Charlestown.

During Grant's trip to Harpers Ferry, Robert Garrett, President of the Baltimore and Ohio Railroad, asked the general how soon it would be safe to send men out to repair the railroad so the country could get some use out of it. Grant's reply was noncommital, but Garrett was told that the general expected to have the answer within a matter of days. Returning after the meeting with Sheridan, Grant again encountered the railroad president, who put the same question to him. "I think you might send your men out next Wednesday," was the reply this time, but Garrett was not informed of the reason for the general's newly acquired confidence.

Sheridan Prepares to Move

Back at his headquarters after the conference with Grant at Charlestown, Sheridan busied himself preparing his army for the advance to Newtown. On September 18 he received a message from Averell that *Early* was moving with an estimated two divisions of infantry on Martinsburg. This important intelligence prompted an immediate change in Sheridan's plan of action, indicating as it did that *Early* had divided his army and exposed it to possible

SHERIDAN'S WAGON

defeat in detail, if Sheridan should be quick enough to exploit the opportunity.

Jubal Early happened to visit the telegraph office in Martinsburg on the morning of September 18. There he learned of Grant's visit to Sheridan and was quick to sense that it portended something more than a social call. *Early* realized at once that he had blundered, that he would have to move fast to repair the potential damage. By forced marching *Gordon* retraced his steps so that by the evening of September 18 he was in bivouac at Bunker Hill, 10 miles north of Winchester on the Martinsburg Road. *Rodes* joined *Breckinridge* at Stephenson's Depot, 4 miles north of Winchester. *Ramseur's division* remained in position astride the Winchester-Berryville Pike two miles east of Winchester, with part of *Lomax's* cavalry covering his right and *Fitz Lee's* his left. *Early's army* had thus rapidly

been reassembled at points within mutual supporting distance, but was still far from being concentrated on a well-defined line to meet a strong enemy attack. Sheridan's battle would not be the walkover that he had pictured in his mind's eye, for *Early's* speedy reaction when he realized his danger had robbed Sheridan of the opportunity to defeat him in detail. Nevertheless, the advantage lay with the Union general for the ratio of total Union combat strength to that of the Confederates was more than two to one, even though neither army commander had accurate knowledge, at the time, of the actual troop strength of his opponent.

LOGAN HOUSE, SHERIDAN'S HEADQUARTERS AFTER THE BATTLE OF WINCHESTER

CHAPTER 9

THE BATTLE OF WINCHESTER (THE OPEQUON)

THE battle fought on September 19, 1864 between *Jubal Early's Valley Army* and Philip Sheridan's Army of the Shenandoah, on and around the plateau east of Winchester, is usually described by Southern historians as the Third Battle of Winchester; by Northern writers as the Battle of the Opequon. The several designations conform to the Civil War pattern by which major battles were named by the South after the nearest town or center of population, whereas the North, whenever possible, chose a familiar terrain feature such as a mountain, river, creek, or similar work of nature, easily recognized as having played a familiar or significant role in the engagement.

Historic Winchester, the oldest English settlement west of the Blue Ridge Mountains, originally established by white frontiersmen in 1744, was called Fredericktown for several years until the Virginia House of Burgesses gave it official recognition by naming it Winchester, after the county seat in England whence came James Wood, the settler who surveyed the area and laid out the streets for the village. It was at Winchester that George Washington received his first military command during the French and Indian War of 1755-56, and from that place accompanied General Braddock on the joint British-American expedition against the French and Indians that ended so disastrously at Fort Duquesne (near Pittsburgh) on the Monongahela River in Pennsylvania. Returning to Winchester after Braddock's defeat, Washington was made a colonel of militia, assigned the mission of protecting the frontier, and at Winchester with his small band of pre-Revolutionary soldiers built Fort Loudoun as a key defense bastion against the rampaging Indians.

Situated on the Valley Pike twenty-two miles south of Martinsburg, West Virginia, and approximately the same distance as the crow flies from Harpers Ferry, Winchester's location, equidistant from North Mountain on the west and the Blue Ridge on the east, became an important objective for the armies of both sides during the Civil War. More than one hundred skirmishes and engagements are said to have occurred within twenty-five miles of the town which boasts of having changed hands seventy-six times during the course of the war.

Stonewall Jackson had given Winchester a measure of fame when he established his headquarters there in November, 1861 and with his small army wintered in the area in preparation for his Shenandoah Valley Campaign

187

in the spring of '62. Thereafter, until the activities of Sheridan's army in the fall of 1864 again put Winchester in the headlines, the only action of major significance in its vicinity occurred in June, 1863, when *Ewell's corps* of *Lee's army* attacked Union General Milroy's occupying force of 8,000 men to clear the way for the second Confederate invasion of Northern soil. Milroy was greatly outnumbered, the two-day battle ending on June 14 with the complete repulse, rout, and scattering of the Northern troops.

Ten miles east of Winchester, not far from the road that crosses the Blue Ridge at Snicker's Gap, a patch of woods near the village of Berryville was chosen as Sheridan's temporary field headquarters while he readied his army for the impending showdown with *Early's* Confederates. Best known as the home of General Daniel Morgan, whose Virginia Riflemen made history during the Revolutionary War, the town of Berryville itself escaped being a direct military target during the Civil War, although armies of the North and South frequently marched and countermarched through its dirt streets on the way to and from battles and skirmishes, and Sheridan's camps filled the nearby countryside before the Battle of Winchester.

Six miles west of Berryville and four miles east of Winchester, Opequon Creek winds its narrow path northward, down the Shenandoah Valley past Martinsburg, to empty into the Potomac River a half-dozen miles south of Williamsport, Maryland. Opequon Creek at this time was important as the boundary line between the two armies, Sheridan's on the east, *Early's* on the west. The stream could be crossed without difficulty at a number of places, but in general it ran deep and its steep banks created a military obstacle for an attacking force which might attempt a crossing other than at the several fords. At the point where the Berryville Road crosses, the creek is practically a gorge, with high tree-covered bluffs close to the stream on either side, somewhat similar to Antietam Creek at Burnside's Bridge. Two parallel streams, Red Bud Creek on the north and Abraham's Creek on the south, run east from the area of Winchester, straddling the Berryville Pike all the way, to empty into Opequon Creek.

Sheridan's Plan of Attack

Sheridan's warning order to his corps commanders and cavalry chief on the morning of September 18 directed them to have their troops ready to march at 9 p. m. that night. All wagons and other impedimenta not actually required for combat were to be sent to Summit Point, there to join the army supply train for convoy to Harpers Ferry at 3 p.m.

Instructions for the approach march to initial battle positions were covered in later orders issued that day to all major elements of the army. It is of interest to note that Sheridan's field order contained no reference to the position or dispositions of *Early's* divisions across the Opequon, despite the fact that the Federal cavalry had been engaged in extensive reconnaissance activities for the preceding ten days and had amassed considerable enemy information. It must therefore be presumed that Sheridan's headquarters had already transmitted important enemy intelligence to his corps commanders in fragmentary form as it was received and evaluated.

Sheridan's directive, over the signature of his experienced, efficient Chief of Staff, Lieut. Colonel James W. Forsyth, graduate of West Point, class of 1856, stated that the army would move at 2 o'clock the following morning (September 19) and indicated the Winchester-Berryville pike as the major axis of movement. Wilson's cavalry division would lead off, with orders to march on Winchester, drive in the enemy cavalry on the Berryville Pike, and "follow them up." The Sixth Corps, Major General Horatio G. Wright commanding, and the Nineteenth Corps under General William H. Emory would move successively on the Berryville Pike after crossing the creek; when the Sixth Corps should reach open country west of the Opequon it would "form line of battle fronting in the direction of Stephenson's Depot." Emory's Nineteenth Corps was instructed to halt when the head of its column reached Opequon Creek, at which time it would come under the command of General Wright, who was charged with assigning battle postions to Emory's divisions. A significant sentence in that part of the order read: "The utmost promptitude should be exercised in the formation of this line of battle," indicating Sheridan's intention to develop his army for attack at an early hour in the morning. Crook's smaller Eighth Corps (the so-called Army of West Virginia) was designated as army reserve, to take position at the same crossing used by the other two corps, and there await subsequent orders for utilization at Sheridan's discretion. The cavalry divisions of Generals Merritt and Averell were told only that they would operate in accordance with orders received from the Chief of Cavalry, General Torbert.

Averell's patrols were active on the north flank of the army area, as that division commander reported in a series of messages to General Torbert during the morning of September 18. Among other items of information Averell spoke of the enemy "showing extraordinary vigilance at Bunker Hill," with the country between that village and the Opequon filled with small Confederate parties.

Torbert's orders to Merritt and Averell were brief. Merritt's cavalry was to operate at the fords near the Winchester Railroad, keep a watchful eye on the enemy, and be prepared for a fight in conjunction with Averell's division. Averell would move to Darkesville* by 6 p. m. Torbert advised that he would join Merritt early on the morning of September 19. Presumably the cavalry would then act in accordance with the situation, and it was understood, if not written into the order, that the cavalry's mission would be to attack *Early's army* in flank if the opportunity offered.

The scheme of maneuver that Sheridan divulged to his staff and corps commanders, at least in part, assigned to the cavalry the initial mission of preceding the infantry-artillery mass to screen the approach march and development of the main body, to brush away the Confederate cavalry screen, if any, and if possible to pin the infantry of *Early's* scattered divisions in place until Wright's and Emory's corps could move off the road into battle formation on the plateau several miles east of Winchester.

The vital role of Wilson's Third Cavalry Division was to dash up the Berryville Pike far enough to secure that road west of the Opequon where it runs for two miles or more through a veritable canyon before reaching open ground at the western end of the defile The steep, tree-covered slopes, rising sharply on both sides of the highway, were impassable for cavalry or artillery and could be negotiated by light infantry only with great difficulty. Confederates, with judiciously placed artillery, could deny this road defile to the Union forces if *Early* should anticipate Sheridan's purpose and move to block the advance of the Federal close-order columns at the Opequon bottleneck. Wilson was therefore the key to the door that must be opened for the main body to reach maneuverable terrain.

---

* This was a single house, but shows on contemporary maps as a village.

The plan for Torbert's other two cavalry divisions was for Merritt and Averell to form a junction near Stephenson's Depot, there to watch alertly for the moment when they could effectively move against *Early's* left and rear, the opportunity for which Sheridan believed would be offered when the Confederate divisions at Bunker Hill and Stephenson's Depot were drawn away to meet the Union infantry. Sheridan in person would follow Wilson's cavalry in order to be on the battleground where he could observe and be prepared to maneuver his troops most advantageously when the Confederates reacted. From that point on he would play it by ear.

The Union commander's battle plan had been carefully thought out to the last detail and was a good one. Its principal weakness, if so it could be called, was that precise execution depended on a strict adherence to a time and space schedule, which rarely works out in practice to the exact result contemplated when poring over maps in the quiet atmosphere of a headquarters tent. The Federal commander hoped to strike his blows early in the morning, so rapidly and with such force that *Early's* separated divisions would be successively broken up before they could effect a junction on the line two miles east of Winchester, where *Ramseur's division* was posted astride the Berryville Pike, its flanks covered by cavalry on Red Bud Creek and Abraham's Creek.

If everything worked out according to plan in the initial stages, Wilson's cavalry, after seizing a forward position which the Sixth and Nineteenth Corps would promptly occupy, was to shift to the left to secure the Union south flank; Merritt and Averell would then circle around *Early's* left to attack the Confederate flank and rear, while Crook's reserve divisions would be thrown beyond Wilson's cavalry across the Valley pike south of Winchester, prepared to block *Early's* expected retreat southward. In effect Sheridan envisaged a double envelopment, that classic maneuver that generals dream about but rarely succeed in bringing off.

EARLY'S ARMY RECONCENTRATES

It will be recalled that *Early* had taken *Gordon's division* to Martinsburg, leaving *Rodes' division* at Bunker Hill, on the morning of September 18; that he had met Averell's division and driven it off in the direction of Charlestown; and at Martinsburg had picked up the intelligence that Grant in person had just conferred with Sheridan. *Early* immediately reversed his direction, returning rapidly with *Gordon* to Bunker Hill. Reaching the latter place late in the day, *Gordon* was ordered to rest his division overnight, but by sunrise on the 19th to be at Stephenson's Depot, to which point *Rodes* was directed to make a night march. *Wharton's division* was already there, which meant that by daylight of September 19 three of *Early's* infantry divisions would be within 4 miles of Winchester, less than two hours' march from the fourth, *Ramseur's*, about the time Sheridan's schedule called for launching his initial attack. It might still be possible for the Federal plan to work if everything clicked perfectly, but there was no margin for Union delay when every minute from daylight on gave *Early* additional time to concentrate his army in a build-up of *Ramseur's* short defense line on the plateau east of Winchester.

Stephenson's Depot, an important supply point on the Winchester, Potomac and Strasburg branch of the Baltimore and Ohio Railroad, which was designated as assembly area for the main body of *Early's* infantry, was located a short distance east of the Winchester-Martinsburg pike, several hundred yards north of the junction with the Charlestown road. Open fields and rolling meadows in that vicinity, with a liberal sprinkling of woods, afforded the kind of terrain over which cavalry could operate to advantage. Today the depot is no longer standing, but the natives recall it more distinctly as the railroad point to which the guerrilla *Mosby*, after capturing an engine from the Federals at Martinsburg, brought the iron horse seventeen miles by road with a team of 120 flesh-and-blood horses, and at Stephenson's Depot placed it on the rails for the use of the Confederates.

STEPHENSON'S DEPOT

The Depot was tactically important as the northern gateway to Winchester, covering as it did the approaches from Martinsburg along the Valley Pike and from Charlestown via the Opequon crossings. It was at Stephenson's that *Edward Johnson* of *Ewell's corps* had put Milroy's troops to rout in the initial stage of *Lee's* 1863 invasion of Pennsylvania, and it was there that *Ramseur* was defeated by Averell's Federal cavalry division during the latter part of July 1864, when one of the North Carolinian's brigades unexpectedly panicked with a loss of four guns, heavy casualties, and the capture by the Union cavalry of 267 unwounded officers and men.

THE BATTLE OPENS

The Union camps were astir shortly after midnight, engaged in the myriad details typical of an army preparing to move into battle. Wilson's Third Cavalry Division, leading off with McIntosh's First Brigade in the van, crossed the Opequon in the darkness, hastened up the Berryville road through the narrow wooded canyon, drove in the Confederate pickets, and deployed to right and left of the pike at the head of the defile.

The division commander, Brigadier General James Harrison Wilson, was a comer in the Union armies. Grant had his eye on the brilliant young West Pointer, whose star was in the ascendancy and who was already recognized as among the most promising of that small group of capable officers who had demonstrated ability with the cavalry corps of the Army of the Potomac under Sheridan. Wilson had a brilliant mind and, like Grant, was a superb horseman. His previous service and experience had been in the engineer corps and on Grant's staff in the West, where the latter found Wilson's military advice so sound and indispensable that he held on to him when he was called east to repair the damage to the Union cause inflicted by Rosecrans' defeat at Chickamauga. Although Wilson had never commanded cavalry troops, Grant thought so highly of his qualifications that, when Sheridan was placed in command of the cavalry corps, Grant relieved Judson Kilpatrick and gave the Third Cavalry Division to Wilson.

Wilson's division, made up of two brigades commanded by Brigadier Generals John B. McIntosh and George H. Chapman, had more than the normal complement of horse artillery, being supported by six batteries of the Regular Army. McIntosh's brigade was strongly constituted, with six regiments from the States of New York, Pennsylvania, Ohio, New Jersey, and Connecticut. While in the vicinity of Washington, en route in August to join Sheridan's Army of the Shenandoah, this brigade had been armed with the seven-shot breechloading Spencer carbine.

IMBODEN
RODES
BRECKINRIDGE
STEPHENSON'S DEPOT
GORDON
McCAUSLAND
LOWELL
LOCKS FOR
1 MILE
RIDGWAY
FORD
LEETOWN

CHARLESTOWN ROAD

MARTINSBURG PIKE

OHIO R.R.

LICK RUN

CLEVEN
FORD

BALTIMORE

BURNT FAC
TANQU
FO

RED BUD RUN

ROCK LED

RED BUD RUN

OPEQUON CREEK

JOHNSON

FACTORY

VIII

ASH HOLLOW

BERRYVILLE CANYON

V CORPS

XIX CORPS

WILSON

CROSS

RUSSELL

ABRAHAM'S CREEK

BERRYVILLE ROAD

JOHNSON

SENSENY ROAD

ABRAHAMS CREEK

JACKSON
FRONT

MILLWOOD

Stone Walls (wood fences omitted)
Swamp
Fences and walls along roads omitted.

SCALE
0   1/4   1/2   3/4   1 MILE
0   1000   2000   3000   4000   5000 FEET

It had been McIntosh's brigade, with their Spencer repeaters, whose aggressive reconnaissance across the Opequon on September 13 had surrounded and captured *Colonel Henagan*, his battle flag, and the entire *Eighth South Carolina Regiment*, together with a handful of men and officers from five Confederate cavalry regiments for a total bag of 16 officers and 127 enlisted men, with the loss of only two of his own men killed and three wounded.

Although it was still dark, the energetic McIntosh wasted no time in executing his mission as soon as Wilson's division had deployed on the eastern edge of the plateau upon which *Ramseur's division* awaited the attack. With Pierce's battery posted to support him, McIntosh attacked *Ramseur's* line with such vigor, in a combined mounted

---

MAP 6. BATTLE OF WINCHESTER, OPENING PHASE

The maps used to illustrate the Battle of Winchester are an adaptation of that shown on Plate 99 of the Atlas. Troops dispositions and movements have been modified in a few instances to agree with the official reports of unit commanders and other sources. The situation shown on this map is that of about 8:45 a.m., September 19, 1864.

Federals. Wilson's cavalry division crossed the Opequon on the Berryville Road and moved rapidly west to attack Ramseur's advanced brigades, which were in earthworks astride the road, as shown. Wilson took this position, and held it against several counterattacks until about 9:00 a.m., when leading units of the VI Corps arrived and began to relieve the cavalry. At the northeast corner of the battlefield Lowell's cavalry brigade of Merritt's division, followed later by Devin's brigade, forced a crossing at Ridgway's Ford. Custer's brigade crossed a mile farther north and linked up with Lowell. Averell's cavalry division, not shown on this map, is moving south astride the Martinsburg Pike.

Confederates. The bulk of Early's infantry up to this time has been concentrated at Stephenson's Depot, with Ramseur guarding the approaches to Winchester from the east, as shown. Johnson's cavalry brigdade of Lomax's division, after screening the front of Ramseur, and picketing the crossings of the Opequon in that front, has fallen back and taken positions on either flank of Ramseur. The map also shows the locations of Lomax's other three brigades—McCausland, Imboden, and Jackson. Fitzhugh Lee's cavalry division is falling back in front of Averell.

When Early became aware of the advance of the Federal columns at Ridgway's Ford and the Berryville Crossing, he started Breckinridge's two brigades under Wharton to reinforce McCausland, and Gordon's and Rodes' divisions to extend Ramseur's position. These movements are shown as just getting under way at about 8:45 a.m.

197

and dismounted formation, that the surprised defenders promptly yielded their advanced earthworks, which McIntosh at once occupied and managed to hold against determined counterattacks from 5 a. m. until 9 a. m., when the head of Wright's Sixth Corps came up to take over.

LEETOWN

Five miles to the north at Ridgway's Ford (Seiver's Crossing), where the Stephenson's Depot-Charlestown road crosses Opequon Creek a short distance east of Leetown, Lowell's Reserve Brigade of Merritt's First Cavalry Division splashed across before dawn, but not without opposition. At the same time Custer forced a crossing at Lock's Ford, and by sunrise had linked up his left with Lowell's right. Devin's brigade followed Lowell across later, and about 11 a. m. started advancing up the road toward Leetown. *McCausland's cavalry,* contesting the crossings, was slowly forced back on Leetown, strongly resisting at every step. Informed of the danger, *Breckinridge* dispatched *Wharton's division* from Stephenson's Depot, having to choose between taking that step or immediately complying with *Early's* order to move south to *Ramseur's* support. His decision, influenced by the current battle developments, was a compromise whereby *Breckinridge* fought a dogged retiring action in the general direction of Stephenson's depot until the overpowering need of help for *Early's* main defense line finally forced him to detach one brigade to continue the retrograde action. The rest of *Wharton's division* was hustled off to *Early*, but by then it would be two o'clock in the afternoon.

Word reached *Jubal Early* about daylight that Sheridan's cavalry had crossed the Opequon at several points. Hastening out to *Ramseur's* position, it was quickly apparent to *Early* that this was more than a mere sideshow. He at once sent word to *Gordon*, whose division was nearest to Winchester, to hasten to *Ramseur's* support. The same order went to *Rodes* and *Breckinridge*, but the latter, as previously noted, already had his hands full meeting the Union cavalry threat on the Charlestown Road. *Rodes* and *Gordon* moved without delay, although it was mid-morning before their two divisions reached Winchester and were fed into the Confederate defense line on the plateau, *Rodes* to the left of *Ramseur, Gordon* on the extreme left. It was about 10:30 a.m. when the reinforcing troops were in position, partly concealed by the extensive woods in the area. By that time, however, *Ramseur's division,* fighting alone, with a fierce determination to restore its damaged reputation, had been forced back half a mile by the heavy pressure from Wright's Sixth Corps to a second position closer to Winchester.

Sheridan's effective force on the field numbered more than 37,000 men, including at least 6,000 cavalry. Opposed to him *Early* could count on about 17,000, including *Lomax's* and *Fitz Lee's cavalry*, whose aggregate strength approximated that of the three Union cavalry divisions. With such a preponderance of total combat strength; in view of Sheridan's extensive preparations for his first major battle in the Shenandoah campaign; and in the face of the scattered positions of the various elements of *Early's army,* all signs pointed to a rapid, decisive engagement in which Confederate defeat in detail appeared to be almost certain.

There was, however, one obvious flaw in Sheridan's otherwise sound plan, which depended for early success on smooth, precision-like, almost flawless execution of that always difficult military maneuver, a combined attack by infantry and cavalry working together on a coordinated basis. The defect was the bottleneck through which one-third of the Union cavalry, all of the infantry and artillery, and most of the combat trains would be required to pass on the approach march through the two-mile long Berry-ville Road defile after crossing the Opequon. It is surprising that Emory's corps was not directed to cross the creek at Tanquary's Ford, a mile north of the Berryville Pike, where a parallel road ran west through Burnt Factory and then angled southwest to a point within half a mile of the principal axis of advance. Utilization of two roads would have reduced by fifty percent the risk of being caught in the defile and should have enabled the two Union infantry corps, the Sixth and Nineteenth, to deploy from parallel columns concurrently instead of in succession, thus avoiding the long delay incurred by Emory's corps while waiting for Wright's divisions and trains to pass the Opequon barrier.

Traffic Jam in Berryville Canyon

The inevitable happened. It may have occurred because the Army march order neglected to specify the position of the corps wagon trains; or Corps Commander Wright may have been unwilling to have his own combat trains delayed to give Emory's divisions the right of way. Whatever the cause, the Sixth Corps trains followed right behind their infantry and artillery, completely blocking the Berry-ville pike until Sheridan himself rode back to see what was holding up the Nineteenth Corps. Angered by what he considered the stupidity responsible for the roadblock, Sheridan ripped out orders to the teamsters, interspersed with hearty soldier oaths, to push the teams off the road. Only then could Emory's corps advance, hours behind schedule, so that it was nearly noon when the Nineteenth Corps moved up on a line abreast and to the right of the Sixth Corps, which had already been engaged for over an hour with three Confederate divisions, now joined on a line between Red Bud Run and Abraham's Creek.

The approach march by the Nineteenth Corps, through the defile to the battlefield, was vividly described by one of the participants, John W. DeForest:

The scene in this swarming gorge was one not easily forgotten. The road was crowded with wagons, ambulances, gun carriages and caissons, getting onward as fast as possible, but so very slowly that one might already divine that we should fight our battle almost without artillery. On the right and on the left endless lines of infantry struggled through underbrush and stumbled over rocks and gutters. On every knoll and under every thicket, gravely watching us pass, sat the hundreds of men who belong to an army but never fight; the cooks, the officer's servants, the hospital gangs, the quartermaster's people, the "present sick" and the habitual skulkers. Here too were jammed squadrons of Wilson's cavalry, who for the present had finished their fighting, having cleared the ford of the Opequon. Presently we met litters loaded with pallid sufferers, and passed a hospital tent where I saw surgeons bending over a table, and beneath it amputated limbs lying in pools of blood. Ahead there was an occasional booming of cannon, deadened to a dull PUM! PUM! by distance. Apparently Wilson's main force had got through the defile and was trying to establish a position for us in the irregular undulating valley east of Winchester where we were to deliver battle.*

---

* From *Sheridan's Battle of Winchester*, first published in Harper's Monthly, 1865; reprinted in *A Volunteer's Adventures* by John William DeForest, Yale University Press, 1946.

Brig. Gen. George Getty

Maj. Gen. James B. Ricketts

Brig. Gen. David A. Russell

Brig. Gen. Cuvier Grover

The fortunes of war thus favored *Jubal Early* during the early stages of the Battle of the Opequon, in spite of the Union superiority in manpower and his own narrow escape from being caught with his divisions widely separated. Instead of overwhelming his opponent by demolishing his scattered divisions one at a time, Sheridan would now have to fight *Early's* smaller but concentrated army on a defensive position of the latter's choosing. It was disappointing, but Sheridan was out to win this battle and had no time to dwell on misfortunes.

Returning to the scene of action, Sheridan addressed himself personally to the task of speeding the deployment of the Sixth and Nineteenth Corps in an effort to make up somewhat for the serious delay caused by the early road jam. When the troops were finally in position for the attack, the Sixth Corps straddled the Berryville pike, with Getty's division to the left, Ricketts' to the right, and Russell's in reserve behind the other two but entirely north of the pike. With only two divisions in the smaller Nineteenth Corps, Grover's, the larger of the two, was placed on Ricketts' right in the front line, while Dwight's was in support, echeloned to Grover's right rear.

Sheridan Launches Coordinated Attack

Shortly before noon Sheridan's three-division infantry assault echelon moved forward in a concerted attack, with minimum artillery support, which would have to come later if the guns should succeed in getting into position through the dense thickets and underbrush. *Early* had profited by the long delay and was ready, with the divisions of *Ramseur, Rodes,* and *Gordon* in line, many of the Confederate troops under cover of heavy woods on either flank and in the ripening corn fields in the center. The Confederates reacted immediately and vigorously all along their line by pouring a heavy fire into the ranks of the

advancing Federals. Getty's division on the left made substantial progress initially against surprisingly light infantry opposition along the Berryville Road, in cooperation with Wilson's cavalry which had taken position beyond the Senseny Road that paralleled the Berryville Road a mile to the south. The weight of the combination of Getty and Ricketts fell largely on the embattled *Ramseur,* who had held the Confederate position single-handedly as long as he was able, but with increasing difficulty as the strength of the two Union corps began to make itself felt.

The arrival of *Rodes* and *Gordon,* which extended *Early's* line north to Red Bud Run, occurred just barely in time to save *Early's* neck. Both Confederate generals were experienced veterans who knew their way around on a battlefield and were aggressive fighters. When the Union attack commenced, the Confederate commanders conferred briefly, sizing up the situation as an effort by Sheridan to turn the Confederate right (which in fact was his plan). They decided to counter the move by an effort to nullify the Union commander's tactics by turning *his* right, or at

---

MAP 7. BATTLE OF WINCHESTER, SECOND PHASE

This portrays the situation from about 11 a.m. to noon. The Federal VI Corps, having driven Ramseur from his initial position, has to wait for about two hours while the XIX Corps struggles through the traffic jam in Berryville canyon. Then, at 11:40 a.m., Sheridan launched these two corps in an attack on the Confederates. The two corps diverged slightly, as shown, offering Gordon an opportunity to drive a wedge between them.

Gordon's leading elements arrived at about 10 a.m. He deployed to the north of Ramseur, leaving an interval for Rodes, who moved in immediately adjacent to Ramseur. Evans, who initially was on the left flank of the Confederate front line, was driven back into the woods by Grover's division of the XIX Corps. This map shows the remaining brigades of Gordon's division arriving to extend the line farther to the left, and Battle's brigade of Rodes' division coming up to rescue Evans.

Wharton is supporting McCausland, while Wickham's brigade of Fitz Lee's division has arrived from the north to cover the immediate left flank of the Confederate position.

The remainder of Fitz Lee's division, and all of Averell's, are still off the map to the north.

205

ATTACK OF WRIGHT'S

least to cause such confusion in the Union ranks as to give the Confederate troops time to stabilize their line.

In conjunction with the advance of the Sixth Corps on the Union left, Grover's division of the Nineteenth Corps attacked on the right with great effect, the blow landing principally on *Evans' brigade* of *Gordon's division,* which was broken and driven back some three hundred yards. The early road jam, together with the steep hills and dense woods which then had to be traversed at a fast pace to hasten Grover's division into line, caused his infantry to make the assault on the army right without benefit of supporting artillery in the initial stage. In spite of the absence of that comforting support and in the face of continuous shelling by the Confederates, Grover's men caught fire as they emerged from the woods into open, rolling country.

VI Corps, On The Left

Their advance developed quickly into so spontaneous a charge that their line officers, far from leading, were virtually sucked into the forward rush of yelling men. Even after they had crossed the fields and entered the second woods that sheltered the Southern defenders, their officers were unable to halt them until they had driven the Confederates to the rear.

GORDON COUNTERATTACKS

Grover's impetuous attack, as so frequently happens in battle, quickly lost cohesion and he was unable to stabilize his forward position against the determined counterattack which *Gordon* and *Rodes* had already planned and now launched. It was at this juncture, as *Rodes* was directing a battery into position, that the gallant Confederate gen-

207

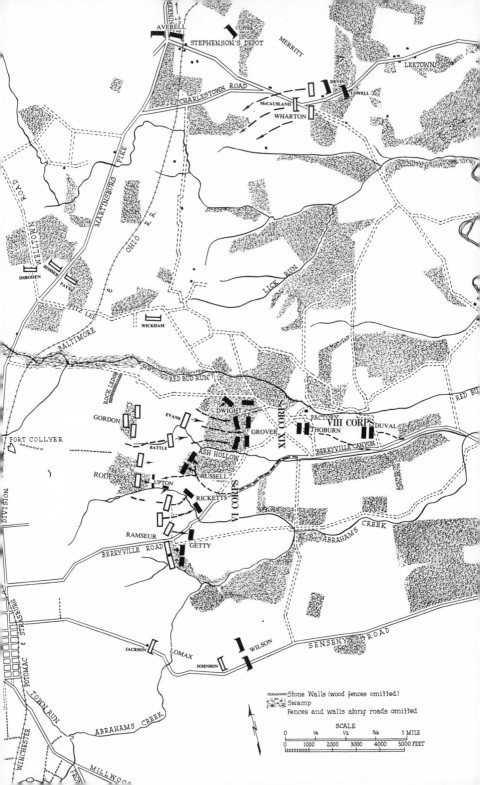

AVERELL

CUSTER

STEPHENSON'S DEPOT

MERRITT

LEETOWN

CHARLESTOWN ROAD

DEVIN

LOWELL

McCAUSLAND

WHARTON

MARTINSBURG PIKE

OHIO R.R.

IMBODEN

ROSSER

PAYNE

FITZ LEE

WICKHAM

BALTIMORE

ROCK LEDGE

RED BUD RUN

LICK RUN

RED BU

FORT COLLYER

GORDON

EVANS

DWIGHT

FACTORY

VIII CORPS

DUVAL

GROVER

XIX CORPS

THOBURN

BATTLE

ASH HOLLOW

BERRYVILLE CANYON

RODES

UPTON

RUSSELL

RICKETTS

VI CORPS

RAMSEUR

GETTY

ABRAHAMS CREEK

BERRYVILLE ROAD

DIVISION

POTOMAC & STRASBURG

JACKSON

LOMAX

WILSON

SENSENY ROAD

JOHNSON

TOWN RUN

ABRAHAMS CREEK

WINCHESTER & FRONT

MILLWOOD

∞∞∞∞∞ Stone Walls (wood fences omitted)
Swamp
Fences and walls along roads omitted

SCALE

0   ¼   ½   ¾   1 MILE

1000   2000   3000   4000   5000 FEET

eral was struck by a shell splinter (probably from Wright's Sixth Corps artillery on the center of the Union line) and mortally wounded as he struggled to control his excited horse.

Saddened but undismayed by the loss of his friend and fellow division-commander, *Gordon* assumed temporary command of the now leaderless division in addition to his own. When *Evans' brigade* of *Gordon's division* had been forced back by Grover's Union division overlapping the Confederate left, the Southern artillery, redoubling its fire, was able to hold Grover in check until *Rodes' absent* brigade, under *Battle's* command, came up and swung into position.

Following Sheridan's orders to advance along the axis of the Winchester-Berryville Road, the Sixth Corps had necessarily diverged somewhat from the Nineteenth as Grover made his attack, because the road turned slightly to the south, with the result that a gap opened in the Union line at the junction of the two corps. Against that vulnerable hinge *Gordon* threw *Battle's brigade,* supported by *Evans,* whose retrograde movement had finally been checked in the woods near Red Bud Run, and the greater

---

MAP 8. BATTLE OF WINCHESTER, GORDON'S COUNTERATTACK

Sometime between 12:30 p.m. and 1 p.m. Gordon threw a counterattack at the gap between the VI and XIX Corps, forcing Ricketts and Grover back in confusion. Russell's reserve division of the VI Corps and Dwight's of the XIX Corps were committed, restoring the situation for Sheridan.

On the north, Merritt's and Averell's cavalry divisions are pushing Wharton and the Confederate cavalry back toward Winchester. On the east, Crook's VIII Corps has been moved up to where it can be launched either to the north or the south in a final blow to crush Early.

Shortly after the action portrayed on this map began to develop, Early moved Wharton's two brigades to a point on the Martinsburg Pike approximately in rear of Gordon.

During this phase, General Rodes was killed, and General Gordon assumed command of Rodes' division in addition to his own. On the Union side, General Russell was killed, and his place taken by General Upton until the latter was wounded, when Colonel Oliver Edwards assumed command.

part of *Rodes'* fresh division. The Confederate counter-attack from front and flanks succeeded in driving back in confusion the Union divisions of Ricketts and Grover. The retreat of these two divisions, against whom General *Gordon* had so effectively turned the tables, threatened to turn into a rout as the Confederate guns poured shells into the men's backs and the counterattacking infantry advanced steadily, yelling and firing as they rushed forward. The fields on both sides of the Berryville Pike were soon filled with panic-stricken fugitives, wounded and unwounded, as the Union line bent and finally buckled. Frenzied generals and staff officers galloped back and forth in a frantic effort to halt the rearward rush, in which it was every man for himself.

Two Dramatic Incidents

At the very moment when all seemed lost, a lone artillery captain, Bradbury of the First Maine battery, serving as a member of Emory's staff, came across an infantry captain from the Twenty-Fourth Iowa, calmly marching a sergeant and twelve men to the rear in formation, much like a detail being relieved from guard duty. At Bradbury's request, the detachment quickly executed a smart "about face" and gave three rousing cheers. The effect was electrical. Panic in that area evaporated, stragglers appeared as if by magic, and in a few minutes the small Iowa squad grew to battalion size with men from half a dozen regiments. About the same time two guns from Bradbury's own battery arrived. The captain quickly wheeled them into position, galloped them forward through musket fire and canister, into the open plain. He opened fire, entirely unsupported for a time, until a line of infantry could be rallied and rushed to the position occupied by the intrepid gunners. Soon the foot soldiers rallied about this island of resistance, as Sheridan ordered a brigade of

Russell's reserve division forward between the right flank of the Sixth Corps and the left of the Nineteenth. This was Upton's outfit, which General Russell accompanied in person as the men charged. It caught the Confederates in flank, and so effectively disrupted their exultant counterattack that the pressure was lifted from Grover's broken brigades, enabling them to halt their retreat and reorganize for further effort. The counterattack of a single Union brigade at the right place and the critical moment very likely saved the day for Sheridan's army.

For *Early's army*, the neutralization of Gordon's near-success marked the high point of the Confederate fortunes of the day. What had come close to a Union disaster was averted by one of those frequent battle episodes that occur when individual heroism on the part of a single officer or a small group of men sets an example or stages a dramatic performance that fires the imagination of his team.

In this instance the spearhead of the Union counterattack, in which General Russell was killed, was a Connecticut heavy artillery volunteer regiment of Upton's brigade, fighting as infantry, and the point of the spear was its colonel, a young West Pointer named Ranald S. Mackenzie, who had graduated from the Military Academy as recently as 1862, with a brilliant future ahead of him as No. 1 in his class. The discipline that he instilled in his regiment was the West Point variety that so irked his easy-going citizen-soldiers as to cause them to swear that the next battle would be his last. The opportunity occurred on September 19, but the denouement was quite different. Their young colonel, with the audacity that later made him a terror to the Indians of the West, galloped up and down in front of his line of advancing men, waving his hat, apparently oblivious to the hail of Confederate bullets, and pointing to the woods from which came the deadly fire. His horse was hit and went down at the same time that its rider took a bullet. The horse was dead, but Mackenzie rose to his feet, shook himself, and continued to lead his men on foot until they entered the woods and drove the Confederates out. From that time on, anyone who made a derogatory remark about Colonel Mackenzie had the entire Second Connecticut Regiment to contend with.

A major general at the age of 24, Mackenzie rose to command of a corps before the fighting ended. Brilliant as his reputation was during the war, his lasting fame rests on his success against the Indians in the seventies. During postwar battles and skirmishes he came to be known, in company with Crook, as the greatest Indian fighter of the age. Grant's opinion set him apart from the ordinary officer in these words: "I regarded him as the most promising young officer in the Army. Graduating at West Point, as he did, during the second year of the war, he had won his way up to the command of a corps before its close. This he did upon his own merit and without influence."

As Sheridan's forces rallied and regained a measure of equilibrium on the flanks of the Confederate penetration, other regiments poured volleys into the backs of *Gordon's* and *Rodes'* most advanced brigades, while still others fired into their faces, causing them in turn to break and retire in confusion over the fields to their main line of resistance.

Much of the fighting during the late morning was in the open fields, without cover, resulting in severe casualties on both sides. In front of Winchester the balance had repeatedly swung back and forth, with neither contestant accomplishing much except to sustain heavy losses. Thus the first phase of the Battle of the Opequon ended with the Confederate defense weakened, but confident and unbroken, while the Union line had receded virtually to the same position from which Sheridan had launched the attack of the Sixth and Nineteenth Corps in the morning.

The hopes of *Early's* Confederates rose with the passing hours and what seemed to them a successful defense against superior numbers. The day was now more than half gone and it appeared not only that Sheridan's massive attack had been halted, but had been "thrown into great confusion and driven from the field" as *Early* was later to report in his *Memoirs*. "A splendid victory had been gained," said *Old Jube*, a strange comment, considering that *Ramseur's* division had been badly mauled; one of the best division commanders, *Robert Rodes*, had been killed along with General *A. C. Godwin* of *Ramseur's division*; *Breckinridge's* troops had been fighting a withdrawal action against a large and aggressive Union cavalry force several miles to the north; *Early's* own cavalry was proving to be a far cry from the superbly mounted, aggressively confident troopers of the early years of the war; the Confederates had already suffered losses that were irreplaceable, and had no reserves to throw into the breach if and when they might be forced to meet another strong Union attack.

Early most certainly was overconfident at this stage of the battle, a condition of mind that had become almost traditional with Confederate generals, who after all had substantial justification insofar as the history of the war in the Shenandoah Valley was concerned. Where *Early* made his greatest mistake was in misjudging the capabilities, the tenacity, the staying quality, the resilience of little Phil Sheridan, who had planned this battle with painstaking foresight and who had no intention of permitting a temporary check to upset the program.

George Crook's two divisions were Sheridan's ace in the hole, to be used as the anvil across the Valley Pike south of Winchester, against which Sheridan had planned to swing the hammer of the combined cavalry divisions of Merritt and Averell, driving down the Martinsburg Road

ATTACK OF EMORY'S

to crush *Early* in the act of retreating. Suggestions were made from time to time by the general's staff during the early afternoon to revise the plan of attack, in view of the delays and setbacks of the morning, by putting Crook's Eighth Corps in on the north flank to turn *Early's* left rather than his right. Sheridan resisted the suggestion, hoping that his cavalry would get into action in time to execute the original plan, but was finally persuaded against his own judgment.

NARROW ESCAPE OF A GENERAL'S WIFE

The Civil War was unique in many ways, none more so than in the custom by which it was possible for the wives of some of the highranking officers, North and South alike, to accompany their husbands in the field, or to visit them

214

XIX Corps, In The Center

for long periods of time between active campaigns, when combat was not imminent.

Mrs. John B. Gordon, wife of one of *Early's* division commanders in the Valley, followed such a practise consistently throughout the war. *Gordon* himself thoroughly approved of the idea and encouraged it, although his superior, General *Early,* a confirmed bachelor, took a dim view of the presence of the weaker sex and was not backward in expressing his opinion without actually issuing prohibitory orders. Mrs. Gordon was an attractive person as well as a determined character and managed to create about her a sympathetic attitude of cooperation and assistance from the Confederate rank and file whenever her horse-drawn carriage should run into difficulty, as occasionally occurred.

215

When her constant presence in the vicinity of his army came to *Early's* attention, he was reported to have expressed the fervent hope that the Yankees would capture and hold her till the war was over. One day he observed a strange conveyance going into the wagon park near Winchester with the regular army trains. Inquiring as to the reason for the presence of the nonregulation vehicle, he was told: "That is Mrs. Gordon's carriage, sir." "Well I'll be damned," exploded *Old Jube,* "If my men would keep up as she does, I'd never issue another order against straggling."*

Hovering in the wings, as it were, when *Early's army* was reconcentrating east of Winchester to meet Sheridan's threat, Mrs. Gordon found herself driving rapidly down the Valley Pike on the morning of September 19, as the divisions of *Rodes* and *Gordon* hastened from Stephenson's Depot to *Ramseur's* support. As she overtook *Rodes'* marching column, a clatter of hoofs signalled the approach of a body of Federal cavalry pursuing the Confederate foot soldiers. General *Rodes,* always gallant, threw a line of men across the road as the carriage dashed by, but the danger was not yet past. As the carriage crossed a wide stream (probably Red Bud Run) north of Winchester, the axle broke, leaving the vehicle stranded in the middle of the stream as the horses kept right on going. Again coming to the rescue, a group of enlisted men manhandled Mrs. Gordon's chariot on to firm ground, made hasty repairs (the Federal cavalry still in the offing), and sent the general's wife safely on her way into Winchester.

THE DAM BREAKS

The Berryville pike west of Opequon Creek was still cluttered with ambulances and ammunition wagons when

---

* *Reminiscences of the Civil War,* by General John B. Gordon. Scribner's, 1903.

Crook was ordered to move his two divisions forward into position on the right rear of the Nineteenth Corps. While halted and awaiting orders at the Opequon Crossing in his capacity as army reserve, the active Crook had become impatient as the hours passed and no instructions were received. Finally he gathered up his staff and rode forward along the highway, where he found General Sheridan at the western end of the gorge, in open country, on a rise of ground just south of the Berryville road. The position afforded an excellent observation post from which much of the impending action could easily be seen, although the Confederate position on the wooded plateau east of Winchester was hidden by the trees. Crook arrived just as Sheridan was issuing final instructions to the corps and division commanders of the two assault corps, and remained with Sheridan during the attack and until he received the order to bring his Eighth Corps into action.

Captain Henry A. DuPont, an officer of the Regular Army and West Point graduate, although as yet only a battery commander, had rendered distinguished service under General David Hunter and was Crook's choice as Chief of Artillery of the Army of West Virginia when the latter became its commander. In that capacity he was with Crook and Sheridan at the army observation post when the Sixth and Nineteenth Corps made their belated attack and suffered the almost disastrous repulse in which more than half of the first Union line of battle was driven back in great disorder under Sheridan's personal observation.

DuPont subsequently wrote a full and illuminating account of Sheridan's Valley campaign,* in which he freely criticized Sheridan for holding Crook's two divisions in army reserve too far removed from the main body instead of posting them at a more accessible spot where they could

_____
* Notes on the Campaign of 1864 in the Valley of Virginia and the Expedition to Lynchburg; New York, 1925.

have been speedily thrown into the action at the psychological moment, when the first assault line was penetrated and driven back. As it happened, it was noon before Sheridan told Crook to bring his corps up as quickly as possible. Crook at once ordered his whole staff except DuPont to ride back at the gallop to speed the movement of the infantry and artillery. As with Crook he awaited the arrival of the corps artillery, DuPont silently watched the battlefield drama, musing that Emory's Nineteenth Corps, while composed of excellent material, appeared to lack the discipline of the Sixth Corps, possibly because many of its regiments had been performing long tours of garrison duty in Louisiana and heretofore had seen very little field service.

As Crook's divisions came up from the Opequon, marching in parallel columns on either side of the Berryville Road, they met on the way hordes of stragglers from the front line who were still retreating even though the Confederate counterattack had been contained. For that reason their progress was distressingly slow, but by two o'clock Thoburn's division was posted on the right of Emory's Nineteenth Corps, while Crook personally led Duval's division further to the right with the intention of feeling his way around the Confederate left flank, the kind of maneuver that was particularly to Crook's liking.

At this stage of the battle the Union situation began to improve. *Wharton's Confederate division,* which had been fighting a slow rearguard type of action against repeated attacks by Merritt's Federal cavalry east of Stephenson's Depot, was finally driven back, its remnants taking position in prolongation of the main Confederate defense line east and north of Winchester, now bent into a right angle salient, with Federal troops lapping steadily around the flank as Crook's fresh divisions came into action.

When the head of the two divisions of the Eighth Corps

had reached the point on the Berryville Road opposite Sheridan's field command post, DuPont quotes the Commanding General as saying to his former classmate at West Point: "Crook, put in your corps to support Emory (Nineteenth Corps) and look well for the right flank." The phraseology of that order, as quoted verbatim by DuPont, was such as to cause some hard feelings because Sheridan in his *Memoirs* later stated that he had directed Crook "to push his command forward as a turning-column, in conjunction with Emory," whereas the loyal followers of Crook's command steadfastly maintained that their general was himself principally responsible for the Union victory as the architect of the culminating flank attack that put *Early's army* to route. Whether the controversy was a valid one will be left to the experts in military semantics to decide.

Of greater interest to the student of the Battle of Winchester is the fact that two future Presidents of the United States performed active roles as officers of Crook's Eighth Corps. Captain William McKinley, a member of the corps staff, was busily employed on liaison duties between the corps commander and his division commanders, and in delivering messages to Sheridan during the action; while Colonel Rutherford B. Hayes, a brigade commander in Duval's division, four times wounded in the course of the war, was one of the principal combat leaders who rendered heroic service in the decisive turning movement which broke the Confederate resistance in the final action of the afternoon battle.

By three o'clock in the afternoon the Confederate cavalry had been pressed back on *Early's* left, exposing the wide plain north and east of Winchester to the unobstructed advance of the Federal cavalry. The Confederate defense line was contracting rapidly as it shrank ever closer to the outskirts of the town. Torbert's Federal horse-

men, with Averell's division west of the Martinsburg Pike and Merritt's to the east, were poised for the knockout blow, as Sheridan renewed his advance all along the line from the east and north.

Breckinridge's troops, chiefly *Wharton's division*, had suffered severe losses and become demoralized in the course of the continuous hammering by Merritt's Union cavalry in the open country east of Stephenson's Depot, all morning and well into the afternoon. When their fighting withdrawal brought them to the main body of the army, *Early* placed them in a position which he thought was in reserve, on a line at a right angle to *Gordon's* on the left flank. But *Breckinridge's* strength had been so depleted that he couldn't stretch his troops to reach the Valley Pike on the extreme left. Merritt was following close on *Breckinridge's* heels, determined to allow him no rest for reorganization or recuperation. *Early's* harassed troopers, covering the

THE WINCHESTER PERIMETER

north flank, were by this time nearly played out and unable to interpose serious resistance when the Union cavalry gathered itself for the supreme effort.

The psychological moment had arrived, and the stage was set. As Merritt continued to press the attack southward along the axis of the turnpike, *Early's* cavalry on the north flank was driven in disorder along the pike, past *Breckinridge's* thinned ranks and into Winchester, the door to which was now wide open from the north. *Jubal Early,* unperturbed and full of fight as he invariably was at moments of crisis, discovered the hole in the dike and immediately pulled part of *Breckinridge's* troops over to the left to close the gap; but the relief was fleeting, despite strong artillery support placed at *Breckinridge's* disposal.

Phil Sheridan was all over the field as the climax of the day-long fight approached. He had committed his reserve, Crook's two divisions, several hours earlier on his right

221

flank, but figured that Wilson's cavalry division, still on the Senseny Road, might be strong enough to block *Early's* probable retreat through Winchester to the south, the task for which Sheridan had been saving Crook's corps since early morning and until his additional strength was needed on the army right flank to restore the balance. Wilson was directed to push forward to the Valley Pike south of Winchester and to close that escape route. Sheridan then galloped over to the center to urge Wright and Emory to renewed efforts to break the Confederate line in conjunction with Crook's swinging door maneuver, as the latter cool-headed general wheeled his two divisions into position to crack down on the Confederate left. Just as Sheridan reached a spot where he could observe the payoff battle, Crook emerged from the Red Bud swamp, off to the northeast, and drove for *Breckinridge's* weakened defense.

This was the moment, about 4:30 in the afternoon, for which Sheridan had planned so carefully, and which had been scheduled for execution many hours earlier. *Early's* inferior strength had been whittled down in repeated hammer blows from two directions by Wright and Emory and Merritt, and Crook was now rapidly edging around the Confederate left flank in a driving attack, gobbling up as he went a large number of enemy cavalrymen who had by that time lost all semblance of organization and were ripe for the plucking.

CROOK'S CLIMACTIC FLANK ATTACK

Crook's flanking maneuver was beautifully executed. As Duval's Second Division completed its wheel and moved resolutely against *Early's* weakened left flank in a long, single line, the men held to a steady pace that never exceeded a walk, enabling them to deliver an effective musketry fire as they advanced, cheering, against a torrent

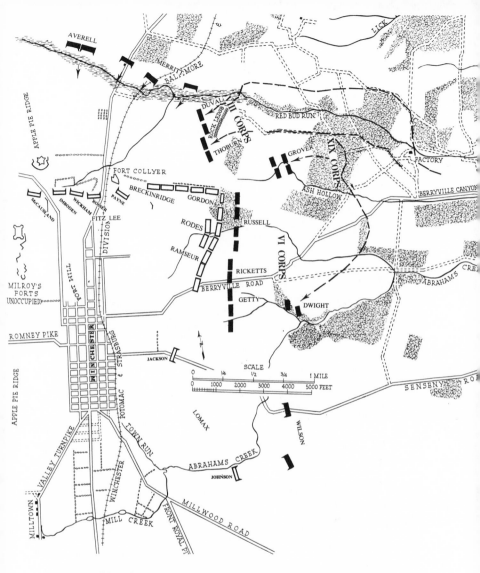

MAP 9. BATTLE OF WINCHESTER, 4:30 P.M. SITUATION

Early's forces were compressed into the defensive perimeter shown. At 4:30 p.m. Sheridan is moving up Crook and Emory in a swinging-door attack to strike the northern face of the Confederate L-shaped position. Merritt's and Averell's cavalry divisions are driving south to participate.

Sheridan moved Dwight's division of Emory's corps to the left of that corps for this final push, but before Dwight had completed the movement Sheridan personally ordered him to the extreme left of the army, where he was told to report to Getty. Dwight moved as shown, but was not committed.

Rodes' division is now under Brig. Gen. Bryan Grimes, and Russell's is under Colonel Oliver Edwards.

223

of bullets from the Confederate defenses that dropped many in their tracks. Crook's First Division, with Thoburn in command, echeloned to the left rear of Duval's division, was ordered to make a frontal attack from its position on the right of the Nineteenth Corps, concurrently with the diagonal flanking attack of the Second Division. As the roar of musketry signalled the opening of Crook's assault, Sheridan's whole line moved forward to join in delivering the coup de grace.

Captain DeForest, waiting expectantly with his regiment for the signal to advance on the right center of Emory's line, in conjunction with Crook's flank attack, recorded his reactions:

I could not see this advance, but I heard it plainly enough. To our right, but hidden from me by the isolated

224

ON THE RIGHT

wood and some rolling land, the broad blue waves surged forward with a yell which lasted for minutes. In response there arose from the northern front of the wood a continuous, deafening wail of musketry without break or tremor. For a time I despaired of the success of the attack, for it did not seem possible that any troops could endure such fire. But the yell came steadily on and triumphed gloriously over the fusillade. The captain of our right company, who could get a view of the charge, afterwards described it to me as grand; the long line tramping forward at the marching step and in perfect order, despite the rearward flow of wounded; only a few of the men firing, and those slowly like cool skirmishers.

Of course we of the Twelfth and Eighth (Vermont) longed to help, and believed that our help was needed. Our men recommenced the file firing and soon shot away their remaining cartridges. Meanwhile Clark and I (impossible now to say which spoke first) told each other that the two regiments ought to charge. Captain Roach (under

225

arrest for something, but present to fight) volunteered to carry the proposition to Colonel Thomas, and ran off stooping on his risky errand. It was a foregone conclusion that the Eighth Vermont and its veteran chief might be relied on for pitching in whenever there was a chance. In three minutes Roach was back unhurt with the message. "The Eighth will advance, and the Twelfth will keep touch with it."

Presently, looking to the left, we saw that the Vermonters were charging; and we jumped forward with a scream, the officers leading and the men hard after them. We were all in a swarm, double-quicking for the wood and yelling like redskins, when we heard behind us a stentorian shout of "Halt! Lie down!" There on our tracks were mounted officers, our brigadier among them, sent by gracious knows whom to stop our wild rush for victory or repulse. But they were caught by the madness of the moment and put no zeal into their orders of recall.

"Well, never mind, boys," I heard McMillan say. "If you want to charge, I am not the man to stop you."

The Twelfth was still rocking back and forth, fluctuating between discipline and impulse, when an officer of Sheridan's staff (a dashing young fellow in embroidered blue shirt, with trousers tucked into his boots) galloped into our front from the direction of Crook's column, and pointed to the wood with his drawn sabre. It was a superb picture of the equestrianism of battle; it was finer than any scene by Horace Vernet or Wouwerman. The whole regiment saw him and rejoiced in him; it flung orders to the winds and leaped out like a runaway horse. The wood was carried in the next minute, our men and Crook's entering it together from different sides, while Gordon's overmatched fellows rushed out of it in the direction of Winchester, many of them throwing away their rifles.

The ranks of the Twelfth Connecticut, having exhausted all their cartridges during the two hours of musketry dueling with the Confederates in front of Winchester, paused after their impetuous charge in a grove to wait for ammunition to come up so they could continue the pressure on *Gordon's* broken regiments. The men watched with interest as an officer galloped up, followed by his orderly, just as a Rebel shell, among the many that were crashing through the woods, burst over his head in a flashing shower of splinters. "Had he come but a trifle slower," wrote Captain DeForest, "it might easily have cost him his life."

" 'That's all right, boys,' he said with a short laugh. 'No matter, we can lick them.' The men laughed also; then a murmur ran along the ranks that it was Sheridan; then came a spontaneous cheer.

" 'What regiment is this?' he asked. 'What are you waiting for?'

" 'The Twelfth Connecticut; waiting for cartridges.'

" 'Get them and come along,' he said, and dashed off in the direction of the firing."

Duval's advance on the extreme right was made virtually at a right angle to Sheridan's main attack, overlapping the Confederate line which had been gradually compressed into an ever-shortening arc on the outskirts of Winchester. Duval ran into difficulties after crossing Red Bud Run, when his troops unexpectedly encountered a deep, miry morass where the Run spreads over low ground to form an almost impassable swamp. This swamp could not be negotiated by horses and indeed was so hazardous a crossing that it was reported to Crook that some of Duval's men were drowned in their efforts to struggle through it. The Confederate left flank was now refused and facing to the north, and protected behind a stone wall that paralleled the Union line of advance until the Federals wheeled to face it frontally. Gordon, having changed front from east to north, was no longer protected on his left by the swamp, but the morass did impede his attackers in their movement to turn southward to the assault, as shown on the map. There was no stopping the excited and exultant Federals, however, so into the swamp plunged Duval's brigades, led by Colonels Rutherford B. Hayes and Daniel D. Johnson, in the face of a destructive fire of muskets and artillery, causing heavy casualties but without halting the attack. The pressure on Duval's division being somewhat relieved by Thoburn's attack, which caught in flank the Confederates who from behind their stone wall had been causing most of Duval's casualties, Crook's two divisions converged, became inextricably mingled, and charged impetuously forward as one unit in happy pursuit of the retreating men and guns of *Breckinridge's* Confederates. In this final, completely victorious charge, division commander Duval was seriously wounded, and Rutherford B. Hayes became acting commander of the Second Division.

Union Cavalry Completes the Rout

As Sheridan watched, Merritt's cavalry charged down the Valley Pike in a mounted attack that came in on *Breckinridge's* left flank and rear, a whirlwind of galloping horses and swinging sabers that irresistibly drove everything in its path. Half a mile to the west of the pike, Averell's cavalry division kept pace with Merritt, but with little opposition since *Early* had no troops available to interpose, now that his own screening cavalry had been effectively dissipated. Devin's brigade of Merritt's division was the first to charge into *Breckinridge,* picking up three battle flags and three hundred prisoners; then pulled back to reorganize, as Lowell's brigade in turn made its attack. Lowell succeeded in capturing flags, prisoners, and two guns. Custer's unused brigade was then brought into line as Merritt prepared to launch the third and final attack with his full division.

Early's right-angle infantry defense had by five o'clock been compressed into a line that extended for less than two miles from the Senseny Road on the right to the

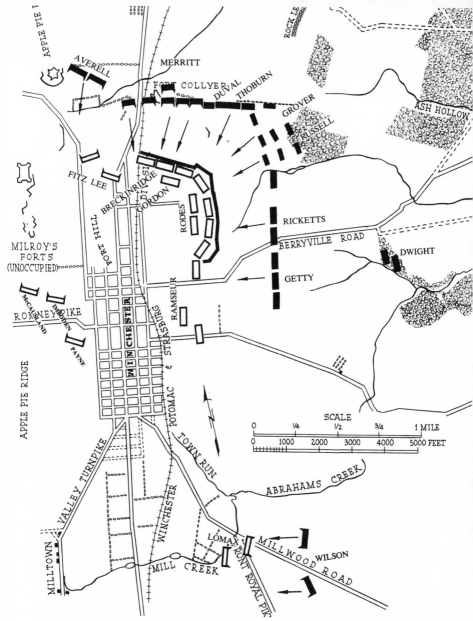

MAP 10. BATTLE OF WINCHESTER, FINAL PHASE

Merritt's cavalry charge against Breckinridge at about 5 p.m. started the rout of the Confederates, which increased rapidly as the Federal infantry corps pressed the attack. By 6 p.m. Early's army was "whirling through Winchester," and down the valley toward Fisher's Hill. The retreat was covered by Lomax's cavalry, but there was little pursuit by the Federals.

229

Valley Pike on the left, with remnants of his cavalry still providing token security on either flank. Against this angled line Sheridan's three corps threw their heavy weight as Wilson's cavalry pressed *Lomax's* troopers steadily back along the Senseny Road in the effort to throw a roadblock against *Early's* withdrawal.

The troops remaining from the divisions of *Gordon, Rodes,* and *Ramseur,* still battling gamely against the unremitting pressure of the Union Sixth and Nineteenth Corps from the east, began to grow uneasy as the noise of battle on their left rear, coming ever closer to Winchester, suggested the always nerve-wracking thought that the enemy was turning their flank and threatening havoc in their rear. Individual soldiers and groups began to drift away to imagined safety, and soon the infection spread through the ranks. A report reached *Early* that the Federals were turning his right as well as his left. He directed a general withdrawal, but promptly cancelled the order when he learned that the alleged enemy was only *Ramseur's division* engaged in rectifying their line to conform to *Rodes* and *Gordon.* It was too late—the damage had been done—there was no stopping the retreat, which got underway at an increased tempo all along the line, particularly astride the Valley Pike where the culminating attack by Merritt's cavalry put the finishing touches to an unaccustomed but highly enjoyable Union experience, that of chasing a fleeing Confederate army.

The net was closing around *Jubal Early* when Merritt threw his entire cavalry division into its third and final powerful mounted attack, three brigades abreast under Devin, Lowell, and Custer. That did it! The heart went out of the Confederate defense as the charging Union cavalry swept forward in a surging mass, sabers slashing and pistols cracking—an onrushing, crushing tidal wave of snorting, half-crazed horses and yelling troopers. Guns were overrun, wagons overturned, Confederate soldiers, wounded and unwounded, fled in all directions as defeat turned into rout and rout into panic.

The streets of Winchester became crowded with Confederate foot troops and cavalry, careening wagons, ambulances, artillery guns and caissons—all seeking to escape. Merritt's division alone, as reported officially by Sheridan's Chief of Cavalry, General Torbert, captured 775 prisoners, of which 70 were officers, 7 battle flags, and 2 pieces of artillery, although General Crook contested the statement, claiming that his own corps had picked up almost 1,000 Confederates, for some of whom the cavalry had claimed credit.

By the time darkness fell, the excitement had somewhat subsided. Wilson's cavalry had been unable to shake loose from *Lomax's* horsemen, who kept contact all the time that Wilson was pushing them back, with the result that by nightfall Wilson was still a mile and a half from the Valley Pike, with *Lomax* hanging grimly on to make certain that *Early's army* would not be interfered with as they disengaged to start their retreat up the Valley from Winchester.

General *Gordon's* wife was still in Winchester when the rout started during the late hours of the day. As *Gordon* reached the town and attempted to rally the men of his disorganized division and to bring order out of the growing chaos, he was startled to come suddenly on a scene in which his wife was the central figure. Shells and bullets from the pursuing Federals were flying about, but to these the general's wife paid little heed as she pleaded with the men to turn and go back. *Gordon* ordered her to get into her carriage and drive south, but her colored attendant could not be found, so once again a handful of Confederate soldiers hitched up the buggy and started her on her way.

Crook's Union command was detailed to conduct the pursuit in the darkness. As any experienced veteran can testify, it is no easy matter to pull an organization into shape to execute a mission of that character at the end of a long day's battle. Crook did his best, following the retreating Confederates as far as Mill Creek, a short distance south of the Winchester outskirts, but there he halted, to the undoubted satisfaction of *Early's* fleeing men.

In company with Crook, Sheridan rode into Winchester after dark, seeking a quiet spot in which to draft a telegram to General Grant to inform him of the victory. Crook appropriately conducted the Commanding General to the home of Miss Wright, the schoolteacher whose information had proven of such great value to Sheridan before the battle. There in the young lady's schoolroom Sheridan composed a short message advising Grant that after a most stubborn and sanguinary engagement, which lasted from early in the morning until 5 o'clock in the evening, the enemy was completely defeated and driven through Winchester; that the Union forces had captured about 2,500 prisoners, five pieces of artillery, nine army flags, and most of the Confederate wounded. "The conduct of the officers and men was most superb," added Sheridan in the brief preliminary telegram; "they charged and carried every position taken up by the Rebels from the Opequon Creek to Winchester. The enemy were strong in number and very obstinate in their fighting."

Chief of Staff Forsyth was a bit more lyrical in his message to General Stevenson, in command at Harper's Ferry, when he wired that Sheridan's army had fought *Early* from daylight to 6 and 7 p.m. and "just sent them a whirling through Winchester." "We are after them tomorrow," wrote Forsyth; "the army behaved splendidly."

The news electrified the North, hungry for a victory. President Lincoln's reaction was one of enthusiastic relief:

> Executive Mansion,
> Washington, September 20, 1864
> "cypher"
> Major General Sheridan,
> Winchester, Va.
> Have just heard of your great victory. God bless you all, officers and men. Strongly inclined to come up and see you.
>
> A. Lincoln

The usually undemonstrative Grant, no doubt gratified that his judgment in selecting Sheridan to command the Army of the Shenandoah had been resoundingly confirmed, waxed enthusiastic, for him, with this telegram to Sheridan:

> I have just received the news of your great victory, and ordered each of the armies here to fire a salute of 100 guns in honor of it at 7 a.m. tomorrow morning. If practicable, push your success and make all you can of it.

At the same time, in prompt appreciation of his success, Grant wired a recommendation to the Secretary of War that Sheridan be appointed to the permanent rank of brigadier general in the Regular Army and his command of the Middle Division (which included the Army of the Shenandoah and other troops at Harpers Ferry and elsewhere) be made permanent. Within hours Secretary Stanton informed Sheridan that both orders had been issued and that a 100-gun salute was fired in Washington "for your great battle and brilliant victory of yesterday."

Perhaps the most amazing result of all was the effect of the victory on the people of the North. Carried along on the emotional crest of a wave of enthusiasm generated by the successful outcome of Sheridan's battle, hard on the heels of Sherman's seizure of Atlanta, proponents of the

233

Peace Party rushed to cover, the price of gold took the healthiest tumble it had experienced since the outbreak of war, optimism took over in the public mind, and the political fortunes of President Lincoln rose from the depths to heights which would carry him through to November re-election for his second term.

EARLY HALTS AT FISHER'S HILL

After marching half of the previous night to their jump-off positions in front of Winchester and fighting off and on all day, Sheridan's army was quite ready to pause for breath after *Early's* men had gone "a-whirling through Winchester and up the Valley." A night pursuit, even for fresh cavalry, is no picnic, and the Union cavalry was far from being fresh after their strenuous efforts during all of September 19. Sheridan wisely decided not to press the pursuit that night, believing that more could be accomplished by giving his men and officers a night's rest with a view to a vigorous follow-up in the early morning.

Finding that the Union army was not pursuing them, the retreating Confederates settled down to a steady march, under orders from *Early* not to halt until they reached Fisher's Hill, a steep ridge about a mile south of Strasburg, twenty miles from Winchester, which extends laterally across the Valley at a narrow point where the Massanutten Mountain range bisects the Valley to afford a defensive position of great natural strength. To that bastion the Confederate army was directed as the nearest position which *Early* believed he could defend with any degree of success.

General *Gordon,* in his *Reminiscences of the Civil War,* wrote movingly of this retreat from Winchester:

Drearily and silently, with burdened brains and aching hearts, leaving our dead and many of the wounded behind us, we rode hour after hour, with our sore-footed,

234

suffering men doing their best to keep up; anxiously inquiring for their commands and eagerly listening for orders to halt and sleep.

Lucky was the Confederate private who on that mournful retreat knew his own captain, and most lucky was the commander who knew where to find the main body of his own troops. The only lamps to guide us were the benignant stars, dimly lighting the gray surface of the broad limestone turnpike. It was, however, a merciful darkness. It came too slowly for our comfort; but it came at last, and screened our weary and confused infantry from further annoyance by Sheridan's horsemen.

By early morning of September 20, long before the slowly pursuing Federals hove into sight, *Early's* divisions were strongly posted, the right flank resting on the towering and virtually impassable Massanuttens, at the point where the North Fork of the Shenandoah River makes a sharp right angle turn; the left flank at the foot of Little North Mountain, not more than four miles to the west. The entire line ran along the prominent ridge of Fisher's Hill, along whose base coursed a small stream known as Tumbling Run, which of itself would serve only as a mental hazard to attacking troops.

Actually *Early's* depleted strength was not sufficient to hold even that limited four-mile frontage with any depth, in addition to which there was the possibility that the energetic Federal cavalry might take it into their heads to barge up the Luray Valley, east of the Massanutten range, to come in on *Early's* rear. To prevent that move, *Fitz Lee's cavalry,* minus their wounded commander, was sent into the next valley, and *Early* dismounted *Lomax's* pitifully small number of troopers to help thicken the attenuated infantry defensive line.

At daylight on the morning of September 20 Torbert's Federal cavalry moved south in pursuit, Averell's division on the Back Road to Cedar Creek, Merritt's on the Valley Pike, and Wilson's along the Front Royal Pike via Stevensburg. The infantry and artillery followed on the main highway and at 9 a.m. Sheridan wired Grant that his army had reached Strasburg and was disposed on the high ground above Cedar Creek. The curtain was about to rise on the second act, the Battle of Fisher's Hill.

Early Blames His Cavalry

The preliminary report which *Early* sent off to General *Lee* failed to tell the full story of his defeat, or *Lee* chose to play it down in his own telegram to the Confederate Secretary of War the day after the battle. *Lee* wrote:

General Early reports that on the morning of the 19th the enemy advanced on Winchester near which place he met his attack, which was resisted from early in the day until near night, when he was compelled to retire. After night he fell back to Newtown and this morning to Fisher's Hill. Our loss is reported severe. Major General Rodes and Brigadier General Godwin were killed nobly doing their duty. Three pieces of artillery of King's battalion were lost. The trains and supplies were brought out safely.

In his later and more detailed report of the battle *Early* rather bitterly threw the blame for his defeat on his cavalry, dislike of which seemed with him to be an obsession. After commenting favorably on the heroic manner in which his infantry and artillery had initially repulsed Sheridan's attack with his whole army, *Early* wrote that he could still have saved the day "if our cavalry would have stopped the enemy's; but so overwhelming was the battle and so demoralized was a larger part of ours, that no assistance was received from it (the cavalry). In this fight I had already defeated the enemy's infantry and could have continued to do so, but the enemy's very great superiority in cavalry and the comparative inefficiency of ours turned the scale

Maj. Gen. Lunsford Lomax

Brig. Gen. Bradley T. Johnson

Brig. Gen. John McCausland

Maj. Gen. Thomas Rosser

against us." The late *Jeb Stuart* would have come out fighting if he could have heard the hard-bitten infantry general traducing his beloved troopers!

Compared to Civil War battles such as Shiloh, Fredericksburg, Chancellorsville, Antietam, Cold Harbor, and others, the casualties at Winchester were not excessive in point of numbers, but the ratio to combat strength on the Confederate side *was* high, 3,921 out of a total strength of 17,700, or approximately 22%. The killed and wounded added up to 2,103, the remaining 1,800 being represented by missing and prisoners. The most severe loss in the infantry was that of General *Rodes,* but *Fitz Lee* was also seriously wounded, to the further disadvantage of the rapidly declining Southern cavalry. Among the infantry brigade commanders, General *Godwin* was killed and Colonel *George S. Patton,** 22nd Virginia Infantry Regiment,* one of *Breckinridge's* officers, was picked up by Union troops with a mortal wound.

In Sheridan's army, with an effective field strength of 37,300, 4,662 were killed and wounded in addition to some 300 captured or missing, a loss of 13 percent. A fairly accurate count was possible because the Union army remained on the battlefield during the night of September 19. The casualties among the Union officers commanding divisions and brigades exceeded those of the Confederates; among those killed being Brigadier General David A. Russell, in command of a division of the Sixth Corps; while the wounded included Generals Upton, McIntosh, and Chapman, all brigade commanders, and Colonels Duval, Johnson, and Sharpe, division and brigade commanders, respectively, in Crook's Eighth Corps.

In his later written account of this battle, *Early's* caustic pen, badly misrepresenting relative statistics, castigated his

---

* Grandfather of General George S. Patton, Jr., famous World War II army commander.

opponent, General Sheridan, for having failed to destroy *Early's* entire force and capture everything he had. "Considering the immense (Confederate) disparity in numbers and equipment," wrote *Early,* "the enemy had very little to boast of. I had lost a few pieces of artillery and some very valuable officers and men, but the main part of my force and all my trains had been saved, and the enemy's loss in killed and wounded was far greater than mine. When I look back to this battle, I can but attribute my escape from utter annihilation to the incapacity of my opponent. . . . I had always thought that instead of being promoted, Sheridan ought to have been cashiered from this battle."

Then, as though to polish off this appraisal, *Early* added this sarcastic postscript: "The enemy has called this battle 'the Battle of the Opequon,' but I know of no claim it has to that title, unless it be in the fact that, after his repulse in the forepart of the day, some of his troops ran back across that stream." One might have thought that the Confederate commander would hesitate to throw the spotlight on troops who ran away, in view of the rapidity of his own departure from the field of Winchester.

VIEW FROM NORTH OF STRASBURG, LOOKING TOWARD FISHER'S HILL

CHAPTER 10

THE FIGHT AT FISHER'S HILL

"GENERAL *Breckinridge,* what do you think of the 'rights of the South in the Territories' now?"

It was *Jubal Early* speaking, his high-pitched voice coming shrilly out of the darkness as the three Confederate generals, *Early, Breckinridge,* and *Gordon,* rode slowly side by side down the pike on the retreat from the Winchester battlefield. This was a typical *Early* jibe which doubtless was intended good-naturedly; but *Old Jube* couldn't seem to resist the tendency to make sarcastic remarks at the most inopportune times, a trait which naturally failed to endear him to his numerous victims, and resulted in estranging many officers who would otherwise have been more kindly disposed toward their fellow-officer.

Although *Early* and *Breckinridge* became friends after the war began, they had been politically hostile during the pre-war years, when *Early* was a confirmed Unionist and

240

outspoken opponent of Secession until his own State of Virginia reluctantly joined her sister states of the Confederacy in cutting the bonds with the Union. *Breckinridge* on the other hand had for years been a distinguished, eloquent proponent of "the rights of the South in the Territories" in the halls of Congress, on the floor of the Senate, as Vice President, and as a candidate for President in 1860 in the role of spokesman for the "Southern Rights" wing of the Democratic party.

EARLY-GORDON RELATIONSHIP

The third member of the group, General *John B. Gordon,* had something less than admiration for *Early* as a man, although he gave him credit for being an able strategist and "one of the coolest and most imperturbable of men under fire and in extremity." According to *Gordon,* *Early* lacked "official courage—the courage of his convictions," in which respect he resembled George B. McClellan and was the direct antithesis of *Lee,* Grant, and *Jackson,* all three of whom, *Gordon* maintained, possessed that quality in the highest degree.

Several of *Early's* marked characteristics of which *Gordon* cordially disapproved were his apparent unwillingness to accept suggestions, however meritorious, from his subordinates, and his chronic distrust of the accuracy of intelligence gathered by his scouts, who *Gordon* insisted were the most reliable and trustworthy men in the army.

As the war progressed, the relationship between *Early* and *Gordon* developed to the place where it was somewhat reminiscent of the armed truce between *Jackson* and *A. P. Hill,* whose feuding was confined to off-battle periods. Perhaps because the destinies of both *Early* and *Gordon* were so closely identified with the famed *Second Corps* and its earlier successive leaders, *Stonewall Jackson* and *"Baldy" Ewell,* the paths of the two generals followed parallel

241

courses. Nevertheless their official relationship, although frequently strained, fell short of reaching the stage of an open break. The possibility existed that West Pointer *Early,* with his sharp tongue and acidulous temperament, may have resented the rapid rise of "civilian-soldier" *Gordon* as at least a potential threat to his own position as successor to *Ewell* in command of the *Second Corps,*

Gordon's record had been spectacular from the very beginning, when as a lawyer with no previous military training he had been elected captain of the "Raccoon Roughs," an aggregation of hardy, homespun, undisciplined mountaineers from the hills of northwestern Georgia. Serving with the *Army of Northern Virginia* in all of its campaigns except for the period when he was convalescing after severe wounds received at Sharpsburg, *Gordon* fought superbly on every field, earned his first star in November 1862, and was made a major general during the Wilderness campaign of 1864. As his military stature grew, the future United States senator and governor came more directly under the eye of the *Commanding General,* until he was finally placed in charge of fully half of *Lee's* small army as the darkness was about to fall on the Confederacy in the wooded country surrounding Appomattox Court House.

Sheridan Takes His Time

The Union victory at Winchester September 19, while it improved Northern morale and satisfied Grant and the Administration at Washington that the right man was in charge in the Valley, had fallen short of achieving the complete result that Sheridan envisaged—the capture or extermination of *Early's* army. Logistics had interposed in the road bottleneck west of Opequon Creek to prevent the early morning attack upon which Sheridan had counted to hit *Early* hard before he could reconcentrate. Then in the afternoon it was found necessary to throw Crook's reserve corps against the Confederate left in order to assure a victory, rather than placing it across the Winchester Pike south of the town to block *Early's* anticipated withdrawal and thus force him to surrender or die. The net effect of these two miscarriages in the precise execution of Sheridan's plan was to permit the escape of that portion of the Confederate army that was still capable of combat, and to allow a short period of grace during which *Early* was enabled to move to a new battlefield possessing stronger characteristics for defense than the field at Winchester; terrain that could have been made virtually impregnable had the Confederate leader shown more perceptive tactical judgment in disposing his troops on the new position.

Criticism of Sheridan's action in allowing three nights and two days to pass before resuming the attack and, on the face of it, granting *Early* sufficient time to recover his poise and to entrench on a strong position across the Valley one mile south of Strasburg, is valid up to a point. Nevertheless such analysts fail to take into consideration some of the military facts of life. True it is that if Sheridan had delayed too long and *Early* in the interim had received the reinforcements *(Kershaw's division)* that arrived on September 26, the Battle of Fisher's Hill, which in effect was merely the second and final stage of the Battle of Winchester, might have ended in Sheridan's repulse instead of a second defeat for *Early*. Although the Confederates had lost Winchester, were forced to retreat twenty miles, and suffered heavy casualties, they were still full of fight and by no means as downhearted as might have been expected. Cocky as ever, they remained confident of their ability to lick the Yankees, although some of their leaders and many of the men had at Winchester gained new respect for the tenacity and fighting ability of their opponents. Though *Jubal Early* may have had second thoughts about Sheridan's qualifications and aggressiveness as a general, he never admitted publicly that his initial impression was erroneous. On the contrary, he wrote that it was only "through the incapacity of my opponent" that his own army had escaped utter annihilation at Winchester.

On the other hand, the principal reason for delaying the follow-up attack was that Sheridan, in view of what happened in the Opequon bottleneck, now planned to allow a greater margin of possible logistical error, and make certain that this time his superiority in strength would be irresistibly applied in such a way that the outcome of the battle would be decisive. In the last analysis, it would be a question of whether Sheridan's field generalship, with perhaps a dash of Irish luck, would pay off.

Early's Troop and Terrain Problems

As though the South's battle losses at Winchester were not enough to make the Confederate situation sufficiently difficult, *Lee* now ordered *Breckinridge* to return with part of his troops to the Department of Southwest Virginia, where the situation required his presence. *Breckinridge's division*, however, under *Wharton*, remained with *Early*. *Early* was informed while at Fisher's Hill that *Kershaw's division*, which before the Battle of Winchester had been ordered back to Richmond but had not traveled further than Culpeper, would soon be returned to him, together with some additional cavalry.

Still another problem confronted *Early* in the two days available to him while awaiting Sheridan's certain resumption of hostilities. That was the matter of reorganization, which imposed certain difficulties in view of a twenty-two percent depletion in strength that had affected every unit in his army. *Early's* solution was to give *Ramseur* the division that was formerly *Rodes'*, and to place *Pegram* in command of *Ramseur's division*, leaving *Gordon* at the head of his own.

244

As already noted, *Early's* right flank was so firmly anchored on the North Fork of the Shenandoah River, secured by the nose of lofty Massanutten Mountain, that no enemy in his right mind would think of wasting time or effort in attacking it. The approach to Fisher's Hill along the pike was flanked on the north side of the highway by a solid wall of towering rocks. The main Confederate position along the ridge was a strong natural bastion with the added protection of previously constructed strong entrenchments and, such as it was, of Tumbling Run in front and at the foot of the ridge.

There was, however, a terrain feature which had a built-in weakness for the Confederates if not properly utilized for tactical defense. Fisher's Hill leads into a series of well-defined parallel ridges and depressions that run in a north-south direction between Massanutten and Little North Mountain. Had General *Early* seriously considered the possibility of a Federal turning movement by way of North Mountain, and posted a strong force of infantry with adequate artillery support on his left flank, Crook would have found it a far more difficult task to roll up the Confederate line than the easy walk-over that almost immediately caused *Early's* entire defense structure to crumble. Little North Mountain, four miles to the west, would have been an equally strong anchor for *Early's* left flank, except that he lacked enough troops to solve all the problems of defense and consequently was forced to take a calculated risk somewhere along the four-mile line. His decision was necessarily a compromise, and it turned out to be the wrong one in that he tried to spread his men over the entire line, with the result that both his left flank *and* the ridge line would prove too weak to do more than offer token resistance when the battle was joined.

From right to left the Confederate line-up showed the divisions of *Wharton, Gordon, Pegram,* and *Ramseur,* in

that order, with *Lomax's* dismounted cavalry thinly holding the extreme left at the foot of Little North Mountain. *Fitzhugh Lee's cavalry,* now under *Wickham,* was up near Milford Pass, prepared to secure Luray Valley against a possible movement by the Federal cavalry to come in on *Early's* rear.

FEDERAL TROOP DISPOSITIONS

Preceded by Averell's cavalry division and half of Merritt's, Sheridan's infantry and artillery followed *Early's* retrograde movement up the Winchester Pike by easy stages, while General Torbert led Wilson's cavalry division, with two of Merritt's brigades, into the Luray Valley to the east of Massanutten Mountain to get south of *Early* and cut off his retreat after he was driven from position. Reaching

246

Cedar Creek at dusk September 20, Merritt's remaining half-division was shifted to the right to connect with Averell, the Sixth and Nineteenth Corps going into position west of Cedar Creek on the high ground overlooking Strasburg; Emory on the left astride the turnpike and extending almost to the Front Royal road; Wright on Emory's right to the west of the pike. Crook's Eighth Corps, the last to arrive, was placed under cover of heavy woods on the north bank of Cedar Creek, in army reserve as at Winchester, for use at the proper time.

In the late afternoon, while the main body of his army was completing its march, Sheridan rode ahead to the Union cavalry position for a personal reconnaissance of *Early's* dispositions at Fisher's Hill. What he saw there convinced him that a frontal attack would encounter heavy

247

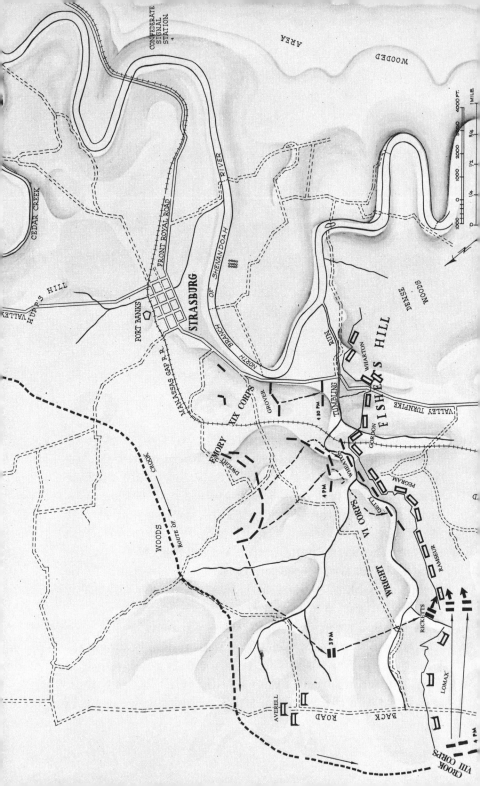

going, but the topography and the width of the valley south of Strasburg suggested the probability that a turning movement against *Early's* left offered a likely opportunity; certainly it would be impracticable to make such an effort against the strongly secured Confederate right flank.

That evening, after telegraphing his arrival to Grant, Sheridan discussed the prospects with his corps commanders and perfected his attack plan down to the last detail, determined that this time there would be no slip-up if it could be prevented by meticulous preparation. As at Winchester a few days earlier, George Crook's corps of two divisions would be employed as the flanking force, while Wright and Emory occupied the Confederates in front.

Sheridan was acutely aware of the existence of a Confederate signal station on top of the northern tip of Massanutten Mountain, known as Three Top Mountain due to its skyline conformation. From that vantage point enemy observers could spot any movement in the open for miles to the north and west. It was obvious that Crook's divisions would have to move at night to escape observation in getting into position on Little North Mountain from which to launch the surprise attack against the Confederate left and rear. At the same time Sheridan decided to turn the apparent Confederate advantage to his own account by freely exposing Wright's and Emory's corps to view without any attempt at concealment, in the hope that *Early* would conclude that the entire Union force was on his immediate front and directly under his eye.

In accordance with that plan, Crook's force lay con-

Map 11. Battle Of Fisher's Hill, September 22, 1864

Showing the routes of the Federal divisions to their assault positions, and the beginning of Crook's attack. The Confederates are behind earthworks which had been constructed previously.

This map is based on the 1873 map prepared for General Sheridan by Lieut. Col. Gillespie, the original being on a scale of 1 inch to 1,000 feet.

cealed in the heavy timber north of Cedar Creek all day September 21, while the other two Union corps were moved closer to the Confederate position. In the course of the movement, Ricketts and Getty engaged in a brisk encounter with the Confederates, who were forced to yield some high ground to the west. When Sheridan's jumpoff position was established to his satisfaction, the Union line was within 700 yards of the Confederates, holding terrain that afforded an unobstructed view of the enemy redoubts and entrenchments and offered good positions for the Union artillery.

CROOK'S FLANK MANEUVER

During the night of the 21st Crook was moved to a concealed position behind Hupp's Hill, between Strasburg and Cedar Creek. The following morning, shielded by woods and ravines from hostile eyes, he continued his series of position shifts by marching to still another covered locality beyond the right flank of the Sixth Corps in the vicinity of the Back Road, along the foot of Little North Mountain.

Sheridan's final tactical strategem, before turning the attack loose, was to push Ricketts' division and Averell's cavalry, on the right of the Union infantry line, forward into contact with the left of *Early's* infantry along Tumbling Run, for the dual purpose of leading *Early* to believe that to be the point of attack and in order to place Ricketts in position to swing around *Early's* left in conjunction with Crook's flanking effort. While Ricketts was engaged in that readjustment and in keeping the attention of the Confederates directed on him, Crook quietly disappeared in the woods of Little North Mountain, moved south in two parallel columns to a position in rear of the Confederate line, then marched his two divisional columns by the left flank, divisions abreast in two lines, down the mountainside to its base. The time was 4 p.m. September 22.

As Crook's leading division emerged into open country from the cover of the woods, the advancing line was of course spotted by the Confederates, who opened at once with their batteries; too few, however, and too late to do more than momentarily harass the advancing infantry. In anticipation of a frontal attack by Sheridan's main force on his front, as Sheridan had hoped, *Early* had posted the mass of his batteries at the center and right of his line, apparently giving little thought to the possibility of a turning movement against his left and rear.

With loud cheers the attackers swept steadily across the rolling and broken terrain, heading for the area in rear of the Confederate entrenchments. In spite of the rocks, underbrush, and dense cedar thickets that impeded the advance and broke up the uniformity of the formations, the lines moved resolutely forward, as Ricketts' division executed a half wheel to the left, in prolongation of Crook's lines, and together the Union infantrymen brushed aside the handful of dismounted cavalrymen who were stationed on the Confederate left flank.

The flank attack of the Union Eighth Corps, which so effectively engulfed the "almost impregnable" Confederate defense as seemingly to give the lie to the meaning of the adjective, was an excellent illustration of one of the basic principles of war: *surprise*. Conversely it exemplified the principle of security, in that *Early* had failed to give proper attention to safeguarding his vulnerable left flank, with the result that he lost the battle almost before it started. Notwithstanding *Early's* helpful contribution to the Union success, the fact that Crook's two divisions so easily threw the entire Confederate army into initial confusion and rapidly succeeding panic and rout, like a row of tenpins which topple successively from the fall of one, detracts no whit from the soldierly performance of those divisions.

251

CROOK AS A LEADER

Crook was the type of general who was all business and no foolishness, who followed orders but exercised intelligence in their execution, who kept his men at their task until the job was fully completed. Other lesser leaders might satisfy their professional ambitions by political maneuvering, currying favor with subordinates, or tacitly permitting actions which would reflect credit on their own records even though the best interests of the service required a different line of action. George Crook was no scholar, and would never be described as articulate. He was constitutionally averse to following the practise of so many generals of conniving to place themselves in a prominent light. Fundamentally he was a solid character, whose good qualities inspired an aggressive loyalty to his person on the part of the officers and men who served under him.

LOOKING EAST

It may have been admiration for their corps commander that made his officers almost combative when it appeared that their leader was being deprived of the credit which they were convinced was his due, both at Winchester and Fisher's Hill. In both battles it was Crook's corps that played the decisive combat role in turning the Confederate flank and assuring a victory. But in both instances it was made to appear that Sheridan had conceived and planned both the strategy and the tactical troop movements that followed. Crook himself remained silent on the subject, but prominent subordinates were less restrained. His Chief of Artillery was outspoken in his censure of Sheridan for allegedly grabbing the credit that DuPont insisted belonged to his general at Winchester, while no less a person than Colonel Rutherford B. Hayes, one of Crook's division commanders at Fisher's Hill, wrote his uncle in Ohio

253

shortly after the battle: "At Fisher's Hill the turning of the Rebel left was planned and executed by Crook against the opinion of the other corps generals. General Sheridan is a whole-souled, brave man and believes in Crook, his old class and roommate at West Point . . . but intellectually he is not General Crook's equal, who is the brains of this army."

The Confederate Stampede

It would seem to the casual observer that there was credit enough for all in the double victory over *Early's* Confederates. The mere fact that Sheridan had chosen Crook on both occasions to be the instrument of victory should be evidence enough of the Commanding General's confidence in the ability of his friend and classmate.

Troops as a rule take their cue from the attitude and actions of their commander. At Fisher's Hill, General *Early* was so confident of the strength of his position that he had ordered his batteries to remove the ammunition chests from the caissons and place them on the ground in rear of the guns; a sure sign to the troops that he expected to remain in possession of the ridge. It was therefore a double shock to his men when they heard the loud cheers of the Yankees moving in great numbers along and *in rear of* the protective entrenchments which faced only to the north. There is nothing in battle that upsets the psychological equilibrium of experienced soldiers so completely as to be outflanked without warning. The fateful word passed like lightning along the Confederate line from left to right even as Wright and Emory moved their corps forward across Tumbling Run.

Early reacted by sending for *Wharton's division* to hurry over from the right, but there was no time for troop movements in the fluid disintegration which quickly affected the entire defense. It was obvious to every Confederate officer and man that retreat or capture were the only alternatives. With unanimous accord, and without waiting for orders, the defenders of Fisher's Hill took off for the rear, in tolerable order at first, then at an accelerated pace, as is usually the case when terror seizes the mind and heart of the individual soldier.

A striking illustration that showed the extent of the panic that fastened on the Confederates when the fearful word "outflanked" reached them was described by Captain DuPont, who accompanied the infantry when the corps artillery had to be left behind because of the character of the terrain on the approach march.*

I personally observed that the sole outlet of a large enclosed fieldwork was completely blocked by the collision of two pieces of Confederate artillery which had attempted to make their exit at the same moment, with the result that both pieces had been overturned with carriages and wheels more or less interlocked, while the twelve horses were pinioned to the ground by their traces and intermingled in all sorts of fantastic attitudes—an incident which effectually prevented the withdrawal from the redoubt of the remaining pieces, which were all captured.

Sheridan described the action by saying that "the stampede was complete, the enemy leaving the field without semblance of organization, abandoning nearly all of his artillery and such other property as was in the works, and the rout extending through the field and over the roads toward Woodstock, Wright and Emory in hot pursuit." Confederate *Gordon* confirmed the result of the engagement, such as it was, with the succinct evaluation: "The retreat was at first stubborn and slow, then rapid, then—a rout."

Even *Jubal Early* had to admit that "the mischief [Crook's flank attack] could not be remedied; after a very

---

* The Campaign of 1864 in the Valley of Virginia, page 137.

brief contest my whole force retired in considerable confusion, but the men and officers of the artillery behaved with great coolness, fighting to the very last, and I had to ride to some of the officers and order them to withdraw their guns before they would move. In some cases they had held out so long, and the roads leading from their positions into the pike were so rugged, that eleven guns fell into the hands of the enemy."

Union casualties of 528 were light compared to the earlier battle at Winchester, in contrast to Confederate losses at Fisher's Hill of 1,235, of whom almost 1,000 were prisoners or stragglers who remained permanently absent. More serious for the Confederate cause than the capture of eleven guns was the loss of the experienced and capable Lieut. Colonel *A. S. "Sandie" Pendleton, Early's* Chief of Staff, who had served in a similar capacity on the corps staff of *Stonewall Jackson* and *Baldy Ewell. Pendleton,* who was known and beloved throughout *Lee's* entire army, was a son of the minister-general, *W. N. Pendleton, Lee's* Chief of Artillery. *Ewell* had offered him a brigade, but *Sandie* preferred to remain on the staff with the rank of lieutenant colonel, where in company with *Kyd Douglas, Jed Hotchkiss,* Doctor *Hunter McGuire, James Power Smith,* Chaplain *Beverly T. Lacy,* and others who had been personally close to General *Jackson,* he aided in contributing to the *Second Corps* a distinctive character all its own.

As *Early's* disorganized masses were streaming up the valley in the early twilight of September 22, *Pendleton* rallied a small group of retreating men with two pieces of artillery and attempted to make a stand across the pike several miles to the south, about midway between Fisher's Hill and Woodstock. It was a brave but fruitless attempt, which ended in the capture of the guns and the mortal wounding of the gallant Confederate officer, who was removed to Woodstock, where he died the following day within the Federal lines.

Sheridan's Dissatisfaction with His Victory

The news of Sheridan's second victory within three days was received with enthusiastic acclaim throughout the North, although Sheridan himself was noticeably disappointed with the net result. He had planned so carefully for a complete victory that would end in the capture or destruction of *Early's* army, and his infantry corps commanders had carried out their assignments so admirably and with such fidelity to the requirements of a coordinated attack, that the failure of his numerous cavalry to do their part stood out the more starkly by comparison.

The army Chief of Cavalry, General Torbert, it will be recalled, had been sent with Wilson's cavalry division, reinforced by Custer's and Lowell's brigades of Merritt's division, up the Luray Valley to seal off *Early's* anticipated retreat once he was driven from his position at Fisher's Hill. It was the same general plan that had been devised before the Battle of Winchester, and again it failed, this time rather miserably. Torbert's superiority over *Fitz Lee's cavalry* and the fact that he had three full days in which to make a forty mile march should have easily allowed him to dislodge the Confederate cavalry, drive it back, recross the Massanutten range at its southern end, and occupy New Market until *Early's* defeated army should move south to encounter the enemy on his rear.

Torbert not only failed to execute his part of the job, but made no real effort to do so, in Sheridan's opinion. Fighting a delaying action, first at Gooney Run, then at Milford Pass, the Confederate cavalry made a stand at the latter place on a strong position that the Union cavalry found it difficult to outflank. The upshot was that *Wickham* outguessed and delayed Torbert long enough to pre-

257

vent the latter from achieving his purpose, whereupon Torbert took his cavalry back to Front Royal and Buckton Ford. When Sheridan was informed of his whereabouts on the morning of September 23, Torbert was bluntly directed to carry out the original mission, but by that time it was too late to slam the door shut on *Early*, who was then on his way to Harrisonburg and points south.

Nor was that all. "Astonished and chagrined" by Torbert's timidity, as Sheridan described his feelings, the mobility-minded commander of the Cavalry Corps of the Army of the Potomac was even more frustrated and angered by the indifference to orders and disinclination to fight displayed by General Averell, whose cavalry division had been placed in a position at Fisher's Hill from which it was expected to execute the historic role of cavalry in the pursuit and exploitation of a retreating foe.

A review of Averell's military record during the Civil War is cause for wonder that he lasted as long as he did as a cavalry division commander. Perhaps it would be generous to state that he lacked the fighting heart that marks the true cavalry leader, and let it go at that. That he was agile-minded in composing his official reports is evident from reading his accounts; there always seemed to be sound reasons for not accomplishing his assigned missions, and he never failed to elaborate at great length. The fact remained, however, that more times than not his division failed to reach the scene of action until after the need for its presence had passed and the enemy had concluded his immediate operations.

General Sheridan reached Woodstock early on the morning of September 23 in company with advance elements of his infantry, expecting to find that Averell's division had been in hot pursuit of the routed Confederates and that the cavalry general would have a glowing report to submit. But Averell wasn't there and no one seemed to know where he was. Devin's brigade of Merritt's cavalry division (the other brigades were with Torbert in the Luray Valley) was at hand, however, so Sheridan pressed them into the pursuit. About noon Averell's division showed up, having taken time out for a good night's rest, followed by a leisurely jaunt over the few miles of road between Fisher's Hill and Woodstock. Sheridan minced no words in upbraiding Averell, and immediately sent him packing after Devin, who had run up against rear-guard opposition at Mount Jackson, but still was making progress despite his small force. It wasn't long after Averell had joined Devin and assumed command of the combined forces that Sheridan received a message from him to the effect that a signal officer had advised him that "a brigade or division of the enemy was turning his flank" and that he thought it prudent to withdraw his division. Sheridan sent back word that Averell should not let the Confederates bluff him so easily; then, thinking it over, he decided he had had enough of that inferior kind of leadership, and dashed off a Special Order that relieved Averell from command and ordered him to Wheeling to await further orders. Colonel William H. Powell was assigned to command of the First Cavalry Division in the same order that brought to an end the military career of the disgruntled William W. Averell.

Early Again Blames His Cavalry

Early's official report to General *Lee* again blamed his cavalry for the defeat at Fisher's Hill, conveniently overlooking his own lack of foresight in failing to provide adequate security for his left flank, where he had placed *Lomax's* thin line of dismounted cavalry. The *Commanding General's* reply told him to be of good cheer, offering the opinion that Sheridan had only 12,000 effective infantrymen (a rank underestimate) and expressing continued confidence in his men and officers. "One victory will put all things right," wrote *Lee,* in an effort to keep the offensive spirit alive in case *Early* may have become discouraged or doubtful of success. But there was a mild criticism as well from the general who rarely found fault with his lieutenants. "As far as I can judge at this distance," said *Lee,* "you have operated more with divisions than with your concentrated strength. Circumstances may have rendered it necessary, but such a course is to be avoided if possible. It will require the greatest watchfulness, the greatest promptness, and the most untiring energy on your part to arrest the progress of the enemy in his present tide of success."

SHERIDAN'S ARMY MARCHING UP THE VALLEY

CHAPTER 11

THE PAUSE BETWEEN BATTLES

FOLLOWING the rout of the Confederates at Fisher's Hill September 22, *Early* had little choice but to fall back as best he could and hope that Sheridan's losses, together with his need for time to pull his forces together after two battles, might combine to lessen the vigor of the Federal pursuit.

It was Averell's job to harry and slow down the retreating Confederates with his cavalry division, and by unremitting pressure against the enemy rear guard to force *Early's* tired infantry to deploy and redeploy constantly. He had failed abjectly in carrying out that mission. Seldom had such an opportunity fallen to the lot of the Union cavalry—the sort of thing to which horse troops were ideally suited—and Averell had muffed it badly, losing his command as indeed he should have. When

261

reporting to Grant his action in firing Averell, Sheridan pinned the onus exclusively on the division commander, explaining that "his indifferent attack was not at all worthy of the excellent soldiers he commanded."

Nevertheless the damage had been done, nor had Torbert been any more successful in getting around *Early's* retiring troops to block their retrograde movement long enough for the Union foot soldiers to catch up. Despite his feelings of frustration at being prevented, for the second time in three days, from carrying out his plan utterly to destroy the elusive *Early,* Sheridan found ample time to enjoy the rare sight of "the bright sun gleaming from the arms and trappings of the thousands of pursuers and pursued" as his army followed the Confederate up the Valley through New Market, artillery on the pike, infantry columns on either side.

An Ineffectual Pursuit

Try as he might, Sheridan was unable to bring his quarry to a halt in order to deliver the final crushing blow. For their part, the Confederates believed they were getting off rather easily, knowing what a large, well-mounted and well-equipped cavalry force Sheridan had at his disposal. General *Gordon* alleged that "General Sheridan followed our retreat very languidly. His cavalry maneuvered before ours, and ours maneuvered before his. His artillery saluted, and ours answered. His infantry made demonstrations, and ours responded by forming lines." One might have thought, from *Gordon's* description, that a large old-fashioned square dance was in progress in the Shenandoah Valley.

The valley for some distance south of New Market is almost entirely cleared, open country, with a few high hills here and there. The Confederates could see and feel the thousands of Yankees in close pursuit, infantry on the rear and cavalry on the flanks, but the retreat was conducted in good order, the rear elements retiring in battle formation with their lines extended across the valley turnpike.

An observant private in the *61st Georgia** wrote in his own account of the retreat: "We often had to fight as we marched along. We would sometimes come in sight of our wagons which could not move fast on account of our having poor, broken-down teams and heavy loads. Our army was very small. I heard a Yankee prisoner say afterwards that they thought it was only our rear guard. They would run cavalry batteries up on top of the hills and shell us severely. We kept in excellent line but we nearly perished for water. We were all nearly exhausted. . . . All the firing ceased and the Yankees camped and began to build fires. We fell back a few miles and camped for the night."

One final effort Sheridan made near New Market to persuade *Early* to stop and fight, when he pushed Devins' small cavalry brigade of five hundred troopers, with two guns, right up to *Early's* lines in the hope that the tempting decoy might cause the Confederate leader to pause for the easy capture. When *Early* ignored the bait and kept right on going, Sheridan gave up the race. For the next day or so contact was lost between the two main bodies. The Union army moved on to Harrisonburg, while *Early* pulled off to the east on the road to Port Republic to facilitate a junction with *Kershaw* who was returning from Culpeper. On September 25 *Fitz Lee's* and *Lomax's* cavalry rejoined the main body between Brown's Gap and Port Republic, and the following day *Kershaw's division,* with *Cutshaw's artillery battalion,* crossed through Swift Run Gap to add 3,800 muskets and additional guns to *Early's* strength. At Port Republic,

---

* Nichols, Pvt. G. W., *A Soldier's Story of his Regiment.* Privately printed in Georgia.

which meanwhile had been occupied by Merritt's Union cavalry division, *Kershaw* accidentally encountered the Federals, attacked, and drove them out.

Meanwhile, Sheridan had sent Torbert with Wilson's cavalry division, through Staunton to Waynesboro, where he was instructed to blow up the railroad bridge and the tunnel through the mountain at Rockfish Gap; then return, burning the mills and all forage and foodstuffs and rounding up as many cattle as he could get his fingers on. While engaged on that expedition, Torbert was attacked by *Pegram's infantry division* and *Wickham's cavalry* and forced back to Staunton. Although he managed to destroy a substantial amount of supplies in the course of the raid, he succeeded only in damaging the bridge and never did reach the tunnel.

Torbert's visit to Waynesboro and the further movement of the Union infantry up the Valley to Mount Crawford caused *Early* to pull all his troops in toward Rockfish Gap, where he remained quietly in camp on the pleasant plateau at Brown's Gap, ringed by the Blue Ridge Mountains, where *Stonewall Jackson* had been wont to rest his troops between battles during his 1862 campaign. While the men rested, *Early* watched to see what Sheridan's next move would be.

The articulate Georgia soldier, Private Nichols, reflected in his later published work the somewhat dejected reaction of *Early's* men at this juncture:

Our army was now reduced to only 5 or 6000 men and seemed badly discouraged and looked like they thought it was useless to fight any longer. We had an elevated position and could see Yankees out in the valley driving off all the horses, cattle, sheep and killing the hogs and burning all the barns and shocks of corn and wheat in the fields, and destroying everything that could feed or shelter man or beast. They burnt nearly all the dwelling houses, the valley was soon filled with smoke. We remained at Port Republic two days and very cautiously moved along some mountain roads to Waynesboro, near the great tunnel thru the mountain, and thru which the Richmond and Staunton railroad passes. We ran a few Yankee cavalry from Waynesboro and occupied it.

Both armies marked time for a week until October 5, when *Early* was further reinforced *by Rosser's cavalry brigade* of 600 troopers. The arrival of *Kershaw, Cutshaw,* and now *Rosser* just about made up his losses at Winchester and Fisher's Hill.

THE DEATH OF MEIGS SPARKS RETALIATION

Distasteful as it may have been for Sheridan, who was not a sadist, to make war on civilians in the execution of his orders to burn out the granary of the Confederacy, an incident occurred on October 3 which set in motion a chain reaction of retaliatory occurrences. As a direct result, application of the philosophy of an eye for an eye and a tooth for a tooth would later involve George A. Custer and *John S. Mosby* as the principals in a hot controversy over which side first started the hanging of captured prisoners. (See Chapter 15). Lieutenant John R. Meigs, the able young engineer who had been so helpful to Sheridan when he first took command in the Valley and who was still his engineer officer, was shot to death within the Union lines by three bushwhackers dressed in Federal uniforms, as he was returning to headquarters with several companions after making a topographical survey of the area around Harrisonburg. The hot-tempered Sheridan, who thought highly of Meigs, and convinced himself that "the murderers" lived in the vicinity, decided it was necessary to invoke drastic measures as a warning to the people of the valley that his army would not tolerate the lending of aid and comfort to unlawful elements. General Custer, recently promoted to command of the Third Cavalry Division when Wilson was transferred to Sherman's army as Chief of Cavalry, was directed to burn all the houses within a radius of five miles. Custer willingly started his task the following morning, but Sheridan upon reflection changed his mind after a few homes had been burned, sending word to Custer to call a halt, and to confine his efforts to gathering in all able-bodied men as prisoners.

Early in his "Memoirs" tells a very different story about Lieutenant Meigs' death. His account states that three of his scouts, armed and in their own uniforms, were reconnoitering in the rear of Sheridan's lines when they ran suddenly into the Union officer, accompanied by two soldiers. When called upon to surrender, Meigs is alleged to have shot and wounded one of the scouts, who in turn killed the lieutenant. The reader must judge for himself which general was giving the true facts; the impulsive Sheridan, motivated possibly by temporary rage at the loss of his valued engineer officer and anxious to find an excuse to discourage civilian assistance to the Confederate partisans infesting the Valley; or *Early,* who was always ready to think the worst of his opponent, even to the point of possibly doctoring the episode in order to remove whatever propaganda value Sheridan might attempt to extract from bushwhacker activities.

The time had now come, in Sheridan's opinion, to go all out in the execution of Grant's instructions to clean out the Valley by killing or removing all live stock, destroying its mills, forage, and foodstuffs, and making it impossible for the Confederate armies to secure from that rich farmland the subsistence which meant life or death to the Confederacy. Sheridan figured that nothing would be gained by remaining inactive in the Harrisonburg area, and furthermore the Union army's line of supply had grown rather too long for comfort. It was the belief of the War Department, in which Grant concurred, that *Early* was licked and probably incapable of causing Sheridan further serious trouble. The Union high command rather anticipated that *Early* would move his forces to the east of the Blue Ridge, preparatory either to rejoining Lee's army or operating along the line of the Virginia Central Railroad.

Sheridan believed it would now be safe to reduce his strength and so recommended to Grant, who concurred, directing him to send Wright's Sixth Corps back to the James River, by way of Culpeper as a precaution against the possibility that *Early* might undertake to cut in on Sheridan's rear while engaged in his work of destruction in the Valley. No such transfer was carried out, however, because it soon became evident that *Early* was determined to make another effort to retrieve his fallen fortunes. Although *Old Jube's* reputation as a fighter had suffered as the result of his two defeats, and the enmities he had built by his unbridled tongue and sarcastic remarks were coming back to plague him in Richmond and elsewhere, General *Lee* did his best to defend him, refusing to take any measures that would lead to his removal or to weaken him by withdrawing troops from the Valley.

Sheridan Retraces His Steps

While Sheridan had been pursuing *Early* up the Valley in the latter part of September, letters and telegrams were exchanged with Grant and Halleck on the subject of repairing the railroads to improve the supply line between Washington and Sheridan's army. Grant inclined to the view that Sheridan should move east through Brown's Gap on Charlottesville and Gordonsville to approach Richmond from that direction, but Sheridan opposed the plan because, he maintained, it would necessitate the dissipa-

tion of too many troops to protect the Orange and Alexandria Railroad against guerrilla raids and at the same time secure the line of the upper Potomac and the Baltimore and Ohio Railroad. He also feared that *Lee* would detach troops from the James River line and enable *Early* with reinforcements to overwhelm him under adverse conditions. He urged Grant to let him retrace his steps down the Valley in order to shorten his supply line and use the time to good advantage by completing the program of destruction which had been a part of his original instructions. Since Sheridan was on the ground and felt so strongly on the subject, Grant left the decision up to him. It was at that point that Sheridan determined to start his

NEAR TOM'S BROOK

return movement, his initial objective being Strasburg and the Cedar Creek line.

SYSTEMATIC DESTRUCTION OF THE VALLEY

On October 6 Sheridan's army started its march north, the infantry and artillery in the lead, Torbert's cavalry covering the rear. The ordered destruction was systematically carried out as the troops proceeded by easy stages. The men were under orders to respect the homes and persons of civilians, but everything of military value was to be destroyed. The job was thoroughly executed, the entire breadth of the Valley being utterly devastated from Staunton to Winchester, with no interference from *Early*

269

except on the part of his cavalry, which nipped at Sheridan's heels from the time his army moved out from Harrisonburg. Merritt's cavalry moved along the eastern half of the valley, using the main turnpike as his axis, while Custer's division followed the Back Road to the west, both outfits spread widely in order to execute with thoroughness the task of destroying the forage-filled barns and mills.

A Confederate chronicler of the campaign, Private Nichols of *Gordon's division*,* briefly reported the return movement of the two armies down the Valley:

> After Sheridan had burned out the upper valley, he fell back to Strasburg and we followed him to New Market. We found that he had burned every barn and nearly every dwelling from Staunton to Strasburg. Most of the dwelling houses in the towns were spared. The distance, I believe, from Staunton to Strasburg is 70 miles, and we heard that Sheridan reported to Lincoln and Grant that— "a crow would perish in the valley." And it was one of the finest and richest I ever saw before this merciless "burn out."

For two days, October 6 and 7, the Confederate cavalry, in two separate commands under *Lomax* and *Thomas W. Rosser,* who had been given *Fitz Lee's division* while the latter was recuperating from the wound received at Winchester, followed the Union army without approaching closely enough to cause any fighting beyond minor brushes between small groups. On the third day *Rosser's* troopers grew bolder, captured some of Custer's battery forges and wagons, and otherwise annoyed his rear guard to such an extent that Sheridan decided to teach them a lesson. That evening the commanding general called Torbert in, told him he had decided to halt the infantry, and directed him "either to give *Rosser* a drubbing next morning or

---

* Nichols, G. W., *op. cit.*

get whipped himself." Sheridan added that he intended to ride out himself to Round Top "mountain," an excellent observation elevation overlooking Tom's Brook, to see the show. That night Merritt's division was bivouacked at the foot of Round Top, with Custer's brigades near Tumbling Run, about six miles northwest of Merritt's camp. Orders were sent to Custer to backtrack before daylight by the Back Road and attack *Rosser's* cavalry at Tom's Brook Crossing, while Merritt would concurrently attack *Lomax* along the Valley Pike.

The Cavalry Fight at Tom's Brook

Sheridan proceeded early in the morning to his observation post and had a front row seat when Custer's division came trotting down the Back Road and met *Rosser* with his three brigades about seven o'clock. Custer and *Rosser* were old West Point friends, both rather given to dramatics, so the clash between them promised fireworks. As the opposing horse artillery batteries opened with a roar that reverberated across the valley, the Blue and Gray brigades deployed for action. Custer's line, extended for a distance of three miles, immediately launched a mounted attack, quickly separating into detachments that charged into *Rosser's* men like scattered shell fragments. At the same moment, Merritt's brigades swept along the pike against *Lomax's* horsemen. For two hours the battle swirled over the hills and dales, with the outcome never in doubt in view of the vastly greater strength of the Union cavalry. The fighting was all mounted, a veritable cavalry Donnybrook. Many of the charges and countercharges were clearly visible to Sheridan and his staff watching eagerly from Round Top.

The Confederates broke first on the flanks and the retreat soon developed into a rout, probably the worst in

FEDERAL CAVALRY COMMANDERS
L. to R.: Merritt, Gregg, Sheridan, Davies, Wilson, Torbert

Confederate cavalry history. The jubilant Union troopers, whooping and hollering, drove *Rosser* and *Lomax* in wild flight up the valley, never stopping until the fleeing Southern horsemen had covered more than twenty-six miles to a haven behind *Early's* infantry at New Market, to which point *Early's* army had countermarched when he learned that Sheridan was moving down the Valley. The "Woodstock Races," as the Confederate debacle was nicknamed by Custer's and Merritt's men, netted for Torbert's two divisions all but one of the enemy's twelve guns, a nice bag of prisoners, and *Rosser's* supply train and headquarters wagons; in fact practically everything on wheels. General *Lomax* was captured during the race, but managed to escape.

The affair at Tom's Brook, coupled with the successful

272

fighting which had fallen to the lot of Sheridan's cavalry in the Battle of Winchester, afforded conclusive evidence that *Early's* horsemen were no longer a match for the Union mounted troops when it came to a showdown fight. Officered at the division, brigade, and regimental level by aggressive leaders, now that Averell had been removed, repeated successes had engendered confidence and Sheridan worked them constantly and hard. Of the cavalry action in the Shenandoah Valley campaign, General Merritt would later write: "Scarcely a day passed when they were not engaged in some affair, and often with considerable loss, as is shown by the fact that in twenty-six engagements, aside from the battles, the cavalry lost an aggregate of 3,205 men and officers." It may be further observed, in appraising the work of their chief, General Torbert, that a more offensive-minded general in his place might have accomplished far greater results for Sheridan with the means at hand. The repeated opportunities that were offered to exploit fully the Union victories at Winchester and Fisher's Hill by rapid movements to get on *Early's* rear and accomplish his destruction at the time of his two extended retreats, had they been effectively grasped by Torbert, should have won for that general a shining reputation as a dashing cavalry commander. But Torbert evidently wasn't the man of the hour.

Viewed objectively, *Early's* attitude toward his own cavalry was hardly calculated to arouse their ambition to excel. There is no evidence that he exerted himself at any time to give them the kind of leadership that Sheridan exemplified in his use of the mounted arm. There was need for effective reorganization of the Confederate cavalry at the start of the Valley campaign, but *Early* had neglected to provide it. Since loyalty works both ways, it is quite possible that *Early's* indifference to its welfare and readiness to blame his mounted force for most of his failures may have contributed substantially to its progressive deterioration. That the Confederate commander recognized Sheridan's superiority in at least that portion of his army is clear from his report on the cavalry battle at Tom's Brook when he wrote: "This is very distressing to me, and God knows I have done all in my power to avert the disasters which have befallen this command; but the fact is the enemy's cavalry is so much superior to ours, both in numbers and equipment, and the country is so favorable to the operations of cavalry, that it is impossible for ours to compete with his."

On October 10, the day following the "Woodstock Races," the Union army resumed its march, crossed to the north side of Cedar Creek, and went into camp on the high ground north of Strasburg. The decision to send Wright's Sixth Corps back to the Army of the Potomac had not yet been revoked. The work of repairing the Manassas Gap branch of the Orange and Alexandria Railroad having been started, Sheridan directed Wright to continue the march by way of Front Royal, which would leave the army at Cedar Creek with only Emory's Nineteenth and Crook's Eighth Corps and the Cavalry Corps.

Early Plans a Comeback

In Confederate circles the talk was going around that *Early* ought to be removed from command in the Shenandoah. After all, he had been roundly defeated, forced to flee at Winchester and Fisher's Hill, and to all intents and purposes driven from the Valley, with Sheridan now engaged in scorching the good earth throughout the length and breadth of the breadbasket of the Confederacy. It was alleged that *Old Jube* had lost the confidence of his men, that their morale was gone, desertions were occurring at an alarming rate, and the physical damage to the crops and livestock had gone so far that it could not be repaired.

Despite the consternation at Richmond, and with full recognition of the severe decline in Southern fortunes due to Sheridan's successes, *Lee* and *Davis* continued to back *Early* by giving him *Kershaw's veteran division* of *Longstreet's corps* and *Rosser's cavalry,* neither of which could with impunity be spared from *Lee's* steadily diminishing strength in eastern Virginia. In *Lee's* view, however, the worsening supply situation, bad as it was, had to be evaluated in context with the need for a victory in the Valley in order to improve the lowered troop morale and as an offset to the boost in Northern morale that Sheridan's victories had brought about. The arrival of *Kershaw* and his division of South Carolinians had been met with enthusiastic cheers by *Early's* men at Brown's Gap. Their fighting spirit, understandably low after their two defeats, was quickly revived as they welcomed the returning division with cheerful jests and queries as to whether they had brought any more guns for Phil Sheridan. The latter referred to an earlier shipment of field guns by the War Department of Richmond, on one of which a practical joker had written with white chalk the words—"Respectfully consigned to General Sheridan through General Early"—and it so happened that very gun did reach Sheridan either at Winchester or Fisher's Hill when it was captured with the inscription still attached.

As for General *Early himself,* there was no defeatism in his make-up. Winchester and Fisher's Hill were in his opinion unfortunate phases in the campaign which he hoped and believed could be neutralized by a surprise victory. His fight with Sheridan was not ended by any means. He had been on the defensive in his first two encounters, and was acutely conscious of the Union superiority in both infantry and cavalry. But he still believed that his infantrymen were better fighters, individually worth two of their opponents. Moreover, he shared with some of his generals the opinion that Sheridan was not the superman that the Northern papers had painted him, else he would have wiped *Early's* army out of existence by this time.

While the Union army was encamped at Harrisonburg, *Early* had moved to initiate his counteroffensive, only to find upon his arrival there that his bird had flown. His own inclination to attack was naturally strengthened by the wholesale burning of barns and mills, the effect of which on the minds of the Southern soldiers is not difficult to imagine. He was also stimulated to assume the offensive by the receipt of several letters from General *Lee*, who informed him that the *Army of Northern Virginia* had been greatly weakened in order to strengthen him, in the expectation that he would prevail over Sheridan to an extent that would make it possible to release at least some of his troops to rejoin *Lee.* "You must not be discouraged," *Lee* wrote, "but continue to try. I rely upon your judgment and ability, and the hearty cooperation of your officers and men to secure it (a victory). With your united force it can be accomplished." Such a letter as that was not only a mandate but, even more, a psychologically urgent appeal to *Jube's* fighting instinct, to which he responded immediately.

RE-ESTABLISHES CONTACT WITH SHERIDAN

The intelligence that Sheridan had sent part of his army back to Grant reached *Early* on October 12, the day he resumed his march from New Market. On the 13th he reoccupied his former position on Fisher's Hill and with part of his force went personally to Hupp's Hill, between Strasburg and Cedar Creek, to reconnoiter. There he found the Union army strongly posted on the high ground north of the creek.

As *Early* examined the terrain and the enemy dispositions, a Union division moved out on the left and stacked arms in an open field. The target was an open invitation which a battery of artillery that had accompanied *Early* could not resist. The guns opened without orders, scattering the Federal infantry like a yard full of chickens. But they reacted strongly and a hot little skirmish ensued, satisfying *Early* that it would be impracticable to bring on a general engagement without more careful planning. He would bide his time for a few days in the hope that Sheridan would attack him again at Fisher's Hill and this time he would make certain that the shoe would be on the other foot. Whereupon he returned with his detachment to Fisher's Hill to sit quietly and await developments.

The lively exchange of compliments at Hupp's Hill, together with the intelligence that *Early's* whole force had reoccupied Fisher's Hill, was sufficient to convince Sheridan that *Early's* intentions were offensive. Orders were immediately dispatched to Wright, who was on his way with the Sixth Corps to Ashby's Gap, to turn around and retrace his steps. Upon its return on October 14, Wright's Corps was placed in position on the west side of Meadow Brook, to the right and rear of Emory's Nineteenth Corps, whose line was along the north bank of Cedar Creek, west of the Valley Pike. The creek was fordable in its upper reaches, but became more of a military obstacle as it neared the Shenandoah River. Crook's Eighth Corps was located to the east of the pike, his two divisions echeloned in depth, and disposed in a southeasterly direction, while the Cavalry Corps was in camp on the right of the Sixth Corps, except for Powell's (formerly Averell's) division, which covered the roads to Front Royal in front and on the east flank of the army. The Sixth Corps was designated as army reserve; the Nineteenth and Eighth were given front line responsibility and ordered to entrench. Army Headquarters was established at the Belle Grove House, a spacious Southern mansion 500 yards west of the pike and in rear of the line of the Nineteenth Corps along the high ground above Cedar Creek.

HALLECK MUDDIES THE WATERS

Before the foregoing events had transpired, however, Sheridan received dispatches from Washington which threatened to upset his carefully planned campaign. On the 12th Halleck wired that Grant wished a position to be taken far enough south to serve as a base for further operations upon Gordonsville and Charlottesville. The dispatch went on to say that the base should be strongly fortified and provisioned, suggesting the vicinity of Manassas Gap as a likely point. Actually Halleck had modified Grant's order by placing his own interpretation on the message, but Sheridan had no way of knowing that. The following day Secretary of War Stanton sent a wire indicating that a conference would be desirable and suggesting that if possible Sheridan repair to Washington for the purpose.

The brew that was being cooked up in Washington was not to Sheridan's liking. It was certainly no time for the Army Commander to absent himself from the field when in contact with the enemy. But since Stanton's invitation was in effect an order, and Sheridan was opposed to the strategic plan that Washington wished to effectuate, he decided it would be wise to make a hurried trip in the hope that he could persuade the War Department to drop the idea and let him run his own show with a minimum of interference.

SHERIDAN GOES TO WASHINGTON

Early's return to Fisher's Hill following his reconnaissance in force to size up the Union position at Cedar

Creek had led Sheridan to believe that an immediate Confederate attack was not imminent, that he could safely visit Washington and return. He thereupon decided to improve the occasion by taking all three divisions of Torbert's cavalry, under Custer, Merritt, and Powell, to Front Royal, from where he would send them south while he himself, with his Chief of Staff and three aides, pushed on to Rectortown and thence took train for Washington. The cavalry mission would be to pass through Chester Gap to Charlottesville to destroy the railroad bridge over the Rivanna River.

At Front Royal a dispatch was received from General Wright, acting army commander during Sheridan's absence, in which Wright expressed concern for his right flank from which Sheridan had withdrawn the cavalry, and enclosing a message which Union signalmen had intercepted as it was transmitted by flag code from the Confederate signal station on Three Top Mountain. The message picked up and translated by Union Signal officers who were familiar with the Confederate code, read as follows:

To Lieutenant General Early:
  Be ready to move as soon as my forces join you, and we will crush Sheridan.
            Longstreet, Lieutenant-General.

Although Sheridan appraised the ruse at its true value (*Longstreet* was in fact still convalescing from the wound received in the Battle of the Wilderness), he thought it best to take no chances. The Charlottesville raid was called off and the cavalry sent packing back to the army.

Sheridan's little group reached Washington about 8 o'clock on the morning of October 17, proceeded to the War Department, and conferred with Stanton and Halleck. In a short discussion the volatile Sheridan convinced his superiors that their plan for him to operate east of the Blue

Ridge should be dropped in favor of establishing a defensive line that could be held in the Valley with reduced forces, so that a large part of the army might be transferred to Grant at Petersburg. Two engineer officers were attached to accompany Sheridan on his return journey for the purpose of developing the proposed defense line.

At 12 noon, four hours after reaching Washington, Sheridan's augmented party boarded a special train for Martinsburg, where they arrived about dark, to find an escort of 300 cavalrymen who had by prearrangement been detailed to escort the commanding general through Winchester to Cedar Creek. Sheridan spent that night at Martinsburg. On the morning of October 18, the party mounted up and started for Winchester, but the two engineer officers were so unaccustomed to horseback journeys that the better part of the day was used up in covering the intervening twenty-eight miles. On reaching Winchester late in the afternoon, Sheridan took the engineers over the heights about Winchester to survey the possibilities for a defense line there.

A mounted messenger whom Sheridan sent to Cedar Creek for information on the situation at the front returned at dark about the time that Sheridan and the engineers reached the Logan house, where Colonel Edwards was staying and where the Army Commander planned to spend the night. The news was reassuring—all quiet at Cedar Creek and Fisher's Hill—so Sheridan turned in at an early hour with the intension of completing his journey in leisurely fashion next morning.

EARLY SURPRISES THE FEDERAL VIII CORPS AT CEDAR CREEK

CHAPTER 12

THE BATTLE OF CEDAR CREEK—FIRST PHASE

THE Battle of Cedar Creek was fought on October 19, one month and a day after the Battle of Winchester (the Opequon). Both at Winchester and Fisher's Hill, three days later, the Confederates, outnumbered at least two to one, had fought defensively, been defeated, routed, and pursued ineffectually by the Union army. During the following weeks Sheridan's cavalry was engaged in thoroughly burning out the Shenandoah Valley, from mountain to mountain, all the way north from Harrisonburg to Strasburg, making it next to impossible for *Early's* army to subsist except by long wagon hauls of forage and rations from the railhead east of the Blue Ridge.

Early was thus faced with a decision either to withdraw entirely from the Valley, leaving Sheridan in undisputed

281

possession, or to attack in the hope of driving him out. The latter would appear, in light of the facts, to be a forlorn hope, but *Early* and his generals didn't see it that way. The arrival of reinforcements had given them fresh strength, and they believed that a well-executed surprise attack would likely meet with success, particularly since, as they thought, part of Sheridan's army had been returned to the Army of the Potomac.

The absence of General Sheridan meant that his army would be commanded temporarily by General Wright, a corps commander who had earned a sound reputation, but was without experience in leading more than a corps in battle. That did not necessarily mean that the army would fall apart if attacked, but there was always the chance that an acting commander might not secure the best results from troops accustomed to the sure hand of a leader who had proven his capacity and in whom they had complete confidence.

General Wesley Merritt, commanding the First Cavalry Division, in his account of the Battle of Cedar Creek, points out that "The occupation of that line was not intended to be permanent; there were many serious objecttions to it as a position for defense. The approaches from all points of the enemy's stronghold at Fisher's Hill were through wooded ravines in which the growth and undulations concealed the movement of troops, and for this reason and its proximity to Fisher's Hill the pickets protecting its front could not be thrown, without danger of capture, sufficiently far to the front to give ample warning of the advance of the enemy."

Accepting Merritt's evaluation of the Union army's position at face value, and assuming that acting army commander Wright held the same view, we have the additional evidence, from Wright's message to Sheridan, en route to Washington, that he was sensitive about his right (west) flank, which in the absence of Torbert's cavalry failed to extend as far as the Back Road, along the base of Little Mountain. Hence, when because of the phony intercepted Confederate flag message two of the cavalry divisions, Custer's and Merritt's, were sent back by Sheridan, leaving Powell with one brigade to operate in the vicinity of Front Royal, Wright placed both of them on his right flank, and no doubt felt easier in his mind as a result. Moore's brigade of Powell's cavalry division was also returned to Wright from Front Royal, eight miles east of Strasburg, but he apparently felt little concern about his left flank, in the mistaken belief that because of the terrain obstacles, Three Top Mountain and the Shenandoah River, there was no danger of a surprise attack from that direction. However, he did assign Moore's brigade to picket Buckton Ford on the Shenandoah River, almost two miles down river from Bowman's Ford and too far distant to be of any use when the Confederates crossed at the latter place.

EARLY PLANS A FLANK ATTACK

Early's decision to attack having been made, it was necessary to determine when, where, and how the decision would be implemented. He did not feel strong enough to make a frontal assault against the entrenched Union position on the high ground north of Cedar Creek. That left only a flank attack. The big question was, which flank?

On October 17 Division Commander *Pegram* was directed to make a reconnaissance as far as Cedar Creek on the front of his division, which covered the Middle Road between the Valley Pike and the Back Road, to ascertain the feasibility of an attack on the enemy right flank. General *Gordon*, accompanied by Brigadier General *Clement A. Evans*, one of his brigade commanders, Major *Robert H. Hunter*, a member of his division staff, and Captain *Jed*

Hotchkiss, topographical engineer on *Early's* staff, was given a similar mission, to examine the enemy dispositions and the terrain on the Union left; both to report back to *Early* with recommendations.

Pegram's reconnaissance developed the fact that the banks of Cedar Creek were steep, with tortuous curves, and strongly guarded by Federals in the sector that marked the Union right; in consequence an attack there would encounter difficulties that might be avoided elsewhere. Thus it was clear that the enemy right would not be *Early's* first choice as a target.

Gordon with his three companions climbed Three Top Mountain on foot, a difficult and tiresome journey, but one that promised rich dividends. General *Evans,* a careful diarist, recorded the journey in a brief entry for October 17: "2½ P.M. in company with General *Gordon* and two or three staff officers went to the signal station on the top of "Three Top" Mountain. From this position the entire camp of the enemy is visible. Also an extent of the country twenty miles wide and thirty miles long."

Looking down from the Confederate signal station on the mountain top, the field glasses of the Confederate officers sought out the roads, streams, and fords, the hills and valleys, the houses and barns, the camps and headquarters of the several components of the Union army. As noted by the observant *Gordon* and confirmed by the meticulous map genius, *Jed Hotchkiss,* who rapidly sketched in the gratifying panorama spread out before them:

Not only the general outlines of Sheridan's breastworks, but every parapet where his heavy guns were mounted, and every piece of artillery, every wagon and tent and supporting line of troops, were in easy range of our vision. I could count, and did count, the number of his guns. I could see distinctly the three colors of trimmings on the jackets respectively of infantry, artillery, and cavalry, and locate each, while the number of flags gave a basis for estimating approximately the forces with which we were to contend in the proposed attack. If, however, the plan of battle which at once suggested itself to my mind should be adopted, it mattered little how large a force General Sheridan had; for the movement which I intended to propose contemplated the turning of Sheridan's flank where he least expected it, a sudden irruption upon his left and rear, and the complete surprise of his entire army.

General *Evans* was equally impressed and so excited by the prospect for a surprise victory that the mountain reconnaissance had disclosed that he took time the following morning to describe his experience in an informative letter to his wife.

Bivouac—Fisher's Hill
near Strasburg, Va.
October 18, 1864

My dearest Allie—
Yesterday I made a reconnaissance with my brigade in the direction of Cedar Creek beyond which the enemy were found to be entrenched on the hills and encamped behind their entrenchments. I returned to camp at 2 P.M. with the brigade and hastily eating dinner set out to go to the top of the mountain on our right where we have a signal station. I rode as far as possible but found that I had to leave my horse and litterly (sic) climb on foot about three quarters of a mile along the crest to get to the signal station. It was so steep that I had to travel on all fours pulling along by the rocks and bushes. The face of the mountain is covered with occasional bushes of mountain growth and small stunted trees. In many places for hundreds of yards it was all rock piled one against the other of various sizes and over these I had to clamber like a coon. My strength was nearly exhausted when I reached the top, although I had rested frequently. But after another short rest I pushed on along the narrow ridge until I arrived at the Signal Station or "look-out," which was the extreme northern end of the mountain where a tremendous pile of over hanging rock makes a precipice down which you may jump half a mile with perfect ease but not

with much safety. What a splendid sight was before me. You can form some idea of it from the view you obtain by reaching the top of Clark's Mountain. But it was far superior to that. Strasburg, Middletown, Newton, and Winchester were in sight visible to the naked eye. The vision was limited by the Blue Ridge on the right, the Alleghanies on the left and before you it melted far off into a hazy horizon,—like a narrow ditch filled with waters of the Shenandoah which wound its way through the plain at the foot of the mountain toward the Blue Ridge, while Cedar Creek, like a placid rill showing here and there between the occasional patches of wood, finally buried itself below Strasburg in the bosom of the Shenandoah. So elevated is the position that the valley presented the appearance of a vast level plain, the highest hills scarcely undertaking its surface. The Valley pike, like a white ribbon lay along the center, the country roads looked like foot paths, the woods like parks and the fields like little gardens with nice fences dividing. But the whole view presented a magnificent natural picture. The interest of the scene was of course heightened by the full view presented of the enemy's camp. Nearly every tent was visible. We were able to locate precisely his cavalry, his artillery, his infantry and his wagon train. We could see precisely where he had run his line of entrenchments and where they stopped. Even the house where Sheridan made his headquarters was pointed out. There all was with the roads leading to it, the place where he could be best attacked and how the lines could move, how far to go and what to do,—just like a large map. I believe that we can litterly route them if we attack their left flank. Tonight we will probably move. Tomorrow, in all probability, we will have a great battle and I trust a brilliant victory. How many poor fellows must die. How many be maimed for life. How many suffer from wounds. Poor men, poor widows, poor orphans, victims of this bloody work. The weather is delightful during the day but the nights are quite cool. I sleep with Capt. Cody and we join our covering thus making enough for comfort . . . Good-bye now. The Good Being keep and preserve you in his care—

Your husband

It was *Gordon's* belief that Sheridan concurred in the generally accepted opinion that the rugged and apparently impassable face of Three Top Mountain ruled out any possibility of a Confederate maneuver that could place a force of men in position to launch an attack on that flank. Clearly Wright held to that opinion, evidenced by his message to Sheridan at Front Royal which revealed his concern for the army right flank, and the additional fact that he placed the bulk of his cavalry on that flank. It should be noted, however, that Sheridan was not quite so blind to the possibility of a move against the Union left, judging by the message he sent back to Wright with the return of Torbert's cavalry: "The cavalry is all ordered back to you . . . Close in Colonel Powell, who will be at this point (presumably Front Royal) . . . Look well to your ground, and be well prepared." (Powell's Second Cavalry Division was operating on the army left, but at too great a distance for close-in security).

As it turned out, Wright was so preoccupied with fears for his right flank that he only partly followed Sheridan's advice to "close in Colonel Powell," whose cavalry was busily engaged in the Front Royal area on a mission of burning bridges, tanneries, mills, and other Confederate property, and in skirmishing with *Mosby's* guerrillas, who were active in the region. Powell's division (except for Moore's brigade) in any event was among the missing when the battle occurred at Cedar Creek, as shown by a sentence in his official report which read: "October 19, all quiet on my front since the 13th."

Hotchkiss reported to his chief that evening when he got back. *Early's* snapping black eyes must have brightened visibly as he examined the engineer's sketch map that nakedly revealed the Union army's innermost tactical secrets. Because neither camouflage nor aerial photographs had yet been invented, the element of surprise, upon which

Early would have to depend for success against Union odds, hinged largely on two vital factors; his ability definitely to ascertain enemy vulnerability, if it existed, and then to find ways and means to exploit the weakness.

The Confederate commander now had the answer to the first question. Sheridan's left flank was not only badly exposed, it was almost entirely unprotected, a cardinal military sin for which Sheridan must share the blame with Wright, upon whom rested the nominal responsibility for security during Sheridan's absence. It may be questioned whether the latter's advice to Wright to pull Powell's cavalry in to cover the army left flank was sufficiently emphatic. Conceivably Sheridan shared the general belief that the character of the terrain in that area made a flank attack improbable. Nevertheless the warning had been given, and if Wright had been alert he would at least have impressed on Crook the need for greater infantry security in view of the lack of cavalry in the area of the Eighth Corps camps.

On the morning of October 18 General *Gordon* personally reported to *Early* to supplement *Hotchkiss'* staff report of the preceding evening. *Early's Memoirs* and *Gordon's Reminiscences of the Civil War* are in disagreement as to who originated the idea for the surprise attack, although the accounts agree on the essentials. According to *Early,* the *Hotchkiss* map, which "designated the roads in the enemy's rear, and the house of a Mr. Cooley as a favorable point for forming an attacking column, after it crossed the river, in order to move against the enemy and strike him on the Valley Pike in rear of his works," was the major factor which caused him to make his tactical decision "if it should prove practicable to move a column between the base of the mountain and the river." According to *Early, Gordon* "confirmed the report of Captain *Hotchkiss,* expressing confidence that the attack could be successfully made on the enemy's left and rear." *Early* wrote that he then sent General *Gordon* and Captain *Hotchkiss* to ascertain the practicability of a possible route at the base of the mountain, and simultaneously gave directions for everything to be in readiness to move that night, October 18, the division commanders to assemble at *Early's* quarters at 2 p.m. to receive final instructions.

In *Gordon's* story of what occurred, he himself conceived the plan to turn the enemy left, while *Early* is represented as having decided initially to attack Sheridan's right and center because of the impossibility of moving troops around his left. *Gordon's* opinion was that, since a surprise attack against the enemy left and rear offered such a favorable opportunity for victory and would be the last thing that the Union army would expect, every effort must be made to locate a route for the approach march. *Gordon* expressed to his own officers the confident belief that such a route *could* be found.

From a careful reading of the two accounts, and keeping in mind the fact that *Early* and *Gordon* seldom saw eye to eye, and that *Gordon's* official report on the Battle of Cedar Creek mysteriously disappeared and was never published, his *Reminiscences* have the ring of truth to the objective reader who takes the trouble to sift both accounts. But regardless of whether the plan was evolved through *Gordon's* initiative and determination in overcoming obstacles to make it work, *Early* had to make the final decision to proceed along that line, and to that extent must be considered the architect of the plan.

In any event, *Gordon* and *Hotchkiss* retraced their steps the morning of October 18, and were rewarded by finding a little-used, narrow, tree-covered pathway only wide enough to accommodate an infantry troop column in single file. A quick calculation revealed that it would take a single corps all night to pass around the nose of the mountain, and it would not be easy. The movement of artillery by that route would be out of the question. From Fisher's Hill to the Shenandoah River, around the nose of Massanutten Mountain to Bowman's Ford, the point selected for crossing the river, would require a march of about five miles; from there to the Cooley House, where the ground was open and the columns could close up and deploy, an additional mile and a half would have to be traversed, all of the distance after crossing the river to be across country, up and down hills, through woods and thickets.

BATTLE ORDERS ARE ISSUED

By two o'clock in the afternoon the plan had been perfected. The division commanders reported as directed and were given their respective missions. *Early* had decided on a movement in four columns, as follows:

The three divisions of the *Second Corps, Gordon's, Ramseur's,* and *Pegram's* under *Gordon's* temporary command, to move over the concealed route around the nose of the mountain and be in position to attack the enemy left and rear at 5 o'clock in the morning, just before daybreak.

Kershaw's and *Wharton's divisions,* with all the artillery, under *Early's* personal command, to move along the Valley Pike through Strasburg to attack the enemy front as soon as *Gordon's corps* should become engaged.

The cavalry brigades of *Rosser* and *Wickham,* under command of the former, to cross Cedar Creek on the Back Road to engage the enemy cavalry at the same time that *Gordon* attacked the opposite flank.

Lomax's cavalry brigade to move by Front Royal, cross the river, and return to strike the enemy on the Valley Pike wherever he might be found, his location to be determined by the sounds of battle.

It was a bold, ambitious undertaking, whose very audacity was perhaps its best recommendation. Only a general of sufficient offensive-mindedness, with equally aggressive subordinates, could envisage such an attack with confidence and equanimity. For a heavily outnumbered, less efficiently equipped army, twice routed by this same opponent, to divide into four echelons of attack with no hope of coordination in the initial stages, for the purpose of making what amounted to a quadruple envelopment from four points of the compass, can only be described as taking a calculated risk with a vengeance. It was a desperate gamble to which *Jubal Early* had committed his army, either from dire necessity to escape from a military straitjacket, or because the exposed position of Sheridan's left flank confirmed in the Confederate commander's mind his original impression that Sheridan's generalship was unequal to his assignment.

Knowledge of the Union countersign for October 19 would be of immeasurable value to the Confederates if somehow it could be obtained. The pains already taken to guarantee surprise indicated the importance of that element in *Early's* plans. The history books do not mention it, but a letter from Sergeant Bell, Company F, 110th Ohio Volunteer Infantry, serving in Crook's corps, informed his family after the battle: "A Confederate woman 'heavy-dated' the countersign out of a Union commander (not Sheridan) and sent her Negro servant to deliver it to the Confederate General, *'Jubal Early.'* Just before daybreak (when the guards would change) Gen. *Early* armed his advance guard with his countersign, and they 'relieved' the Union pickets thus opening the way for General *Early's* attack, in the 'gray of the morning.'"

Sergeant Bell does not take the trouble to explain how the information about the romantic Union officer and his alleged treasonable carelessness may have filtered down to the ranks. He might even have conjured up the incident to entertain the folks back home with a bit of innocent Munchausen-like battle news, but it *could* have happened the way the sergeant told it.

Supplementary instructions issued by *Early* included the hasty construction of a temporary bridge across the Shenandoah River one mile east of Fisher's Hill, to accommodate the first crossing of that river by the *Second Corps*. *Gordon* was told, when he should reach the Cooley farm, to point his attack for the Belle Grove house, west of the Valley Pike, where Sheridan's headquarters were known to have been established (although *Early* doesn't say how that information was acquired); a guide familiar with the country would be assigned him to point the way. *Colonel Payne's* force of three hundred cavalrymen was attached to *Gordon's* corps to accompany that column for the express purpose of capturing General Sheridan. *Rosser's cavalry* was to attack up the Back Road before daylight, simultaneously with *Gordon's* attack, in the hope of surprising the Federal cavalry on the Union right while in their camps, before they could get to their horses. The artillery would mass during the night on the pike west of Fisher's Hill, prepared to gallop forward to Hupp's Hill at 5 a.m., the hour designated for the attack on both flanks, any movement prior thereto being forbidden lest the noise of the wheels on the hard road give advance warning to the Federals.

Watches were synchronized and the division commanders then returned to their units to pass the orders down the line. Canteens, swords, and every other item of personal equipment that might make a noise were turned in to the supply sergeants in the *Second Corps* and the men were instructed not to strike matches or speak above a whisper when they reached and started around the mountain path, lest the Union pickets along the river below should hear them and become suspicious. The surprise must be complete—a careless slip by a single soldier might jeopardize the entire project.

The Night March of the Second Corps

Gordon's men entered into the spirit of the affair with enthusiasm, since theirs would be the most important part in the enterprise. His three divisions moved out as soon as night fell. In single file, closed up to make certain that no soldier should lose contact with the man in front, the long column wound its snakelike way across the river and around the mountain, all night long. As an added guarantee against anyone losing his way, *Gordon* had arranged to have a courier stationed at every road fork along the selected route, right up to the crossing point at Bowman's Ford.

As the column neared the river, one of the Confederate scouts in advance of the main body saw in the darkness what looked like two Federal pickets, standing guard along the side of the road. It was a ticklish moment and could very well give the whole show away if the bluecoats should open fire. While the column halted, *Gordon* sent a staff officer with several scouts to crawl along on hands and knees until close enough to pounce on the pickets before they could awaken to their danger. The task was accomplished in the scouts' best cloak-and-dagger style, but just as they were about to seize the pickets and force their surrender, the enemy turned out to be two cedar bushes in the corner of a rail fence!

The approach march to the river having been completed without further incident and in good time, the troops of the *Second Corps* rested to await the attack hour specified in *Early's* order. *Gordon* has left a dramatic description of that moment:

For nearly an hour we waited for the appointed time, resting near the bank of the river in the middle of which the Union vedettes sat upon their horses, wholly unconscious of the presence of the gray-jacketed foe, who from the ambush of night, like crouching lions from the jungle, were ready to spring upon them. The whole situation was unspeakably impressive. Everything conspired to make the conditions both thrilling and weird. The men were resting, lying in long lines on the thickly matted grass or reclining in groups, their hearts thumping, their ears eagerly listening for the orders: "Attention, men!" "Fall in!" "Forward!" At brief intervals members of the staff withdrew to a point where they could safely strike a match and examine watches in order to keep me advised of the time. In the still starlit night, the only sounds heard were the gentle rustle of leaves by the October wind, the low murmur of the Shenandoah flowing swiftly along its rocky bed and dashing against the limestone cliffs that bordered it, the churning of the water by the feet of horses on which sat Sheridan's faithful pickets, and the subdued tones or half-whispers of my men as they thoughtfully communed with each other as to the fate which might befall each in the next hour.

Concurrently with the stealthy approach march of *Gordon's divisions, Kershaw* and *Wharton* moved during the night to their jumpoff positions. For this phase of the army attack *Early* had modified his original plan so that *Kershaw's division,* after passing through Strasburg, would angle off to the right from the pike, cross Cedar Creek at Bowman's Mill, and assault the Union left flank at the same time that *Gordon* was launching his attack in a westerly direction from the Cooley house, against Sheridan's left and rear, a mile and a half further north. No change was made in the orders to *Wharton's division,* which would simultaneously engage the enemy frontally along the Valley Pike and at the same time cover the Confederate artillery in the vicinity of Hupp's Hill.

The almost complete lack of security precautions on the left of the Union army at Cedar Creek, in view of the probability of a Confederate attack, is one of those things which has never been adequately explained. In the official report of the battle of October 19 filed by the acting army commander, General Wright stated that about 9 o'clock on the evening of October 18, General Crook reported to him that an infantry brigade sent out that day to reconnoiter the enemy position had returned with the information that "nothing was to be found in his old camp and that he had doubtless retreated up the valley." Wright went on to say that the reconnaissance report sounded plausible on the premise that the Union officers, anticipating for some days that because of the destruction of all the food supplies in the Valley *Early* would have to either attack or withdraw, accepted the report as an indication that the withdrawal was at least probable. To confirm the reconnaissance party's report, however, Wright ordered two additional reconnaissances to be made at daylight the following morning, by an infantry brigade of Emory's corps up the Valley Pike and by a cavalry brigade along the Back Road on the west.

There can be no doubt that Crook's "Army of Western Virginia," or Eighth Corps as it was variably called, was lulled into a sense of false security by the negative report of its reconnaissance brigade. We are not told how far the brigade traveled, but it certainly turned in a poor performance, in the light of events the next morning. It doesn't take long for news to circulate through army ranks, so it is likely that Crook's divisions, in their semi-detached position on the army left, north of Cedar Creek and about a mile east of the left flank of the neighboring Nineteenth Corps, turned in to their bunks that night with a confident feeling that the Rebs were pulling out and would not disturb the peace of their camp.

A curious incident that occurred during the night should have shaken General Crook's assurance to the extent of making him a bit more alert to the situation than seems to have been the case. He himself has stated in his autobiography that his Officer of the Day, while making his nightly rounds, heard noises outside the picket line. "In the belief that the noise was made by Union cavalry," Crook wrote, "The officer went out to investigate and was captured by the enemy without being able to give the alarm." In the Army service of security, the officer of the day is the important representative of the commander upon whose shoulders rests a vital responsibility for the safety of the command, and the night-long disappearance of such a one would not ordinarily be treated as a routine occurrence, without sparking a prompt and positive reaction from his commanding officer. The Eighth Corps, from General Crook on down, would appear to have had much to explain had a court of inquiry been assembled following the Battle of Cedar Creek.

George Crook, a cavalryman serving with infantry, who was destined in post-Civil War years to gain a large measure of fame as an Indian fighter on the Western frontier, seems to have considered it the sole responsibility of the cavalry to provide the covering screen for the army. His autobiography records the statement that about the middle of October "General Sheridan took the cavalry pickets from my front on Cedar Creek, leaving several fords unpicketed. Soon after General Sheridan left (on his quick trip to Washington), I called General Wright's attention to the pickets having been taken off, and he promised to replace them." Nevertheless, Crook must have been conversant with Sheridan's well-known policy of keeping his cavalry concentrated for effective utilization in a combat role, and cannot be excused for failure to provide his own infantry security protection, with or without cavalry.

Crook's camp had been pitched on open, level ground along the upper edge of a steep, narrow ravine through which Cedar Creek follows a southeasterly course on its way to join the Shenandoah River a half mile to the west of Bowman's Ford, where *Gordon's* Confederates effected their crossing. The locale of the camp was a half-mile east of the pike where Cedar Creek makes a sharp right bend. To the south the ground sloped downward from the camp, to meet the aforementioned ravine a mile further along. To the east and north, however, the terrain was wide open, a fact of which the Confederates took full advantage in planning the approach route that they had spotted from Three Top Mountain.

So unsuspecting was army headquarters of the Confederate plan for a surprise attack that General Crook, by invitation of General Sheridan, made his personal headquarters with Sheridan at Belle Grove, a good mile from the camp of the Eighth Corps as the crow flies and even further by road. Sheridan held a high opinion of Crook's military judgment and capabilities and may have felt that the latter's actual presence at army headquarters would add a measure of insurance when the army was committed to Wright's command during Sheridan's trip to Washington.

Defense positions for the two divisions of Crook's corps had been selected and breastworks of a sort constructed by Colonel Thoburn's First Division, which was posted in an isolated position on a hill top a mile south of the camp, some distance east and north of Cedar Creek. Colonel R. B. Hayes' undersized Second Division was cast in the role of corps reserve, without any specific terrain assignment; a tactical anomaly the fallacy of which was soon to be revealed by the Confederate surprise envelopment of the left rear of Sheridan's army. Crook had one other infantry detachment at his disposal, a small provisional brigade under Colonel J. H. Kitching, stationed several hundred yards north of the Second Division, a half-mile east of the Valley Pike and just off the country road that led to the west past Union army headquarters at Belle Grove House. Neither Hayes' nor Kitching's camps were protected by earthworks.

Crook's artillery, commanded by Captain Henry A. Du-Pont, consisting of three batteries whose armament added up to sixteen guns, was posted on two high, narrow, diverging ridges dominating the main highway and the Cedar Creek ford and bridge in front of the camp. The caissons, horses, and trains were hidden in the narrow, V-shaped ravine between the ridges.

A Confederate Tidal Wave

Jubal Early's scheme of maneuver had been planned with great care. The key to its success would be the simultaneous attack on Sheridan's front, flanks, and rear—all based on the principle of surprise. The several elements of his army were all in their initial attack positions well before daylight, shivering in the cold air of late October and drenched with the moisture of a light fog which hugged the low ground along the streams and in the ravines and depressions which abound in the Strasburg area.

As General *Gordon's* watch ticked off the seconds, he calculated the length of time it would take his leading division to reach the Cooley house, where his force would be on Sheridan's flank and rear, in position to launch the surprise attack on the Union camp at 5 o'clock, the hour designated by General *Early*. When the moment arrived, he gave the go-ahead signal to General *Payne*, whose cavalry would precede the infantry on its specific mission to

MAP 12. BATTLE OF CEDAR CREEK, OCTOBER 19, 1864, OPENING PHASE

This shows the routes taken by the Confederates to their jumpoff positions; and the start of the attack is portrayed. The weight of the initial assault fell on Crook's VIII Corps, then on the XIX Corps, both of which were forced north, the VIII in great confusion. The Confederate demonstration at Cupp's Ford lacked authenticity and was easily fended off by part of Custer's division. This left the bulk of Custer's division and all of Merritt's available for close-in support of the Federal infantry. Two of Dupont's batteries are in front of Thoburn's division. The one on the east, Battery D, 1st Pennsylvania Light, was overrun; the other, Battery B, 5th U. S., and the third, Battery L, 1st Ohio (shown just south of the camp), were withdrawn along the pike to the 2d position, where they rendered good service.

This map is based on the Gillespie map mentioned under Map 11. The Jed Hotchkiss map, Plate 82 (9), was also consulted for Confederate dispositions.

HILL AT CEDAR CREEK OCCUPIED BY SHERIDAN'S LEFT

drive directly for Sheridan's headquarters.

Payne's troopers at once rode into the shallow water of the river, galloped across the ford, firing as they rode, and drove the surprised handful of Federal pickets in wild flight to the rear. *Gordon's division,* under command of its senior brigadier, General *Evans,* rushed through the chill waters behind the cavalry, followed in turn by the divisions of *Ramseur* and *Pegram.* The cold waters of the Shenandoah lent added stimulus to the martial exuberance of the excited soldiers, to induce a "double-quick" pace that brought them in short order to their assault position a mile or so beyond the river.

Wheeling into line at the Cooley house, the *Second Corps* faced west, with *Ramseur* on the right, *Evans* on the left, *Pegram* in support, and moved rapidly forward to engulf the unsuspecting, completely surprised Union camp of Crook's Eighth Corps, many of whose men were still sleeping peacefully in their tents. *Payne's* troopers, galloping in a heavy mass through part of the camp, naturally aroused many of Crook's men, but *Gordon's* infantry followed so closely on the heels of the cavalry that the Union breastworks were only partly manned by half-dressed men whose initial surprise quickly turned to confused terror as wave after wave of yelling, shooting Confederate footsoldiers poured into and through their camp.

Private *G. W. Nichols, 61st Georgia,* a unit of *Evans' brigade* of *Gordon's division,* recounted his personal experience and observaticns in the course of the Confederate attack on Crook's camps:*

We advanced up the road at double quick to a certain place and stopped. We faced the Yankees' camp and advanced thru the wood in fine order. The enemy was not aware of our being anywhere near them till a few of their camp guards began to shoot at us. It was then light enough for us to see their camps.

We advanced in a run and raised the Rebel yell. At this signal Kershaw advanced from a different place and raised a terrible yell. The Yankees fired a few cannon shot at Kershaw's men and then fled. We were soon in their camp. The most of them were still in bed when we raised the yell and began firing at them. They jumped up running, and did not take time to put on their clothing, but fled in their night clothes, without their guns, hats or shoes. We were shooting them as fast as we could, and yelling as loud as we could to see them run. It was the worst stampede I ever saw. We captured about 20 stands of colors and some of Sheridan's men told me in Savannah Ga. the next June that some of the Yankees ran to Winchester, which is 15 miles away, in their night-clothes, without shoes or hats. We took many prisoners and captured nearly all of their wagons, artillery, ambulances, horses, mules and a great deal of clothing, shoes, blankets, tents, etc. I saw one Union soldier who had been killed with only one shoe on. We ran in pursuit of them until we had gotten about two miles from their camp, then everything was halted. A great many

---

* G. W. Nichols, *op. cit.*

of us went back to their camp after blankets, shoes, clothing, etc. and to my surprise, General Early had his own wagons and artillery brought over Cedar Creek. It seemed that there were no Yankees in our front. Everything was quiet as death. Some of our boys went to sleep while the others were plundering the camps. I got two nice new tent flies, two fine blankets, a fine rubber cloth, two new overshirts and two pair of new shoes. In fact, we could get anything we wanted except Yankee money.

Kershaw's division, which under *Early's* modified plan had been given a combined frontal and flank attack mission in Crook's sector, advanced in complete silence to Robert's Ford, near Bowman's Mill, where Cedar Creek makes a complete 360-degree loop. *Kershaw's* outfit neared the creek somewhat ahead of schedule, while *Gordon's divisions* were still crossing the river, and *Rosser's cavalry* on the left was moving along the Back Road to its position. All in all, however, the preliminary approach march and development of the several subdivisions of *Early's army* was conducted in a superior manner, and if the synchronization of the widely separated divisions and brigades was not perfect the margin was very slim indeed.

At Robert's Ford a previously instructed detachment of *Kershaw's division* dashed with a minimum of noise across the creek in the darkness a few minutes before five o'clock, surprising and capturing nearly all of the Union pickets assigned to guard the ford. Still observing silence, *Kershaw* crossed his division and advanced without throwing forward the customary skirmishers. Within a matter of minutes his fanned-out columns overran and outflanked the partially manned entrenchments that were the responsibility of Thoburn's division. Having received no warning from their pickets along Cedar Creek, most of whom *Kershaw* had quietly gathered in, the Federals in Thoburn's line, or most of them, were awakened from peaceful sleep to find the Confederates swarming over and around their works. Thoburn's men fled in confusion to the rear, the enemy firing happily at those who ran to avoid capture, their pace being undoubtedly quickened by the noise of heavy musketry to the northeast, which indicated that the enemy was already in rear of Crook's base camp.

While *Kershaw's division* was engaged in driving Thoburn's east of Cedar Creek, *Wharton's division* had moved forward in the darkness to occupy Hupp's Hill, straddling the Valley Pike one mile north of Strasburg, where the division quietly deployed to cover *Early's artillery,* the latter under orders to gallop forward to that prominent landmark as soon as the attack opened and there would be no further need for secrecy. Upon the arrival of the guns, *Wharton* was to advance for the purpose of seizing the bridge on the pike where it crossed Cedar Creek near Burnt Mill, directly in front of the defense line of Emory's Nineteenth Corps.

Captain DuPont, Crook's artillery chief, recorded the start of the battle as between 4:30 and 5 o'clock, when he "was aroused by some distant firing on our extreme right which was caused by *Rosser's* demonstration on the Back Road, and a few minutes later there were some scattered shots along our front." "Not being fully awake," DuPont remarked, "my first impression was that our pickets were chopping wood to make fires, the night being quite cool, but as the firing did not cease I jumped up, put on my clothes, ordered my horse, called the chief bugler and directed him to sound the 'reveille,' which, repeated at the different battery camps, turned the men out for roll call. My first impulse was to have 'boots and saddles' sounded—which would have meant that horses were to be harnessed and batteries made ready for immediate action; but upon reflecting that under orders from Army Headquarters we had stood to arms at 2 a.m. for three or four nights previously, and that no such instructions had been given for the past night (presumably for some good reason), I concluded that 'boots and saddles' might needlessly alarm our infantry; and then, too, a surprise seemed unlikely, as it was generally known that a brigade of the Nineteenth Corps was ordered to make a reconnaissance in force at daybreak to feel the enemy. As the men of Light Battery B were answering to their names at roll call, a tremendous sound of volley firing suddenly burst forth at the entrenchments on the heights above (*Gordon's* attack on the army left rear).''

As the tidal wave of *Kershaw's* advance washed over Thoburn's position and moved on, DuPont's immobilized Pennsylvania battery of six ten-pounder Parrott guns, deprived of all infantry support, was captured after a desperate hand-to-hand encounter in which a number of the gunners were bayoneted or knocked down by clubbed muskets beside their pieces, unable to spot any targets because of the dim light and fog.

DuPont's own Regular battery, Light Battery B, Fifth U. S. Artillery posted about 400 yards from the Pennsylvania battery, was removed from the axis of *Kershaw's* advance, but nevertheless in danger of imminent capture. Under a withering fire of enemy muskets, and unable to see the Confederates because of the fog, Battery B (six 3-inch rifled guns), its guns loaded with canister, was ordered by DuPont to open fire, target or no target, aiming in the direction of the sound, so that the thunder of their cannon would alert the rest of the army to the onrushing danger. Lieutenant Brewerton, the battery commander, was directed to stand firm until the forms of enemy soldiers became visible through the fog, then abandon the limbers and run the guns by hand down into the ravine, where the caisson limbers would be waiting to be attached to the pieces and gallop to safety. That difficult order was efficiently executed under Confederate fire, with the result that five of the six guns were extricated from the battery's surrounded position and were available to perform a vital function in the latter stage of the battle.

DuPont's third battery, L of the First Ohio Artillery (four 12-pounder Napoleon guns), Captain Gibbs commanding, which occupied a small field-work on the extreme right of Crook's corps on the lower part of the second ridge covering the ford and bridge over Cedar Creek, opened with two guns in the semi-darkness at the approach of *Wharton's division.* The artillerymen saw only the flashes from the muzzles of the enemy muskets, but their fire was so accurately delivered that it brought the enemy advance up the pike to a halt until the Confederate artillery galloped up to Hupp's Hill, unlimbered, and poured its concentrated fire into the gallant Ohio battery. Only then, as *Wharton's* infantry advanced in overwhelming force, did the guns retire in safety, after delaying the attack of an entire Confederate division and gaining priceless time for DuPont's Regular battery to escape from its trap in the ravine and for many of Thoburn's infantrymen to make good their retreat.

As Gibbs' battery withdrew, Captain DuPont took charge, placing it in a new position about 800 yards farther along the turnpike, where it again opened fire on the advancing Confederates, protected by nearby infantry of the Sixth Corps. Soon however that corps also commenced its retirement, so the battery leapfrogged to the rear for the last time, to join the remaining five guns of DuPont's battery in position north of Middletown.

Two Union Corps Submerged

The Confederate surprise attack on the Union center and left had proven brilliantly successful, driving the half-

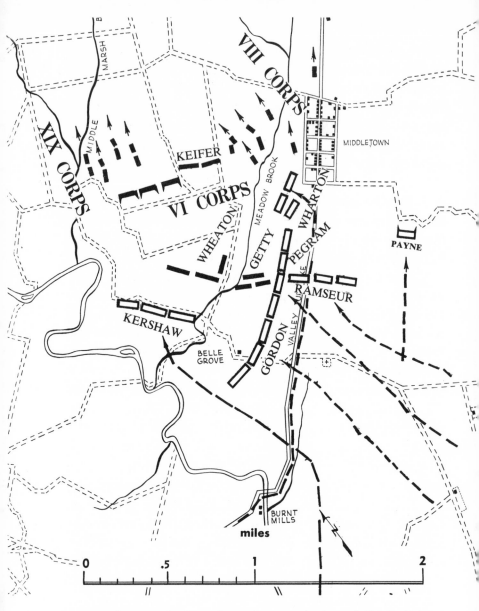

MAP 13. BATTLE OF CEDAR CREEK—SITUATION AT ABOUT 7:30-8:30 A.M.

The Confederate attack is losing some of its steam, as many of the men stop to loot the camps of the VIII and XIX Corps. The VIII Corps is withdrawing in disorder to the north. This is shown here somewhat schematically, for there is little or no cohesion in the units. The XIX is also retreating precipitately, though in better order than the VIII Corps. The VI Corps, supported on the right rear by the cavalry, is covering the withdrawal.

awake and mostly unarmed units of Crook's Eighth and Emory's Nineteenth Corps in frantic fright to the rear, and in the process capturing 18 guns, 11 of Emory's and 7 of Crook's. Just as *Early's* disciplined veterans had panicked at Fisher's Hill when terror seized the men individually and collectively with the realization that the enemy in large numbers had penetrated their flank and rear, so now at Cedar Creek the tables were turned, with Sheridan's troops on the receiving end. At such times even the firmest discipline gives way to confusion, so that it is every man for himself.

General *Early* in person accompanied *Kershaw*, watched his division cross Cedar Creek and take Thoburn's breastworks with virtually no opposition, then rode rapidly to Hupp's Hill, which he reached about the same time as his artillery. The heavy firing from *Gordon's corps* in the Union rear satisfied him that the attack in that quarter was proceeding as ordered.

The first mission of the Confederate artillery was to neutralize the fire of the guns of DuPont's Ohio battery, then holding up the advance of *Wharton's division.* This was accomplished just as the sun rose and the fog began to lift. *Wharton's division* and the artillery then moved forward, accompanied by *Early.* On the hill beyond Cedar Creek *Early* met *Gordon,* whose three divisions by then had completely dispersed Crook's two small divisions. *Kershaw's division,* coming up from the south, joined *Gordon's* leading units on the pike and the two forces pushed on to the west and north in pursuit of Crook's corps and the two divisions of Emory's Nineteenth Corps, which in turn had been badly outflanked when Crook's camps were overrun. Emory's corps, although alerted by the Eighth Corps' discomfiture and retreat, failed to profit by the warning and offered little if any resistance. One of Grover's brigades, already formed to make the ordered daylight reconnaissance in force on the army left, might have been expected to establish a defense line facing east, upon which the rest of the corps could rally when the Confederates attacked; instead of which Grover immediately ordered his men into their entrenchments, which faced south and permitted his left flank to remain exposed. Consequently Emory's unhinged corps, unnecessarily, was caught flat-footed even as Crook's had been, and its departure from the battlefield to the rear was equally prompt and disorganized.

General Wright, acting army commander, could do little to halt the rush to the rear, in spite of his efforts to form a line from the Nineteenth Corps to meet Gordon's attack. It was evident that Wright lacked the spark that seemed to fire the troops whenever Sheridan rode among them, for he was unable to stem the panic or even to stimulate their own officers to rally the men of the retreating Nineteenth. Wright thereupon sent orders to General Ricketts, acting commander of his own reliable Sixth Corps, which as yet undisturbed was standing firm on its reserve position to the right rear of the Nineteenth Corps, to move back to a new, more tenable position upon which Emory's corps could rally.

On the right of the Union position, where two divisions of cavalry protected what Wright had erroneously thought was his vulnerable flank, *Rosser's* demonstration up the Back Road with *Fitz Lee's cavalry* made no impression whatsoever, one reason being that Merritt's and Custer's Union cavalry divisions were neither surprised nor intimidated by the excitement on the army left and center. In contrast with the infantry, when *Rosser* advanced the cavalry was wide awake and half-way through breakfast, in conformity with the Sheridan-instilled doctrine that in the immediate presence of the enemy the cavalry must be ready to meet any dawn attack their opponents might choose to deliver. The cavalry reconnaissance brigade that Wright

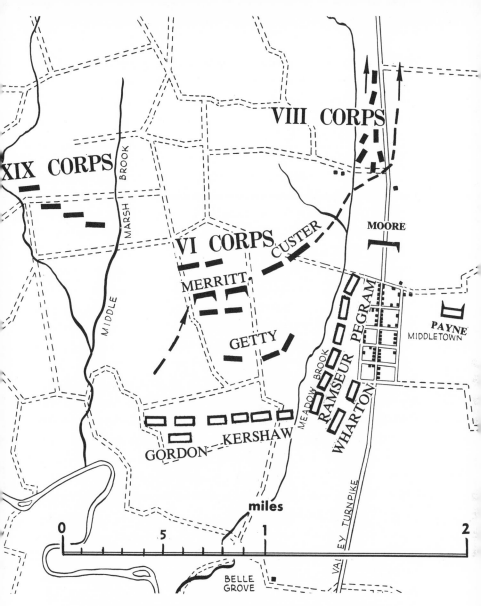

MAP 14. BATTLE OF CEDAR CREEK—SITUATION ABOUT 9:30 A.M.

The VI Corps continues to cover the withdrawal of the XIX and VII Corps, while the Confederates follow leisurely. Moore's brigade of Powell's cavalry division, brought up from Buckton Ford, and Merritt's cavalry division, are supporting the VI Corps. Custer, who assisted Merritt on the Federal right for about an hour, has been ordered to the extreme east flank, and is moving via the route shown. Merritt will also be moved, within the next half hour, to positions north of Middletown, to help cover that flank.

the evening before had ordered to move at daylight was on the road and opened on *Rosser's* cavalry with its carbines before *Rosser* had even come within sight of his objective, the cavalry camps. That firing appears to have opened the battle, as heard and reported by Captain DuPont of Crook's corps, several miles to the southeast.

While the retrograde movement of the Sixth Corps was proceeding in reasonably good order to its new position, Ricketts was severely wounded, the corps command thereupon devolving on division commander Getty. Between 8 and 9 a.m., and despite the loss of six artillery pieces to the Confederates, Getty conducted the withdrawal calmly and efficiently, checking the slowed-down Confederate advance by occasional counterattacks, and finally bringing the retrograde movement to a halt on a line facing the enemy about 1½ miles north of Middletown, with the left of the corps resting on the turnpike. Torbert's cavalry was pulled in from the right and redisposed to cover the corps flanks, while Emory was engaged in reassembling his scattered divisions on the right of the Sixth Corps in the direction of the Back Road. Farther to the north Crook established a rallying point for his Eighth Corps, but it would be quite some time before that badly disorganized and disrupted organization would be able to offer any serious opposition to the Confederates.

Early Hesitates

This was the moment, in the thinking of General *John B. Gordon,* field commander of three-fifths of *Early's* infantry, for the reunited Confederate army to exploit its stunning initial success by an all-out, concentrated, renewed attack which *Gordon* believed would complete the rout of the Union army by demolishing the still undefeated Sixth Corps. *Gordon* was of the opinion (although mistakenly) that Sheridan's cavalry had been driven by

Rosser on the Union right and that the Sixth Corps was vulnerable, with both flanks unprotected. In consultation with *Early's* able Chief of Artillery, Colonel *Thomas H. Carter, Gordon* informed him that most of Sheridan's artillery had already been captured and that he had ordered the three divisions under his *(Gordon's)* command to attack the Union Sixth Corps simultaneously in front and on both flanks. Were *Carter* to gallop along the turnpike with all his batteries and the captured pieces "to pour an incessant stream of shot and shell upon this solitary remaining corps," as *Gordon* expressed it, there was nothing that could save it from destruction. *Carter's* enthusiastic reply was to this effect: "General, you will need no infantry. With enfilade fire from my batteries I will destroy that corps in twenty minutes."

It is today a nice question whether or not *Gordon* was right in his conviction that a final massive Confederate attack would in fact have driven the Union forces from the field or destroyed them. In support of *Gordon's* thesis, Crook's artillery chief, West Pointer DuPont, wrote that *Early's* mistake was in pressing the attack on a broad front rather than sending a powerful column directly up the turnpike, which might well have turned the Sixth Corps' newly established flank, resting on the pike about a mile north of Middletown.

On the other hand, and despite the fact that two corps, more than half of the infantry of the Union army, had been overrun and dispersed in wild flight, the remaining Sixth Corps had neither panicked nor fled, while the powerful cavalry divisions under Custer and Merritt were still virtually intact and capable, if intelligently employed, of making *Early* pay dearly for any ill-advised tactical move that could expose his own tiring troops to a painful or even fatal reverse.

Wright's Sixth Corps was a strong, dependable, veteran

outfit, temporarily commanded by General Getty, who succeeded Ricketts when the latter was severely wounded in the early stages of the battle. But even the Sixth was unable to stem the rising Confederate tide when the Eighth and Nineteenth had been successively flanked and overrun. The First and Third Divisions of the Sixth Corps, in line parallel to the turnpike, had sustained the full force of the attack by *Gordon* and *Kershaw;* then their flanks were also turned and after a stubborn resistance they too had moved to the rear. Getty's own division, the Second, which was posted some distance from the other two, found itself the only organized unit, except the two cavalry divisions and two of DuPont's artillery batteries, left holding the field against the entire Confederate army.

If any one Union officer may be said to have contributed to *Early's* failure to exploit his initial success by acting upon the optimistic appraisal of his subordinate, *Gordon,* it was Brigadier General George W. Getty. When he discovered that the divisions on his right and left had pulled out, the acting corps commander calmly led his remaining division back across Meadow Branch and placed it on a strong defensive position upon a wooded eminence in rear of the stream. There he was shortly attacked by Confederates *Ramseur* and *Pegram.* Getty ordered his men to withhold their fire until the enemy was within thirty yards of them, when the Federals opened with a terrific volley. The Confederates broke and fell back in disorder. Reforming, they came forward in a second charge, and again were driven back. *Early* ordered up *Wharton's division* to assist *Ramseur* and *Pegram* in overcoming the strongly resisting Union island of defense. This time the three division attack was directed simultaneously against Getty's front and flank. For two hours he had held *Early* in check, but there was a limit. Displaying excellent judgment, Getty fell back, without confusion, placing his division at the junction of

312

a road crossing the turnpike 1½ miles north of Middletown where it became the anchor of the Union defense line upon which to rebuild the shattered fortunes of Sheridan's army. Here the Union retreat came to an end. *Early's* divisions required time to reorganize almost as badly as the Federals, who were for the moment relieved of the pressure of the Confederate pursuit. Federal officers rallied a portion of their men upon positions to which the more terrified of the runners would return as soon as they came to their senses and discovered that the world had not really come to an end.

By mid-day *Jubal Early's* ideas differed strongly from *Gordon's* as to what his next move should be, after it became apparent, according to the tenor of *Early's* report, that three vicious attacks on the Union Sixth Corps (actually only Getty's division of that corps) had merely caused that fighting organization to recoil smoothly and then each time strike swiftly back before taking another retrograde step toward its ultimate defense line north of Middletown. *Early* recognized Sheridan's great superiority in cavalry, held it in considerable respect, and had no valid reason for believing that *Rosser* had accomplished more than a demonstration on the Confederate left. Furthermore he had personally observed how *Wharton's division* had reeled back from one of the Federal Sixth Corps' sharp counterattacks. When the fog lifted he had seen for himself the strong defensive position upon which Wright's corps had finally settled down, and it was reported to him that a heavy force of Federal cavalry had been observed moving south, east of the turnpike, to pose a serious threat to his right flank and rear. He also stated, in postwar rebuttal of *Gordon's* contention that an attack up the turnpike to turn the Federal left would have put the finishing touch to the initial Confederate victory, that such a move was impracticable "because the approach in that direction was through an open flat and across a boggy stream with deep banks." The stream to which *Early* referred was called Meadow Brook, which paralleled the turnpike about 400 yards to the west and was indeed a tactical obstacle, although not by any means impassable.

To what extent *Early* was rationalizing, in stating the reasons why he thought it best to pause rather than to risk all in a grand finale, is a matter of opinion, but to General *Gordon* it was a bitter disappointment. The latter, in his *Reminiscences of the Civil War*, recounts the following interesting colloquy that, *Gordon* said, occurred immediately following the exchange of views between Colonel *Carter* and himself, which appears on page 311.

At this moment General Early came upon the field and said: "Well, Gordon, this is glory enough for one day. This is the 19th. Precisely one month ago today we were going in the opposite direction."

His allusion was to our flight from Winchester on the 19th of September. I replied, "It is very well so far, general; but we have one more blow to strike, and then there will not be left an organized company of infantry in Sheridan's army."

I pointed to the Sixth Corps and explained the movements that I had ordered, which I felt sure would compass the capture of that corps—certainly its destruction. When I had finished, he said: "No use in that; they will all go directly."

"That is the Sixth Corps, general. It will not go unless we drive it from the field."

"Yes, it will go too, directly."

My heart went into my boots; visions of the fatal halt on the first day at Gettysburg, and of the whole day's hesitation to permit an assault on Grant's exposed flank on the 6th of May in the Wilderness, rose before me. And so it came to pass that the fatal halting, the hesitation, the spasmodic firing, and the isolated movements in the face of the sullen, slow, and orderly retreat of this superb Federal corps, lost us the great opportunity, and converted the brilliant victory of the morning into disastrous defeat in the evening.

Instead of attacking the Sixth Corps on its left flank, for the reasons previously mentioned, *Early* decided to send *Gordon* (who had now reverted to the command of his own division) over to the left of the Confederate line for an advance against the Union right, to attack in conjunction with *Kershaw*, whose division was ordered to assail the enemy frontally. *Kershaw* sent back word that his troops were very much scattered, a cavalry force was threatening him in front, and he was consequently in no condition to make an attack. The staff officer detailed to carry the order to *Gordon* reported back that he had not delivered it because he could see for himself that *Gordon's division* was also scattered and in no condition to execute the order if transmitted, an unwarranted assumption with which *Gordon* would have violently disagreed had he known of it.

"It was now apparent," said *Early* in his official report of the battle, "that it would not do to press my troops further. They had been up all night and were much jaded. In passing over rough ground to attack the enemy in the early morning their own ranks had been much disordered and the men scattered, and it had required time to re-form them. Their ranks, moreover, were much thinned by the absence of the men engaged in plundering the enemy's camps. The delay which had unavoidably occurred had enabled the enemy to rally a portion of his routed troops, and his immense force of cavalry, which remained intact, was threatening both of our flanks in an open country, which of itself rendered an advance extremely hazardous. I determined, therefore, to try and hold what had been gained, and orders were given for carrying off the captured and abandoned artillery, small-arms, and wagons."

GORDON'S BITTER DISAPPOINTMENT

General *Gordon* felt very deeply the lost opportunity, which he attributed solely to his superior, General *Early*. The post-war Governor and United States Senator, many years after the war, published his own account of the reversal at Cedar Creek, a colorful narrative that differed radically from *Early's* official report.

It was *Gordon's* firm conviction that one more heavy, concerted blow "with every gun and every exultant soldier of *Early's* army" would have given the Confederates a complete and inexpensive victory. In support of his thesis he pointed to the fact that the preponderance of combat strength at the point of contact had shifted from the Union to the Confederate army by reason of the rout of the Federal Eighth and Nineteenth Corps, and that the fighting morale of *Early's* men was at a high pitch while that of the Federals was correspondingly low. Even the steady, veteran Sixth Corps, which had not been badly hurt in the initial encounter, would not in *Gordon's* opinion have been able to stand against the concentrated fire of *Carter's* artillery and the captured Federal pieces.

In measured but scornful words *Gordon* described the lost opportunity as he and other Confederate officers saw the picture: "The concentration was stopped; the blow was not delivered. We halted, we hesitated, we dallied, firing a few shots here, attacking with a brigade or a division there, and before such feeble assaults the superb Union corps retired at intervals and by short stages. We waited, waited for weary hours; waited till the routed men in blue found that no foe was pursuing them and until they had time to recover their normal composure and courage; waited till Confederate officers lost hope and the fires had gone out in the hearts of the privates."

Gordon's bitter disappointment at his superior's implied timidity in failing to exploit what *Gordon* felt certain could have been a glorious and comparatively easy victory is understandable. For it was he, in company with *Jed Hotchkiss,* who had climbed Three Top Mountain and discovered the vulnerability of the Federal left flank; and the following morning it was he who, in command of the *Second Corps,* had exploited the enemy's weak point and set the Union army up for the kill which *Early* declined to execute. *Gordon's* recollections of *Early's* similar unwillingness to press the advantage at Gettysburg and in the Wilderness when opportunity offered undoubtedly influenced his feelings on this occasion. In the case of the previous battles, *Gordon's* tactical judgment, which involved taking a calculated risk that accorded with General *Lee's* battle plans, was overruled by *Early,* who in turn was overruled by *Lee* when he learned of *Gordon's* recommendation during the Battle of the Wilderness. At Cedar Creek there was no *Lee* to appeal to when *Early,* disregarding *Gordon,* elected to mark time until victory, eluding him, was transformed into a shocking defeat.

Military analysts may or may not concur in *Gordon's* findings. Although he was able to make out a stronge case that, if accepted, was a damning indictment of *Jubal Early,* he could not have known the quality of the defense line that Wright may have constructed around the unpanicked Sixth Corps north of Middletown, nor how strongly it might have reacted to a renewed attack, which must have been a frontal one. Moreover, he completely disregarded in his conclusions two pertinent factors which could have been vital—the capability of the two powerful cavalry divisions of Merritt and Custer, neither of which had been engaged, and the uncertainty of the ability of *Early's army* to stage a further sustained assault until his divisions could be reshuffled after their headlong dash of the early morning. Nevertheless, those who believe in the power of the offensive and recognize the ease with which the retreat of a disorganized army, however brave, can be converted into a rout by an energetic, already victorious opponent, will on balance support *Gordon's* belief that *Jubal Early* missed his great opportunity at Cedar Creek.

VALLEY PIKE, WHERE SHERIDAN REJOINED THE ARMY

CHAPTER 13

SHERIDAN RIDES TO FAME

WHEN General John J. Pershing, commanding the American Expeditionary Forces of the First World War, stepped on French soil in advance of his troops, he reportedly saluted our allies with the symbolic phrase: "Lafayette, we are here!" Although the words were actually coined by a member of Pershing's staff, it would be difficult to convince Americans of that fact. Which perhaps is just as well.

Popular legends about famous historical characters are usually compounded of fact and fiction, which with the passage of time cannot be separated, particularly if the myth has already captured the imagination of the public. Thus the name of Phil Sheridan is universally associated with his historic ride "from Winchester, twenty miles away," when according to the poem by Thomas Buchanan Read

319

the fiery little general on his powerful big gelding, Rienzi, galloped over hill and dale to turn back his broken, retreating army, galvanize the men to a cheering counterattack, and snatch glorious victory from humiliating defeat. That the poet employed poetic license in describing the affair, mixing fact and fiction in his thrilling account, may have been histrionically legitimate, but Sheridan's reputation as a great military leader was acquired as the result of solid achievement, not through happy chance, and it cannot detract one whit from his historic stature to screen out the fiction to bring the event into military focus.

EARLY WORKS WHILE SHERIDAN SLEEPS

While Sheridan was sleeping peacefully at the Logan home in Winchester the night of October 18, on his return trip from Washington, his mind at ease over the situation at the front, *Early's divisions* were secretly moving into positions, under cover of night, from which to launch their surprise thunderbolt against the unsuspecting Union army before daylight on the morning of October 19.

Shortly before six o'clock in the morning, almost an hour after the Confederate storm had broken on Crook's startled troops, Sheridan was wakened by the duty officer at Winchester with the report that he heard irregular artillery firing at Cedar Creek. Recalling the reconnaissance in force that Wright had scheduled for that morning, Sheridan went back to bed to finish his sleep, but his mind became so restless that he soon rose and dressed. A few minutes later the officer again advised him that the firing had not ceased, but in answer to an inquiry from the general said that it did not sound like a battle. Becoming suspicious that trouble might be brewing, however, Sheridan ordered breakfast to be speeded up, the horses saddled, and everything readied for a quick move.

Between 8:30 and 9 o'clock Sheridan's party mounted and rode through the streets of Winchester to the Valley Pike, where his escort, the 17th Pennsylvania Volunteer Cavalry, was waiting at Mill Creek, a half-mile beyond the outskirts of town. Every now and then Sheridan would bend forward toward the pommel of his saddle and listen intently in an effort to evaluate the sound of the firing, which by this time had risen to a steady rumble. As the horsemen moved along at the regulation gait, the noise seemed to increase at a more rapid cadence than could be explained by their own rate of movement, leading the general to speculate on the dire possibility that his own army might be falling back.

In Sheridan's own words: "Just as we made the crest of the rise beyond the stream (Mill Creek) there burst upon our view the appalling spectacle of a panic-stricken army—hundreds of slightly wounded men, throngs of others unhurt but utterly demoralized, and baggage-wagons by the score, all pressing to the rear in hopeless confusion, telling only too plainly that a disaster had occurred at the front. On accosting some of the fugitives, they assured me that the army was broken up, in full retreat, and that all was lost; all this with a manner true to that peculiar indifference that takes possession of panic-stricken men."

It is at such moments as this, recognizable by every military officer who in time of war has faced the responsibility for making split-second decisions upon which hang important events, that the competence of a commander faces its most severe test. Sheridan was a man of decision, a commanding general who had risen by sheer merit from an obscure quartermaster captain to leader of an army, one who had never lost a battle, an officer of sound judgment in whom his men had absolute confidence. He had learned

321

at West Point and in four years of war the vital importance of carefully estimating every situation, and on this historic occasion his training and experience did not fail him or his army.

Concerned as he naturally was at the vision which without warning burst on his view—hundreds of wounded and unwounded fugitives and vehicles from a battlefield more than a dozen miles distant—Sheridan's trained soldier mind reacted immediately. An order was promptly transmitted to Colonel Oliver Edwards, commanding the brigade stationed in Winchester, to string out his men in a.cordon across the valley near Mill Creek to halt the fugitives, bring disciplined order out of military chaos, and allow the wagons to pass through for parking on the north side of Winchester. Sheridan then continued on his way, at a walk, it should be noted, to allow time to consider the problem and to reach a sound decision as to the next step.

His first thought was to form a new defense line at the southern edge of Winchester with the several elements of the routed army as they arrived. The recollection of the intercepted Confederate message indicating the approach of *Longstreet's* reinforcing troops persisted in his mind, even though it had not been confirmed. Then came more positive, aggressive ideas, typical of Sheridan the fighter. Musing that his troops had shown confidence in him because he had always appeared at the front to lead rather than direct them from the safety of a command post, the feeling that he must in person do what he could to restore their shattered ranks soon crowded out every other consideration. In the time that it took him to walk his horse only a few hundred yards, Sheridan made up his mind. He would return to his army as rapidly as possible and either salvage what he could from the early morning debacle or go down to defeat with his men. As he was reaching that decision, his chief commissary officer met him on the road with the additional intelligence that "everything was gone, army headquarters captured, and the troops dispersed." Leaving his chief of staff, Colonel Forsyth, with two other staff officers and most of the cavalry escort to round up the fugitives, Sheridan started on his dramatic ride with two aides and twenty troopers, down the valley pike to glory or ruin, whichever it might be.

In his own account of the ride from Winchester, Sheridan makes no reference to his gait, but a simple calculation on the distance covered, approximately 12 miles from Mill Creek to the position where he came up with his disorganized army 1½ miles north of Middletown, proves rather conclusively that he did not proceed at an extended gallop, as the poet would have us believe. Had he done so, even allowing for the frequency with which he was forced to take to the fields to avoid the jam of vehicles and runaway soldiers on the highway, he would have reached the army somewhat earlier than 10:30 o'clock, the actual hour of his arrival. Furthermore, as every experienced horse cavalryman can testify, a steady, alternating gait gets a horse and rider over a long distance more expeditiously, and in shape to function efficiently at the terminal point, than the mad, continuous gallop favored by the script writers. Knowing this, Sheridan, who was perceptive enough to employ dramatics only when they served a useful purpose, set a rapid but sensible pace that nevertheless ate up the miles in short order.

Several miles below Winchester Sheridan was able to return to the highway, having passed most of the walking wounded and the motley procession of wagons and ambulances. From that point it may be assumed that he accelerated his pace. Soon he observed that the road on either side was crowded with soldiers who, having fled beyond pursuit, had recovered some measure of composure and were no longer so concerned about putting additional distance be-

tween the Confederates and themselves. These were the unwounded and least panicked men of the army and, typical
of soldiers from time immemorial, they were now mostly concerned with their creature comforts, many busily engaged
in the pleasant but unwarlike task of boiling coffee. Somewhat ashamed of themselves, perhaps, but at the same time
stimulated by the appearance of their jaunty little commander heading for the battlefield they had so uncere-
moniously abandoned, these men almost with one accord
tossed their hats in the air, pushed aside their cooking
utensils, shouldered their muskets and fell into an unorganized column to follow the rapidly receding figure of
their commanding general.

"COME ON BACK, BOYS, GIVE 'EM HELL!"

The news spread rapidly, as officer after officer galloped
across fields to pass the word that Sheridan had come back.
In Sheridan's own circumspect description of the scene it
may be taken for granted that his words were somewhat
saltier than he reported them:

They, too (the men who were farther back from the
road), turned their faces to the front and marched toward
the enemy, changing in a moment from the depths of depression to the extreme of enthusiasm. I already knew that
even in the ordinary condition of mind enthusiasm is a
potent element with soldiers, but what I saw that day convinced me that if it can be excited from a state of despon-
dency its power is almost irresistible. I said nothing except
to remark, as I rode among those on the road: "If I had
been with you this morning this disaster would not have
happened. We must face the other way; we will go back
and recover our camps."

A more realistic account, and one more likely to be accepted by the knowledgeable American veteran, is found in
a letter written by Sergeant L. L. Bell, Company F, 110th

Ohio Volunteer Infantry, a regiment in Crook's Eighth Corps, one of the Union soldiers whose outfit was overrun by *Gordon's* Confederates and who dressed "on the flat of his back" when his tent was knocked down in the rush. Instead of the poetic phrase attributed to Sheridan by the history text, "Turn boys, turn, we're going back," Sergeant Bell quotes the general as having said, in pungent soldier language: "Come on back, boys—Give 'em Hell, G— D— 'em. We'll make coffee out of Cedar Creek tonight."

Just north of Newtown the now fast-moving Sheridan reined in his horse to inquire of a passing rider how things looked at the front. The individual addressed happened to be a chaplain, "making for the rear with all possible speed," as Sheridan described the encounter. "Everything is lost; but all will be right when you get there," replied the nervous dominie, who thereupon clapped heels to the sides of his winded horse to resume his breathless pace to the rear.

The streets of Newtown were so congested with fugitives from the army that Sheridan was forced to detour around the village, in the course of which he met Major William McKinley of Crook's staff. The major lost no time in spreading the good news of the general's return to the officers and men of Crook's divisions, who of all the army were most in need of encouragement and spine-stiffening.

The Army Experiences a Transfusion

Just south of Newtown, about three-quarters of a mile west of the Valley Pike, Sheridan spotted a body of troops which appeared to be in good shape—the first evidence that his army had not completely disintegrated in his absence. These troops turned out to Ricketts' and Wheaton's divisions of Wright's Sixth Corps, to the right rear of which was the rallied Nineteenth Corps. Somewhat closer to the front he came up to the rear of Getty's division, which to-

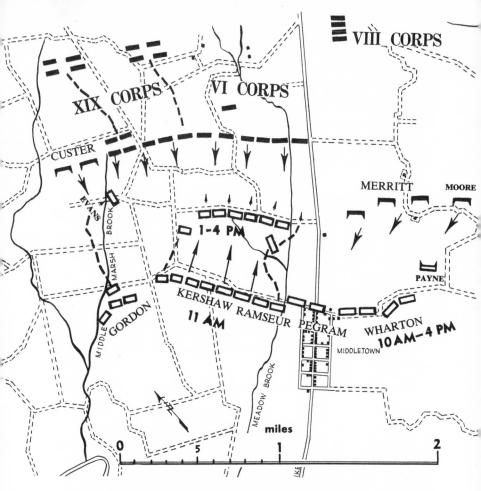

MAP 15. BATTLE OF CEDAR CREEK, SEMI-FINAL PHASE

By 11 a.m. the Confederates had advanced to the road which runs perpendicular to the turnpike just north of Middletown, where Early held them for several hours despite the impatience, of Gordon and other commanders to continue the attack. Meantime Sheridan had arrived from Winchester after his famous ride and had re-formed his line of battle on the position established by Getty. Merritt's cavalry division and Moore's brigade were on the left flank, but at 11 a.m. Custer was shifted back to the right flank.

At about 3:45 p.m. the three Confederate divisions on their left made a feeble attack, Wharton and Pegram not participating. During this short advance a gap developed between Kershaw and Gordon, which was exploited by the Federals when they launched a general attack at 4 p.m. This assault resulted in driving the Confederates from the field in increasing disorder.

The development of this final advance, and the pursuit that followed, constitute the final phase of the battle, which cannot well be portrayed graphically. The Union victory was complete, and brought the campaign virtually to a close.

326

gether with Lowell's cavalry brigade (a part of Merritt's division) was the only unit in contact with and interposing organized resistance to the enemy.

"My God! I'm glad you've come," was the heartfelt greeting from cavalry General Torbert, while the irrepressible George Custer, an old friend of Sheridan's, threw both arms around his superior in a welcome gesture that expressed the universal relief that the boss was back and things would now begin to move.

Getty's division, about a mile north of Middletown, in contact with enemy pickets, was posted on the reverse slope of a rise of ground behind a barricade of hastily-formed fence-rails. Sheridan jumped his horse over the fence, rode to the crest, took off his little round hat and waved it. The men rose to their feet with cheers as Sheridan moved along the crest to show himself to as many of the troops as possible. As he turned back to the rear of Getty's division, a line of regimental flags, assembled from Crook's dispersed corps, rose up to show themselves. This meeting with merely a symbolic representation of Crook's demoralized divisions, which included only a handful of unpanicked officers and color-bearers—among them one of the brigade commanders, Rutherford B. Hayes, later President of the United States, formed a colorful climax to Sheridan's ride from Winchester. It was exactly 10:30 a.m. and the time for dramatics was past. The word of Sheridan's return had spread like a forest fire and he could now get down to the serious business of planning countermeasures.

Sheridan Prepares to Counterattack

His first orders were to bring the Nineteenth Corps and the remaining two divisions of the Sixth Corps forward to the line occupied by Getty's anchor division, placing the Nineteenth on the right. The two unbroken batteries of the Eighth Corps under Captain DuPont, the only organized troops of Crook's corps that were still on the field and ready for action, were posted on the pike between Wright's Sixth Corps and the cavalry. While these movements were in progress, Sheridan rode to the fields east of the pike for a good view of the front preparatory to further reshuffling of his troops. He then sent Custer's cavalry division back to the right flank, from which original position it had been moved by Wright to help strengthen the Union island of resistance on the left when the infantry had fallen apart during the early morning action. Merritt's cavalry division and Moore's brigade of Powell's divison remained in place to cover the army left flank.

By twelve-thirty, two hours after his arrival, the new line was pretty well established. It was then that one of Sheridan's aides, whose thinking demonstrated the capabilities of a twentieth century public relations expert, proposed that the general ride along the entire front of the army to make certain that every soldier should see with his own eyes that his Commanding General was actually there in the flesh. Nothing loath, Sheridan did so, hat in hand, to the evident pleasure of his troops and with results in the way of rousing their fighting spirit that would shortly be measured in a satisfyingly practical way.

Not long after he had "inspected" his line of battle, the Confederates launched a half-hearted attack on Emory's Nineteenth Corps, which was easily repulsed, convincing the Union commander that there was no particular hurry about initiating his counterattack. The possibility that *Longstreet's corps* might actually have come up as reinforcements still lingered in the back of his mind, so he decided to have Merritt's cavalry pick up some prisoners for interrogation. This was promptly done, Sheridan himself questioning the captured Confederates in his persuasive way. Their answers indicated that none of *Longstreet's* divisions were present except *Kershaw's,* which latter was not news, but the negative information served to clear the air. Sheridan was fully satisfied that he could now attack with reasonably accurate knowledge of the Confederate strength available to *Early.* All of these adjustments and movements had taken a long time, so that it was nearly four o'clock before Sheridan was prepared to turn the army loose. "Now we are ready to go back to our camps," he kept repeating to one group of men after another; "we are going to get a twist on those fellows. We are going to lick them out of their boots." And the men loved it! This was the kind of fighting talk they liked to hear. It restored their self-respect and went a long way toward putting them in the frame of mind of a football team that has had a setback in the first half of the game, but is conscious of its own power and needs only a lively pep talk to win.

Sheridan's plan of attack was to advance the infantry line in a swinging movement, pivoting on the Sixth Corps, with Emory's Nineteenth Corps sweeping around like a scythe and striking *Early's* line at an oblique angle to drive the Confederates off the wooded crests which had become their strong points of resistance. When this movement should be well underway and the enemy hotly engaged, the Sixth Corps, flanked by several brigades of cavalry, would launch a vigorous frontal assault aimed at driving *Early* southward along the Valley Pike.

THE BATTLE IS RENEWED

When the order was given to start the attack, the lines moved forward with a steadiness and enthusiasm that boded ill to the Southerners who earlier had taken far too much that rightly belonged to Sheridan's divisions—their camps, most of their artillery, and some 1,400 prisoners. Their attitude was pretty well illustrated by the comment of one veteran, who remarked philosophically: "We may

SHERIDAN'S COUNTERATTACK

as well whip them tonight; if we don't, we'll have to do it tomorrow. Sheridan will get it out of us sometime."

The Confederates reacted promptly and violently. Screaming shells crashed down on the advancing Federals as musketry crackled all along the front. But Sheridan's troops were fully aroused and in no mood to be halted by mere shells and bullets. Dwight's brigades rushed with loud cheers over the most advanced Confederate position, located in a grove and behind a stone wall which had been extended by partly-finished earthworks. With their confidence restored by this easy initial success, the Nineteenth Corps was spurred to greater effort, and the charge gained momentum.

DuPont's two batteries opened as Emory's troops moved out, directing enfilading fire against an enemy battery and a portion of *Gordon's* infantry which was offering determined resistance to the flanking maneuver of the Nineteenth Corps. The support of these Union guns, about all that were available for the counterattack, had a marked effect in helping Dwight's division of Emory's corps to break the Confederate obstacle and to start the process of rolling up *Early's* line from left to right.

Gordon's division, which was on *Early's* right early in the morning, had swept all the way across the Confederate front in their headlong attack and pursuit of the fleeing Federals. When the Union counterattack was launched, *Gordon* occupied a position on the extreme left of *Early's* line, with a wide gap between his division and the rest of the Confederate line. Flag signals from their station on Three Top Mountain sent repeated warnings that the Federals had rallied and were massing for attack, with concentrations of cavalry on either flank and beyond the flank to the east of the pike. *Gordon* sent several staff officers to *Early* to apprise him of the danger, but no counteraction was undertaken by the army commander. Finally *Gordon* himself rode over to see *Early* and was finally directed to extend his own division to cover the gap and to post a gun battery on the left.

THE UNION BREAKTHROUGH

By the time *Gordon* got back to his own division it was too late. Emory's corps had broken through, and was lapping around *Gordon's* partly isolated troops, who were fighting desperately to extricate themselves. By that time, also, Wright's Sixth Corps was bearing down on the main Confederate line with crushing force. Custer's cavalry division, operating on the Union right flank, moved in from Middle Marsh Brook just at that moment to execute, in typically Custer fashion, a mopping up charge that was able to exploit the infantry breakthrough and ultimately to convert the Confederate attempts at organized withdrawal into a rout as complete as the one that Crook's corps had suffered in the early morning.

Regiment after regiment on *Gordon's* flank was rolled up and disintegrated in much the same way that ten pins are toppled, one after another, by a glancing blow against the one on the end. The Confederate crumbling process, commencing slowly, quickly spread to all ranks until, amidst the smoke of battle and the twilight, *Early's entire army*, with the exception of *Carter's artillery*, caught the infection. It soon became a matter of every man for himself, as the Confederates repeated in reverse the earlier rapid break-up of the Union Eighth and Nineteenth Corps. Nor did it take any longer for Sheridan's army to achieve the same result.

As the Confederates gave ground in confusion that quickly developed into a rout, DuPont moved his nine guns straight down the turnpike, first at a trot and then at a gallop. Arriving at the high ground overlooking Cedar Creek, the Union artillerymen observed the enemy in full retreat about 600 yards away, crowding the turnpike in a disordered mass of fleeing men. It was an opportunity of a lifetime for an experienced artilleryman, of which DuPont took full advantage. In his own words:

I immediately opened fire—the five rifled guns directing their shots towards the head of the column and the four 12-pounders further to the rear. Our shooting was very accurate and almost every shell exploded directly in the midst of the crowded masses before us. After a very few rounds, evidence of complete demoralization could be plainly discerned—field-pieces and caissons, wagons and ambulances, were abandoned by their drivers and dashed along the road in wild confusion, damaging or destroying each other by collisions, while swarms of the retreating enemy left the road and scattered through the fields. I gave the order to cease firing as soon as the Union cavalry had advanced far enough to be endangered by our projectiles, when our mounted troops promptly captured everything in sight.

DuPont's gunners did not come through their pleasant adventure entirely unscathed, for *Early's* retreat was ably covered in the beginning by effective fire from a Confederate battery, which directed its attention on the Union guns that were creating havoc in the Confederate ranks. Although the total casualties of Crook's three artillery batteries for the entire day's fighting were only fifty-one, this final exploit, added to their excellent performance in retarding the rush of *Gordon's Second Corps* during its dawn surprise attack, stood out in stark contrast to the attitude of the infantry of the Eighth Corps, whose precipitous rout of the early morning fell far short of being described as valorous.

Crook's official report of the battle gave his artillery the recognition they had so justly earned by stating that "Captain DuPont, Chief of Artillery, and the officers and men of his batteries are deserving of particular mention for their conspicuous gallantry and the valuable services rendered that day." And later, in a more concrete way, this distinguished artilleryman was granted appropriate recognition by the award of a Congressional Medal of Honor for his work at Cedar Creek.

Darkness descended over the battlefield while the rout was still on, which proved a blessing to the dejected Confederates even as it had at the close of the Battle of Winchester in September. The day had been a tough one for both armies, involving a long tour of unrelieved duty which included loss of sleep and much running and fighting and killing. Everywhere dead and wounded men and horses, dismounted guns, broken muskets, demolished caissons, and pools of blood on the heights and in the ravines testified to the bitterness of the battle. In spite of the fact that Sheridan's numerous cavalry had lost no more than 200 men killed, wounded, and missing, the great number of dead horses showed that the Union cavalry had taken a prominent part in the fighting, and it was also clear that the artillery of both armies had taken plenty of punishment.

An Exciting Pursuit

Now it became the mission of Merritt's and Custer's troopers to carry on the pursuit, which they undertook with enthusiasm, while the infantry of Sheridan's three corps moved back into their old camps, filled with the dead and wounded of both armies. There was, however, still a job to be done, that of recovering the 24 guns that *Early* had captured in the morning battle, and which the Confederates were making an effort to haul away.

The usually resilient Confederate infantry seemed to have lost their accustomed powers of recuperation. Perhaps the shocking change in a few hours from an exciting victory to a depressing defeat had numbed their senses, or they were just too tired and discouraged to care about anything except reaching a place of safety and relief from the strenuous events of the past twenty-four hours. Or it may have been that an oppressive cloud of hopeless dejection had settled over the Southern army when this third strike had been called on it—Winchester, Fisher's Hill, and now Cedar Creek. Whatever it was, discipline and organization quickly vanished as the streaming thousands of Confederates took off to the south in a frantic effort to get away.

There was little that *Early's* officers could do to stem the tide of retreat, so they gave up trying, as regiments and brigades became hopelessly intermingled. A Union colonel, spurring his horse into a fleeing squad of Confederates, grabbed a regimental battle flag from the startled hands of the color sergeant and escaped without injury.

A Yankee cavalryman caught up with a Rebel baggage wagon, slashed the driver with his saber, and returned triumphantly with the vehicle and a load of prisoners. An artillery lieutenant rode up to a retiring battery, announced himself as a Union officer, and directed the whole battery to "countermarch immediately," an order which was promptly complied with, the lieutenant bringing up the rear.

A Confederate lieutenant amusedly told a Union captain after the war that he had surrendered five times during the retreat, but finally escaped. "Two hundred of our men," he said, "would throw down their arms to twenty or thirty of your cavalry. Then the chief of the troop would order, 'now you stay there!' and spur off after more prisoners. Then we officers would tell our men, 'now scatter, boys; take to the bushes and hollows; get back to Fisher's Hill.' Well, what with the nightfall and the rough country, the biggest part of us sneaked out of our scrape."

Some of the more vivid descriptions of the kaleidoscopic events that marked the battle and its aftermath are found in General *Gordon's* comprehensive and surprisingly objective *Reminiscences*. Writing of the wild confusion incident to the retirement of *Early's* army in the gathering darkness, *Gordon* dramatizes the awe-inspiring effect that large masses of galloping enemy cavalry can produce on routed troops:

The steady roll of musketry, punctuated now and then by peals of thunder from retreating or advancing batteries, suddenly ceased; and resistance ended as the last organized regiment of Early's literally overwhelmed army broke and fled in the darkness. As the tumult of battle died away, there came from the north side of the plain a dull, heavy swelling sound like the roaring of a distant cyclone, the omen of additional disaster. It was unmistakable.

335

Sheridan's horsemen were riding furiously across the open fields of grass to intercept the Confederates before they crossed Cedar Creek. Many were cut off and captured. As the sullen roar from horses' hoofs beating the soft turf of the plain told of the near approach of the cavalry, all effort at orderly retreat was abandoned. The only possibility of saving the rear regiments was in unrestrained flight—every man for himself. Mounted officers gathered here and there squads of brave men who poured volleys into the advancing lines of blue; but it was too late to make effective resistance.

Death of the Gallant Ramseur

Perhaps the most severe individual blow to the Confederate cause during the confusion of the retreat was the mortal wounding of 27-year-old Major General *Stephen Dodson Ramseur,* the gallant North Carolinian who had previously taken wounds at Malvern Hill, Chancellorsville, and Spotsylvania Court House. Always in the thick of the battle, he exerted every effort to stay the rout on his portion of the field, but without effect. First he received a wound to which he paid no attention. Then his horse was shot under him. The same thing happened to another that he mounted. A moment later a Union bullet drilled through both lungs and he was carried to the rear, wondering when or if he should see the baby daughter who had been born to him only three days before the battle. The news had come to him by telegraphic message which was relayed from signal station to signal station along the mountain ridge, and he had told his intimates beforehand that he wanted badly to win this battle so that he might secure leave to become acquainted with the new arrival.

Surgeon Knight of Crook's artillery brigade, captured in his tent at daybreak, had been kept on the field and pressed into service to help the Confederate surgeons attend to the wounded. When the retreat occurred, and Knight was marching along as a prisoner, he happened to be walking alongside the ambulance that was taking the wounded *Ramseur* to the rear. The approach of the Union cavalry led a major on *Ramseur's* staff to decide that under the circumstances discretion was the better part of valor. Looking about him, he spied a Union officer, who happened to be surgeon Knight. "We surrender to you sir,!" remarked *Ramseur's* aide, which suited Knight perfectly. Ordering the ambulance to turn about, he conducted the wounded general, two staff officers and two orderlies, to Sheridan's headquarters at the Belle Grove House.

Late that evening, word having spread of the wounded *Ramseur's* presence at army headquarters, classmates and friends who had known him at West Point in the late 1850's flocked to the Belle Grove House to see and talk with their old friend. Cavalryman Wesley Merritt and artilleryman DuPont, class of 1860 along with *Ramseur,* were followed by George Custer and others. *Ramseur* and DuPont had been intimates at the Academy, and it was to the latter that the Southerner turned for comfort when his suffering became so intense that an anaesthetic had to be administered. The next morning he died without recovering consciousness.

Although *Ramseur* was the only Confederate general to meet his death at Cedar Creek, the South came very close to losing another distinguished division commander, General *Gordon,* although not directly from shell or bullet. After crossing Cedar Creek in the course of the retreat, *Gordon* managed to collect a small, heterogenous group of men from several different divisions who were cajoled into forming a thin line across the turnpike in the hope of checking, at least temporarily, the ardor of the Federal pursuit. It was a noble gesture, but a fruitless one, as might have been expected, for the men soon vanished from *Gordon's* sight in the dim starlight.

At the point where *Gordon* attempted to make a stand, the pike ran along the edge of a limestone cliff, on which one flank of this momentary line of resistance rested. As his small group evaporated, *Gordon* suddenly realized that he was surrounded on three sides, all except the cliff, by Union cavalry, who were engaged in the exhilarating task of gathering in as many prisoners as they could handle. *Gordon* had the choice of a Yankee bullet, surrender, or flight over the precipice. He chose the latter. Sinking his spurs into the flanks of his startled horse, the two of them plunged into the empty void, the steed tumbling in one direction, *Gordon* in another.

In recounting this adventure, the general humorously compared his dilemma to that of General Israel Putnam, escaping from British dragoons at Horse Neck in 1779. *Gordon* didn't know whether Putnam had ridden, rolled, or slid down *his* precipice. But whatever method Putnam used, *Gordon* declared he had "gone him two better," because he did all three at Cedar Creek, and was knocked unconscious upon landing at the bottom. Miraculously the Confederate general was only stunned, as was his horse, and both of them in a short time recovered their senses. Finding himself in a dark glen well below the level of the turnpike, *Gordon* listened for a time to the movement of the Federals pursuing down the pike, then quietly walked his mount across open country, unmolested, until he had passed around the Union forces to the south of him and rejoined his own army.

The Cavalry Recovers the Lost Guns

As though defeat and rout were not enough to fill their cup of sorrow, *Early's* harried troops were forced to undergo further humiliation by losing in turn all the

CAPTURED MATERIEL AT BELLE GROVE

guns, ordnance, wagons, and other equipment they had
taken from the Federals during their morning success.
The resistance of *Rosser's* cavalry on *Early's* left had only
slightly delayed the advance of the Union horsemen on
the west flank. When *Rosser's* troopers retired, the coast
was clear for Custer's division to sweep across country in
a southeasterly direction, to strike the Valley Pike near
Hupp's Hill, west of Cedar Creek and about a mile north
of Strasburg, where they created havoc among the retreating Confederate wagons and artillery. About the same time
that Custer's troopers reached the scene, Merritt's cavalry
angled in from the Union left across the creek, and together the two divisions fulfilled the cavalryman's dream
of turning enemy defeat into disaster.

Some of the cavalry pushed on through the fields,
around the straining mass of men and vehicles, through
Strasburg to Spangler's Mill, several hundred yards be-

yond the western outskirts of the town, where they broke up a wooden bridge on the turnpike which had earlier been damaged and repaired. This bridge crossed a small creek flowing through a ravine near the point where the turnpike to Fisher's Hill passes through a veritable canyon, with the Shenandoah River on one side and tall, steep, rugged formations of bare rock on the other. *Early's* report indicates that he had sent the Union prisoners and captured materiel up the valley for safety, but it seems that everyone was too occupied with other matters to effectively carry out the orders. Although the Union prisoners had been marched beyond reach, the caravan of captured guns and vehicles had not passed beyond Strasburg, so that the broken bridge west of the town became the Confederate Achilles' heel, the Blue horsemen recapturing all of Sheridan's 24 guns, together with 25 of *Early's* own, and more than 1,000 prisoners.

The number of captured Confederate guns was verified by actual count of several Union officers, one of them an aide to General Sheridan, who assured the skeptical army commander that he was certain of the number "because he had laid his hand on every one." The other reporter was Captain DeForest, Twelfth Connecticut Volunteers, who personally counted 49 field pieces, captured and recaptured, together with other Confederate materiel including 50 wagons, 65 ambulances, and 1,600 rifles.

Union casualties at Cedar Creek were listed as 644 killed, 3,430 wounded, 1,591 captured and missing for a total of 5,665. *Early* reported for the Confederates 1,860 killed and wounded, which with 1,050 captured added up to 2,910, exclusive of the "missing." As at Winchester, however, he was forced to leave many of his wounded behind, and had no opportunity to count the dead, so that his figures cannot be regarded as more than approximations, probably arrived at by a process of deducting the number present for duty, when his army reassembled at New Market several days later, from his effective strength before the battle of October 19. The much heavier Union losses were attributed by DeForest to the fact that "the Confederates were obviously the best shots, and their open-order style of fighting was an economical one. Moreover, when they retreated, they went in a swarm and at full speed, thus presenting a poor mark for musketry. We, on the contrary, sought to retire in regular order, and suffered heavily for it."

EARLY RETREATS TO NEW MARKET

Early made a fleeting halt in the entrenchments at Fisher's Hill during the night of October 19, resting his men for a few brief hours, but before dawn the following morning his greatly reduced force of infantry and artillery resumed the retreat up the valley, with *Rosser's* cavalry acting as rear guard. The Confederates ended their retrograde movement at New Market. There *Early* established a defensive position.

The initiative was now in the hands of the victorious General Sheridan, whose army nevertheless had a few wounds of its own. He was wisely content for the moment to let developments shape his course. Although he had not by any means destroyed *Early's army,* he had for all practical purposes rendered the Shenandoah Valley useless to the Confederacy, which was the major purpose for which he had been sent.

Sheridan rested his army in their camps at Cedar Creek for several weeks, then moved back to Kernstown, where it had been decided to construct a defensive position that could be held against any possible move *Early* might undertake, and at the same time make it possible for Sheridan with safety to detach a number of divisions for transfer to Grant in the Petersburg area.

341

SHERIDAN'S TROOPS MARCHING THROUGH MIDDLETOWN

CHAPTER 14

REPERCUSSIONS AND RECRIMINATIONS

SHERIDAN'S dispatches to Grant on October 20 and 21 waxed increasingly enthusiastic as Union prisoners began to straggle back to the army after escaping from their captors during the march up the valley. From their accounts, and reports from the pursuing cavalry, the completeness of the rout of *Early's* army became apparent. "For ten miles on the line of retreat the road and country was covered with small arms, thrown away by the flying rebels, and other debris," Sheridan wrote. "General, I want Getty, and the brave boys, Merritt and Custer, promoted by brevet," he added, explaining that when the enemy was attacked, the two cavalrymen, under Torbert's direction, "fiercely attacked the enemy's flanks, and when he broke, closed in after dark and secured the artillery, trains, etc."

It was clear that the former commander of Grant's famed Cavalry Corps of the Army of the Potomac was proud and delighted that two of his young men of the mounted arm had played so important a part in exploiting the breakthrough at Cedar Creek. The inclusion of infantry division commander Getty among the three whom Sheridan singled out for immediate commendation was well-merited recognition of that officer's lone courageous stand, at the head of his division, when the rest of the army infantry was retiring to a place of safety beyond Middletown.

The North Cheers Sheridan's Victory

The reaction to Sheridan's victory in Washington and throughout the North surpassed even the enthusiasm that had greeted *Early's* defeat and rout at Winchester and Fisher's Hill. For here was conclusive evidence that "little Phil" was a bulldog who refused to let go, and a leader who could inspire men to supreme effort. The Union had waited long and eagerly for a military hero. Popular imagination was inflamed by the somewhat exaggerated story of his rapid ride from Winchester, but it served its purpose, and the facts were not so greatly distorted as to defy credulity.

As soon as the news reached him, General Grant again ordered a salute of one hundred guns to be fired into the Confederate lines at Petersburg. President Lincoln, who at the start had been humorously doubtful of the generalship of so short a man as Sheridan, but who now confessed enthusiastically that "five feet, five inches was about the right height" to fill the bill, dashed off a note extending the thanks and admiration of the nation to Sheridan and his army. Even more to Sheridan's satisfaction was the recognition afforded by his promotion, a few weeks later, to the rank of major general in the United States Army, and the general acceptance in political circles of the fact that his successes in the Valley coupled with

343

VOTING IN THE FIELD—SHERIDAN'S SOLDIERS HELP REELECT LINCOLN

those of Sherman in Georgia, had practically assured Lincoln's re-election on November 8. For the Northern Peace Party, backing Democrat General McClellan in opposition to Lincoln, had been neatly deprived of its justification for existence, with the result that Lincoln received 212 electoral votes to Little Mac's 21.

Sheridan might have been pardoned for making the most of his ride from Winchester in view of its thrilling aftermath, but it is much to his credit that he apparently regarded it as all in the day's work and no more than his duty. His reference to the ride is so surprisingly brief and lacking in drama, in his official report of the Shenandoah campaign, that it bears reprinting:

On reaching Mill Creek, half a mile south of Winchester, the head of the fugitives appeared in sight, trains and men coming to the rear with appalling rapidity. . . . Taking twenty men from my escort, I pushed on to the

344

front, leaving the balance under General Forsyth and Colonels Thom and Alexander to do what they could in stemming the torrent of fugitives. I am happy to say that hundreds of the men, when on reflection found they had not done themselves justice, came back with cheers.

Nevertheless, the victorious general understood very well the psychological effect that the success of the Union army would produce on the public mind, and that much of the adulation would center on his person. His friend and lieutenant, General George Crook, described Sheridan's real feelings in this fashion, the evening following the battle:

"Sitting around the campfires that night," wrote Crook, "Gen. Sheridan was feeling very good. He said, 'Crook, I am going to get much more credit for this than I deserve, for, had I been here in the morning, the same thing would have taken place.' "

Crook Deprecates Sheridan's Part in the Battle

Later it appeared that Crook's opinion of Sheridan underwent a drastic change, in the belief, which grew with the passing years, that he and his Eighth Corps had never received full justice for their part in the Valley Campaign. Crook claimed subsequently that Sheridan had deliberately withheld proper credit from those to whom it belonged and had assumed for himself undue credit not justified by the circumstances. Twenty-five years after the battle, Crook revisited the scene at Cedar Creek and Fisher's Hill and bitterly recorded his thoughts in his diary:

"After examining the ground and the position of the troops after twenty-five years which have elapsed and in the light of subsequent events, it renders Gen. Sheridan's claims and his subsequent actions in allowing the general public to remain under the impressions regarding his part in these battles, when he knew they were fiction, all the more contemptible. The adulations heaped on him by a grateful nation for his supposed genius turned his head, which, added to his natural disposition, caused him to bloat his little carcass with debauchery and dissipation, which carried him off prematurely."

Crook's contemptuous one-sentence obituary of his former fellow cadet at West Point and superior officer in the Valley and later in the post-war Army, was typical of the slow-thinking, reticent, but scrupulously honest-minded farm boy who had graduated thirty-eighth in a class of forty-three cadets at the Military Academy, and who thus became the lowest-ranking student in the history of that institution to attain the rank of major general, United States Army. It took Crook some time to come to the conclusion that Sheridan had not played fair with him, possibly because his own unobtrusive character made him reluctant to think badly of his friend until he could be convinced in his own mind by a process of reasoning that took into account all the facts in the case. On the other hand, he was not slow to express freely his unfavorable opinion of the shortcomings, as he saw them, of many others of his fellow officers such as Averell, Duffie, Emory, and Hunter. In reading his *Autobiography* one gains the impression that "everybody is out of step but Johnny," the similarity between *Jubal Early* and George Crook in that respect being rather striking. The difference was that *Early* spoke out for all to hear, while the taciturn Crook confided his blasts chiefly to his private papers, which were not published until more than fifty years after his death.*

The quoted entry from Crook's diary was made by the General only three months before his death from a heart

---

* *General George Crook, His Autobiography.* Edited by Martin F. Schmitt, University of Oklahoma Press, 1946, 1960.

attack in March, 1890. He was not in the best of health at the time, but the caustic nature of the remarks about Sheridan's alleged perfidy sound very much as though the thought had been simmering under the surface of Crook's mind for a quarter of a century and that his return to the scenes of the 1864 Valley Campaign caused pent-up emotions to be released in a rush of words.

Grant and Sheridan both held Crook in high regard, as did most of the officers and men of his various commands, of whose loyalty and affection for their commanding officer there could be no doubt, even though such feelings may have blinded them to his own occasional lapses and errors of omission. One of his strongest supporters was Rutherford B. Hayes, who served under Crook successively as brigade and division commander during the Campaign of 1864.

Conceivably professional jealousy on Crook's part may have contributed something to his modified attitude towards Sheridan. Crook gained the impression, in the spring of 1865, that Grant planned to place him in command of the cavalry of the Army of the Potomac for the renewal of the campaign against *Lee*. Instead Sheridan rejoined Grant at the conclusion of the Valley Campaign and resumed command of the cavalry corps, in which Crook was given a division composed of the cavalry brigades which had remained with Meade when the rest of the corps became a part of Sheridan's Army of the Shenandoah. That too may have rankled in his mind to feed the flames of doubt about Sheridan that were kindled as the result of events at Winchester, Fisher's Hill, and Cedar Creek.

Significance of Confederate Loss of the Valley

The almost mortal blow inflicted on the Confederate armies by the loss of the food supply heretofore furnished from the fruitful farms of the Shenandoah Valley was soon to be confirmed in telegrams and letters from *Lee* at Petersburg, from North Carolina, and elsewhere. A typical example was Lee's telegram of December 14 to President *Jefferson Davis:*

"Chief Commissary of this Army received notice yesterday from Richmond that there was no salt meat there to send him, but would forward preserved meat. He thinks he may get enough to last tomorrow. Neither meat nor corn are now coming over the Southern Roads, and I have heard there was meat in Wilmington."

A week later, December 22, the War Department having sent *Braxton Bragg* to Wilmington to take charge of the defense forces in that area, *Lee* wired *Davis* that *Bragg* had reported "his inability to subsist troops and that his District was exhausted." *Lee* added that *Bragg* would consume his remaining supply of meat in one day and inquired if there was anything the authorities at Richmond could do about it.

Apparently there was little that the War Department could do, since it had already exhausted most of its small supply of miracles. Rail transportation, never adequate in the South, had deteriorated in quantity and quality, but the basic fact was that the Confederate bread-basket, the Shenandoah Valley, would no longer be available as a primary food source for the Confederacy, now that Sheridan controlled it and *Early's* reduced army was relatively impotent.

That Sheridan's cavalry had performed a thorough job of devastating the economy of the Confederates who lived in the valley may be judged from the accounting rendered by but one of the Union divisions, under Wesley Merritt's command. Between September 29 and October 8, Merritt's cavalry swept the area from Waynesboro and Staunton to as far north as Tom's Brook, burning barns and mills

348

SCORCHED EARTH—DESTRUCTION NEAR WOODSTOCK

and driving off cattle. The value of property destroyed and captured was estimated at $3,304,672 and included 630 barns, 47 flouring mills, 4 saw mills, 1 woolen mill, 3,455 tons of hay, 410,000 bushels of wheat, as well as smaller quantities of corn, oats, and straw. The livestock reported driven off added up to 1,347 cattle, 1,231 sheep, and 725 swine. And that report represented the destruction accomplished by only one of the three cavalry divisions in a single area of the Valley during the short period of ten days.

EARLY'S ERRORS OF JUDGMENT

Humility was a quality foreign to *Jubal Early's* character. Had it been otherwise, and had he been less given to acid comment in dealing with fellow officers and civilians, he might have elicited qualified sympathy, if not commendation, from the Southern press for having put up a stiff fight against heavy odds during the critical battles of Winchester and Cedar Creek.

Early's inflexibility of mind was such that to his dying

349

day he insisted that his two major defeats were caused chiefly by military deficiencies of his own troops. At Winchester he had personally exuded confidence of victory following the initial repulse of Sheridan's morning attack; in *Early's* words, "we deserved the victory, and would have had it, but for the enemy's immense superiority in cavalry, which alone gave it to him." Unlike the more open-minded *John B. Gordon,* who was able to recognize merit in an opponent when deserved, *Early* completely discounted the courage and vigor of Sheridan's infantry divisions and gave no credit whatsoever to the Union commander himself, whether for strategy, tactics, or influence on the battle by his personal, magnetic leadership.

The even more humiliating reversal and defeat at Cedar Creek, after his daring and imaginative battle plan had been so successfully executed in the early morning by his generals and the men of their several commands, was no fault of *Early's,* if we are to believe his own explanation: "This was the case of a glorious victory given up by my own troops after they had won it, and it is to be accounted for on the ground of the partial demoralization caused by the plunder of the enemy's camps, and from the fact that the men undertook to judge for themselves when it was proper for them to retire. Had they but waited, the mischief on the left would have been remedied. I have never been able to satisfy myself that the enemy's attack, in the afternoon, was not a demonstration to cover his retreat during the night."

Not a few Confederates in high places, although recognizing *Early's* zeal and loyalty to the cause once he had thrown himself wholeheartedly into it, and while giving him full credit for personal courage and aggressiveness as a military commander, nevertheless considered him to be lacking in judgment on too many occasions. His failure to evaluate with any degree of accuracy the capabilities of his opponent, General Sheridan, was a glaring weakness for which both he and his army paid a heavy penalty. What started out as simply an unflattering opinion of Sheridan's capacity quickly became a fixation, despite the fact that the little Irishman within a month decisively defeated him and drove his army in confusion from the field in three successive battles. Even after Cedar Creek, *Early* stubbornly adhered to his belief that Sheridan had had nothing to do with the outcome, remarking that the Union commander had been absent at the beginning of the fight and, "although he returned in the afternoon before the change in the fortunes of the day, nevertheless I saw no reason to change the estimate I had formed of him."

Not by a single word would the self-sufficient Confederate commander ever admit publicly that he might have committed an error of judgment in not pushing the attack on the morning of October 19 when every advantage lay with his own army. His only remark on that score was when he privately told *Jed Hotchkiss*, who hand-carried *Early's* report of the battle to *Lee:* "not to inform General *Lee* that we ought to have advanced during the morning at Middletown, for we should have done so." *Early* doubtless assumed that his trusted staff officer would keep the comment to himself, but *Hotchkiss* recorded it in his diary, which years later came to public attention in the Official Records of the war.

Even less praiseworthy was the suppression, if such was actually the case, of the official report of General *Gordon,* which certainly reached *Early's* headquarters for consolidation with those of other subordinate commanders before forwarding to Richmond. If *Early* saw and read *Gordon's* report, and who can doubt it, he would have felt certain that the expressed views of so highly respected a general, which differed radically from his own report

351

as to the reasons for his defeat, would carry weight with *Lee* and the *War Department.* Although *Gordon* in later years was careful to avoid the direct accusation that his report had been suppressed, it seems incredible that the only one that was "lost" happened to be that of the general who had led the corps whose surprise flank attack set up the Union army for the kill from which *Early* had for hours withheld his army, and until Sheridan had time to stage and execute his overwhelming counterattack.

One further example of questionable military judgment on *Early's* part should be mentioned. This had to do with inept employment of most of his cavalry at the Battle of Cedar Creek. It will be recalled that in planning his ambitious concentric attack for the morning of October 19, *Rosser's* cavalry, about 1,200 strong, was assigned to the left flank to occupy the attention of the greatly superior Union cavalry whose camps had been spotted, from the top of Three Top Mountain, on Sheridan's right flank. The major portion of the rest of *Early's* mounted troops, about 1,700 officers and men of *Lomax's* command, were assigned a long-range mission that reflected either supreme confidence on Early's part or very faulty judgment as to the capabilities of his troopers.

The orders given to *Lomax* called for him to march by way of Front Royal, cross the Shenandoah River at that point, and circle back to the Valley Pike for the purpose of attacking the Union rear wherever they should be found. Three hundred troopers under *Payne,* attached to the *Second Corps,* would precede *Gordon's* flank approach march in an effort to capture Sheridan in his headquarters at Belle Grove. The question in the minds of those who enjoy ex post facto reconstruction of battles is this: Would *Early* not have exercised better judgment by sending *Payne's* 300 on the long night march by way of Front Royal, at the same time holding *Lomax's* 1,700 in a position of close-in readiness to fully exploit whatever success *Gordon's* infantry might be able to achieve? *Early* was acutely aware of his inferiority in cavalry, which had been amply demonstrated at Winchester and Fisher's Hill, at Tom's Brook, and elsewhere in the Valley, and his reports made frequent reference to Sheridan's superiority in that arm. He had also referred to the fact that there was open country on his right flank which rendered it vulnerable to attack by the numerous Federal cavalry, which makes it doubly surprising that he frittered away on a vague distant mission the very force that could have been used to excellent advantage so much closer to home. Even though *Early* would defend this action by saying that he was providing for his right flank protection by having *Lomax* maneuvering on the Federal left and rear, it is obvious that there was little that cavalry could do at such a distance from the battlefield; the possibility of disrupting Sheridan's rear areas was too long a chance to be considered wise as against the certainty that 1,700 cavalrymen could render a far more useful service to the Confederates by at least partly neutralizing the greater strength in mounted troops which Sheridan enjoyed.

In the final analysis there is good reason to conclude that lack of judgment in both the administration and employment of the cavalry under his command stemmed from the same cause that made the Federal cavalry so ineffectual during the first half of the war—ignorance on the part of infantry trained generals of the capabilities and limitations of the mounted arm. The record shows clearly, to those who analyze the matter from a basis of understanding as to what cavalry can and cannot do, that *Early's* low opinion of his cavalry simply reflected his own failure to use it properly and to the best advantage.

Long after the war, when the ghosts of Winchester and Cedar Creek were being resurrected, *Early* believed the time had come to tell his side of the story in full. In a published account he made a strong point of his belief that he had been called upon to lead a forlorn hope in the Shenandoah Valley during the fall of 1864. Rationalizing undoubtedly played a part in his conclusions, but there was something to be said for his viewpoint, even though it could have been used with the same justification on many other occasions when Confederate armies were greatly outnumbered.

To be assigned a mission in 1864, similar to the one that triggered *Stonewall Jackson's* amazing marches and battles over the same ground in early 1862, of itself offered a basis for comparison that would inevitably place *Early* at a disadvantage vis-a-vis *Jackson*. First of all, while *Early* was a vigorous fighter and during the war earned a high rating as a brigade and division commander on many famous battlefields, where on several occasions his driving force at a psychological moment either assured a Confederate victory or restored the balance in favor of the army of which he was a part, there were other times when his actions left much to be desired. On the record it is unlikely that *Old Jube,* any more than *Baldy Ewell,* can by any stretch of the imagination be said to have been cast in the mold of the great *Stonewall.*

Secondly, weight must be given, in comparing the two campaigns, to the relative quality of *Jackson's* second-rate opponents and General Sheridan, against whom *Early* had to contend. Granted that *Jackson* faced greater numerical odds than *Early,* even though the Confederate strength was pretty much the same in the Valley in '62 and '64, there was no Federal unity of command to direct the efforts of *Jackson's* opponents, nor any semblance of co-ordination between the three independent Union commands in their frenzied, ineffectual moves to pin down the elusive Confederate as he ranged freely up and down the Valley, striking at will and almost with impunity whenever one or another of the Federal generals was caught with his logistics down. Conversely, *Early* was confronted with a skilful, experienced combat leader in Phil Sheridan, who was in sole charge of his theater of operations and was supported to the hilt by a General-in-Chief who knew how to give a soldier a mission and then leave him alone to carry it out in his own way.

On the credit side, *Early* deserved a high rating for constructive achievement in drawing away from Grant's army before Petersburg one full army corps, the Sixth, two-thirds of another, the Nineteenth, and several divisions of cavalry, the effect of which was to delay, for whatever use it may have been to *Lee*, the beginning of the end of the armed resistance of the Confederacy.

Early did suffer unjustly in public esteem throughout the South, because of a misconception by *Lee* as to the odds that faced his army in the Valley. The usually accurate *Lee*, whose information normally enabled him to come very close in estimating enemy strength, was for once far off the mark in appraising Sheridan's numbers. Out of respect for *Lee*, *Early* did not offer this in his own defense, but the fact was that the *Commanding General* consistently and seriously underestimated the size of the force arrayed against his lieutenant. Whether it would have been possible to detach additional troops from *Lee's army* at that time to reinforce *Early* may be doubted, but *Lee's* thinking must have been influenced to some extent by the miscalculation.

The cordial relations that existed between *Lee* and *Early* were not noticeably upset by *Early's* reverses, whatever *Lee* may privately have thought about the outcome in the Valley. Always generous in giving his subordinates the benefit of the doubt, and equally ready to assume responsibility for failures, *Lee* may have belatedly recognized his own error in evaluating Sheridan's strength, and in so doing mitigated the faults that would otherwise appear so glaring in *Early's* conduct of operations. He would certainly not have failed to recall his mild criticism of *Early* in the letter written to the *Valley Commander* after Winchester, wherein *Lee* pointed out that *Early* seemed to have "operated more with divisions than with your concentrated strength," adding the caution that "such a course is to be avoided if possible." Many a corps and army commander, before and after *Early,* has been tempted and fallen into that military error, and it will happen again in all armies, but *Lee* was one general who knew the value of delegating authority in company with responsibility, and conversely how much damage can be done within an army by circumscribing, even though unconsciously, the full exercise of the command functions of subordinates. While that may not have been exactly what *Lee* intended to convey by his implication about fighting his army piecemeal, the criticism was justified.

Implausible as it may appear at first glance, the possibility exists that *Lee's* polite criticism of *Early's* generalship on the field of Winchester, mild as it was, made such an impression on *Early's* mind that it was uppermost in his thoughts at Cedar Creek. That it influenced the character of his plan of attack is certain, because in assigning missions for October 19 to the several elements of his command, not a single unit was held back as army reserve, which was indeed interpreting *Lee's* advice to an absurd degree, for that experienced commander would have been the last to counsel throwing of fundamental principles to the four winds.

356

It was in that same letter of September 27 that *Lee* had obliquely implied that *Early's* handling of his cavalry showed room for improvement. "As regards the western cavalry," *Lee* wrote, "I think for the present the best thing you can do is to separate it; perhaps there is a lack of confidence between officers and men. The men are all good and only require instructions and discipline . . . The enemy's force cannot be so greatly superior to yours. His effective infantry, I do not think, exceeds 12,000 men."

EARLY OFFERS TO QUIT

Two days after the Battle of Cedar Creek, back at New Market where his army was finally halted in its retreat, *Early* drafted and sent off to General *Lee* a full account of the events of October 19 and his own opinion of the reasons for the rout, which in his own words was "as thorough and disgraceful as ever happened to our army." But near the end of the report, almost as though he had reread and reflected upon those paragraphs which utterly castigated his own troops for plundering the enemy camps and thus losing the opportunity to seal the victory, and for later panicking and refusing to rally, the crusty general added a paragraph which for him sounded almost out of character:

"It is mortifying to me, general, to have to make these explanations of my reverses. They are due to no want of effort on my part, though it may be that I have not the capacity or judgment to prevent them. I have labored faithfully to gain success, and I have not failed to expose my person and to set an example to my men. I know that I shall have to endure censure from those who do not understand my position and difficulties, but I am still willing to make renewed efforts. If you think, however, that the interests of the service would be promoted by a change of commanders, I beg you will have no hesitation in making the change. The interests of the service are far beyond any mere personal considerations, and if they require it I am willing to surrender my command into other hands."

Coming from *Jubal Early* that was a most unusual display of humility, and may have been enough to counterbalance in *Lee's* mind the adverse publicity that followed the setting of the Confederate sun in the Valley, as the Southern newspapers went after *Early* like a pack in full cry. Conceivably *Early* would have been better off and received a more sympathetic press, despite his reverses, if instead of shifting the blame to his troops he had stated flatly for the benefit of the public what he told *Jed Hotchkiss* in private, and which the latter duly recorded in his Journal after the Battle of Cedar Creek: "The Yankees got whipped and we got scared."

And so *Jubal Early* remained in command of the depleted Confederate forces in the upper Valley, an area so devastated by the calculated scorched-earth policy which Sheridan's cavalry under Grant's instructions had faithfully carried out that the crows henceforth were constrained to "carry their own rations." The probabilities are that, with the increasing pressures being exerted simultaneously in all the military theaters in accordance with Grant's strategy, there was no one whom *Lee* could spare to relieve *Early* even if he had been disposed to follow the demands of the press. As it had turned out, the "forlorn hope," as *Early* called his Valley Campaign, had now become a lost hope to the revival of which no supporting troops could possibly be spared from other sectors; all any Confederate commander could do from now on, whether *Early* or his successor, would be to shadow-box the Federal army to discourage the occupation of further territory by the invaders.

Early's official charge of wholesale plundering by his Confederates was taken up after the war and strongly challenged by *Gordon*, whose opinion of his immediate superior as a field general had become more and more unfavorable as the war progressed. Nor did *Early's* unconcealed objection to the almost constant presence of Mrs. Gordon in the field endear him to the *Gordons*. And once more, for the third time in a major test of strength on the battlefield, *Early's* apparent reluctance to allow his army to clinch its initial victory at Cedar Creek had confirmed *Gordon's* growing belief that his superior was deficient in the moral courage so essential in a commander of large bodies of troops. *Gordon's* adverse opinion had naturally been strengthened when Sheridan counterattacked later in the day to drive the Confederates in confusion from the field. As a result, bitter feelings were engendered that led to a lively controversy over the Battle of Cedar Creek and the causes of *Early's* defeat which still reverberates whenever the spotlight is thrown on the 1864 campaign in the Shenandoah Valley.

Early's account stated that in passing over Cedar Creek after Crook's corps had been driven from their camps, he discovered a number of men engaged in plundering, and ordered a battalion of *Wharton's* temporarily inactive division to clear the camps and force the men to return to their organizations. Sometime later he was advised that a great many men from various units were doing the same thing, whereupon every available staff officer was sent to stop the plundering if possible and at the same time orders went to the division commanders to take the necessary action to recall all men of their own divisions so engaged.

Early's official report to General *Lee,* written on October 21, two days after the battle, when he had had opportunity for reflection, placed the blame for his defeat solely on the acts of plunder and the panic of the men of his army when they were counterattacked. Said *Early,* avoiding any implication of failure in generalship on his own part: "We had within our grasp a glorious victory, and lost it, by the uncontrollable propensity of our men for plunder, in the first place, and the subsequent panic of those who had kept their places, which was without sufficient cause, for I believe that the enemy had only made the movement against us as a demonstration, hoping to protect his stores, etc. at Winchester . . . The truth is, we have very few field or company officers worth anything, almost all our good officers of that kind having been killed, wounded, or captured, and it is impossible to preserve discipline without good field and company officers . . . the victory already gained was lost by the subsequent bad conduct of the troops."

Not until thirty-nine years had elapsed was any real effort made to vindicate the Confederate fighting men against *Early's* charge that it was they whose "bad conduct" had brought disaster to the army. By that time the Official Records had been published, but without *Gordon's* report of the part he and his *Second Corps* had played. Nine years after *Early's* death (March 2, 1894), and only four months before his own death on January 4, 1904, *Gordon's Reminiscences of the Civil War* appeared in book form. His account of the Battle of Cedar Creek absolves the Confederate combat troops of the charge of plundering, and instead places full responsibility for the defeat squarely on the shoulders of *Early* himself. *Gordon* states:

I am writing reminiscences; but if they are to be of any value they must also stand the test applied to witnesses in courts of justice. The unexpected and unexplained absence of my official report of Cedar Creek from the list of those published with General Early's in the War Records makes clear my duty to record in these reminiscences some statements which appear to me essential to the truth of history.
Captain Jed Hotchkiss, of General Early's staff, has fortunately left a Journal in which he recorded events as they occurred day by day. In that Journal, which has been pub-

lished by the Government among official papers in the records of the "War of the Rebellion" (First Series, Vol. XLIII, Part I, pp. 567-599), Captain Hotchkiss made at the time this memorandum: "Saturday, October 29th . . . A contention between Generals Gordon and Early about the battle of Cedar Creek," etc.

There were a number of strongly controverted points between us; but the only one in which the whole country is concerned, involving as it does the character of Southern soldiery, the only one which I feel compelled to notice in this book, is the question as to the responsibility for the disaster at Cedar Creek after the signal victory had been won . . . General Early insisted, and so stated in his now published report, that the "bad conduct" of his own men caused the astounding disaster; while I was convinced that it was due solely to the unfortunate halting and delay after the morning victory. I insisted then, and still insist, that our men deserved only unstinted praise. I believed then, and I believe now, that neither General Sheridan nor any other commander could have prevented the complete destruction of his infantry if in the early hours of the morning we had concentrated our fire and assaults upon his only remaining corps.

If my official report of the battle of Cedar Creek had been published with General Early's, it would perhaps not be necessary for me to speak of the "contention" mentioned by Captain Hotchkiss in his Journal, which I have recently seen for the first time. Justice to others, however, to the living and the dead, demands that I now make record in this book of some facts connected with that "contention," and that I send to posterity this record in connection with his report.

It is due to General Early to say that his physical strength was not sufficient to enable him to ascend Massanutten Mountain and survey the field from that lofty peak. He had not, therefore, the opportunity to take in the tremendous possibilities which that view revealed. He had not been permitted to stand upon that summit and trace with his own eye the inviting lines for the Confederate night march; to see for himself, in the conditions immediately before him, the sure prophecy of Confederate victory, and to have his brain set on fire by clearly perceiving that the movement, if adopted and executed with vigor and pressed to the end, must inevitably result in bringing to Sheridan's army, in quick succession, complete surprise, universal dismay, boundless panic, and finally rout, capture or annihilation. Again, General Early was not on that portion of the field which was struck by the Confederate cyclone at dawn; nor did he witness its destructive sweep through Sheridan's camps and along his breastworks, leaving in its wide track not a Federal soldier with arms in his hands.

Gordon's story goes on to quote from Sheridan's official report to support his contention that *Early's* decision not to vigorously press the attack, when the Union army was disorganized and in retreat, was principally responsible for the subsequent Confederate defeat. In Sheridan's own words *Gordon* repeats that "the whole army (Union) had been driven back in confusion"; "there was not left in a large portion of the Union infantry a company organization"; "the torrent of fugitives" had gone to the rear with such "appalling rapidity" as to have reached Mill Creek, eight or ten miles away, by nine o'clock in the morning.

Gordon was not the only Confederate who felt strongly on the subject. Statements by other prominent participants in the battle expressed similar views. Colonel *Thomas H. Carter, Early's* chief of artillery, said that *Early* "made a fatal mistake in stopping the pursuit of the enemy, with the Sixth Corps retiring before artillery alone and the other two corps in full and disorganized flight at nine o'clock in the morning."

Major *R. W. Hunter,* Chief of Staff, *Second Corps,* somewhat lyrically declaimed that "neither the famous Macedonian phalanx, nor Caesar's Tenth Legion, nor the Old Guard of Napoleon, nor Wellington's hollow squares, which saved him at Waterloo, nor any possible combination of troops, could have withstood the combined assault of infantry, artillery, and cavalry that it was in our power to have made upon the Sixth Corps on that eventful morning after the complete rout of the Eighth and Nineteenth Corps. Why was not that concentrated assault made?"

Jed Hotchkiss referred to the "inexcusable delay"; General *Thomas L. Rosser,* cavalry commander, declared that if the fight had continued as it was begun, the legend of Sheridan's famous ride from Winchester would never have been born; and General *Gabriel C. Wharton,* one of *Early's* division commanders, contributed to the testimony a description of his own reactions immediately after the two Union corps were routed: "I expected every minute orders to advance; but no orders came, and there we stood —no enemy in our front for hours, except some troops moving about in the woodland on a hill nearly a mile in our front. I have never been able to understand why General *Early* did not advance, or why he remained in line for four or five hours after the brilliant victory of the morning."

REFUTES CHARGE OF PLUNDERING

On the premise that Confederate posterity in particular would be profoundly interested in the question of whether *Early's* officers and men forgot their duty in plundering the captured Union camps and thus turning victory into defeat, *Gordon* carefully marshalled evidence to prove the falsity of *Early's* charge that he would have defeated Sheridan's whole force "but for the bad conduct of my troops."

In extenuation of *"Old Jube,"* who in *Gordon's* view was as brave and loyal to the Confederate cause as any officer, while at the same time extremely obstinate in sticking to his own opinions, right or wrong—*Gordon's* account said that *Early* was *misled* about the plundering. It was true, *Gordon* pointed out, that Confederate soldiers *did* straggle and plunder, but they were noncombatants, men who had been wounded in the summer campaign and had come up for medical check, or unarmed men who as casuals were not part of the fighting troops. These were the men, according to the Rev. *A. C. Hopkins,* a Confederate chaplain who was unassigned to any particular unit at Cedar Creek and hence free to visit all parts of the battlefield at will, "who came like a division down the pike behind *Wharton,* and soon scattered over the field and camps and helped themselves. They were not on duty. But there can be no doubt that General *Early* mistook them for men who had fallen out of ranks."

As a clincher to the rebuttal, *Wharton* was quoted as saying that the reports of the combat soldiers straggling and pillaging was not correct, nor did it have any connection with the disaster to the army, while *Gordon* made the additional point that of all the official reports that were published, not a single one, even remotely, suggested that plundering was the cause of the Confederate reverses.

The truth about the plundering seems to lie somewhere between the extreme viewpoints expressed by *Early* on the one hand, and *Gordon* and his adherents on the other. It is understandable that the Confederate generals would be reluctant to advertise to the world that they had so little discipline in their organizations that their soldiers turned aside from their duty in the midst of battle in order to satisfy the natural urge for booty. It was normal procedure for the Confederate soldier to improve his own deficient wardrobe by taking the better clothing, boots, etc. from Federal soldiers, even to the extent of stripping the bodies of the dead. But that usually occurred after the battle was over.

Two extracts from the diary of General *Clement A. Evans,* a close friend and loyal supporter of *Gordon's* who commanded *Gordon's* division at Cedar Creek, furnish an interesting commentary on the controversy:

October 21 '64—Camp Shirley—The victory is due to the plan and management of Gordon, the defeat is due to Early. When shall we be relieved of his heavy incubus? The immense amount of plunder on the battlefield caused a great deal of the straggling and proper steps were not taken to prevent it. I have seldom seen a richer battlefield. Oct. 30 '64—Camp Shirley—The unhappy state of feeling between General Gordon and Early has been increased by the recent "address" of Early to his troops in which some pointed allusions understood to refer to Gordon are made.—Early desperately jealous and will do everything in his power to work the downfall of General Gordon for he feels that Gordon's genius will obscure him as a Dept Commander in the same way it did last year as a Division Commander. If the government will consult the interest of affairs here, Gordon and Early—by removal of Early from Command. There was plundering done as on every battlefield, but, it was Early's miserable generalship which lost the battle.

CAPTURE OF WAGONS NEAR RIPON BY MOSBY'S GUERRILLAS

CHAPTER 15

CONCLUSION OF THE VALLEY CAMPAIGN

RELUCTANT to acknowledge the military facts of life inherent in three successive defeats and routs, and despite the weakened condition of his greatly reduced army, by November 11 *Jubal Early* had reassembled enough strength at New Market to make one last quasi-offensive move in the direction of Sheridan's army, then encamped around Kernstown and relaxing in peaceful comfort as the men and officers looked forward to a winter of relief from campaigning. The Confederate gesture, which may have been intended merely as a reconnaissance in force, turned out to be a feeble one. If *Early* thought to catch Sheridan napping, he soon discovered his mistake, for the Union cavalry under Merritt and Custer met the Confederate cavalry of *Rosser* and *Lomax* at Cedar Creek and easily drove them back in a brief encounter that must

366

have convinced *Early* the Valley Campaign was indeed over. In the early part of December, when it was apparent that further active campaigning for the winter was impracticable, Wright's Sixth Corps was returned to Grant and the *Confederate Second Corps,* together with *Kershaw's division,* rejoined *Lee.*

Sheridan now found time to turn his attention to the problem posed by the intermittent harassment of small Union detachments at the hands of Colonel *Mosby's* guerrillas, officially recognized by the Southern hierarchy as the *Forty-Third Battalion, Virginia Cavalry.* That designation by the *War Department* had been conferred ostensibly to throw about the tough, independent *Rangers* a cloak of military respectability, however diaphanous the covering may have appeared to their Federal victims.

The Fabulous John S. Mosby

John Singleton Mosby, one of the more glamorous of the many Confederate leaders who achieved renown against the background of romance and chivalry that was as natural to the South as mint juleps, beautiful women, and blooded horses, was a product of his environment. A lawyer in civil life, he had entered the service as a private in the *1st Virginia Cavalry* before First Bull Run, and served in *Jeb Stuart's* command until after the Battle of Fredericksburg in December 1862. Small in stature, and weighing only 125 pounds, he was active in mind and body, becoming restive when faced with another winter of inactivity devoted mostly to foraging in rear areas for supplies. It was then that his keen imagination conceived the idea of taking a small detail of cavalrymen over to Loudoun County where, as the then lieutenant told *Stuart,* he "thought he could make things lively during the winter months." It was the type of adventure that would appeal to *Stuart,* who readily approved the suggestion, never suspecting the extent to which the initial venture into irregular warfare would carry the high-spirited young cavalryman. Had *Stuart* known then how greatly the carefree, unconventional partisan service would appeal to the more adventuresome of the Confederate troopers, in marked contrast to the regimented discipline of the regular service, he might have had second thoughts about the wisdom of turning *Mosby* loose to attract men from his own squadrons.

Photographs of *Mosby* reveal a determined, straightforward, clean-cut countenance with deep-set eyes, broad forehead, firm lips and well-formed nose. Slender and wiry, neither tall nor short, his quiet appearance, although indicating alertness and the suggestion of great physical endurance, was in marked contrast to what one might expect from reading of his fabulous exploits in the last two years of the war.

By the summer of 1864, *Mosby's* incursions, together with those of other irregulars such as *Gilmor, White,* and *McNeil,* had been so successful that the Union high command was forced to reckon with him as an important factor in the consideration of overall strategy. Sheridan was well aware of *Mosby's* gadfly propensities when he planned his Shenandoah campaign, but probably had little idea, until he learned the hard way, that *Mosby's* comparative handful of men would be able by their bold, hit-run methods to pin down so large a proportion of Federal combat effectives for guarding depots and rail communications and escorting supply trains. The Confederate guerrillas, Sheridan advised Grant, had "annoyed him during the entire campaign," particularly "*Mosby,* the most redoubtable of these leaders, whose force was made up from the country around Upperville, east of the Blue Ridge, to which section he always fled for a hiding place when he scented danger."

Mosby did not of course devote all his time to aiding

JOHN SINGLETON MOSBY AND GROUP OF RAIDERS

Early's operations in the Valley by engaging in raids on Sheridan's rear areas. Loudoun County came in time to be known as part of "Mosby's Confederacy" through serving as the base from which his lightning forays were launched, and to which his hard riding horsemen would return individually after completing a mission. In addition *Mosby* ranged over a wide area of northern Virginia and southern Maryland, with special attention to the outposts guarding the approaches to the Washington defenses, which extended in a long curving line from the upper to the lower Potomac. How many Union troops *Mosby's Rangers* succeeded in keeping occupied can never be known, but the number must have run into the tens of thousands. So sensitive had the authorities at the Capital become in their fear of *Mosby* that General Hooker was alleged to have said that in the spring of 1863 the planks on Chain Bridge over the Potomac were taken up every night to keep him out of Washington. That Federal precaution was undertaken in the early stages of *Mosby's* career as a partisan, when he commanded only about twenty men, every one of whom however was equivalent to a troop of cavalry in immobilizing enemy combat forces. The canny Confederate operated on the premise that a small force that moved rapidly and secretly to threaten many points on a defensive line could neutralize a hundred times its own number, for the simple reason that the line must be stronger at every point than the attacking force to avoid being broken.

One incident will serve to illustrate the great value to the Confederacy of *Mosby's* methods, and incidentally his sense of humor as well. Operating along the Potomac with his small detachment in early 1863, he learned from friendly citizens where every Union picket was stationed. "A certain Major-General came after me with a division of cavalry and a battery of artillery," wrote *Mosby* in a reminiscent account of his experiences; "after shelling the woods in every direction so as to be sure of my extermination, and destroying many bats and owls, he took off as prisoners all the old men he could find. He had the idea that I was a myth and those old men were the raiders. He returned with his prizes to camp, but I was there almost as soon as he was."

It was *John Mosby* who set the Civil War fashion of tracking down and seizing Union generals in their beds in the dead of night. And if the area chosen happened to be close to Washington and the prospective victims were presumably safe and secure in the midst of large bodies of troops, that merely added spice to the raid. Such adventures, however, carried within themselves the seeds of their own failure, in forcing the opposition to take extra precautions whenever *Mosby* was known to be operating in the vicinity.

Mosby's "Greatest Exploit"

The capture of Brigadier General Edwin H. Stoughton, 25-year old West Pointer, a brigade commander on the line of Union outposts near Centerville in early 1863, was an adventure which *Mosby* himself declared to have been his greatest exploit. Stoughton was asleep in his quarters* at Fairfax Courthouse, with hundreds of Federal infantry and cavalry soldiers in the immediate vicinity, when *Mosby* led 29 mounted *Rangers* through the Union lines one dark, rainy night, seized Stoughton and 31 others, along with 58 horses, and escorted them back to Confederate territory, despite desperate efforts by aroused Federal cavalry to block his escape and recover the prisoners.

The officer *Mosby* was really after on his Fairfax raid was an Englishman, Colonel Percy Wyndham, who was serving as a cavalry brigade commander in the Union Army. *Mosby* had been persistent in attacking the Englishman's pickets and had irritated Wyndham to the point where the latter took to sending the partisan leader messages in which he called him a horse-thief and other uncomplimentary names. *Mosby* concluded that Wyndham had gone beyond the bounds of sportsmanship and it was time to teach him a lesson. It so happened, however, that General Stoughton became the principal prize in the absence of Wyndham, who was visiting in Washington the night *Mosby's* party chose to pay their call.

Mosby's guide on this occasion was a deserter from the 5th New York Cavalry, one Sergeant *Ames,* who held a deep grudge against the men of his outfit for an alleged affront that had made him very vindictive. The regiment from which *Ames* deserted was part of Wyndham's brigade, a fact that probably influenced *Mosby* to act when he did. Nevertheless, to make certain that *Ames* would not double-cross him, he put the defector through a number of severe tests before setting the date for the raid.

Sergeant *Ames* entered upon his traitorous assignment

_____
* A 2-story brick house near the court house, and still in use.

with such willing enthusiasm that, once the stealthy Confederates had safely passed within the Union lines, representing themselves to be a Federal cavalry detachment, *Mosby* split his group into two parts and sent *Ames* with several companions to capture Colonel Wyndham. Although *Ames* failed to find Wyndham, he brought back his own former troop commander, Captain Barker, two members of Wyndham's staff, and a uniform belonging to the Englishman, in recognition of which feat *Mosby* promoted him to the rank of lieutenant in what was then only a *Ranger* company.

There is a sequel to the story of Lieutenant *Ames,* who, *Mosby* recorded, continued to serve with him "until he was killed in October 1864." It goes without saying that *Ames* was a marked man, who would be roughly treated if he should ever fall into the hands of his former fellow-troopers. The fate that befell him came to light in the following letter written to his wife by one Cornelious Raver, a Union soldier whose organization is not identified, but who was probably a member of Colonel Young's battalion of scouts, organized by Sheridan in the fall of 1864 to counteract and contain *Mosby's Rangers.*

Elexandre October the 16 1864

Mrs Elizabeth Raver
  Cavettsville PO
    Westmoreland Co.
     Penna.

dear Wife and dear little Babie after my love to you all I will informe you that I am well and hartey I hope you are all the same Well I will informe you that we have had some Big times since I rote Before on the night of the (?) at half past nine oclock we marched about nine miles and Captured 9 Rebels and then we heard that the Rebels had hid 4 pieses of artillery and then Company E ower one Company started up the mountain about 2 miles then We poot out a skurmish lien and surcled the Woods till we found them fore pieses of artillery that they had bin pepering us with all the time so We took it and did not fier a gun to take it Before We Started the mager told us if we Captured it We should have a big Bounty for it so We will look for it We hulled them 4 pieses of artillery 10 miles by hand Back to Camp and did not git back till about 7 oclock the next morning then we poot them on the cars and We was sent Back to Elexander along to gard them so we are hear this the morning of the 16 I expect we will go Back today We are all Well and hartey Conner and me stick together like two ticks Well I must tell you that We had the pleasure of bering Mosbeys first liutenant he went by the name of yankey Ames one of our Boys shot him on last monday throu the hart he was the sunofabitch that cut so many of ower mens throats so he is gon up the spout at last Well I wish you Would send me some money Please send it in Shin Plasters We cant git it chainged hear Well this is about all at present Please Right Soon direct as Before good by for this time

Cornelious Raver

While Private Raver's letter may not have won plaudits for spelling or punctuation, he did manage to pack a lot of news in a few sentences, and to convey in pungent language the satisfaction he and his buddies evidently experienced in sending Yankee Ames "up the spout!"

General Grant himself had a narrow escape from falling into the hands of the famous guerrilla leader in one of the weekly trips by rail that he was in the habit of taking to the Capital from his headquarters at Culpeper, following his appointment as General-in-Chief and prior to the opening of the Wilderness Campaign in the spring of 1864. As the unguarded train in which he was riding approached Warrenton Junction, Grant noticed a heavy cloud of dust a short distance from the tracks, "as if made by a body of cavalry on a charge." Halting the train at the Junction, the General was informed by the lone dispatcher at the station that *Mosby* had just crossed at full speed in pursuit of a detachment of Federal cavalry. It is not recorded that *Mosby* learned at the time of the rich prize so nearly within his grasp, nor how closely he may have come to changing the course of the war, but the two of them must have exchanged views on the episode at some time during their postwar relationship, which Grant in his *Memoirs* describes as intimate.

SHERIDAN CONCENTRATES ON THE IRREGULARS

During the lull that occurred following the elimination of *Early,* Sheridan concluded that he would concentrate on the Confederate "irregulars." This was a matter of unfinished business in any event, but it was made more pressing in Sheridan's mind by the recent killing by *Mosby* men, within the Union lines, of Colonel Tolles, his chief quartermaster, and his medical inspector, one Ohlenschlager. This latest stroke, added to the previous headaches that *Mosby* had induced throughout Sheridan's active campaign against *Early,* meant to *Mosby* merely one more notch on his gun stock, figuratively speaking. But the timing was significant in that Sheridan now found himself in position to take positive measures to pay off some old scores, among which was the much-publicized, spectacular "Greenback Raid."

When *Early's* Confederates had crossed the Potomac on their bold raid against the National Capital in early July, *Mosby* sent a detachment into Maryland to cut communications and prevent, or at least delay, information of *Early's* march from reaching the defenders of Washington. With that assignment completed, the Rangers returned to home territory. Later in the fall they engaged in a sharp encounter with the Eighth Illinois Cavalry near The Plains (also called White Plains), where that regiment was .assisting a force of Union infantry in guarding the workmen who were relaying the tracks of the Manassas Gap Railroad. Halting trains and tearing up tracks of that

374

particular railroad proved to be productive of little reward in the form of booty to *Mosby's* men, so in order to keep morale at a high pitch their leader shifted them over to the Shenandoah Valley, where his scouts had advised him that Baltimore and Ohio Railroad trains were ripe for plucking and offered greater potential gain.

THE GREENBACK RAID

Between Winchester and Martinsburg the *Rangers* took position in a woods near the turnpike and spent all of one day, October 14, watching parties of Federals moving up and down, occasionally dashing out to engage in the competitive sport of horse-racing in various directions, depending on the size and combativeness of their casual opponents. That night *Mosby* and his band moved to another body of woods, dismounted, left their horses with a detail, and crossed a field to the railroad at a spot where it passed through a deep cut. There they jacked up one side of the track on fence rails and old ties so that the engine would be certain to overturn when it reached that point. The men then lay down along the bank to await the coming of the train.

As the headlight of the engine appeared around a curve in the road, *Mosby* and his eager followers poised for action. There was a tremendous thump as the engine rose and fell, the scream of escaping steam, and the sound of a single shot. "Board her, boys!" was *Mosby's* sharp command, as the conductor jumped down to the track and hastily called out that he surrendered the train.

The famed desperadoes and train robbers of the western frontier could not have done a more thorough job of looting and burning, after the passengers of both sexes had been evacuated from the cars. The occupants of one car were immigrants who knew no English and sat frozen to their seats until *Mosby* conceived the idea of getting across to them the fate that words failed to convey. A bundle of newspapers was set afire and thrown into the car. That was something they understood. In a flash the car was ludicrously emptied as the poor creatures dived headling through the windows to safety.

The payoff came when a heavy tin box was discovered under a blanket and an innocent-looking satchel was appropriated from a Union officer in the search for plunder. The Yankee paymaster, believing that his tin box had not been found before the cars were consigned to the flames, boasted to his captors that they had overlooked more than $200,000 in greenbacks. When his error was pointed out, the major's crestfallen countenance afforded the raiders their best laugh of the evening. How much more in paper money was seized from the satchel was not reported, but one of the *Rangers* recorded the gratifying intelligence that each of the participant's shares came to $2,200 when the distribution was made the following day.

FEDERAL COUNTERMEASURES

Mosby's dramatic and highly effective sorties and raids achieved so much notoriety that it might be supposed he had everything his own way so long as the conventional Federal forces were preoccupied with field operations against Confederate armies. Actually that was not the case, for countermeasures were introduced with the creation by Sheridan, during the summer of 1864, of a battalion of military scouts under the then Major Young, who emulated *Mosby's* methods and in time developed his bold recruits into a hard core of independent scouts who became an admitted thorn in *Mosby's* side. One such body, under command of Captain Blazer, spent the greater part of its time tracking down the Confederate Rangers and killing as many as possible. In the period between August 18 and October 24, ranging up and down the Shenandoah

Valley between Harpers Ferry and Berryville, Blazer kept count of his actions and reported that his force of scouts had killed forty-four, wounded twelve, and captured twelve of *Mosby's* men with a loss to himself of five killed, seven wounded, and eight prisoners. Subsequent to that report, and apparently in a determined effort to remove the Blazer threat, *Mosby* sent two companies to wipe him out. In a big woods northeast of Berryville the two forces met on November 18, maneuvered warily for position, and finally clashed. Blazer's company was ambushed, fought desperately, but was defeated and put to rout, all of his men being either killed or captured. Among the latter was Captain Blazer himself, who was sent off to Libby Prison.

The Official Records, for those with the patience to search the voluminous documents, disclose a storehouse of information on every phase of the Civil War. There one finds occasional reports from Sheridan to Grant, and from *Mosby* to *Lee,* touching on the activities of the famous partisan specialist. On August 17, shortly after Sheridan took command of the Army of the Shenandoah, he sent a dispatch to Grant which read: "*Mosby* has annoyed me and captured a few wagons. We hanged one and shot six of his men yesterday." And again on August 22: "We have disposed of quite a number of *Mosby's* men."

It was not until after the Battle of Cedar Creek, however, that the more or less sporting aspects of guerrilla warfare in the Valley were transformed into grim and grisly tactics that left no room for anything but ruthless killing without quarter. The cold facts of a major incident which initiated the eye-for-an-eye treatment are found in *Mosby's* dispatch to *Lee* dated October 29, 1864:

During my absence from my command the enemy captured six of my men near Front Royal. These were immediately hanged by order, and in the presence of General

Custer. They also hanged another lately in Rappahannock. It is my purpose to hang an equal number of Custer's men whenever I capture them.

The preceding dispatch was indorsed by *Lee* to the *Secretary of War* with the comment: "I have directed Colonel *Mosby* to hang an equal number of Custer's men in retaliation for those executed by him."

As might be expected, the Confederates and the Federals gave very different accounts of the events that preceded the start of wholesale hangings and their justification, or lack of it. The Custer men claimed that in an encounter near Front Royal a Union officer, struck down along the road, was fired into by the *Rangers* as they rode past the wounded man, causing several additional wounds, none of which fortunately proved fatal. The *Rangers,* although they did not refute the charge, were infuriated more by the cold-blooded manner as they put it, in which the retaliation was conducted. According to their account, Custer's six captives were led through the streets of Front Royal with ropes around their necks before being led to their execution on a hill outside the town. After which a placard was attached to one of the swinging bodies that read: "This shall be the fate of all of Mosby's men."

Some weeks later a guerrilla raid in the Valley captured twenty-six of Custer's troopers, at which time the promise *Mosby* had made in his dispatch to *Lee* was fulfilled. The Union prisoners were formed in line, the adjutant read them an order, and twenty-six slips of paper were placed in a hat, six of them with numbers which, drawn by lot, would doom the unfortunates who were unlucky enough to pick other than blanks. As described by one of the less hardened *Rangers,* it was "one of the most pathetic chapters in human experience." The eyes of some of the Confederates filled with tears as they watched the harrowing experience, and one of the men who had led many of the

Rangers' most desperate charges actually broke down and wept like a child. With that hanging the debt had been paid in full, after which, significantly, there was no further stringing up of *Mosby* men by Custer or anyone else.

MERRITT RAIDS "MOSBY'S CONFEDERACY"

Toward the end of November Sheridan detached Merritt's cavalry division with instructions to cross the Blue Ridge into Loudoun County, operate against *Mosby* in his own bailiwick, and clear the area of forage and subsistence, as had been done so thoroughly in the Shenandoah Valley. Loudoun County, or *"Mosby's* Confederacy," covered five hundred square miles of lush horse country in which nestled such communities as Upperville, Middleburg, Leesburg and the like—a cavalryman's paradise that *John Singleton Mosby* had appropriated to his own use and that had served his purpose beautifully. Sheridan's decision to devastate Loudoun County was entirely logical, in fact an essential element in the scorched-earth policy that Grant had set forth in plain language when Sheridan was given his Valley mission in mid-summer.

Merritt made a wide swing through northwestern Virginia, to such distant and widely separated points as Centerville, Fairfax Court House, and Leesburg, meanwhile sweeping the countryside as far north as the Potomac River, burning grain and bringing in large herds of cattle, sheep, and hogs. While the Union cavalry was engaged in this expedition, *Rosser* with two brigades of Confederate cavalry crossed North Mountain into West Virginia, attacked a Union military post at New Creek, captured five hundred prisoners, destroyed the garrison's supplies, and tore up the Baltimore and Ohio Railroad tracks in the vicinity. That evidence, however inconclusive, of a latent Confederate spark of resistance and the continuing will to undertake aggressive measures, led Sheridan to send General Crook with one division of his small corps back to West Virginia to stamp out the spark, Crook's other division being returned to Grant at City Point.

The earlier departure of the Federal Sixth Corps to rejoin the Army of the Potomac, followed by the transfer of Crook's Eighth Corps, left only Torbert's cavalry of two divisions and Emory's small Nineteenth Corps to pass the winter in the Valley. The pathetically shrunken remnants of *Early's army,* by that time composed of *Wharton's lone division* of infantry and a corporal's guard of cavalry (compared to the strength of the Union horsemen), had gone into winter quarters at Staunton.

Torbert's Cavalry Scores a Failure

Back in October, prior to the Battle of Cedar Creek, Grant had advised Sheridan of his desire to have the railroads broken up in the Gordonsville-Charlottesville area, particularly *Lee's* supply life-line, the strategic Virginia Central, which ran directly to Richmond, and the almost equally vital James River Canal. That had been the message, routed through Halleck's office to Sheridan, which the meddlesome Chief-of-Staff had modified to suit himself and which, by the time it reached Sheridan, was distorted to such an extent that Sheridan found it necessary to pay his pre-Cedar Creek Battle visit to Washington in order to persuade the War Department to let him carry out his own plan.

Disruption of rail communications at critical Gordonsville, east of the Blue Ridge, remained on the time-table of the tenacious Grant who again urged Sheridan to do something about the matter. It was mid-December and very cold. The thermometer had already dipped to zero once or twice and the Valley would look back on the winter of '64-'65 as a particularly severe one during which snow fell on several occasions to the depth of several inches. The season was unsuitable for cavalry operations, but the troopers weren't making the decisions. So on December 19 Torbert moved out with Merritt's and Powell's cavalry divisions through Chester Gap, while Custer headed for Staunton to keep *Early's* force occupied if possible. The Confederate cavalry, however, smarting under their succession of reverses at the hands of the Blue cavalry, caught Custer's outfit in bivouac before daylight one morning near Lacey Spring, driving him in retreat down the Valley, with a loss of some prisoners and horses, and a large number of saddles and bridles that the Federals had not had time to place on the horses, so sudden was the Confederate attack.

Wharton's infantry division was sent to Gordonsville to counter the Union horsemen in conjunction with *Lomax's cavalry,* which in the meantime had already accomplished its mission of discouraging Torbert, a relatively easy matter considering the weather conditions. *Early's* counterintelligence, gathered through the efforts of his own cavalry as well as information from the more than willing citizens of the Valley, was so effective that the expedition turned out to be an utter failure, many of the Union troopers suffering frostbite and other discomforts of campaigning in bitter cold weather.

Sheridan, with but one division of infantry and three of cavalry, now went into winter cantonments at Winchester; *Early,* with one division of infantry and three brigades of cavalry at Staunton. To all intents and purposes, the Valley Campaign was over, although each commander kept a wary eye on the other as a matter of insurance against the remote possibility that his opponent might be foolish enough to risk a serious encounter under impossible weather conditions. Sheridan's "independent scouts" under the leadership of Colonel Young had by that time become seasoned campaigners in the art of ferreting out information from within *Early's* lines, serving Sheridan well during the winter both in the Valley and in West Virginia against the guerrillas who operated in certain anti-Union areas of that State under the noted *Harry Gilmor*.

TIT FOR TAT

Having little else to do as the winter months passed, Sheridan's headquarters staff spent their time dreaming up adventures for Young and his men. Some one figured that it would be helpful if Young could dispose of *Gilmor* and thus remove from the scene one of the most persistent of the Confederate troublemakers. Word had reached Sheridan from his scouts that *Gilmor* was at Moorefield, about ninety miles southwest of Winchester, in West Virginia, where he had called a meeting to which he expected a sizeable body of new recruits to repair from various sections of the country. It was accordingly arranged that Young would take twenty men, disguised as Confederates on their way to *Gilmor's* rendezvous to be followed at an appropriate distance by a squadron of Union cavalry, ostensibly engaged in the task of pursuing the fleeing "Confederates."

The scheme worked beautifully and without a hitch. The disguised Federals received a cordial welcome from the country folk whom they encountered on the way and on entering Moorefield had no difficulty in locating the house where *Gilmor* was sleeping. On the night of February 5, with the Union cavalry "in pursuit" at a respectful distance, Young gained access to the house, roughly awakened the surprised *Gilmor*, placed a pistol at his head, and informed him that he was a prisoner of one of Sheridan's staff officers. *Gilmor's* men, who in the meantime had gotten wind of the fact that something was wrong, started to the rescue about the time the Union cavalry rode up, driving the guerrillas off in every direction. Colonel Young, escorted by Sheridan's cavalry, rode back to Winchester, turned *Gilmor* over to superior authority, and that episode was marked Closed in the Federal files.

The incident, however, rankled with *Gilmor's* followers, who didn't fancy having the hated Yankees playing tricks that they considered to be more properly in their own department. With their own leader a prisoner, *Gilmor's* faithful followers joined up with guerrillas to plot revenge.

Several weeks after the Moorefield encounter, young *Jesse McNeil,* son of Captain *"Hanse" McNeil,* one of the more widely known partisans who had been killed in a scrap in the Valley in the fall of 1864, led a group of seventy bold raiders to Cumberland, Maryland, to repay the compliment and square the account. The elder *McNeil* had for several years nourished a grudge against Union General Ben Kelley, the perennial commander of Federal troops guarding the line of the Baltimore and Ohio Railroad, for an alleged affront in 1862, having to do with Kelley's refusal to permit *McNeil's* wife to pass through the Union lines to reach her Moorefield home and convalescent husband, who was recuperating from an earlier wound. The hot-blooded, hot-headed *Jesse* thus had several good reasons for staging a spectacular raid that, if successful, would permit his father to rest comfortably in his grave, avenge the "family honor," and wipe out the stain of the Yankee capture of his former leader, Captain *Gilmor.*

Whether by accident or design, the raid started in the midst of a heavy snow storm, the kind of weather that no self-respecting Federal would expect the toughest guerrilla to combat. Young *McNeil* and his numerous colleagues, dressed in Federal uniforms, covered a distance of fifty miles to cross the Potomac near Cumberland, where General George Crook's two Union divisions were hibernating. Making short shrift of the few Federal pickets encountered along the road to Cumberland, the raiders entered the town without opposition and then split into two groups to descend on the separate hotels in which Crook and Kelley had their respective headquarters.

It was all over in a few minutes. Disposing of sleepy, unsuspecting sentinels was easy. Nor was there any resistance offered when the two generals were wakened and ordered to dress and accompany their captors. There was of course a great uproar as soon as the *Rangers* left with their guests, and Union cavalry from all over galloped the countryside in an effort to round up the raiders and effect a release of the generals and their headquarters flags. But the cagey *McNeil* was not to be foiled in his getaway, with the result that he outmaneuvered the several pursuing detachments, reached *Early's* headquarters at Harrisonburg, and turned his prisoners over to the tender mercies of Crook's fellow West Pointer. Both generals were promptly sent to Richmond, but according to custom were released to await official exchange, which occurred within a matter of weeks.

THE BATTLE OF WAYNESBORO

In compliance with Grant's several times repeated instructions to Sheridan to operate against the Virginia Central Railroad, to render it and the James River Canal useless to *Lee*, Sheridan found it convenient to initiate the undertaking in the closing days of February, 1865. Little Phil's seeming reluctance to leave the Valley was unquestionably related to the new project, following the execution of which it had been suggested by Grant that Sheridan attempt to capture Lynchburg and then, depending on the circumstances at the time, either join Sherman's army in North Carolina or return to Winchester. The prospect of being attached to Sherman carried no appeal for Sheridan, who thought he foresaw an early end to the war and wanted to have his boys in at the kill with Grant, under whose immediate command the cavalry corps had been given the freedom of action that Sheridan had needed to establish its reputation as a foeman worthy of *Jeb Stuart's* steel. To return to Winchester after the scheduled expedition would simply be to vegetate in comparative idleness. Sheridan made up his mind that he was going to take his cavalry back to the Army of the Potomac even if it should become necessary to slightly alter events to bring it about within the bounds of military propriety.

Wesley Merritt had succeeded Torbert, on leave of absence, as Sheridan's Chief of Cavalry, a reassignment that placed in command a more aggressive and competent cavalry leader than Torbert had proven himself to be. Leaving his only remaining infantry division to hold the fort at Winchester (the other had in the meantime been returned to Grant), and with Merritt in field command of the two cavalry divisions, Custer's and Merritt's (the latter now under Devin), accompanied by two sections of artillery, a pontoon train of eight canvas boats, and an undersized ammunition and supply train, the 10,000 man column moved out from Winchester on February 27 on what would prove to be the final engagement that marked the end of organized Confederate resistance in the Shenandoah Valley.

A heavy rain was falling as the troopers rode up the turnpike, followed by the artillery and trains. It was still cold, but the rain, which had persisted into the second and third days, was melting the snow and turning the side roads into muddy streams that held little promise of pleasurable travel once the column was forced to leave the hard-surfaced turnpike. Crossing the North Fork of the Shenandoah on the pontoons, the column reached Lacey Spring at the end of the second day without meeting an enemy except a few guerrillas who paralleled the march of the cavalry without offering any opposition.

Early had of course been informed of Sheridan's move and sent *Rosser's* cavalry, several hundred strong, to delay the march. *Rosser* encountered the Federals at Mt. Crawford, where he tried to burn the bridges over the Middle Fork, but was outflanked and driven back by two regiments of Capehart's brigade who swam their horses across the swollen stream and attacked, taking thirty prisoners and twenty ambulances and wagons.

Immediately on learning of Sheridan's departure from Winchester, or possibly even before, *Early* had sent instructions to *Lomax* at Millboro, forty miles west of Staunton, to assemble his cavalry and be prepared to harass and delay Sheridan if he should turn toward Lynchburg. He also wired *Echols*, in southwestern Virginia, to entrain his infantry brigade for Lynchburg. *Early* then departed from Staunton, riding toward Waynesboro, and gathering up en route all the troops that remained to him other than *Echols' brigade* and *Lomax's* cavalry. That pathetic remnant would be *Wharton's* two brigades, with a battalion of artillery, hardly more than 1,500 men, who had passed the winter near Fisherville, between Staunton and Waynesboro.

On the morning of March 2 the still defiant Confederate general took up a defensive position along a ridge just west of Waynesboro, where he posted *Wharton's* little force in the hope of delaying the Federal advance for a few hours to permit the removal from the town of some supplies and a half-dozen pieces of artillery for which no horses could be found.

When Sheridan arrived at Staunton on the morning of March 1, only to find that *Early* had departed, leaving word that he intended to make a stand at Waynesboro, he had the choice of punching through *Early's* expected defense line there or marching directly to Lynchburg, the latter a move which would expose his rear to a possible Confederate attack. His decision was to send Merritt with Custer's division in the lead, followed by Devin's division, on the road to Waynesboro.

The rains, continuing without a pause ever since the column had left Winchester, had turned the roads into one continuous mudhole, so that men and horses were plastered with the gooey substance until all individuality had been obliterated and recognition became difficult. Approaching Waynesboro, Custer discovered the enemy ensconced behind temporary breastworks on the ridge west of the town. A reconnaissance disclosed that *Early's* left was somewhat exposed, which prompted Custer to mount a combined frontal and flank attack, using a dismounted brigade for the turning movement while the remainder of the division, two brigades, assaulted the position partly mounted and partly dismounted.

The Last, Weak Stand of Jubal Early

The flank attack, as usual, accomplished its purpose, causing the defenders to take off from there without ceremony, while the frontal assault rolled over and through the barely resisting, confused, and overwhelmed Confederates. Two mounted regiments, seeing the enemy bewilderment, charged the enemy position in column at such a pace that their momentum carried them right through Waynesboro and on across South River, where they finally reined in their horses to discover that they had unwittingly but fortuitously gotten themselves on *Early's* rear. Whereupon a fast thinking officer spread them out in a cordon along the east bank of the river, blocking the Confederate retreat, until the entire force had surrendered except *Rosser's* cavalry, which eluded Custer, and a coterie of generals including *Early, Wharton, Long,* and about twenty men, all of whom managed to escape into the mountains.

"I went to the top of a hill to reconnoitre," *Early* explained in his *Reminiscenses,*" and had the mortification of seeing the greater part of my command being carried off as prisoners, and a force of the enemy moving rapidly towards Rockfish Gap. I then rode with the greater part of my staff and 15 or 20 others, including General *Long,* across the mountain north of the Gap. . . . . ."

In this affair, which resulted in a minimum of casualties to either side, Custer captured "the greater part of my command," according to *Early;* 1,600 men according to Sheridan's report. Both agreed on eleven as the number of guns taken, and Custer claimed in addition that he had seized seventeen battle flags, which was typically Custerian, in refuting which *Early* made the dry remark that he couldn't imagine where Custer could have gotten so many flags. Escorted by a regiment of cavalry, the Confederate prisoners were marched back to Winchester, marking the final act in Sheridan's Shenandoah Valley Campaign.

Early's last battle, if the relatively bloodless encounter at Waynesboro can fairly be designated a battle, was recognized at the time for what history would record as the terminal point for organized warfare in the Valley, that vital corridor to the North which had made and broken more than one Union general throughout the four years in which it had served as a cockpit. It was the end for *Jubal Early,* the loser; but for Philip Sheridan, the accomplishment of his first and only major mission as commander of an independent army was but a phase, albeit a most important one, in his rise from obscurity to rank with Grant and Sherman as one of the three principal architects of final victory in the closing weeks of the war.

FIVE WEEKS TO APPOMATTOX

It is beyond the scope of this narrative to follow Sheridan and his cavalry through the remaining period of five weeks that would elapse before *Lee's* surrender to Grant at Appomattox Court House. Suffice it to say that, having made up his mind that he wanted desperately to rejoin the Army of the Potomac for the final stages of the war whose early end he foresaw in company with plenty of other leading figures of the South as well as the North, Sheridan hastened to satisfy the minimum requirements of Grant's directive that he break up the Virginia Central Railroad and the James River Canal. As to whether he would exercise the discretion allowed him on the subject of seizing Lynchburg and then joining Sherman or returning to Winchester—well, Sheridan would cross those bridges when he came to them, or would figure a plausible explanation to give Grant when he should reach Petersburg.

The Union cavalry, Custer in the lead, moved on Charlottesville, but the rains and spring thaws had so softened the roads that the wagons made slow progress and the horses were badly in need of rest when the column reached unprotected Charlottesville, which the mayor, accompanied by a group of citizens, ceremoniously surrendered to General Custer. Sheridan decided to remain several days in historic Charlottesville to give horses and men a breather, at the same time sending detachments to destroy the railroad in the direction of Lynchburg. Custer was given the job of tearing up the railroad; Merritt was dispatched to destroy the canal. The two divisions were to meet at Newmarket preparatory to crossing the James River at a point east of Lynchburg.

What with high water making the James River unfordable, the accompanying pontoons being too short to span the river, the available bridges burned by the Confederates, and reports that Lynchburg was being fortified and reinforced—Sheridan happily concluded that it had become impracticable for him to join Sherman, and foolish to return to Winchester. Apparently the only sensible solution would be to do what he had planned all along, rejoin Grant before Petersburg, concurrently destroying further stretches of the railroad and canal as the cavalry marched east.

It was quite a march, all things considered, by the time Sheridan and his two cavalry divisions reached White House Landing on the Pamunkey River March 18. There they found awaiting them the supplies which they badly needed after a sixteen day march in almost incessant rain. "The hardships of this march," Sheridan wrote, "far exceeded those of any previous campaigns by the cavalry."

Early Bows off the Stage

Early continued, with a handful of men in place of an army, to Charlottesville, only to discover that the town was in the hands of the Federals. He then turned back with his little party, following a circuitous route to Gordonsville, where he found General *Wharton*, whom he dispatched to Lynchburg to take command of *Echols' brigade* for the defense of that city. Remaining at Gordonsville for several days, *Early* rode on towards Richmond, barely escaping capture at the hands of a Federal cavalry force. Reaching army headquarters, he reported to General *Lee*, who directed him to send *Rosser's* and *McCausland's* cavalry to Petersburg and himself return to the Valley to reorganize what was left of his command. While engaged in that rather hopeless and unrewarding occupation, *Jubal Early* on March 30 (one week only before *Lee's* surrender) received a telegram from *Lee*, instructing him to turn over the command in southwestern Virginia to *Echols* and the remnants in the Valley to *Lomax*, and return to his home, where he would receive a letter of explanation.

The letter explained in diplomatic language that *Early* was no longer able to command the cheerful support of the people and the full confidence of the soldiers so essential to success. "While my own confidence in your ability, zeal, and devotion to the cause, is unimpaired," wrote *Lee*, "I have nevertheless felt that I could not oppose what seems to be the current of opinion, without injustice to your reputation and injury to the service . . . Thanking you for the fidelity and energy with which you have always supported my efforts, and for the courage and devotion you have ever manifested in the service of the country, I am, etc."

Lieutenant General *Jubal A. Early,* a distinguished officer without a command, was a tragic if not pathetic figure during the last few days of the Confederacy, although he would have been the last to admit it. On the 30th of March, after turning over his "command" to General *Echols,* he contracted a heavy cold and cough that prostrated him for several days. When he was again able to travel, an ambulance conveyed him to his home in Lynchburg, in the course of which journey the news reached him of *Lee's* surrender. He then proceeded on horseback to join *Edmund Kirby Smith* in the Trans-Mississippi Department, only to learn that *Kirby Smith* too had surrendered his army. Unwilling to subject himself to the humiliation of conforming to the will of the victor, the thoroughly "unreconstructed" *Early* left the country in disguise, to find refuge in Mexico, a voluntary exile from the reunited Nation whose dissolution he had fought so hard to sustain.

THANKSGIVING—ARMY OF SHENANDOAH RECEIVES GIFTS OF TURKEYS
FROM THE HOME FRONT

CHAPTER 16

SUMMARY OF THE CAMPAIGN

IN studying the Shenandoah Valley Campaign of 1864 the temptation is strong to draw parallels between it and *Stonewall Jackson's* campaign in the same area during the spring of '62. The Confederate strategy was identical in both campaigns, to secure the Valley for the South, to draw troops from the Army of the Potomac, and to keep the Washington Administration off balance. On the Union side the strategy in 1862 was neither well-defined nor intelligently executed, whereas in 1864 unity of command had at long last been achieved and a capable, determined, fighting general led the Union forces in a carefully prepared campaign for extermination of the opposing army *and* the war potential of the Valley.

The relative capabilities of the opposing commanders

in '62 and '64 were vastly different. The assertion that Sheridan was worth any two of his predecessors in the Valley can hardly be questioned. As between *Jackson* and *Early* the contrast, although less notable, was sufficiently marked to raise an interesting speculation as to what the outcome might have been had it been *Jackson* rather than *Early* with whom Sheridan had to contend. One might express the viewpoint that *Early*, while making a successful effort to emulate his illustrious fellow West Pointer in the rapidity of his marches and the flexibility of his operations, was less endowed with the qualities of moral courage, personal magnetism, and stern asceticism that characterized *Stonewall Jackson*. It has also been stated that *Early* lacked the courage of his convictions and, if the testimony of General *Gordon* be accepted as valid, there were other character traits which he considered to be less than admirable.

Did *Early* accomplish the three-fold mission assigned him by General *Lee*, to save Lynchburg, drive Hunter from the Valley, and conduct a threatening raid on Washington? He most certainly did, with amazing celerity, and was so successful in alarming the Federal authorities that Grant was compelled to detach two army corps from Meade's command, delay his own war of attrition against *Lee's army*, and finally shift the major portion of his cavalry corps to the Valley to give Sheridan sufficient combat power to deal effectively with *Early's* comparatively small, but able and aggressive force.

It is doubtful that *Stonewall Jackson* would have done better or accomplished more than *Jubal Early* on his 450-mile expedition. In weighing the after effects, however, it is debatable whether in the long run the Confederate cause was well-served. Driving Hunter from the Valley preserved Lynchburg and permitted the Valley farmers to harvest their crops, but only to have most of the garnered hay and grain burned to the ground a few weeks later, and with it

Executive Mansion
Washington, Oct 22. 1864.

Major General Sheridan

With great pleasure I tender to you and your brave army, the thanks of the Nation, and my own personal administration and gratitude, for the months operation in the Shenandoah Valley; and especially for the splendid work of October 19. 1864.

Your Ob.^t Servt
Abraham Lincoln.

FACSIMILE OF LETTER OF CONGRATULATIONS FROM THE PRESIDENT

the mills and barns, which was a much more serious matter for the saddened inhabitants.

More significant in its implications, Washington's narrow escape from capture and possible burning hardened the determination of the Lincoln Administration to end that perennial threat once and for all, which in turn led to long overdue policy decisions and actions by the War Department whereby military sense was introduced into the command structure. The ensuing chain of events, from Sheridan's transfer to the Valley, through the late summer and early fall maneuvers, to the successive victories at Winchester, Fisher's Hill, and Cedar Creek, provided a badly needed tonic without which the stalemate in the Richmond-Petersburg area might have continued indefinitely, George B. McClellan could possibly have squeaked through to the Presidency, and the United States might have become two recognized nations under different flags.

Was *Early's* postwar claim, that he was called upon to lead what he described as a "forlorn hope," a valid one? *Lee* didn't think so, or he would scarcely have weakened his *Army of Northern Virginia* by detaching to *Early's* force the entire *Second Corps*, followed later by several brigades of cavalry and a portion of *Longstreet's corps*. Nor is it likely that *Early* himself would have so characterized his failures if he had made good his initial surprise victory at Cedar Creek.

That *Early* was a loyal, personally brave, hard-working and hard-fighting leader of troops was admitted even by those who could not agree with him and who may have felt the whiplash of his caustic, sarcastic, unbridled tongue. But many questioned the soundness of his judgment, and many more resented his readiness to shift the blame for his errors and deficiencies on to the handiest scapegoat, whether it happened to be his cavalry, his junior officers, his generals, or even his soldiers—with blanket indictments that were hastily made with little effort to sift the truth, and stubbornly adhered to regardless of evidence to the contrary.

"*Old Jube*" was ambitious, opinionated, dogmatic, and self-centered, unwilling to accept the views of his generals unless they coincided with his own, and surprisingly skeptical even of the reports of his experienced intelligence scouts. Among his pet prejudices the cavalry occupied a high priority, possibly because he knew so little about its capabilities and limitations and made no effort to learn.

One of his unfortunate characteristics was a lack of frankness, bordering on intellectual dishonesty, as in the instance when he admitted to *Jed Hotchkiss* that he should have continued the attack at Cedar Creek, at the same time cautioning that staff officer not to inform General *Lee* of what he had said. Instead *Early* persisted in his public statement that plundering by his soldiers had prevented the victory. And if, as seems likely, he was instrumental in suppressing *Gordon's* official report of that battle because it placed on *Early* himself personal responsibility for the disaster to Southern arms, then indeed he deserved to be condemned for lack of moral courage. Truly a paradoxical character, one is puzzled whether to class him among the top echelon of Confederate generals for his undoubtedly great contribution to Confederate arms, or to expand *Lee's* reference to him as "my bad old man" beyond the *Commanding General's* restricted meaning (*Early's* cussing and fondness for apple jack) by applying it more broadly to his general character.

It is a far simpler task to evaluate Philip Sheridan, who in many respects was the antithesis of *Jubal Early*. Whether or not General Crook was being entirely candid in writing that Sheridan became dissipated in his later years, his character and abilities during the war and early postwar years were such that he earned the respect, confidence, and admiration of the world as well as that of the men and officers of the Union armies, his own and others.

Sheridan was an extrovert, *Early* an introvert. Sheridan was the outgiving type, who was interested in other people and had much to offer them. Both generals were thoroughly self-confident and with good reason, having earned excellent combat reputations as brigade and division commanders in many major battles. Sheridan's personality attracted men and inspired them to do their best because they instinctively liked him and admired his courage and the quality of his leadership. Conversely, *Early* repelled many of his colleagues and juniors by his sharp tongue, and engendered distrust by his own failure to recognize merit in others beside himself.

In considering the strictly military capabilities of the two leaders, a persuasive case can be built for either, but in the final analysis the weight of evidence favors Sheridan.

While it is a fact that his army outnumbered *Early's,* and he was especially strong in cavalry, Confederate armies in other campaigns had overwhelmingly defeated Union armies with an even greater disparity in combat strength. Both commanders generally handled their divisions skilfully, but on balance Sheridan's utilization of his combined strength in infantry and cavalry was markedly superior to that of *Early,* who neither understood nor had confidence in the capabilities of the mounted arm.

Insofar as the execution of their several strategic missions was concerned, it would be difficult to find fault with either. *Early* accomplished the initial purpose for which he was sent to the Valley, but in subsequently losing three major battles against superior forces he was rated by the Confederacy a failure, which is the usual fate of the losing commander, regardless of extenuating circumstances. On the other hand, Sheridan, who also accomplished his assigned mission, achieved it through a series of carefully planned and executed troop movements, skilful employment of terrain and logistics, and aggressive combat tactics in spite of fumbles by his corps commanders, several of which (at Winchester and Cedar Creek) narrowly avoided becoming disasters.

In comparing the quality and effectiveness of the several corps and division commanders serving with the respective armies, generalization is dangerous, but in the aggregate it appears that *Early* was more fortunate than Sheridan. Some of the best and most distinguished Confederate generals served under *Early—Gordon, Breckinridge, Ramseur,* and *Rodes* for example. Neither Wright nor Emory on the Union side were considered top-flight commanders, and Crook certainly did not increase his stature at Cedar Creek.

On the score of military judgment, Sheridan was clearly superior. *Early* was criticized by *Lee* for fighting his army by divisions. Sheridan made no such mistake. After being defeated and put to rout at Winchester by being out-flanked, *Early* failed to profit by the lesson and was again outflanked in a similar manner at Fisher's Hill because he neglected to secure his vulnerable left flank. At Cedar Creek, in Sheridan's absence, *Early* sprang a complete sur-prise on the Union army under Wright and should by all the rules of war have exploited his initial success to achieve a complete victory. But he hesitated too long and was overwhelmed by a determined adversary who reached the battlefield in time to restore the fortunes of his own con-fused and discomfited army. In retrospect, weighing the factors that contributed to the Union victories and Con-federate defeats, *Early's* gross underestimate of the capabil-ities of his opponent was perhaps his most egregious error, a cardinal military sin that he compounded by persisting in his opinion even after being badly defeated three times in a row.

There were officers in the Union army who believed that if Sheridan had been present, *Early's* surprise at Cedar Creek would never have occurred, because the Union gen-eral would have seen to it that Powell's cavalry division was properly closed in to secure his left flank; the Con-federate divisions would not have been able to cross the Shenandoah without discovery and strong opposition; and the chain reaction of subsequent events might have been prevented. Speculation after the event, to be sure, but it was typical of Sheridan to see that such details were not left to chance, and he *had* warned Wright to order Powell in on the army left.

Whether Sheridan deserved the hero-worship that the public showered on him for his dramatic reversal of the fortunes of war after his ride from Winchester is a matter of opinion, but it cannot be denied that he pulled it off, put heart into a defeated army, threw a carefully planned coordinated counterattack at a victorious foe, and drove him in utter confusion from the field.

Stubborn in defense, aggressive in attack, Sheridan possessed the will to win in far greater measure than most Union generals, and was never willing to admit defeat, regardless of the odds. He never lost a battle, a unique distinction in itself. More importantly, he took such pains in advance to assure the best possible chance of victory by his deliberate, meticulous preparation for battle, logistically and tactically, committing his troops only when he was satisfied that all was ready, that on the record he seems to have earned the smiles with which Fortune favored him. When he struck, it was with his full force. Finally, because the world loves a winner, whatever errors of omission or commission may be charged to Phil Sheridan pale into insignificance when contrasted with his accomplishments. Without question he was a tenacious bulldog with a dynamic personality and a fighting heart, and deserved the plaudits and gratitude of the Nation which he had done so much to preserve.

BIBLIOGRAPHY

Appendix A

Abbott, John S. C., *History of the Civil War in America* (2 vols.), New York, 1863.

Alexander, John H., *Mosby's Men*. The Neale Publishing Co., 1907.

Bean, William G., *Stonewall's Man, Sandie Pendleton*. University of North Carolina Press, 1959.

Boatner, Lieut. Colonel Mark M. III, *The Civil War Dictionary*. David McKay Company, 1959.

Cooke, John Esten, *Wearing of the Gray*. Edited by Philip Van Doren Stern. Indiana University Press, 1959.

Cullum, Bvt. Major General George W., *Register of the Officers and Graduates of the U. S. Military Academy*, Boston, 1891,

DeForest, J. W., *A Volunteer's Adventures*, Yale University Press, 1946.

DuPont, Henry Algernon, *The Campaign of 1864 in the Valley of Virginia and the Expedition to Lynchburg*. New York, 1925.

Dyer, Frederick H. A., *A Compendium of the War of the Rebellion*. (3 vols.), Thomas Yoseloff, 1959.

Early, J. B., *Autobiography of Lieut. General Jubal A. Early, C. S. A.* J. B. Lippincott, 1912.

Evans, Clement A., *Diary*. Unpublished Ms. in collection of Mrs. George E. Lippincott.

Freeman, Douglas S., *Lee's Lieutenants* (3 vols.). Chas. Scribner's Sons, 1935 and 1944.

Freeman, Douglas S., *R. E. Lee* (4 vols.). Chas Scribner's Sons, 1935.

Gordon, General John B., *Reminiscences of the Civil War*. Charles Scribner's Sons, 1905.

Grant, U. S., *Personal Memoirs*. The World Publishing Co. 1952.

Herr, Major General John K. and Wallace, Edward S., *The Story of the U. S. Cavalry*. Boston, 1953.

Hoke, Jacob, *Gettysburg, the Great Invasion of 1863, with Appendix: The Burning of Chambersburg*. Dayton, 1887.

Jones, Virgil C., *Ranger Mosby*. Chapel Hill, 1944.

Livermore, Thomas L., *Numbers and Losses in the Civil War*. Indiana University Press, 1957.

McCartney, Clarence E., *Grant and His Generals*. New York, 1953.

Nichols, Pvt. G. W., *A Soldier's Story of His Regiment*. Privately printed in Georgia.

O'Connor, Richard, *Sheridan the Inevitable*. The Bobbs-Merrill Company, 1953.

Pratt, Fletcher, *Eleven Generals*. William Sloane Associates, 1949.

Schenck, Rev. B. S., *The Burning of Chambersburg*. Philadelphia, 1864.

Sheridan, P. H., *Personal Memoirs* (2 vols.). New York, 1888.

Steele, Matthew F., *American Campaigns* (2 vols.). War Department Document No. 324.

Stern, Philip Van Doren, *Secret Missions of the Civil War*. Rand McNally & Company, 1959.

Vandiver, Frank, *Jubal's Raid*. McGraw-Hill, 1960.

Warner, Ezra J., *Generals in Gray*. Louisiana State University Press, 1959.

Wise, Jennings C., *The Long Arm of Lee*. New York, 1959.

Battles and Leaders of the Civil War, Vol. IV. The Century Company, 1884.

General George Crook, His Autobiography. Edited by Martin F. Schmitt, University of Oklahoma Press, 1946, 1960.

Lee's Dispatches to Jefferson Davis and the War Department, C. S. A. Edited by Douglas S. Freeman and Grady McWhiney. G. P. Putnam's Sons, 1957.

The Memoirs of Colonel John S. Mosby, Indiana University Press, 1959.

Register of Graduates and Former Cadets of the U. S. Military Academy, 1802-1957. The West Point Alumni Foundation, 1957.

War of the Rebellion: *Official Records of the Union and Confederate Armies*. Government Printing Office, 1882-1900.

APPENDIX B—ORGANIZATION, STRENGTH, LOSSES

Note: Data are incomplete and inaccurate, and in the case of the Confederates are mainly estimates. Sources consulted: *Official Records*, Vol. XLIII, Parts I and II; Livermore, *Numbers & Losses in the Civil War*; and *Battles and Leaders*, Vol. IV.

TABLE I. *BATTLE OF THE MONOCACY, JULY 9, 1864.*

FEDERAL FORCE, MAJ. GEN. LEWIS WALLACE

Unit	Commander	Strength	Losses Killed	Wounded	Captured or Missing	Total
1st Separate Brigade	Brig. Gen. Erastus B. Tyler }	2,700	.....	.....	.....	.....
Cavalry	Lieut. Col. D. R. Clendenin }					
3d Division, VI Corps (2 brigs)	Brig. Gen. Jas. B. Ricketts	3,350	98	594	1,188	1,880
(4 brigs)	Totals	6,050				

CONFEDERATE FORCE, LIEUT. GEN. JUBAL A. EARLY

Unit	Commander	Strength	Killed	Wounded	Captured or Missing	Total
Gordon's division (3 brigs)	Maj. Gen. John B. Gordon	.....	...	...	.....	.....
Breckenridge's division (3 brigs)	Brig. Gen. John Echols	.....	...	...	.....	.....
Rodes' division (4 brigs)	Maj. Gen. Robert E. Rodes	.....	...	...	.....	.....
Ramseur's division (3 brigs)	Maj. Gen. Stephen D. Ramseur	.....	...	...	.....	.....
Cavalry (5 brigs)	Maj. Gen. Robert Ransom	.....	...	...	.....	.....
Artillery (3 bns)	Lieut. Col. Floyd King		not reported			700
(18 brigs)	Totals	20,000				

Note: During General Breckinridge's service with Early's army in the Valley campaign, from the Lynchburg affair until immediately after the Battle of Winchester, his assignment was in effect that of a corps commander, his own division at all times being under his immediate direction; from time to time General Early attached other divisions to his force.

TABLE 2. *BATTLE OF WINCHESTER* (OPEQUON), SEPT. 19, 1864

ARMY OF THE SHENANDOAH, MAJ. GEN. PHILIP H. SHERIDAN

Unit	Commander	Strength (effectives)	Losses			Total
			Killed	Wounded	Captured or Missing	
VI Corps						
1st Division (3 brigs)	Maj. Gen. Horatio G. Wright					
	Brig. Gen. David A. Russell		72	443	9	524
	Brig. Gen. Emory Upton					
	Col. Oliver Edwards					
2d Division (3 brigs)	Brig. Gen. George W. Getty		56	483	20	559
3d Division (2 brigs)	Brig. Gen. Jas. B. Ricketts		83	500	17	600
Artillery (6 btrys)	Col. Chas. H. Tompkins			16		16
Totals, VI Corps		5,500	211	1,442	46	1,699
XIX Corps						
1st Division (2 brigs)	Bvt. Maj. Gen. William H. Emory		80	460	2	542
2d Division (4 brigs)	Brig. Gen. William Dwight		234	1,089	204	1,527
Reserve Artillery (2 btrys)	Brig. Gen. Cuvier Grover					
	Capt. Elijah D. Taft			5		5
Totals, XIX Corps		12,100	314	1,554	206	2,074
VIII Corps (Army of W. Va.)	Bvt. Maj. Gen. George Crook					
1st Division (3 brigs)	Col. Joseph Thoburn		67	394	6	467
2d Division (2 brigs)	Col. Isaac H. Duval; Col.		37	289	1	327
	Rutherford B. Hayes					
Artillery Brigade (3 btrys)	Capt. Henry A. DuPont			not stated		
Totals, VIII Corps		7,000	104	683	7	794
Cavalry						
1st Division (3 brigs)	Bvt. Maj. Gen. Alfred T. A. Torbert					
2d Division (2 brigs)	Brig. Gen. Wesley Merritt		39	193	56	288
3d Division (2 brigs)	Bvt. Maj. Gen. William W. Averell		7	24	4	35
Horse Artillery	Brig. Gen. Jas H. Wilson		22	72	19	113
	Capt. La Rhett L. Livingston			15		15
Totals, Cavalry		5,500	68	304	79	451
(26 brigs)	Aggregate	37,300	697	3,983	338	5,018

404

SECOND CORPS, ARMY OF NORTHERN VIRGINIA, LIEUT. GEN. JUBAL A. EARLY

Command						
Gordon's division (4 brigs) .... Maj. Gen. John B. Gordon	2,900	....	....	....	....	....
Breckenridge's division (2 brigs) ..... Maj. Gen. John C. Breckinridge	1,600	....	....	....	....	....
Ramseur's division (4 brigs) .... Maj. Gen. Stephen D. Ramseur	2,400	....	....	....	....	....
Rodes' division (4 brigs) .... Maj. Gen. Robert E. Rodes	3,300	....	....	....	....	....
Fitz Lee's cavalry division (3 brigs) . Maj. Gen. Fitzhugh Lee ....}	2,900	....	....	....	....	....
Lomax's cavalry division (3 brigs) .. Maj. Gen. Lunsford L. Lomax ......}						
Artillery (3 bns) .... Lieut. Col. William Nelson	900	276	1,827	1,818	....	....
Aggregate	17,700	276	1,827	1,818	3,921	
(20 brigs)						

TABLE 3. *BATTLE OF FISHER'S HILL*, SEPT. 21-22, 1864
ARMY OF THE SHENANDOAH, MAJ. GEN. PHILIP H. SHERIDAN

Unit	Commander	Strength	Losses			
			Killed	Wounded	Captured or Missing	Total
VI Corps	Maj. Gen. Horatio G. Wright					
1st Division (2 brigs)	Brig. Gen. Frank Wheaton	....	5	36	1	42
2d Division (3 brigs)	Brig. Gen. Geo. W. Getty	....	12	101	1	114
3d Division (2 brigs)	Brig. Gen. Jas. B. Ricketts	....	10	70	1	81
Artillery (5 btrys)	Col. Chas. H. Tompkins	....	...	1	...	1
	Totals, VI Corps	3,000	27	208	3	238
XIX Corps	Bvt. Maj. Gen. William H. Emory					
1st Division (2 brigs)	Brig. Gen. William Dwight	....	4	29	...	33
2d Division (4 brigs)	Brig. Gen. Cuvier Grover	....	11	57	13	81
Reserve Artillery (2 btrys)	Capt. Elijah D. Taft	....				
	Totals, XIX Corps	8,300	15	86	13	114
VIII Corps	Bvt. Maj. Gen. George Crook					
1st Division (2 brigs)	Col. Joseph Thoburn	....	1	77	1	79
2d Division (2 brigs)	Col. Rutherford B. Hayes	....	7	75	1	83
Artillery (3 btrys)	Capt. Henry A. DuPont	....				
	Totals, VIII Corps	4,900	8	152	2	162
Cavalry						
2d Division (2 brigs)	Bvt. Maj. Gen. William W. Averell	....	2	11	1	14
	Totals, Cavalry	1,800	2	11	1	14
(19 brigs)	Aggregate	20,000	52	457	19	528
SECOND CORPS, ARMY OF NORTHERN VIRGINIA, LIEUT. GEN. JUBAL A. EARLY						
Gordon's division	Maj. Gen. John B. Gordon	....	...	...	...	...
Wharton's division	Brig. Gen. Gabriel C. Wharton	....	...	...	...	...
Ramseur's division	Brig. Gen. John Pegram	....	...	...	...	...
Rodes' division	Maj. Gen. Stephen D. Ramseur	....	...	...	...	...
Lomax's division (dismtd cav)	Maj. Gen. Lunsford Lomax	....	...	...	...	...
Artillery	Lieut. Col. William Nelson	....	...	...	...	...
	Aggregate	12,000	30	210	995	1,235

TABLE 4. *BATTLE OF CEDAR CREEK, OCT. 19, 1864*

ARMY OF THE SHENANDOAH, BVT. MAJ. GEN. HORATIO G. WRIGHT; MAJ. GEN. PHILIP H. SHERIDAN

Unit	Commander	Strength	Losses			
			Killed	Wounded	Captured or Missing	Total
VI Corps	Brig. Gen. Jas. B. Ricketts	.....	.....	2	.....	2
	Brig. Gen. Geo. W. Getty	.....	.....	.....	.....	.....
	Maj. Gen. H. G. Wright	.....	.....	.....	.....	.....
1st Division (3 brigs)	Brig. Gen. Frank Wheaton	.....	69	401	99	569
2d Division (3 brigs)	Brig. Gen. Geo. Getty	.....	107	570	61	738
	Brig. Gen. Lewis A. Grant	.....	.....	.....	.....	.....
	Brig. Gen. Getty	.....	.....	.....	.....	.....
3d Division (2 brigs)	Col. J. Warren Keifer	.....	108	562	36	706
Artillery	Col. Chas. H. Tompkins	.....	14	93	4	111
	Totals, VI Corps	.....	298	1,628	200	2,126
XIX Corps	Bvt. Maj. Gen. W. H. Emory	.....	.....	2	.....	2
1st Division (2 brigs)	Brig. Gen. Jas. W. McMillan	.....	156	689	216	1,061
	Brig. Gen. W. Dwight	.....	.....	.....	.....	.....
2d Division (4 brigs)	Brig. Gen. Cuvier Grover	.....	96	628	568	1,292
	Brig. Gen. H. W. Birge	.....	.....	.....	.....	.....
Reserve Artillery (2 btrys)	Maj. Albert W. Bradbury	.....	5	17	6	28
	Totals, XIX Corps	.....	257	1,336	790	2,383
VIII Corps	Bvt. Maj. Gen. Geo. Crook	.....	1	.....	.....	1
1st Division (2 brigs)	Col. Jos. Thoburn	.....	14	97	474	585
	Col. Thos. M. Harris	.....	.....	.....	.....	.....
2d Division (2 brigs)	Col. Rutherford B. Hayes	.....	25	157	39	221
Artillery (3 btrys)	Capt. Henry A. DuPont	.....	8	16	27	51
	Totals, VIII Corps	.....	48	270	540	858
Provisional Division (2 brigs)	Col. J. Howard Kitching	.....	12	72	18	102
Cavalry	Bvt. Maj. Gen. A. T. A. Torbert	.....	.....	.....	.....	.....
1st Division (3 brigs)	Brig. Gen. Wesley Merritt	.....	24	91	34	149
2d Division (2 brigs)	Col. William H. Powell	.....	1	8	1	10

Losses

Unit	Commander	Strength	Killed	Wounded	Captured or Missing	Total
3d Division (2 brigs) ....Brig. Gen. Geo. A. Custer		.....	2	24	8	34
Horse Artillery (5 btrys)		.....	2	1	.....	3
Totals, Cavalry		.....				196
(27 brigs)	Aggregate	40,000*	29	124	43	5,665
			644	3,430	1,591	

ARMY OF THE VALLEY,† LIEUT. GEN. JUBAL A. EARLY

Unit	Commander	Strength	Killed	Wounded	Captured or Missing	Total
II Corps, Army of Northern Virginia	Maj. Gen. John B. Gordon	.....	...	...	...	...
Ramseur's division (4 brigs)	......Maj. Gen. Stephen D. Ramseur	.....	...	...	...	...
Pegram's division (3 brigs)	.........Brig. Gen. John Pegram	.....	...	...	...	...
Gordon's division (4 brigs)	.........Brig. Gen. Clement A. Evans	.....	...	...	...	...
Kershaw's division (4 brigs)	.........Maj. Gen. Joseph B. Kershaw	.....	...	...	...	...
Wharton's division (3 brigs)	.........Brig. Gen. Gabriel C. Wharton	.....	...	...	...	...
Artillery (5 bns) ....Col. Thos. H. Carter		.....	...	...	...	...
Cavalry						
Lomax's division (4 brigs)	.........Maj. Gen. Lunsford L. Lomax	.....	...	...	...	...
Rosser's division (3 brigs)	.........Maj. Gen. Thos. L. Rosser	.....	...	...	...	...
Horse artillery (7 btrys)						
Total (25 brigs)		12,500	320	1,540	1,050	2,910

*The figure 40,000 represents "effectives," arbitrarily taken as 93% of "present" strength.

†This is the organization shown in I or Vol. XLII, Pt. I, pp. 564-567, except that the table given there does not show the temporary corps command of Gordon, mentioned in Early's report, p. 561. Elsewhere in this volume (p. 1011) Early's force on Aug. 31 was titled Army of Valley District.

TABLE 5. RECAPITULATION OF LOSSES

	Losses			
	Killed	Wounded	Captured or Missing	Total
Federals, campaign	1,938	11,893	3,121	16,952
Federals, 4 battles (Tables 1-4)**	1,491	8,464	3,136	13,091
Confederates, Early's estimate	726	4,077	3,963****	8,766

**Does not include 25 minor engagements.

****However, Col. B. W. Crowninshield, Provost Marshal General of Sheridan's command, reported 7,000 unwounded Confederate prisoners; and his successor reported 13,000 prisoners received Aug. 1, 1864–Mar. 1, 1865.

COMMENTARY

by D. Scott Hartwig

Sheridan in the Shenandoah is perhaps the best of the several campaign studies that General Edward Stackpole produced during the 1950s and 1960s. His appraisal of the opposing generals, Sheridan and Early, was fair and impartial, and his narrative of this important campaign was crisply written and easily followed. General Stackpole made almost exclusive use of secondary sources, however, such as Douglas S. Freeman's magnificent three volume work *Lee's Lieutenants*. He also drew on the postwar reminiscences and recollections of a few key participants in the campaign. At the time, the reliability and accuracy of these sources was accepted without question. In the thirty years since *Sheridan in the Shenandoah* was published, that has changed. For example, although *Lee's Lieutenants* still remains a brilliant work, various opinions and interpretations held by Douglas Freeman have been challenged by recent scholarship. The postwar reminiscences and recollections of men like Sheridan, Early, and Gordon, written long after the event, were frequently tainted by hindsight, professional jealousies, and distance, in time, from the event described. What these men had to say long after the war often differed greatly from how they felt, or what they did, or what they could have done, at the time of the event. Only by consulting their wartime private and official correspondence will a more rounded, and accurate, picture emerge. This commentary will explore several points that were made in *Sheridan in the Shenandoah* that deserve comment. Some were accepted as fact in 1961, but today they are not.

In his *Reminiscences of the Civil War*, published in 1903, Major General John B. Gordon wrote:

On July 11, 1864, the second day after the battle of Monocacy, we were at the defences of Washington . . . It is true that, as we approached, Rodes's division had driven in some skirmishers, and during the day (July 11th) another small affair had occurred on the Seventh Street road; but all the Federals encountered on this approach could not have manned any considerable portion of the defences. Undoubtedly we could have marched into Washington (Gordon, p. 314).

General Stackpole accepted Gordon's version and wrote that the Confederates might have entered Washington "with only minor casualties" and "possibly have captured President Lincoln, burned the White House and other public buildings, and gotten away before Wright's troops arrived" (p. 73). Was Gordon correct? Did Early miss a brilliant opportunity to score a stunning political/military triumph by smashing up the capitol then stealing away with the President in tow as a prisoner? Long afterwards it makes for exciting reading, but at the time, no such opportunity was perceived by Early and his lieutenants, or indeed, even existed.

The leading elements of Early's army — "a small body of cavalry" — did not arrive within sight of the capitol's defenses until "a little after noon." According to Early, "the main body of my command did not get up until some two or three hours later." His leading brigade of infantry did not deploy into line before 2:00 P.M., and the main body of his army was not deployed "before four o'clock." By this time, two divisions of the federal 6th Corps and elements of the 19th Corps had arrived by water and they were debarking and marching to the front. Brigadier General Frank Wheaton, who led the 1st

Brigade, 2nd Division, of the 6th Corps, reported that he arrived in Washington on the 11th at 12 meridian (noon). Major General Horatio G. Wright, commander of the 6th Corps, in a dispatch sent from Fort Stevens at 4:10 P.M., July 11, wrote that the head of his column "has nearly reached the front." Clearly, Early's, Wright's, and Wheaton's testimonies establish that Early's army could not have "marched into Washington," as Gordon claimed, without meeting fierce resistance from the veteran 6th and 19th corps (Early, 1881, Vol. 9, pp. 298–99, 308–9; *O.R.* Vol. 37, Pt. 2, p. 275; Pt. 1, p. 265).

Even if the 6th and 19th corps had not arrived in Washington in the nick of time, it should not be presumed that Early might have cakewalked down Seventh Street to the Capitol. The fortifications ringing Washington, of which Fort Stevens was a part, were the most powerful in the entire country. The formidable nature of these works was described by Brigadier General J. G. Barnard, a distinguished engineer who had figured prominently in their construction. He wrote that they consisted of "a connected system of fortifications by which every prominent point, at intervals of eight hundred to one thousand yards, was occupied by an inclosed field-fort, every important approach or depression of ground unseen from the forts swept by a battery of field guns, and the whole connected by rifle trenches. . . ." Early's veterans, having learned during the early weeks of the spring 1864 campaign the immense advantages that hastily thrown up field works gave to the defender, contemplated Washington's powerful fortifications with great respect. As they knew, even second-rate troops when well protected could exact a terrible toll from an attacker (Early, 1881, p. 304).

Contrary to another popular myth, the capitol, although not garrisoned by first-line troops, was not defended solely by frightened government clerks. Among those immediately available to confront Early when his advance arrived before the capitol were 600 dismounted troopers of the 2nd Cavalry

Division of the Army of the Potomac. The official returns for the Department of Washington on July 10 reported there were 458 officers and 12,342 enlisted men present for duty north of the Potomac River. Granted, nearly all these troops were second-rate, rear echelon men, and they were not all deployed in Early's front. But sheltered behind the fortifications of the capitol, a relatively weak force could have inflicted heavy losses on Early's regiments as they advanced over open ground (*O.R.* Vol. 37, Pt. 1, p. 231; Pt. 2, p. 171).

JOHN B. GORDON

The point of all this has been to establish that it would not have been a trifling matter for General Early to have entered Washington on July 11. It has also been to make the reader wary of accepting unhesitatingly the statements of a single eyewitness, particularly when they were written nearly thirty years after the event. John B. Gordon is a case in point. He was a magnificent soldier, who compiled an excellent record in the war, and a gifted writer, with a knack for telling a story well. With his wartime record and brilliant postwar political career to lend him credibility, the accuracy of Gordon's reminiscence of the war was unquestioned. Until recently.

One of the famous human-interest stories of the Battle of Gettysburg was the Barlow-Gordon incident, which occurred on the first day of the battle. Gordon told that during the fighting on July 1, his brigade overran a federal position held by troops of Brigadier General Francis C. Barlow's division of the Union 11th Corps. Barlow was seriously wounded and Gordon related, in great detail, how he assisted the stricken federal officer. The story was accepted as fact until 1985, when William F. Hanna, in an article in *Civil War Times Illustrated* challenged Gordon's account; indeed, he questioned whether Gordon had even personally encountered Barlow on the field. By consulting Barlow's wartime letters concerning Gettysburg, the first of which was written on July 7, Hanna discovered that Barlow's version did not agree at all with Gordon's. Not once did Barlow mention a General Gordon. In fact, he credited a "Major Pitzera" of General Early's staff as the good samaritan (this was actually Lieutenant A. L. Pitzer, who served as an aide to Early).

"Among the leading examples of participants whose postwar writing must be used with great care is John B. Gordon," writes Dr. Gary Gallagher. The reason is that "few witnesses matched either Gordon's egocentrism or his willingness to play loose with the truth." Gordon enjoyed placing himself at center stage and embellishing his stories. In the case of the Shenandoah Valley Campaign of 1864, he and his commanding officer, Jubal Early, did not see eye to eye. Gordon, quite naturally, sought to champion his point of view in his reminiscences. Early, in his reminiscence, sought to defend his actions in the valley, many of which Gordon freely criticized. Professional jealousy colored the accuracy of their accounts, particularly Gordon's. This was also true of the recollections of Philip Sheridan and George Crook, two close wartime friends who became bitter enemies long after the war (Gallagher, 1992, pp. 37, 39).

SHERIDAN AND CROOK

General Stackpole made liberal use of both Crook's and Sheridan's postwar memoirs. Yet, the general noted that Crook's version of the Valley Campaign was tainted by the Ohioan's opinion, expressed twenty-five years later, that, in General Stackpole's words, "Sheridan had deliberately withheld proper credit from those to whom it belonged and had assumed for himself undue credit not justified by the circumstances." To a degree, this was probably true, but did Crook feel this way in 1862, or was his opinion of Sheridan soured as a result of professional jealousies and differences of opinion and philosophy that arose between the two men during the Indian Wars?

In 1875, Crook was assigned to command of the Department of the Platte, a geographic military unit within the vast Division of the Missouri, which Philip Sheridan had commanded since 1869. Crook arrived with an already proven reputation as one of the most successful Indian Wars officers in the field. But Crook and Sheridan differed widely on how to handle the Native Americans. Crook, although a dogged opponent in the field, sympathized with Native Americans and treated them with dignity and respect. Sheridan, on the other hand, saw the trouble with the Indians as a "clear-cut struggle of civilization against barbarism," according to Paul A. Hutton, author of the excellent *Phil Sheridan and His Army*. With such divergent points of view, it was inevitable that the two men would clash over policy. Hutton wrote that "Sheridan, who tended to see sinister motivation behind every action he disagreed with, viewed Crook's gestures of moderation . . . as self-serving actions to win glory by having the Indians surrender to him" (Hutton, p. 129).

It was Crook's command of the Department of Arizona, which he assumed in 1882, that destroyed the once strong friendship of these men and turned Crook into a bitter enemy of Sheridan. The dispute arose over Crook's methods, specifically the use of Apache scouts, to bring the Apache Geronimo to bay and the generous terms Crook offered Geronimo when the Apache was at last forced to negotiate a surrender—one he later managed to back out of. Crook offered to resign and Sheridan accepted. Geronimo was eventually captured and imprisoned in Florida along with many of the Chiricahua Apache scouts who had served Crook so faithfully, but who Sheridan thought had been of dubious loyalty. Crook, wrote Hutton, "never forgave Sheridan, and their long but stormy relationship came to a sad close." The Ohioan's sharply critical words for Sheridan in the Shenandoah Valley Campaign, which General Stackpole cites, were all written with the memory of Sheridan's handling of the Apache problem fresh in Crook's mind (Hutton, p. 368).

What the stories of Crook, Sheridan, and Gordon illustrate is that while postwar reminiscences have their value, using them solely to support a conclusion is unwise. They must be balanced by the statements of other eyewitnesses and by wartime correspondence and records.

GENERAL GRANT

A more thorough perusal of the sources might have prompted General Stackpole to omit the unfortunate story on page 86 that claims that General Grant "blew his top" and went on a drinking binge when he learned Lincoln had placed Halleck in command of the consolidated departments that exercised jurisdiction over the valley. The story is absolutely untrue and unfair to Grant. A more thorough explanation is necessary.

General Stackpole wrote that Grant evidenced reluctance to detach troops from the Petersburg–Richmond front to confront the threat raised by Early's movement north of the Potomac (p. 84). While it is true that it took several days for Grant to determine just what Early was up to, once it was clear that the Confederate intended to cross into Maryland, Grant showed no reluctance to detach troops. He wired Halleck on July 5, "I can send an army corps from here to meet them or cut off their return south." Halleck responded that same day that he did not think Grant needed to send an entire corps to Washington; forwarding the dismounted cavalry of Sheridan's cavalry corps would be sufficient. Grant thought differently and at midnight directed Meade to send a division from the 6th Corps and all of Sheridan's dismounted troopers. He wired Halleck after coming to this decision, "We now want to crush out and destroy any force the enemy have sent north. Force enough can be spared away from here to do it." (*O.R.* Vol. 40, Pt. 3, pp. 3–4; Catton, pp. 310–11).

By July 9 Halleck was growing increasingly worried and wired Grant that the forces in Maryland were not sufficient to handle Early. Grant responded, "If you think it necessary order the Nineteenth Corps as it arrives at Fortress Monroe to Washington. About the 18th or 20th is the time I should like to have a large force here [Petersburg]; but if the rebel force now north can be captured or destroyed I would willingly postpone aggressive operations to destroy them, and could send in addition to the Nineteenth Corps the balance of the Sixth Corps." Up to this point Grant had demonstrated no "lack of political perception." If anything, the record shows that he had been highly sensitive and concerned about the implications of Early's incursion into the north and had actively sought to shift powerful forces north in order to destroy the Confederates (*O.R.* Vol. 40, Pt. 3, p. 91).

Grant decided on his own to send the balance of the 6th Corps to Washington. After issuing the necessary orders, he wired Halleck again (still on July 9) explaining that force enough had been dispatched north to handle anything Early had with him, and, he continued, if Lincoln thought it advisable for him to come north to Washington, he could leave "in an hour after receiving notice." Lincoln responded that he thought it would be a good idea if Grant did come north and thought he should take personal command of the effort against Early. It was a suggestion, however, not an order. Grant reflected on it and decided that Horatio Wright of the 6th Corps was an "excellent officer" and fully capable of taking care of Early. Grant also thought it was a bad time to leave the Petersburg front. General Stackpole claims (p. 87) that this was a mistake on Grant's part, that he should have gone to the capitol and met with Lincoln and Halleck to at least work out some command arrangement. This presumes that Grant knew that problems in the command arrangement were going to arise, which on July 10 he did not, and that Grant could have left the Petersburg front (*O.R.* Vol. 40, Pt. 3, p. 92).

In his outstanding work, *Grant Takes Command,* Bruce Catton wrote, "One thing that influenced Grant was the belief that if he himself went to Washington to direct the operations against Early both friend and foe would assume, with much reason, that the whole Petersburg campaign had been a flat failure." He would not go to Washington because, as he told his staff, "this is probably just what Lee wants me to do." Yet another reason Grant did not go north to Washington was that in his absence, the ranking federal officer in Virginia would be Major General Benjamin Butler. Catton commented that "the thought of letting this man direct all of the operations against Robert E. Lee was enough to make a soldier shudder" (Catton, pp. 313, 326).

General Stackpole briefly reviews the frustrating efforts of Grant to organize an effective command structure to deal with Early (pp. 84–86). Grant did, as General Stackpole writes, propose the names of both Franklin and Meade to command the forces arrayed against Early. In the case of Meade, it may have reflected Grant's opinion of that officer, but not in a negative sense. There was nothing secret about Meade's nomination. Grant discussed it with him and Meade responded that he was ready to follow any orders he might be given. Privately, to his wife, Meade wrote that he liked the idea of having an independent command. Obviously, Meade, who possessed a pricklish pride, did not feel Grant was in any way attempting to dispose of him to a second-rate theater of operations.

There was considerable discussion over Grant's nominations for command, which meant that the ineffectual command structure continued to hamper operations against Early. General Stackpole writes that during the latter part of July, Early again began to make threatening moves in the valley, and Lincoln, "without consulting Grant," placed Halleck in command of the four departments that the valley fell within (p. 86). It was this decision by the President that, we are told, sent the despondent Grant on a drinking binge, presumably because he thought Halleck such an ineffective soldier.

That it was Lincoln's idea to put Halleck in command does not agree with the record. It was at Grant's, and not Lincoln's, insistence that Secretary of War Stanton informed Halleck on July 27 that he was responsible for direct control over the valley departments. Grant certainly did not want Halleck to have permanent command over these forces, but if he was the one to prod Stanton to put Halleck in at least temporary command, it stands to reason that Grant was not upset with the arrangement and there was no reason for the general to go on a drinking binge. So why did he? Or did he go on a drinking binge at all?

The drinking story actually had nothing to do with the problems associated with naming a commander in the Shenandoah Valley. It originated with a rather unpleasant officer named Major General William F. Smith. Grant actually had a high opinion of Smith as a combat officer and had attempted, in early July, to reorganize the forces under the command of Benjamin Butler so that Smith would command Butler's troops in the field, while the incompetent Butler would be gently nudged into an elevated position where he could do no harm. Grant had to handle the matter delicately, for Butler held enormous political power and the presidential election was four months away. The deal eventually collapsed, and Smith, who misunderstood the attempted reorganization, was furious. Smith thought the intention was to place him in command of Butler's department and relieve Butler outright. On July 10 Smith visited Grant at his headquarters and spoke his mind in a venomous manner about Butler, whom he detested, and also about Meade, whom Smith thought was a miserable army commander. Catton wrote of Grant, "if there was one thing he disliked more than anything else it was a soldier who carried personal criticism of a brother officer to his commanding general." Grant decided he could do without Smith's type in the army, and on July 19 he issued orders relieving Smith from command of the 18th Corps (Catton, p. 330).

Smith considered that Grant had betrayed him and set out to seek revenge. He wrote a letter to Vermont Senator Solomon Foot in which he reduced the entire affair to the charge that Grant had behaved the way he had because he was drunk. According to Smith, Ben Butler had primed the army commander with drink during a visit to Smith's headquarters on July 1. Grant left drunk, said Smith, and the incident provided Butler with leverage to expose Grant if it proved necessary. Obviously, to Smith, Butler had played his card when Grant attempted to reorganize Butler's department, and Grant had backed down. John A. Rawlins, Grant's chief of staff, "who of all living mortals was the first to look for evidence that Grant had been drunk," dismissed Smith's story as without foundation. Nevertheless, the damage was done. "To this day, the heart of the legend that Grant was a periodic alcoholic in wartime is the story Smith told," wrote Catton (pp. 334–35).

CEDAR CREEK

Just as Smith created the legend that Grant was a periodic wartime alcoholic, so too did John B. Gordon create the notion that Jubal Early threw away a fabulous opportunity to deliver the coup de grace to Sheridan's beaten army at Cedar Creek. Following the defeat and rout of the federal 8th and 19th corps, when only the 6th Corps retained any organization on the field, Gordon claimed Early hesitated. The time was approximately 10:30 A.M. He wrote, "But the concentration [of Confederate forces] was stopped; the blow was not delivered. We halted, we hesitated, we dallied, firing a few shots here, attacking with a brigade or a division there, and before such feeble assaults the superb Union corps [6th] retired at intervals and by short stages. We waited—for what? . . . We waited—waited for weary hours; waited till those stirring, driving, and able Federal leaders, Wright, Crook, and Getty, could gather again their shattered fragments." Gordon included an entire chapter in his reminiscence entitled "The Fatal Halt at Cedar Creek." From this chapter was born the notion that there had been a "fatal halt" by Early during the battle. General Stackpole did not entirely accept Gordon's account but concluded that "those who believe in the power of the offensive and recognize the ease with which the retreat of a disorganized army, however brave, can be converted into a rout by an energetic, already victorious opponent, will on the balance support Gordon's belief that Jubal Early missed his great opportunity at Cedar Creek." But does the record support Gordon, or is it merely our opinion, colored by Gordon's skillful writing, that supports the Georgian?

Jeffery Wert, a careful student of the 1864 Valley Campaign, disposed of Gordon's claim with the statement that "the facts or events, placed in their proper sequence, destroy this assertion of a 'fatal halt.'" Gordon wrote that after the defeat of the 8th and 19th corps, he encountered the steady 6th Corps standing in his path "like a granite breakwater." The 6th was heavily outnumbered by the advancing Confederate forces and Gordon wrote, "I had directed every Confederate command then subject to my orders to assail it in front and upon both flanks simultaneously." These orders, Gordon felt certain, "would compass the capture of that corps — certainly its destruction." Wert questions, "to whom did Gordon issue this order?" Of the Valley Army's five infantry divisions, Pegram, Wharton, and Ramseur were under Early's direct command at this point of the battle. As for Kershaw and Evans, Kershaw had informed an officer of Early's staff that his division could not advance due to a heavy force of cavalry in their front and because many men had left the ranks to plunder the Federal camps. Evans's division was reported to be in a similar condition. Gordon's statement, wrote Wert, "lacks credibility" (Wert, p. 217).

The situation at 10:30 A.M. (approximately the time Gordon claimed to have met Early and informed him that he had ordered a general forward movement) was not as promising for the Confederate army as Gordon described. Pegram, Wharton, and a brigade of Kershaw's division were confronted east of Middletown by 7,500 well armed, determined Federal cavalry, supported by five horse batteries. This powerful force posed a grave threat to Early's right flank and tied down Pegram's and Wharton's divisions. The three other Confederate divisions were moving forward to take up positions on the left of Pegram's and were not ready or positioned to attack. There was also the controversial question of straggling from the ranks to plunder the abandoned Union camps.

In his report and memoirs, Early cited the straggling from the ranks in search of plunder and food as a critical factor in his defeat at Cedar Creek. Gordon challenged this statement. To support his claim that there was no straggling from the combat ranks, Gordon cited letters, in his reminiscences, from several Confederate officers present during the battle, all of whom upheld Gordon. "Who, then," wrote Gordon, "were the men in the captured camps who were reported to General Early? They were men without arms, the partially disabled, whom the army surgeons had pronounced scarcely strong enough for the long and rough night march and the strenuous work of the battle" (p. 370). Gordon's effort to shield the Confederate fighting man at Cedar Creek was commendable, but inaccurate. Many combat soldiers admitted either personally straggling to plunder the Union camps or observing large-scale straggling. The historian of the 12th North Carolina wrote, "The Confederate lines had been very much thinned from straggling and the plundering of the captured camps of the enemy." A member of the 6th North Carolina testified that "the rout seemed to be so complete that the half-famished and poorly clothed men of the Early's army found the rich spoils in the captured camp and stores of the federal sutlers too tempting, and so many of them straggled that when General Wright, who was in command of the federals, reformed his line near Newtown, and General Sheridan came riding in from Winchester and took command, our lines were too weak to resist their attack." Private George W. Nichols, of the 61st Georgia, recorded, "A great many of us went back to their camp after blankets, shoes, clothing. . . . I got two nice new tent flies, two fine blankets, a fine rubber cloth, two new overshirts and two pair of new shoes." D. Augustus Dickert of Kershaw's division observed "stragglers, who looked like half the army, laden with every imaginable kind of plunder," when he looked to the rear after the federal camps had been overrun. Testimony contrary to Gordon's could continue to be quoted at length, but the above is sufficient evidence to establish that large-scale straggling did occur and did weaken the southern army's ability to maintain the offensive and to resist Sheridan's eventual counterattack (Clark, Vol. 1, pp. 327, 649; Nichols, p. 195; Dickert, p. 449).

Just as Gordon's claim that no fighting men straggled from the ranks is inaccurate, so too is Jubal Early's statement that he lost the battle because of the straggling. The absentees from the ranks undoubtedly reduced the firepower of Early's brigades and damaged their offensive and defensive capabilities, but they were not alone responsible for the defeat. Early mishandled his cavalry and failed to take decisive action before Sheridan's counterattack fell, when he was informed that his left flank was in danger. He also might have put more fire into the feeble attack he eventually sent forward against the 19th Corps in the early afternoon. There is also the possibility that even if Early had not made the mistakes he did and his men had not straggled in heavy numbers, he still would have lost the battle because Philip Sheridan refused to be beaten. Answers to some of these questions and debates will never be found, simply because definite answers do not exist. The key is to arrive at the best informed interpretation or opinion by consulting the widest range of sources. Only then can we do true justice to the men who made history in our American Civil War.

The return of *Sheridan in the Shenandoah* comes at a most important time. The effort to preserve many of the battlefields described by General Stackpole is at a critical stage. Perhaps this work will lend its hand to the preservation effort by generating increased awareness of the momentous and far-reaching events that gripped the picturesque valley in the fall of 1864.

BIBLIOGRAPHY

Catton, Bruce. *Grant Takes Command.* Boston and Toronto: Little, Brown and Co., 1968.

Civil War, Vol. XX. The entire magazine is devoted to the Shenandoah Valley Campaign, 1989.

Clark, Walter, ed. *Histories of the Several Regiments and Battalions from North Carolina, in the Great War.* 5 Vols. Raleigh: Pub. by the State, 1902.

Dickert, D. Augustus. *History of Kershaw's Brigade.* Newbury, S.C.: Elbert H. Aull Co., 1899; Reprint Edition, with Introduction by Dr. Wm. Stanley Hoole. Dayton: Press of Morningside Bookshop, 1973.

Early, Jubal A. *Autobiographical Sketch and Narrative of the War Between the States.* Philadelphia and London: J. B. Lippincott Co., 1912.

Early, Jubal A. "The Advance on Washington in 1864," *Southern Historical Society Papers,* Vol. 9, pp. 297–312, 1881.

Gallagher, Gary W. "Confederate Corps Leadership on the First Day at Gettysburg: A. P. Hill and Richard S. Ewell in a Difficult Debut," in Gary W. Gallagher, ed. *The First Day at Gettysburg: Essays on Confederate and Union Leadership* (Kent, Ohio: Kent State University Press, 1992), pp. 37, 39.

Gordon, John B. *Reminiscences of the Civil War.* New York: Charles Scribner's Sons, 1903.

Hanna, William H. "A Gettysburg Myth Exploded," *Civil War Times Illustrated,* Vol. XXIV, No. 3 (May, 1985), pp. 43–47.

Hutton, Paul A. *Phil Sheridan and His Army.* Lincoln and London: University of Nebraska Press, 1985.

Nichols, G. W. *A Soldier's Story of His Regiment.* Kennesaw, Ga.: Continental Book Co., 1961.

Sheridan, Philip H. *Personal Memoirs of P. H. Sheridan, General United States Army.* New York: Charles L. Webster Co., 1888.

Taylor, James E. *With Sheridan up the Shenandoah Valley in 1864.* Dayton: Morningside House, 1989. An indispensable work on the federal army during the campaign.

The War of the Rebellion: A Compilation of the Official Records (O.R.) of the Union and Confederate Armies. Washington D.C.: U.S. Government Printing Office, 1880–1901.

Wert, Jeffery D. *From Winchester to Cedar Creek.* Carlisle, Pa.: South Mountain Press, 1987.

Worthington, Glenn H. *Fighting for Time.* Frederick, Md.: Frederick County Historical Society, 1932.

INDEX

A

Abraham's Creek, 181, 192, 201
Adams, Capt. Jack, CSA, 175
Aldie, 119
Alexander, Col. Barton S., 345
Ames, "Yankee," 371, 372
Anderson, Lt. Gen. Richard S., CSA, 5, 156, 173. 174, 177
Antietam, Battle of, 11, 26, 52, 53
Army of Northern Virginia, 2, 4, 5, 19, 53, 137, 144, 157, 173, 242, 276, 395
Army of the Potomac, 1, 3, 4, 13, 53, 56, 72, 84, 105, 117, 118, 120, 121, 122, 125, 126, 130, 138, 149, 154, 157, 195, 282, 342, 385, 388
Army of the Shenandoah, 147, 170, 186, 233, 377
Army of West Virginia (see also Eighth Corps), 149, 190, 295
Artillery, Confederate, 42, 57, 95, 178, 209, 275, 277, 305, 307, 311, 316
Artillery, Federal, 37, 42, 95, 195, 210, 298, 303, 304, 305, 307, 312, 330, 332, 333
Ashby's Gap, 174, 277
Ashby, Col. Turner, CSA, 118
Ashland, 136
Averell, Maj. Gen William W, 25, 33, 35, 40, 88, 91-102, 145, 146, 149, 165, 178, 183, 190, 192-94, 213, 220, 235, 250, 258, 259, 261

B

Back Road, 143, 236, 250, 270, 283, 295, 302, 308, 310
Baltimore and Ohio RR, 48, 49, 51, 60, 67, 145, 146, 154, 178, 183, 268
Banks, Maj. Gen. Nathaniel P., 83, 179
Bard, Thos. R., 98, 101, 102
Barksdale, Brig. Gen. William, CSA, 12
Battery B, 5th US Artillery, 304
Battery L, 1st Ohio Artillery, 305
Battle, Brig. Gen. Cullen A., CSA, 209
Beauregard, Pierre G., CSA, 136
Beaver Dam Station, 134
Bell, Sgt., Co. F, 110th Ohio, 291, 324
Berkeley Springs, 88
Bermuda Hundred, 100, 136
Belle Grove, 297, 337, 352
Berryville, 76, 154, 155, 174; pike, 195, 200, 205, 209, 216, 219
Berryville Canyon, 200-03
Blackwater Creek, 41
Blair, Montgomery, 73
Blazer, Capt. (of Scouts) Richard, 376, 377
Blue Ridge Mountains, 20, 25, 143, 148, 159, 174, 187, 188, 281, 368, 380
Bolivar Heights, 49
Booneville, Battle of, 115
Boonsboro, 52
Botetourt Spring, 45
Bowman's Ford, 290, 297; mill, 302
Bradbury, Maj. Albert W., 210
Bragg, Gen. Braxton, CSA, 117, 348, 137
Brandy Station, 119, 126
Breckinridge, Maj. Gen. John C., CSA, 19, 21, 22, 25, 27, 28-32, 40, 47-8, 51-4, 139, 170, 184, 198-222, 228, 240-41, 244
Brewerton, Lt. Henry F., 304
Brock's Gap, 48
Brown's Gap, 263, 264, 267, 275
Brown, Widow Lizinka, 6, 16
Buford's Gap, 44
Bunker Hill, Va., 154, 184, 192, 193
Buckton Ford, 258
Burnt Mill, 303
Butler, Maj. Gen. Benjamin F., 130, 136

C

Cameron's Depot, 167
Campbell Court House, 41
Capehart's brigade, 386
Carbines, 131
Carter, Col. Thos. H., CSA, (Carter's Artillery), 311, 332, 362
Castleman's Ferry fight, 88
Catoctin Mountain, 53, 55, 56
Cavalry, Early's (see Lee, F; Lomax; Johnson, B; Jackson; McCausland, Rosser) 21, 22, 30, 36, 37, 39, 41, 44, 49, 52, 54, 55, 56, 58, 61, 63, 65, 71, 74, 89, 90-102, 120, 127, 134, 135, 138, 145, 153, 154, 169, 190, 199, 236, 246, 257-60, 270-74, 290, 309, 395
Cavalry, Federal, Sheridan's (see also Averell, Custer, Gregg, Merritt, Powell, Lowell, Devin, Torbert), 21, 25, 30, 35, 36, 39, 41, 55, 56, 117, 120, 122, 126, 129, 130, 138-54, 160, 164-65, 170, 173, 190-95, 198, 218, 220, 228-31, 246, 257, 261-62, 131, 132, 136, 137, 160, 264, 270-74, 282, 283, 287, 307, 331, 335, 338, 342, 379, 380, 385, 389
Cedar Creek, 156, 157, 247, 269, 274, 276, 283, 284, 285, 286, 295, 297, 298, 302, 303, 305, 307, 320, 339; Battle of, 281-341
Cedarville fight, 164
Chalmers, Brig. Gen. James R., CSA, 115
Chambersburg, 89-102, 145
Chapman, Brig. Gen. Geo. H., 195, 238
Charlestown, W. Va., 165, 167, 168, 181, 186, 193
Charlottesville, 25, 30, 104, 138, 148, 267, 389, 390
Chesapeake & Ohio Canal, 49, 52, 145
Chesterfield Station, 136
Chester Gap, 155
Cherry Run, 91
City Point, 103, 106
Clark's Mountain, 286
Clendenin, Col. D.R., 55
Clifton, 154
Clifton-Berryville line, 174
Cold Harbor, 26, 81, 82, 83
Comparison of Early and Sheridan, 393-99
Confederate signal station on Three Top Mountain, 249
Cooley House, 290, 298
Couch, Maj. Gen. Darius N., 92, 93, 95, 99, 100, 101
Crampton's Gap, 54
Crook, Maj. Gen. George, 25, 33, 35, 38, 39, 40, 42, 87, 88, 92, 95, 104, 111, 145, 149, 150, 165, 176, 190, 217, 218, 221, 222, 224, 226, 231, 232, 238, 242, 249, 252, 274, 295, 296, 300, 301, 302, 307, 308, 310, 311, 312, 320, 325, 327, 328, 332, 345, 383, 384
Cross Keys, 144
Culpeper, 178, 263
Cumberland Valley, Pa., 12, 52, 92
Cumberland Valley RR, 98
Curtis, Maj. Gen. Samuel R., 113
Custer, Brig. Gen. George A., 131, 134, 150, 151, 198, 228, 230, 257, 265, 266, 270, 271, 279, 283, 308, 311, 317, 327, 331, 337, 342, 366, 387, 388, 389
Cutshaw's artillery, 177, 178, 263, 265

D

Darkesville, 191
Davis, Jefferson, 20, 29, 35, 348
Death of Meigs, 265

428

429